Respectably
Catholic
& Scientific

Respectably Catholic & Scientific

Evolution and Birth Control between the World Wars

Alexander Pavuk

The Catholic University of America Press
Washington, D.C.

The paper used in this publication meets the requirements
of American National Standards for Information Science—
Permanence of Paper for Printed Library Materials,
ANSI Z39.48-1992.
∞

Cataloging-in-Publication Data available from the
Library of Congress
ISBN 978-0-8132-3431-1

In memory of my father, Thomas

Contents

Acknowledgments

How can I thank you all?

My deepest appreciation goes to the many erudite and generous scholars who have helped me, directly or indirectly, with this book project. Thanks also to Trevor Lipscombe and the entire staff of the Catholic University of America Press; to William J. Shepherd and the staff of the American Catholic History Research Center and University Archives; to the copy editor, Clare Jensen; to the archival staffs of the American Philosophical Society and Georgetown University Rare Books and Special Collections. I am grateful to Cambridge University Press for permission to reprint part of my article from *Religion and American Culture* 26 (2016) in chapter 2.

To my family, especially my mother, Lubov, who always says that when I think something nice about people I should tell them, thank you.

Three old friends, in particular, have provided endless hours of intellectual stimulation and laughter over the years: Tom Rylko, Dan Gioffre, and John Hosler, the latter of whom is a talented academic and a former colleague at Morgan State University. All of them in their own ways challenged me to think through various ideas in this book, and I thank them.

Thanks, most of all, to my wife, Arezoo, without whom I could not have begun the process of finishing this book, or of starting real life's adventure, particularly now with our little boy.

For any ambiguities or errors of interpretation in these pages, I have no one to thank but myself.

Abbreviations

AAAS   American Association for the Advancement of Science

ACLU   American Civil Liberties Union

ACUA   American Catholic Research Center and University Archive

AES   American Eugenics Society

APS   American Philosophical Society

ASHA   American Social Hygiene Association

CC   Pius XI, *Casti Connubii*

CRTS   Catholic Roundtable of Science

FCCC   Federal Council of Churches of Christ

GURBSC Georgetown University Rare Books and Special Collections

NCWC   National Catholic Welfare Conference

experience facilitated what he described as his inevitable rejection of religion.[4] What is perhaps most striking in this story is that the shift to unbelief came not from rebellion against the priests' mandated curriculum but rather in tandem with it or even as a result of it. My own confession is that this book has nothing to do with George Carlin, nor will it focus on events after the start of World War II. But Carlin's story about his Catholic priests hoping to reach and positively influence him through progressive and scientific education is relevant by way of analogy.

Forty years before Carlin's performance, John Anthony O'Brien (1893–1980), an educational psychologist and Catholic priest, beamed with satisfaction as he finished reading the latest book review from the internationally renowned *Scientific Book Club*. In it, decorated embryologist Edwin Grant Conklin of Princeton University had glowingly commended O'Brien's recent book, *Evolution and Religion*. Such high praise from Conklin, one of America's most influential scientists and popularizers of evolution, only served to intensify the pride O'Brien felt on receiving a letter from paleontologist Henry Fairfield Osborn, the director of the Museum of Natural History in New York City and an even more famous evolution popularizer than Conklin. In his letter, Osborn commended O'Brien "for his liberalism" in the new book.[5] Similar plaudits from public scientists followed O'Brien's 1934 pamphlet (later expanded into a book in 1938) endorsing the rhythm method of birth control on the authority of various sciences. O'Brien was the first American Catholic priest to receive a PhD from a non-Catholic university—a degree

---

4. The liner notes to *Class Clown* list the priests and nuns of Corpus Christi School whom Carlin discussed throughout the album. He once explained, "I wanted people to know that the disrespect I had for the dogmatic aspect ... was tempered with an affection and a gratitude that I had for this wonderful setting that I considered like a garden ... where they let me grow, ... be a creative person and think for myself there, so I kind of wanted to illustrate that, and go, thanks and no thanks." George Carlin, Bravo's *Inside the Actors Studio*, October 31, 2004. See also David Gonzalez, "George Carlin Didn't Shun School That Ejected Him," *New York Times*, June 24, 2008.

5. On these and other scientists' positive evaluations of O'Brien's *Evolution and Religion*, see John L. Morrison, "A History of American Catholic Opinion on the Theory of Evolution, 1859–1950" (PhD diss., University of Missouri, 1951), 344–45.

in educational psychology from the University of Illinois in 1920.[6]

Father O'Brien was reaping the rewards of his contributions to realms of American public discourse that had rarely included the likes of Catholics before World War I. He had accessed the cultural space where the country's most important scientist-popularizers—like Conklin, Osborn, and others—actively framed how human origins and development would be discussed, debated, and understood in the public square in the interwar period. O'Brien addressed a number of his own books and articles to non-Catholic intellectual elites in particular, though he certainly hoped Catholics would read his work. O'Brien was part of a small but disproportionately influential cadre of like-minded liberal-progressive Catholics who sought to reach and, if possible, join the ranks of widely-received non-Catholic American thinkers whose own influence spread through the lingua franca of science. Two others of the most important and visibly liberal Catholic thinkers pursuing the same goal were, like O'Brien, not only priests but also practicing social scientists: industrial economist Fr. John Augustine Ryan (1869–1945), and anthropologist-ethnologist Fr. John Montgomery Cooper (1881–1949).

These three priests all shared the experience of social science training within a span of time incorporating the fin de siècle and the Progressive Era, a period when both positivist philosophy and a broader scientism were significantly influencing the still-coalescing social sciences. They also shared an intellectual connection to the Catholic University of America and its social science faculty. Ryan and O'Brien undertook some portion of graduate study at the school. Cooper and Ryan taught in the social sciences at the school for decades. In Ryan's case, Catholic University hosted both his graduate study and the great majority of his career as a professor.

Significant social science professors at Catholic University in

6. His dissertation was "Some Factors in the Development of Speed in Silent Reading" (PhD diss., University of Illinois, 1920), published the following year by MacMillan as *Silent Reading: With Special Reference to Methods for Developing Speed*.

the late nineteenth and early twentieth century exerted important influence on the intellectual course of the school, in general, and especially on the developing social science department there. These included Fr. William Kerby (whose own dissertation supervisor at Catholic University, Thomas Bouquillon, had first incorporated practical sociological principles into the school's moral theology curriculum), Fr. Edward Pace (who wrote his dissertation on Herbert Spencer and evolution), and other figures connected to mainline social science. They not only facilitated elements of their respective fields' steady scientism in the departmental milieu but also gave safe harbor there to strands of two intellectual movements in the church, movements that were ultimately condemned by papal decree in 1899 and 1907 but which had previously enjoyed strongholds at Catholic University. These were the Americanist and the modernist movements.[7] Even after the condemnations, lingering influences from both these traditions remained at the school in a subaltern state outside of theology classrooms, particularly in the social science departments.[8]

The social science faculty who mentored our figures, and later our figures themselves, worked continually to incorporate the most up-to-date scientific approaches from the coalescing professionalizing disciplines into the departments. At the same time, they rejected the idea entertained by some other Catholics who argued for the insertion of a separate "Catholic social science" in American intellectual culture.[9]

7. Addressing some of this residual influence in a later period is Nicholas K. Rademacher, *Paul Hanly Furfey: Priest, Scientist, Social Reformer* (New York: Fordham University Press, 2017), 37–38, 49, 58–61. See also the work of Christopher Kauffman, especially *Tradition and Transformation in Catholic Culture: The Priests of Saint Sulpice in the United States from 1791 to the Present* (New York: Macmillan, 1988), and the work of R. Scott Appleby, especially *Church and Age Unite!* (Notre Dame: University of Notre Dame Press, 1992). On modernism in the United States context, see William L. Portier, *Divided Friends: Portraits of the Roman Catholic Modernist Crisis in the United States* (Washington, D.C.: The Catholic University of America Press, 2013).

8. The early post-*Pascendi* years following the encyclical condemning modernism were skillfully broached some years ago in Elizabeth McKeown's "From *Pascendi* to *Primitive Man*: The Apologetics and Anthropology of John Montgomery Cooper," *U.S. Catholic Historian* 13 (1995): 1–21.

9. See, for example, C. Joseph Neusse, "William Joseph Kerby (1870–1936): The Approach

Both the Americanist-modernist internal Catholic influence
and the technocratic expertise approach of the social sciences
would exert an important pull on all three of our figures. Indeed,
those pulls had their own overlaps.[10] Americanism and modernism dealt with incorporating modernity's philosophical viewpoints
and techniques, especially scientific techniques, into Catholicism.[11]
Likewise, though purporting philosophical objectivity, the nascent
social science fields themselves featured deeply embedded Victorian era assumptions. These included the idea that human mastery
of nature accelerated in progressive history as the scientific method
guided social development. From proto–social scientists Auguste
Comte and John Stuart Mill's influence on American sociologists
Albion Small and Lester Ward to other neo-Comtist thinkers' effects on nascent social science fields, a related series of presuppositions permeated the foundations of social science scholarship and,
thus, our figures. Both strands of influence dovetailed in a true enthusiasm for science and for an intellectual and social engagement
on scientific terms with the broader culture, especially around the
Progressive movement.[12]

It is, thus, no coincidence that all three figures later sought involvement with the post-World War I organization known as the
National Catholic Welfare Conference (NCWC), an organization

to His Field of the First American Catholic Sociologist," *American Catholic Studies* 111 (2000):
77–96.

10. Acknowledging both the complexity and the contested nature of each of these
terms—*Americanism* and *modernism*—in both the contemporary and historical literature, I
note that my use of the terms is not meant to imply one way or another whether they genuinely qualified as coherent "movements" or were merely individual orientations encompassing
transatlantic connections; it is enough here to say they were communities of discourse. I also
do not argue here the question of their absolute relationship to one another other than to note
that they have been seen to share affinities while in no way being synonymous.

11. Some figures, such as earlier twentieth-century Presbyterian modernist Charles Augustine Briggs, have seen substantial connections between Protestant and Catholic modern-
isms. See Charles A. Briggs, "Modernism Mediating the Coming Catholicism," *North American Review* 187 (1908): 877–89. See also Mark Massa, *Charles Augustus Briggs and the Crisis of
Historical Criticism* (Minneapolis: Fortress Press, 1990).

12. See Gillis J. Harp, *Positivist Republic: Auguste Comte and the Reconstruction of American Liberalism, 1865–1920* (University Park: Pennsylvania State University Press, 1995), esp.
156–65. See also Dorothy Ross, *The Origins of American Social Science* (Cambridge: Cambridge University Press, 1991), 104–6.

tied to Catholic social science reform streams and outreach to non-Catholic America. It was an organization accused by some more conservative American Catholics of being an open recapitulation of Americanism.[13]

It was, thus, with shared perspectives deriving from both their Catholic and secular intellectual forays that Frs. Ryan, Cooper, and O'Brien sought to engage mainline intellectuals on the latter's terms. They hoped, by doing so, to overcome longstanding anti-Catholic strains in American history and intellectual life, strains accusing Catholics of employing obscurantist and authoritarian reasoning. But they also employed mainline science's language from their own beliefs in the perspectives themselves and in the idea that engagement through scientific lenses would produce the most effective interface of church and culture. All three ultimately shared a fervent desire to translate the Catholic ethos, as they understood it, into the vocabulary of the modern age, the vocabulary of science.

This did not seem a bad bet at the time. After all, as Frederick Lewis Allen, influential observer of the cultural norms in that era, noted, "the prestige of science was colossal."[14] This was particularly true where key issues about the origins, nature, and development of humanity were being hashed out in public intellectual debates.

In those years, much of this public intellectual engagement and exchange occurred in nationally distributed print media comprising books, middlebrow-highbrow magazine pieces, and, in some cases, newspapers. Aside from letters and other archival records, this media is where many of the important exchanges documented in this book took place. Such sources facilitate our asking—and finding some likely answers to—one particular question: how did the place of religious and theological language shift as a prime cul-

13. On the NCWC and its association with Catholic liberalism, see Douglas J. Slawson, *The Foundation and First Decade of the National Catholic Welfare Council* (Washington, D.C.: The Catholic University of America Press, 1992).

14. Frederick Lewis Allen, *Only Yesterday: An Informal History of the 1920s* (New York: Harper and Brothers, 1931), 197.

tural reference point over time—in relation to science and professional scientists' authority—in public discourse about evolution and contraception with the complicity of our three Fr. Johns?[15] More than is often acknowledged, it has been through the complex involvement of liberal religious figures that evolution and birth control came to be reconstructed in public culture as bodies of knowledge and practice ripe for controlled human planning by scientific elites rather than as issues of moral concern needing the primary mediation, interpretation, and guidance of religious or moral-philosophical figures.[16]

Human Origins and Development: Contraception and Evolution Connections

Evolution and contraception were increasingly intertwined both in the rubric of human origins controversies and in social movements on the eve of World War I. This process continued and accelerated in the interwar years. In certain senses, the two subjects deeply intersected well before that. Some biologists and social scientists in the later nineteenth century (such as philosopher Herbert Spencer, psychologist G. Stanley Hall, and others) had argued—in a vein often associated with German embryologist Ernst Haeckel—that each developing human fetus recapitulated the full-scale evolution-

15. As with numerous students of intellectual history, my views on discursive webs and the rhetoric of science have been influenced by David Hollinger's classic essay "Historians and the Discourse of Intellectuals," in *Religion and Twentieth Century Intellectual Life*, ed. Michael J. Lacey (Cambridge: Cambridge University Press, 1989), 116–35, and by Jon H. Roberts, "Religion, Secularization, and Cultural Spaces in America," in *American Catholic Traditions: Resources for Renewal*, ed. Sandra Yocum Mize and William Portier (Maryknoll, N.Y.: Orbis Books, 1997), 185–205. I have also found useful Andreas Daum's "Varieties of Popular Science and the Transformations of Public Knowledge: Some Historical Reflections," *Isis* (2009): 319–32, esp. 323.

16. In this realm lay early twentieth-century intellectuals' preoccupation with efficiency, subsequently called "scientific social control," and finally, "planning." See John Jordan, *Machine Age Ideology: Social Engineering and American Liberalism, 1911–1939* (Chapel Hill: University of North Carolina Press, 1994), 141. The era was replete with "hyperbolic representations of scientific knowledge as an agent, if not a mystical force." David Hollinger, *Science, Jews, and Secular Culture* (Princeton: Princeton University Press, 1996), 103.

social problems, politics, and human history.[18] Modern methods of textual analysis also interested many liberals. Having said that, several caveats are in order. Father Ryan, giving voice to the position, characterized Catholic liberalism as idiosyncratic since it contained some of what was considered liberal thought and some of what was considered conservative thought. He pointed out that people can be liberal in some fields while holding to conservative or authoritarian views—in this case, Catholic dogmatic positions—in others. Ryan contended that the term *liberalism* carried different connotations depending on location and other factors, such as Continental liberalism's association with anticlericalism since the nineteenth century.[19] In this view, a Catholic could accept the church's absolute authority in matters of faith and morals while tolerating, or even personally entertaining, various perspectives on society with respect to governmental policy, education, and social conventions.

As scholars have demonstrated, liberal Catholics in America endorsed numerous aspects of the broader Progressive reform movement, especially its faith in the efficacy of science to solve social problems.[20] Keeping this interface in mind, the terms *progressive Catholic* and *liberal Catholic* are used mostly synonymously here even though progressivism and liberalism, per se, have had distinct meanings in politics, economics, and various other aspects of history.

Unlike ultramontane Catholics, some of whom staffed the

18. Robert Cross, *The Emergence of Liberal Catholicism in America* (Cambridge, Mass.: Harvard University Press, 1958), 13–14.

19. Lester Kurtz pointed out that European anticlericalists had a preexisting affinity with Darwinian evolution, connected as it was with the legitimization of social, not just individual, evolution. See Kurtz, *The Politics of Heresy: The Modernist Crisis in Roman Catholicism* (Berkeley: University of California Press, 1988), 24.

20. See, for example, Dorothy M. Brown and Elizabeth McKeown, *The Poor Belong to Us: Catholic Charities and American Welfare* (Cambridge, Mass.: Harvard University Press, 1997); Dierdre M. Moloney, *American Catholic Lay Groups and Transatlantic Social Reform in the Progressive Era* (Chapel Hill: University of North Carolina Press, 2002); and portions referring to liberal Catholics in Thomas E. Woods Jr., *The Church Confronts Modernity: Catholic Intellectuals and the Progressive Era* (New York: Columbia University Press, 2004).

American hierarchy, many liberal Catholics welcomed the separation of church and state rather than pining for a church-controlled commonwealth.[21] Like other American liberals and progressives, they, too thought that the secular state's decisions should be informed and guided by the continually updating fruits of rational social science and expertise. Indeed, liberal American Catholics sought rapprochement with modern America writ large, urging Catholics to accept and supplement public education rather than to overly exert themselves for the cause of separate parochial schools. Such liberals' belief in gradual and progressive development could even apply to the church itself as part of culture.

At the same time, there were limits to the connectedness; liberal-progressive Catholics adhered to the Social Gospel in general but not its pan-Protestant, anti-dogmatic impulse. All three of our main figures believed that a liberal and engaged form of Catholicism, tied into the scientific currents of the age, had particular and unique qualities to offer America beyond what Protestantism offered. Catholic-derived ideas had even informed the incipient American nation. Thus, in contrast to its caricature by mainline progressives, Catholicism could not be reduced to an outsider immigrant body seeking to import foreign ways.

Ultimately, liberal-progressive Catholics sought a selective appropriation of what they saw as useful in the progressive reform tradition while claiming to eschew aspects of modern philosophy and scholarly fashions irreconcilable with Catholicism, such as pragmatism. It was their modus operandi to challenge, both overtly and subtly, the idea that this negotiation could not succeed

21. For a nuanced view of conservative Catholicism in the context of the American church in the decades around the turn of the twentieth century, see R. Laurence Moore, *Religious Outsiders and the Making of Americans* (New York: Oxford University Press, 1986). For conservative and progressive Catholics in debate over public and private education, see Philip Gleason, *Contending with Modernity: Catholic Higher Education in the Twentieth Century* (New York: Oxford University Press, 1995), especially parts 1 and 2. A more recent discussion of conservatism in both Rome and the American church as related to the philosophy of science in the fin de siècle is found in John Slattery's *Faith and Science at Notre Dame: John Zahm, Evolution, and the Catholic Church* (Notre Dame, Ind.: University of Notre Dame Press, 2019).

due to overall incompatibilities. They challenged the idea of such incompatibility whether it was voiced by more conservative and cautious Catholics or by non-Catholic progressives. They would shrink from no obstacle on their quest to successfully interface with modern intellectual culture and its major trends as deeply as possible.[22]

It is also necessary to clarify what liberal-progressive Catholics were not. Without forgetting Ryan's qualifications, the term *conservative Catholic* is here used to characterize that bloc within the institutional church directly or indirectly opposing our figures and their goals. In the realm that concerns us here—intellectual life in America—this book characterizes as conservative those Catholics who consistently framed their public arguments, even when aimed at non-Catholics, in the neoscholastic models advocated by Pope Leo XIII (r. 1878–1903) in his encyclical *Aeterni Patris* (On the Restoration of Christian Philosophy) of 1879.[23] Likewise, a distaste for neoscholastic expression and even neoscholastic thinking almost always characterized liberal Catholics. That said, some liberal Catholics used neoscholastic language when writing to convince other Catholics. When writing for non-Catholics, however, they avoided it.

As philosopher Michael Heller has noted, the philosophy of science endorsed by twentieth-century neoscholastics had two root layers, one of which was Aristotle's cosmology honed by Thomas Aquinas. The other was creative adaptation of that model in subsequent centuries by various Catholic philosophers such as Francisco Suárez and, by the nineteenth century, figures like Gaetano Sanseverino. In the first half of the twentieth century, this adaptation is best represented by the work of the renowned Jacques Maritain. Acknowledging the danger of oversimplification that often besets descriptions of neoscholasticism, one can still speak of certain fun-

22. Cross, *Emergence of Liberal Catholicism*, 14.
    23. For the text of the encyclical, see Pope Leo XIII, *The Leonine Encyclicals, 1878–1902* (McPherson, Kans.: Agnus Dei Publishing, 2014), 17–40.

damental contours inhering in it. Doing so here, in brief, is necessary if we are to appreciate not only its advocates' position but also, more importantly, those aspects of it that liberal Catholics and others who turned away from it found particularly objectionable. Its key was the epistemological distinction between levels of abstraction, placing the object and method of observation in the physical sciences on one level; in the mathematically grounded sciences on a second level; and in metaphysics on a third level.[24]

According to the neoscholastics, that third level—the site of the divine essences underpinning reality—was not approachable by the tools of physical or mathematical science. Then again, it did not have to be, since essences could be approached by philosophy, and only philosophy.[25] From the perspective of the neoscholastic Catholic conservative, the result of embracing neoscholasticism was by no means an eschewal of modern thought or an avoidance of the new sciences. On the contrary, it provided the ideal lens through which to engage with both of them, since it offered not only a clear framework for assessing the material at hand but also a rigorous method for discerning the limits of the new ideas. Natural science could and should be pursued, but its limits were as important to define as its reach.

Holding this philosophy of science in the early twentieth century would not affect one's practical approach to bench science. Neither, however, would it offer any particular incentive for pursuing the biological or social sciences as a profession. After all, the philosopher, not the modern scientist, occupied the prized position of approaching the First Cause out from which the subjects of all the natural and physical sciences themselves emerged. Scientific study, though laudable as inquiry into the objective natural order and the workings of secondary causes, still only encompassed one aspect of the broader pursuit of God's truth.

24. Michael Haller, *Creative Tension: Essays on Science and Religion* (Philadelphia: Templeton Press, 2003), 72. On varieties of Catholic neoscholasticism, see Gerald McCool, *The Neo-Thomists* (Milwaukee: Marquette University Press, 1994).
25. Haller, *Creative Tension*, 72.

In American public intellectual discourse, those who did focus on the sciences from within the neoscholastic philosophical mold found themselves girded in opposition to the dominant professionalizing Anglo-American science community. A good part of this dissonance derived from the latter having embraced positivism and the uniformity of nature as key identifiers of professional status and, indeed, legitimate scientific discourse. That the positivist-professional tie seemed natural and inevitable in America derived in no small part from the efforts of Edward Youmans and his magazine *Popular Science Monthly* in the later nineteenth century.[26] A newly constructed story of science's historical development also emerged to reify this connection back into natural science's earliest emergence and its struggle over time against purported religious obscurantism. Positivism not only elevated science and its method to the top spot in the hierarchy of knowledge but also could elevate the professional scientist to the role of ultimate cultural authority.[27]

An atmosphere of growing scientism in broader public culture saw the positivist view of science employed to deny the existence

26. For the conflation of professionalization and adherence to the uniformity of nature, see Matthew Stanley, "The Uniformity of Nature Laws in Victorian Britain: Naturalism, Theism, and Scientific Practice," *Zygon* 46 (2011): 536–60, and Stanley, *Huxley's Church and Maxwell's Demon: From Theistic to Natural Science* (Chicago: University of Chicago Press, 2015). Particularly for the United States context, see an article published in Edward Youmans's magazine by W. D. LeSueur: "A Defense of Modern Thought," *Popular Science Monthly* 24 (1883–84): 780–95. See also R. Clinton Ohlers, "The End of Miracles: Naturalism's Rise in American Science, 1830–1931" (PhD diss., University of Pennsylvania, 2007); William J. Leverette, "E. L. Youmans' Crusade for Scientific Autonomy and Respectability," *American Quarterly* 17 (1965): 12–32; Eva Marie Garroutte, "The Positivist Attack on Baconian Science and Religious Knowledge in the 1870s," in *The Secular Revolution: Power, Interests, and Conflict in the Secularization of American Public Life*, ed. Christian Smith (Berkeley: University of California Press, 2003), 187–215.

27. The so-called warfare metaphor or conflict thesis of science and religion history came from this invention, one which firmly advanced positivism. Its most well-known and influential example is John William Draper's *History of the Conflict between Religion and Science* (New York: D. Appleton and Co., 1874). See also Andrew Dickson White, *A History of the Warfare of Science with Theology in Christendom*, 2 vols. (London: Macmillan and Co., 1896). White first advanced his general view in an 1869 lecture covered by Horace Greeley. See "First of the Course of Scientific Lectures—Prof. White on 'The Battlefields of Science,'" *New York Herald Tribune* (December 18, 1869), 4. The conflict thesis has been soundly refuted by historians of science. See, for example, Jeff Hardin, Ronald L. Numbers, and Ronald A. Binzley, eds., *The Warfare between Science and Religion: The Idea That Wouldn't Die* (Baltimore: Johns Hopkins University Press, 2018).

of the noumenal world. Neoscholastic Catholics believed their co-religionists were acquiescing to this positivism and, therefore, fostering religious indifferentism and even philosophical relativism. As an outside observer of all of this, Russian philosopher Nicholas Berdyaev observed in 1925 that, for the neoscholastics, accepting a natural world as outside God, yet ordered by God and approachable through natural reason, is "the cornerstone of civilization."[28] This helps show why neoscholastic Catholic opponents of our liberal subjects saw the latter as such a threat to the good of the church and of society itself. But the latter felt the same way about the former's efforts in trying to "stunt" the unfolding modern age. In many ways, liberal Catholics refused to accept neoscholasticism because it aimed philosophical timelessness at the historicism so central to the fabric of intellectual life by the turn of the twentieth century.[29]

A likely insurmountable problem for Leo XIII's project was inherent in all neoscholastics' efforts. This is because, as historian Peter Harrison has ably shown, what constituted *science* by the second half of the nineteenth century did not exist in Aquinas's late medieval period, or, for that matter, at any time until the second half of the nineteenth century. It is not merely an issue of less complete facts or methods in earlier eras. Rather, natural historians and natural philosophers through the early modern period did not see themselves doing anything akin to what the later scientists understood as the point of their undertakings.[30] *Scientia*, in con-

---

28. N. A. Berdyaev, "Neothomism," *Journal Put'* 1 (1925): 170–71. This was Berdyaev's review of Réginald Garrigou-Lagrange's "Le sens commun: La philosophie de l'être et les formules dogmatiques" and Jacques Maritain's "Reflexions sur l'intelligence et sur sa vie propere." Berdyaev pointed out that as an Eastern Orthodox, he believed "there is ... no such split between the natural and the supernatural" (171).

29. Catholics who agreed with the likes of Catholic University's James Fox—who noted in 1899 that facts enjoyed much more influence with their contemporary hearers than did philosophical postulates—were bound to reject neoscholasticism as a form for engaging non-Catholics. See Michael Connolly, "The 'Grave Emergency' of 1909: Modernism and the Paulist Fathers," *U.S. Catholic Historian* 20 (2002): 53.

30. See Peter Harrison, *The Territories of Science and Religion* (Chicago: University of Chicago Press, 2015).

trast to what later became *science*, constituted a wholly different sensorium, featuring entirely different goals. This was true both for when Aquinas originally undertook his project of reconciliation between reason and faith and in the subsequent centuries leading to the nineteenth century. Leo XIII, in other words, pursued a neo-scholastic revival at precisely the time when a new conception of *science*, and *scientist*, was emerging—in uniformitarian garb. Neo-scholasticism's disjuncture with this emerging construct is hard to overestimate.

In negotiating these discourses, our liberal American Catholics sought to carve out a via media between presuppositions and perspectives of institutional Catholics, modernists and social scientists, and secular progressives and Protestant modernists. But the Catholics also brought another concern to the table: a strong desire to avoid any cooperation, perceived or otherwise, with conservative Protestants. This was for both theological and socio-political reasons. Theologically, Catholic biblical exegesis rejected the strict literalism of said Protestants and, thus, a set of conclusions derived from it. Politically, many Catholics of all stripes equated conservative Protestantism with backward nativism and a long cultural habit of anti-Catholic prejudice.

This book contends that our liberal-progressive Catholics' near-exclusive use of naturalistic argumentation in mainline public debate between the world wars unintentionally helped excise traditional religious language and frameworks from the discourse on evolution and birth control. These discursive shifts, to which the liberal Catholics contributed, not only involved new terminology; they also helped alter the categories under discussion, revise the basis of debates, and change how related problems were conceived and resolved. The debated subjects themselves were transformed into technical, biosocial matters fully in the domain of scientific experts.

Liberal Catholics and their allies fought hard to defend evolution both on the merits and as a chosen cause symbolizing intellectual sophistication. The latter was intended to contrast with conservative Protestant obscurantism and with conflict thesis-derived views of Catholicism as antiscientific and narrow. However, the manner in which they executed this defense of evolution backfired. The problem centered not only on their aforementioned use of wholly naturalistic language in debate but also on their approach to evolution as an abstract scientific matter unconnected to biologized social initiatives with eugenic underpinnings. In effectively disarming themselves this way, they were unable to wield convincing arguments when opposing other professional experts who were willing to intertwine evolution with philosophical and religious language and with biopolitical causes.

Likewise, our liberal-progressive Catholics also acted in ways that undermined many of their own interests in birth control debates. Initially, in the 1920s, they opposed contraception with medical and psychological arguments. By the early Depression years, they actually defended the rational planning of births in the form of the rhythm method while simultaneously opposing it in the form of artificial contraception. In both cases, they used science-centered, quasi-utilitarian arguments in the broader cultural conversation. This science-centered double standard could in no way counter increasingly prevalent claims by non-Catholic scientists and religious figures (including liberal Protestants and Jews), who, by 1930, contended that artificial birth control was not only healthy but also morally acceptable and economically just. The liberal-progressive Catholics' strategy unintentionally contributed to a larger conceptual separation of sex from procreation in the American mentality, the very separation the Catholic church itself sought to avoid.

These Catholics' careful adherence to scientific language in the human origins debates also opened up their own rhetoric to successful co-optation by both putatively secular public scientists—such as Osborn, Conklin, and others—and various social engineering activists, including Sanger. In certain cases, such popularizers redeployed the Catholics' own rhetoric against conservative Protestants and even sometimes against conservative Catholics. Interestingly, the language of these popularizers was itself not always so secular or strictly naturalistic as that of our Catholics. Osborn, Conklin, and others embedded quasi-theological claims into their popular science writings (and Sanger was willing, at times, to quote the Bible against Catholics) such that a role reversal, of sorts, took place as to who was actually secularizing the discourse.

With a few exceptions, when Catholicism has been considered at all in the history of American science or general histories of birth control and evolution, liberal Catholic perspectives have been blurred or elided in favor of conservatives, especially those within the institutional hierarchy. The latter serve as contrasts to America's science-oriented public intellectuals and advocates for individual freedoms. The implication is that traditional voices were the only ones affecting these cultural encounters. This, in turn, makes it tempting to place Catholicism under an overly broad umbrella in such histories.

Catholics have also tended to be cast in general histories as the lone source of uniform opposition to birth control in America, particularly after 1930, although that was not the case at any point in the interwar era.[31] The arguments, even by standards of contraception history, depict Catholics as a bloc opposing birth control advocates polemically and politically.[32]

31. See the nuanced work by Kathleen A. Tobin, *The American Religious Debate over Birth Control, 1907–1937* (Jefferson, N.C.: McFarland, 2001), 180–82. John McGreevy's *Catholicism and American Freedom: A History* (New York: W. W. Norton, 2004), and Leslie Woodcock Tentler's *Catholics and Contraception: An American History* (Ithaca: Cornell University Press, 2004), have successfully re-addressed and given substantial nuance to the picture of Catholicism with respect to birth control in America. McGreevy places the issue in the stream of broader cultural shifts in America with notions of contingent morality and freedom of choice. Tentler's study is a fine social history concerned primarily with pastoral approaches and actual practices, although intellectual debates are also addressed.

32. See the still influential history of birth control in America by Linda Gordon, *Woman's Body, Woman's Right: A Social History of Birth Control in America* (New York: Grossman Publishers, 1976), reframed and reissued as Gordon, *The Moral Property of Women: A History of Birth Control Politics in America* (Champaign: University of Illinois Press, 2002). Its author mentions Catholics only in terms of vocal opposition to birth control. See especially pages 315–16

Likewise, the broader American debate over evolution in the first half of the twentieth century is characterized by a substantial literature, much of it tied to the 1925 Scopes Trial, but here, too, the public Catholic voice has received surprisingly little attention. Presumed to have stood with conservative religion, Catholics were assumed to have shown little particular interest in the sciences (a presumption tied to the widespread mythology on Catholics and science from the warfare metaphor). In this case, the oversight includes both conservative and liberal Catholic voices. Neither contingent fits into the lingering creationist versus evolutionist paradigm that has been constructed to explain the larger debate and the Scopes Trial. It was, however, true that neoscholastic Catholic conservatives in America hesitated to support evolution for humans, although their philosophy of science did not preclude that. An almost singular focus on Protestantism in American evolution history results in marginalizing dissenting voices that cannot be accurately fit into the prevailing paradigm.[33]

Beyond integrating the influential voices of progressive Catholics into the American contraception and evolution narratives, this book intends to further the complexity thesis on the historical relationship in culture between science and religion, a thesis first articulated in John Hedley Brooke's seminal *Science and Religion* (1991).[34]

(1976) for her argument that Catholics—presented as a bloc—politically intimidated FDR and New-Deal-era social workers into avoiding the contraception issue. There is little in the way of discerning the difference between liberal Catholics and other Catholics, or whether there was there any unexpected fallout from Catholics' activities. See also James Reed, *From Private Vice to Public Virtue: The Birth Control Movement and American Society since 1830* (New York: Basic Books, 1978). Reed argues that physicians who opposed birth control around the turn of the century were responding as social conservatives *rather than* as scientists, not as both (45). For Catholics, he depicts an uncomplicated American Catholic opposition centering on papal decrees against birth control and those who mimicked those decrees.

33. Even the book that is still the standard of the field for the Scopes Trial—Edward Larson's Pulitzer Prize–winning *Summer for the Gods: The Scopes Trial and America's Continuing Debate over Science and Religion* (New York: Basic Books, 1997)—does not address the imbalance where Catholics are involved. It virtually ignores the role of the Catholic intellectual response to Scopes. Larson cited only a single contemporary Catholic source, the *Chicago Tribune* (*Summer for the Gods*, 127).

34. John Hedley Brooke, *Science and Religion: Some Historical Perspectives* (Cambridge: Cambridge University Press, 1991).

Catholics' science-centered outreach. Covering the later 1920s and the 1930s, this chapter emphasizes Cooper and O'Brien's "scientific apostleship." This "scientific apostleship" consisted of efforts in the public square to advance their interests in the language of science alongside strident attempts to stimulate Catholics' own interest in scientific research. Both figures interacted extensively with broad intellectual networks and professional organizations, reaping approval as symbols of open-minded religion's embrace of evolution, and, by extension, its embrace of the authority of science in general.

Chapter 4 moves to human conception and contraception in the 1920s, beginning with the shifting image of contraception in the Protestant-inflected environment. After a brief overview of the church's approach to contraception since the nineteenth century, this chapter looks at Ryan's substantial role in constructing Catholicism's public image on birth control in the 1920s through both intellectual and polemical engagement. Ryan's and Cooper's efforts to challenge the organized contraception movement with their own science-centered language saw them walk a tightrope in mainline public dialogue, a tightrope that ultimately worked against their own interests. The chapter concludes with an in-depth discussion of episodes late in the decade in which Ryan and Cooper debated their co-religionists over the propriety of using neoscholastic propositions in contraception debate, instead defending ends-based logic as an alternative method of argumentation.

Chapter 5 centers on crucial 1920s processes whereby several progressive and science-centered research and reform efforts came together in the interest of eugenically managing evolution. The field of genetics provided the necessary underpinnings for scientists who worked with Margaret Sanger to reconceptualize birth control from its prior associations with radicalism to the medicalized eugenic bridge that would unite in its rhetoric both controlled conception and controlled evolution. Chapter 5 also looks at the fostered transition whereby older moral and mental associations tying uncontrolled lust to disorder and weak character were reversed such that self-control in continence became the road to psycho-physiological pathology. It includes a look at how previously dissonant movements for social hygiene, eugenics, birth control, and demographic-based reform came together in a union of perceived shared interest. The scientized efforts of Cooper in the American Social Hygiene Association (ASHA) and of both Ryan and Cooper in the American Eugenics Society (AES) are shown to have unintentionally assisted in these shifts even as Ryan and Cooper tried to oppose some of them.

Chapter 6 advances the story of contraception through the 1930s, where the Great Depression itself, in tandem with a nexus of movements endorsing artificial birth control on economic and eugenic grounds, resulted in shifts in key public organizations' stances on contraception. These shifts spanned from mainline Protestant churches to, eventually, physicians' associations and legal entities. Although not endorsing artificial contraception, our liberal Catholics nonetheless contributed to this larger shift by the way they changed the emphases of their own arguments. Previously using science to argue for the dangers of contraception, by the early-to-mid-1930s, they instead argued in favor of what they called natural regulation of births, made possible by applying new scientific research into the physiology of female ovulation. Liberal Catholics enthusiastically recommended the rhythm method of birth regulation, an endorsement eventually yielding a swath of unforeseen consequences discussed here. These Catholics are shown to have played a substantive role in shearing the culture's perceived connection between intercourse and procreation, a fracture the institutional church had long fought to prevent. Both the nature of arguments (and responses to them) in O'Brien's influential publications and Ryan's engagement with Sanger, both in Congress and in the public arena, constitute the Catholic center-of-gravity in this chapter.

The conclusion evaluates, by way of illustrative episodes, the overall consequences of liberal-progressive Catholics' interwar efforts. It is followed by a short postscript considering reverberations into the 1950s, where echoes of some of our priests' arguments may, ironically, have helped encourage Catholic physician John Rock in co-developing the first birth control pill.

Three Father Johns

Liberal, Progressive, and Scientific

Directive sociology … sets up the true ends of human
association and describes the manner in which it should
be controlled for the realization of those ends.

—Fr. William Kerby (1912)

Father John Augustine Ryan, midwestern farm boy–cum–Catholic
hotline to FDR, never won any contests for charisma. Not long
after assuming his post at the Catholic University of America in
1915, he solidified his reputation as an uninspiring and even mo-
notonous lecturer, with one student later conferring upon him the
questionable distinction of worst teacher he ever had.[1] Colleagues
and students alike had a hand in assigning him the nickname "Fog
Ryan" as a nod to his ever-present distractedness. His topsy-turvy
appearance did little to compensate for these defects; rumpled suits
occasionally replete with evidence of recent meals did little to hide
the increasing softness of his frame over time. Unkempt eyebrows
surmounting large, hollow eyes crowned his rather puffy face,

---

Epigraph is from William Kerby, "Sociology," in *The Catholic Encyclopedia* (1912), quoted
in Neusse, "William Joseph Kerby," 89.

1. "Who Was John A. Ryan?," American Catholic History Classroom, https://cuomeka
.wrlc.org/exhibits/show/bishops/ryan/1919ryan-intro (accessed January 25, 2021).

giving Ryan an owl-like appearance especially as he aged. Yet this man possessed a character and tenacity that could not be weighed by mere physiognomy or lecture room persona. Chief among his virtues were a populist sense of fair play, curiosity, and a direct honesty that could border on bluntness but never degenerated into cheap shots or virulence. He was stubborn when it came to what he believed was right, but he could also see other perspectives.[2] One of the characteristics that brought him into bad repute with some of his more hesitant co-religionists was a tendency to find any common denominator by which he could justify cooperating even with the irreligious if it meant advancing his social justice interests—even at the expense of framing the questions religiously.[3] By his death in 1945, the New York Times eulogized Ryan as "the economist ... leader of the liberal wing of the Catholic church in America [with an] international reputation and a prestige outside his communion in America that equaled his influence within it."[4] One day after this obituary ran, President Harry Truman said of his death, "a powerful influence in our American life is lost."[5]

John Ryan arrived in the American populist heartland of Vermillion, Minnesota, on May 25, 1869, to parents William and Mary Luby Ryan, first-generation Irish Catholic immigrants from County Tipperary, who had fled the lingering ravages of Ireland's infamous potato famine. The rest of the spare homes in Vermillion, twenty miles south of St. Paul, sheltered other families of a similar ethno-religious makeup and class. All had come to America seeking a life better than that they experienced in the political and economic tempests of rural Ireland.

The eldest of ten children who survived infancy, Ryan later

2. Francis L. Broderick, Right Reverend New Dealer: John A. Ryan (London: Macmillan, 1963), 2.

3. Broderick, Right Reverend New Dealer, 67.

4. "Msgr. John A. Ryan, Economist, 76, Dies," New York Times (September 17, 1945), 19, in John Augustine Ryan Papers, box 74, folder 6, American Catholic History Research Center and University Archive, The Catholic University of America, Washington, D.C. (henceforth ACUA).

5. New York Times (September 18, 1945), in Ryan Papers, box 74, folder 6, ACUA.

recalled a household imbued with "strict Roman Catholic principles."[6] His father, a mill worker turned small farmer, exuded stiffness and formality, playing to a tee the role of stern and humorless disciplinarian. By the age of sixteen, young Ryan had had enough of his father's ways, even temporarily running away to a relative's farm. On the other hand, Ryan had only praise for his mother, invoking words like "warm," "intuitive," and others of that ilk to describe her.[7]

Ryan grew up broad-shouldered from his work on the family farm, a farm to which he would return for summer chores years after he left home to attend seminary. Over time, he grew into a softer version of his once-athletic, baseball-playing youth and was characterizable by words like "gruff, chubby, and earthy."[8] By the time he established himself, he was much more likely to be found intensely grinding away at his desk than performing any but the minimum socializing expected of him in his faculty and priestly positions.[9] Even when he was in his seventies, hard work and a direct manner remained trademarks. His biographer, Francis Broderick, astutely notes that these qualities veiled what was, in fact, a lack of both introspection and sensitivity to the subtleties of human motivation, whether others' or his own.[10] He says that Ryan's notes from his personal journal in 1894 could have been mistaken for a populist political tract.[11]

Bereft of verbal eloquence himself, Ryan could nevertheless be stirred by oratory provided that the topic interested him. He frequently felt mesmerized as a young man by the elocution of certain Farmer's Alliance leaders' speeches, especially those given by a man named Ignatius Donnelly on farm grievances. Donnelly

6. John A. Ryan, *Social Doctrine in Action: A Personal History* (New York: Harper and Brothers, 1941), 7.

7. Ryan quoted in Broderick, *Right Reverend New Dealer*, 2–4, 5.

8. Broderick, *Right Reverend New Dealer*, 6–7, 77.

9. Broderick, *Right Reverend New Dealer*, 36–37.

10. Broderick, *Right Reverend New Dealer*, 168.

11. Broderick, *Right Reverend New Dealer*, 18.

represented a coalition of rural reform clubs that would eventually coalesce into the People's Party.[12]

It was an Anglo-Protestant version of Ryan's midwestern milieu that produced the famous populist-progressive orator William Jennings Bryan. Although both were cut from much the same cloth, these two figures would eventually see themselves on opposite sides of key debates of the 1920s, such as the Scopes Trial and Prohibition (the latter only after Ryan changed his mind and reversed his initial support). One man who *would* agree with Ryan on the Scopes Trial and much else, yet who emerged from very different circumstances, was Fr. John Montgomery Cooper.

Cooper was born October 28, 1881, in Rockville, Maryland, into a socially established Catholic family in circumstances markedly contrasting with the Ryans' rural immigrant enclave. Raised in an upper-crust section of Baltimore, along with two siblings, by James and Emma Tolou Cooper, Cooper came from a lineage that traced all the way back to colonial Quakers on his father's side. John's mother, Emma, was of French Catholic lineage; her family had immigrated in the early nineteenth century to Maryland, America's oldest concentrated Catholic milieu.[13] The precocious Cooper received an excellent early education in Baltimore from the erudite priests of the Sulpician order, a group hailing from France known for its intimate connection with liberal Catholic thought.[14] Quite unlike Ryan, Cooper showed artistic talent as a youth; Ryan's farm family had little time for such things. Cooper and Ryan did, how-

12. "After Mass on Sunday ... Hugh McGuire, the town radical, ... harangued about the railroad monopoly, [and] John was always nearby. If neighbors dropped in to talk over Alliance issues with William [his father], John was at hand" (Broderick, *Right Reverend New Dealer*, 18).

13. McKeown, "From *Pascendi* to *Primitive Man*," 2n2. On Cooper's paternal family, see Regina Flannery, "John Montgomery Cooper, 1881–1949," *American Anthropologist*, New Series 52 (January–March 1950): 64. Flannery traces Cooper's father's side to James Cooper, who arrived in Pennsylvania's Darby township from Mayfield, England, in 1684. For more on Cooper's lineage, see Paul Hanly Furfey, "John Montgomery Cooper, 1881–1949," *Primitive Man* 23 (July 1950): 49–50.

14. For a history of the Baltimore Sulpicians and their modernism, see Kauffman, *Tradition and Transformation*. It was the Sulpician order—under priests trained in the Baltimore seminary—that ran the famously modernist St. Joseph's Seminary in Dunwoodie, New York.

ever, share certain characteristics. Both were athletic when growing
up, their training perhaps helping to shape disciplined personali-
ties that would translate into lifelong mutual reputations for relent-
less effort in all their undertakings.[15]

Growing into adulthood, Cooper assumed a lean, wiry form,
the sharpness of his angular features softened by expressive and
clear eyes. As dissimilar as his physicality was compared to Ryan's,
so, too, was Cooper's youthful experience unlike Ryan's in terms
of exposure to common folk. Cooper's genteel background largely insulated him from the struggles of the marginalized. However,
both his parents' teachings and his subsequent experiences with
American tribes quashed any possibility of personal elitism or
detachment. Indeed, Cooper developed strong concern and respect for simple folk and their customs in his many encounters
with native peoples in anthropological field expeditions spanning
the Western United States and Canada as well as through extensive study of South American native communities. His encounters
with primitive cultures he termed "inter-marginal" cultivated in
him deep respect for their folkways and practices, especially where
child-rearing was concerned.[16]

Cooper also possessed a personal touch in relating to peers
throughout his illustrious career in academia. He believed that
informal exchanges—sometimes over good German beer—were
as important as the conference hall in cultivating new ideas and
perspectives.[17] Throughout his academic career, Cooper's public
persona remained consistently polished, his slim physique and fas-
tidious attire cutting a sharp contrast with the rumpled Ryan.

Our third and final central figure also bore the name Fr. John,
and he, too, grew up to be a progressive Catholic social scientist
who made a mark in the American public square. Born John An-

15. McKeown, "From *Pascendi* to *Primitive Man*," 2n2.

16. McKeown, "From *Pascendi* to *Primitive Man*," 3, 4n5, 5n8.

17. This is a reference to Cooper's particular mention of collegial discussions at the
Hofbrau restaurant in New Haven at a conference he attended at Yale University (McKeown
"From *Pascendi* to *Primitive Man*," 6n9).

thony O'Brien to John F. and Elizabeth T. Powers O'Brien of Peoria, Illinois, on January 20, 1893, O'Brien was, like Ryan, a product of the Irish Catholic upper Midwest. However, the difference in his home life compared to Ryan's is apparent in O'Brien's warm words about his "devoted" father in his published recollections. O'Brien constructed an image of his upbringing that evokes a pleasing hearth: "my father reading aloud after the supper table was cleared while mother sewed and the children listened."[18] His images of his "devout" mother reveal not only genuine fondness but also admiration of this schoolteacher with a "retentive memory" who early on stimulated his interest in learning. O'Brien specifically credited his mother and her frequent habit of quoting good literature with his own blossoming love of the literary arts.[19]

O'Brien also recalled his early schooling with affection. His precollegiate studies—first with "those great educators," the Sisters of Notre Dame at St. Patrick School, and then with the Brothers of Mary at Spalding Institute—culminated with his high school graduation as class valedictorian.[20] Following one year in Massachusetts at the College of the Holy Cross "perched in a room … overlooking one of the largest textile mills in New England … reading … anthologies of prose and poetry," homesickness prompted his transfer to St. Viator's College back in his home state in 1913. There he spent his time not only studying but also participating in activities that took him out of his room, including playing second string on the college's football team.[21]

By that point, O'Brien had grown into a handsome young man with a square chin and cheerful eyes whose fashionable inclinations led him to adopt the kind of swooping pompadour-style haircut combed up for volume popular around the war era. Soon taken under the wing of Fr. William J. Bergin, CSV, whom he called

18. O'Brien quoted in Walter Romig, ed. *Book of Catholic Authors*, 2nd ser. (Detroit: Walter Romig and Co., 1943), 242.
19. O'Brien quoted in Romig, *Book of Catholic Authors*, 242.
20. O'Brien quoted in Romig, *Book of Catholic Authors*, 242.
21. O'Brien quoted in Romig, *Book of Catholic Authors*, 244.

a deep thinker, excellent teacher, and "a great admirer of Orestes Brownson," O'Brien cultivated a lasting friendship with Bergin that ultimately led him to team with Bergin later in his career at the University of Illinois.[22]

With this trio of Fr. Johns, we have three people with diverse backgrounds and experiences who nevertheless came together in a set of intellectual overlaps amid interlocking careers via the common font of Catholic progressive liberalism. Their coherence as a set stems not only from their mutual interactions in a common universe of discourse but also partly from sharing common opposition within their church. Further drawing them together were their encounters with broader progressivism and with liberal movements within the church at institutions nurturing them. These helped form their shared visions as liberal Catholics who particularly sought to engage thinkers outside an insulated Catholic American subculture. Perhaps their most common denominator was a belief that the language of science was the Rosetta stone that would crack the wall between them and Catholic intellectual respectability in the American public square while providing access to the broader intellectual communities they sought to both reach and influence.

However one assesses the positions taken by Frs. Ryan, Cooper, and O'Brien, one thing not in dispute is their courage. They took on what was a powerful conservative ultramontane cadre within Catholicism—among whom were most of the American bishops— set to oppose much of what they sought and especially how they sought it. They also found themselves trying to negotiate what they saw as their church's authentic position as a place of real influence in an American public culture that saw substantial and even new anti-Catholic sentiments, sentiments seen in everything from the subtle anti-Catholicism in elite journals of opinion like *The Nation* to the Al Smith presidential campaign down to the second Ku Klux Klan.

---

22. O'Brien quoted in Romig, *Book of Catholic Authors*, 243. Brownson, the Protestant transcendentalist-cum-Catholic, was a mentor of Isaac Hecker.

By the 1920s, overtly political anti-Catholicism restored itself and was centered in the new northern Klan.[23] The Klan's membership skyrocketed from five thousand in 1920 to five million by 1924.[24] The northern Klan maintained an alliance with the various fundamentalist Protestant churches, many of which were located in the North. Affiliates of this new Klan were expected to participate in a Protestant congregation, uphold Prohibition, and evince family and patriotic values. Nevertheless, fundamentalism was not the whole story of Protestantism and the Klan. At times, Klan leaders attempted to create a pan-Protestant phalanx against Catholic threats, a populist version of the very Christian unity moves marking the elite Protestant ecumenical movement fashioned through the Federal Council of Churches."[25]

From the early twentieth century, the politics of education, too, was a venue for significant anti-Catholicism. In the curricula of higher education, educators who were increasingly oriented toward secular science models of education battled the old guard Protestant elites for control. One common bond between the two groups, however, was distaste for what they saw as Catholic casuistry. Programmatic positivists in the social and biological science fields were colonizing the curricula of universities and beginning to successfully reorient American higher education toward a nationwide vision of specialized secular scholarship.[26] The college-educated

23. A Klan handbill popular in Indiana in the early 1920s read: "Remember, every criminal, every gambler, every thug, every libertine, every girl ruiner, every home wrecker, every wife beater, ... every crooked politician, every pagan Papist priest, every shyster lawyer, every K. of C. [Knight of Columbus], ... every Rome controlled newspaper ... is fighting the Klan." Quoted in Martin E. Marty, *The Noise of Conflict: 1919–1941*, vol. 2 of *Modern American Religion* (Chicago: University of Chicago Press, 1991), 95.

24. Glen Jeansonne, *A Time of Paradox: America Since 1890* (Lanham, Md.: Rowman and Littlefield, 2006), 107. The new Klan was created in 1915 by a former Protestant minister named William J. Simmons who used public relations experts to increase membership (Jeansonne, 108).

25. Marty, *Noise of Conflict*, 94.

26. Christian Smith, "Rethinking the Secularization of American Public Life," in *The Secular Revolution: Power, Interests, and Conflict in the Secularization of American Public Life*, ed. Christian Smith (Berkeley: University of California Press, 2003), 75. This trend represented, in fact, the importation and implementation of the late nineteenth-century (*Kulturkampf*-era) German university model. Added to that was an increasingly prevalent trend by the second

public was schooled in a binding narrative of professionalization and efficiency that was reinforced by industry's drive for advanced scientific research. There was supposedly no place in this vision of public life for Catholic intellectuals, who were viewed as wedded to outmoded Aristotelian conceptions of science that were, by definition, impractical for the needs of a technocratic economy.

But the three Fr. Johns never fit the bill of the anti-Catholic caricatures. Indeed, the landscape of progressivism was a transatlantic intellectual environment whose powerful winds strongly blew through the lives of all three. Ryan's and Cooper's graduate study and maturation took place during the Progressive movement itself. O'Brien matured while a partially transformed American progressivism maintained an essential role in intellectual life even after World War I. Its currents circulated at Catholic University in the decades surrounding the turn of the twentieth century where they mingled together with Americanist and modernist currents. We will consider below how these intellectual orientations operated together at that university.

The eldest of our central figures—and the one who, once appointed to the faculty, spent the entirety of his professional academic career at the Catholic University of America—was Fr. Ryan. The man most responsible for getting him there was one of the American church's most famous Americanist hierarchs.

Although John Ryan's biological father was present in the home throughout his upbringing, Ryan spent the first seventeen years of life without the emotional and intellectual support of a father figure to whom he could turn for trustworthy guidance. At age eighteen, Ryan found that figure in the Americanist, Bishop John Ireland of St. Paul, Minnesota. Ryan had enrolled at the diocese of St. Paul's junior seminary, Saint Thomas, and then at its major seminary, St. Paul's—named not only for the patron saint of the city where it

---

decade of the twentieth century whereby "the naturalistic definition of science was rapidly being transformed from a methodology into a dominant academic worldview." George M. Marsden, "Evangelicals and the Scientific Culture: An Overview," in *Religion and Twentieth Century American Intellectual Life*, ed. Michael J. Lacey (Cambridge: Cambridge University Press, 1989), 42.

resided but also for the patron of the religious order spawning the Americanist movement itself, the Paulists.

Ireland ordained Ryan to the priesthood in 1898 and served as his most significant formative mentor. Ireland represented both a break from and a continuation of certain trajectories in the American Catholic episcopate since the country's first territorial bishop, John Carroll, assumed his see in 1789. The break was with a number of Ireland's contemporary episcopal colleagues over his approach to church-government relations and the desire for a particularly American Catholic community geared to appeal to Protestants. The continuity was that, in the longer view, much of Ireland's thought in these matters enjoyed precedents in the earlier history of the American episcopate.

The above-mentioned John Carroll, brother of the sole Catholic signer of the Declaration of Independence and relative of Maryland colony's founders, had served as first provincial bishop of Baltimore. In Carroll, one already finds kernels of precedent for Ireland's socio-political and ecclesiological views. Carroll represented a republican and Enlightenment strand of Catholicism concerned with how the American Catholic church might interface with a culture then in rebellion against the English monarchy. Like America's founders, Carroll believed strongly in the autonomy of the individual and in the primacy of natural reason. He saw this combination as the obvious grounding for the church's relationship to any state—but especially to America given the principles of the United States.[27] It was Carroll who introduced the French-originating Sulpician order into the American Catholic epicenter in Baltimore and into its education system. Sulpicians had played a part in educating Ireland in France and, later, Sulpician schools helped shape Cooper, Ryan, and, to an extent, O'Brien.[28] As in

27. See Patrick W. Carey, ed., *American Catholic Religious Thought: The Shaping of a Theological and Social Tradition* (Milwaukee: Marquette University Press, 2004), 14–16.

28. As Christopher Kauffman points out, the Sulpician priest and philosopher Louis Branchereau, author of a well-known philosophy manual, substantially influenced Ireland when the latter studied in France. See Kauffman, *Tradition and Transformation*, 158.

France, the Sulpicians became known in America for their liberal theology and their conciliar Gallican view of church organization.[29]

American bishops after Carroll's 1815 death oversaw a period often described as the era of Romantic Catholicism, which lasted through the 1860s; during that time, Sulpician Romanticist hierarchs led key eastern and midwestern dioceses.[30] This environment, in conjunction with an additional influx of French-educated priests bringing a theological emphasis on the internal workings of the Holy Spirit, laid the groundwork for the kind of Catholicism Ireland would try to cultivate in the late nineteenth and early twentieth century.[31]

America's own indigenous Romantic movement also produced well-known figures who emphasized intuition and internal spiritual guidance. It is not too surprising that the conjunction of these two contexts saw intellectual heavyweight Orestes Brownson (1803–76) and his like-minded disciple Isaac Thomas Hecker (1819–88), founder of the Paulist Order, convert to Catholicism from transcendentalist Protestantism as they searched for a path containing not only order and tradition but also a theology of the vivifying Spirit.[32] Catholics such as Brownson and Hecker understood the Holy Spirit working with fervor in the hearts and souls of the faithful as the same Spirit guiding and refashioning American

29. See Kauffman, *Tradition and Transformation*, 154–60. For examples of their ecumenical outreach in the early decades of the nineteenth century, see 92–93. On Baltimore's Sulpicians, see chap. 5.

30. Examples include the pro-American and liberal French Sulpician Benedict Joseph Flaget of Bardstown, Kentucky; Bishop Ambrose Maréchal (r. 1817–28), Carroll's own second successor to the see of Baltimore; and others. See Kauffman, *Tradition and Transformation*, 154, 160–61.

31. The above-mentioned Branchereau's work was strongly scrutinized by the Catholic censors on suspicion of ontologism, a view that heavily emphasized the key role of individual intuition in religious awareness. As Kauffman noted, Branchereau's views have been traced to the Americanists' emphasis on "the agency of the Holy Spirit in the church in the modern world" (*Tradition and Transformation*, 158).

32. On Hecker's transcendentalism, see Philip Gleason, "Boundlessness, Consolidation, and Discontinuity between Generations: Catholic Seminary Studies in Antebellum America," *Church History* 73 (September 2004): 583.

society and culture writ large.[33] For Brownson, Hecker, and other thinkers in this Romantic Catholicism, what would come to be
seen as the post-Kantian world's emphasis on subject over object
meant an exciting new era of the Holy Spirit acting through Christian social development, or, as they called it, the Spirit of the Age.[34]
Hecker and his ilk took to this message as their prime apologetic
emphasis.[35] The echo is clearly discernible in Ireland, who wrote
of the turn-of-the-century American church "grow[ing] with the
growth of the country ... [and] well-fitted for the work of religion
and a new people in a new age."[36]

By contrast, the ultramontane movement's triumph in Vatican I (1871) saw the rise of a very different tradition of American
bishops—one focused on uniformity, papal centralization, and, especially, the utter rejection of what they saw as a very dangerous
development: Kantian-influenced theology.[37] By the time Ireland
and his close colleague in Baltimore, Cardinal James Gibbons (r.
1877–1921), were manning their sees, a not-so-subtle struggle had
developed within the American episcopate between the Americanists and the conservatives, with the former two bishops clearly
planted in the Americanist camp.[38] Those Catholics in America
later tied to the ideas of the conservative movement would repre-

33. See Carey, *American Catholic Religious Thought*, 38–39.

34. Hecker's essays arguing Catholicism's deep connection with American ideals and
bearing this perspective were collected and published in the year of his death under the title
The Church and the Age (1888).

35. This analysis of Hecker is directly adopted from Carey. See Carey, *American Catholic
Religious Thought*, 35–48.

36. John Ireland, *The Church and Modern Society: Lectures and Addresses*, vol. 1 (St. Paul,
Minn.: Pioneer Press, 1904), 22. Patrick Carey has rightly argued that for the likes of Ireland
and Gibbons vis-à-vis progressivism, "a quasi-immanentist understanding of the relationship
of the sacred to the secular lay behind the Americanist call for Catholics to identify themselves with American ideals and institutions" (*American Catholic Religious Thought*, 51).

37. On the intellectual and political developments resonating from Vatican I, see John
W. O'Malley, *Vatican I: The Council and the Making of the Ultramontane Church* (Cambridge,
Mass.: Belknap Press of Harvard University Press, 2018).

38. On the nuances of Catholic bishops' Americanist-conservative debates, see R. Laurence Moore, *Religious Outsiders*, especially 48–71. Thomas W. Spalding characterized Gibbons as essentially "a reincarnation of James Carroll" in light of his "devotion to American
principles, his deep-felt patriotism, his civic sense, his all-embracing ecumenism." Thomas
W. Spalding, *The Premier See: A History of the Archdiocese of Baltimore, 1789–1989* (Baltimore:
Johns Hopkins University Press, 1989), 233.

sent a key force of suspicion and opposition to the three Fr. Johns.

The Americanist Ireland, serving in the United States, was deeply influenced by its Protestant Social Gospel. He purposefully plugged himself into the American Progressive movement and inherited the latter's deep faith in the scientific method's role in both social and moral reconstruction.[39] As such, Ireland mandated modern science instruction at all his seminaries. His mentor's insistence on social science courses initiated Ryan into the intellectual models that would come to define him.[40] Ryan also gained a solid foundation in the biological sciences at St. Paul's, a curricular feature unusual for Catholic diocesan seminaries at that time and stemming partly from railroad magnate James T. Hill's major benefaction of St. Paul's seminary. Hill insisted that science courses—and thoroughly equipped modern laboratories—contribute to all seminary students' formation.[41] Finally, like all Catholic seminarians at the time, Ryan received his grounding in philosophy, mostly through formulaic and legalistic manuals in neoscholastic thought.[42]

Ryan accepted neoscholastic natural law presuppositions, but this acceptance represented no culmination of deep intellectual examination on the subject. Instead, the seeming clarity and definitiveness of natural law reasoning when applied to social-moral problems found already fallow fields in Ryan. Creative, in-depth

39. See Carey, *American Catholic Religious Thought*, 49. Ireland's own calls for Catholic patriotism and assimilationism reinforce this. As an example, Ireland wrote that "the Catholic Church of America received into its bosom sons and daughters of many races in order that by assimilating to itself virtues of various types it should grow with the growth of the country into a new and vigorous spiritual commonwealth" (*Church and Modern Society*, 1:22). As scholar Thomas Wangler characterized Ireland's thought: "The idea was that '[w]hen the American people came to realize that Catholicism stood guard over their own civic ideals, and that a commitment to it involved no essentially foreign entanglement, Ireland was convinced that conversions would abound.'" Thomas Wangler, "The Ecclesiology of Archbishop John Ireland: Its Nature, Development, and Influence" (PhD diss., Marquette University, 1968), 238.

40. Ryan, *Social Doctrine*, 7.

41. Broderick, *Right Reverend New Dealer*, 16.

42. One of the most famous and widely used was Jesuit John Gury's *Compendium of Moral Theology*, itself based on the Scholastic theologian Alphonsus Liguori's *Moral Theology* (1748). See John T. Noonan Jr., *Contraception: A History of Its Treatment by the Catholic Theologians and Canonists* (Cambridge, Mass.: Harvard University Press, 1965), 320, 396.

theological reflection never attracted his attention. His mind and temperament always gravitated toward practical outcomes. Recalling his seminary studies in biblical interpretation, he once noted:

I devoted an exceptional amount of time to the various theories then current on the inspiration of Scripture and to the different opinions concerning the effects of original sin ..., [but] there are a number of ... questions concerning which even the authoritative specialists are not in full agreement. In this broad field of theological opinion there are very few views for which a student cannot invoke the authority of a distinguished theologian, and frequently an entire "school" of theologians.[43]

This sort of open-ended engagement did not appeal to him. He preferred the apparent definitiveness of social science, admitting that his "deepest and most sustained interest ... was not in questions of dogma or Scripture or church history but in those treatises of moral theology which dealt with the morality of economic transactions," adding that "my collateral reading took in ... a fair amount of books and magazines which fell under the head of sociology and economics."[44] Ryan believed it would not be the standard fields of Scripture or dogmatics that would most lead people toward salvation in the industrial age but rather lessons in economic opportunity: "It seemed to me ... that the salvation of millions of souls depended largely upon the economic opportunity to live decently."[45] Ryan's rhetoric of salvation had a very temporal cast to it, not unlike that of a postmillennialist Protestant progressive.

Unlike the questions of biblical theology, Ryan extensively contemplated the effects of the machine age upon human beings and their social interactions, writing in his diary early in seminary: "As the nature of men has become mechanical, in their dealings with one another, they do not hesitate to treat their brothers as machines, considering them as useful only for the amount of ma-

43. Ryan, *Social Doctrine*, 58. These various biblical interpretive theories he mentions were the historical-critical, or scientific-critical, approaches.

44. Ryan, *Social Doctrine*, 59.

45. Ryan, *Social Doctrine*, 59.

terial profit to be derived from them."[46] Ryan's dream as a semi-
narian was to change this—partly through moral exhortation but
mostly through practical social proposals. He later reminisced on
his fondness in those years for English Catholic economist W. S.
Lily alongside American political economists Henry George and
Richard T. Ely of Johns Hopkins University and the University of
Wisconsin, respectively.[47]

At the same time—as a prescient historian rightly pointed out
more recently—for such Catholics as Ryan, the economic question
was and would increasingly become intertwined with questions of
sexual morality, especially birth control.[48] Evolution's relationship
to genetics and, ultimately, eugenics tied Ryan and his social question to these concerns as well. With all of these contexts in mind,
we can foresee from early in Ryan's priesthood a trajectory that
would lead him squarely into the central debates of this book.

Ryan's sympathies with the liberal wing of the church only increased after 1898 when Archbishop Ireland sent him off to graduate studies at the then epicenter of Catholic liberalism in American
higher education, the Catholic University of America in Washington, D.C.[49] This venue saw a culmination of Americanist trends
stretching from Carroll through the French Sulpicians to the Ro-
mantics and Hecker. The school's emergence and growth in an era
of reform and progressivism in education also helped set its course
as an early bridge between the Catholic subculture and the wider
American intellectual milieu. While approval from Rome obviously enabled the university's creation, once founded, the school's

46. John A. Ryan, "Journal 1892–1898," 20, in Ryan Papers, box 69, folder 22, ACUA.

47. Ryan, *Social Doctrine*, 40–54.

48. McGreevy, *Catholicism and American Freedom*, 163. McGreevy also points out that
by the interwar era, "noting the similarities in the arguments made by proponents of birth
control, involuntary sterilization, and euthanasia, Catholics warned that the pragmatic criterion of usefulness might move from the right to procreate to the lives of the elderly and the
infirm" (226).

49. Broderick, *Right Reverend New Dealer*, 14–15. Quoting Fr. Joseph McSorley, whose
student days at the university overlapped with Ryan's, Broderick points out that the former
recalled that "the atmosphere was heavy with liberalism" (McSorley quoted in Broderick,
Right Reverend New Dealer, 30).

broad impetus came from its own leaders and the faculty's desire to connect Catholics with non-Catholic America. As this was also the desire of all three Fr. Johns, it is no coincidence that all of them had ties to this university either as professors or as graduate students—and, in the case of Ryan, as both.

The American bishops' formal blessing for the school had come in 1884 at Baltimore's Third Plenary Council; throughout the 1870s, a set of insistent and forceful visionaries, one of whom was Isaac Hecker himself, advocated for the school. [50] Hecker and other early proponents insisted that the new university be of a caliber and form distinct from all other Catholic institutions previously existing in the United States, a concern directed at the intellectual poverty of American Catholic colleges. That concern had only grown amid the university reform movement led by the likes of Andrew Dickson White and Charles W. Eliot. Part of the remedy was to model the university's new graduate program on the pattern of the German research universities.[51] That model led to a concerted faculty recruitment effort designed to bring cutting-edge research models to the school by its opening in 1887. These models included higher biblical criticism, historicism, and developmentalist views of dogma. On the other hand, whatever new ideas the Catholic University of America's faculty might have in store, the anti-Catholic American intellectual and social milieu still obtaining in the 1880s meant the school's advocates knew their university would have its work cut out for it to connect with non-Catholic America.

A most troubling aspect of this prejudice was the press's often overt presumption of Catholic hostility to the sciences. A myth about Catholic anti-scientific animus traced at least as far back as Voltaire's distortions of the Galileo incident;[52] the incident had been accentuated to sensational effect in the 1870s by American

50. John Tracy Ellis, *The Formative Years of the Catholic University of America*. (Washington, D.C.: American Catholic Historical Association, 1946), 57.

51. Gleason, *Contending with Modernity*, 169.

52. On the subsequent distortions of the Galileo case and effects on Catholic writers' insecurity about it, see Artigas, Glick, and Martínez, *Negotiating Darwin*, 281–83.

physician John William Draper in his popular 1874 book *History of the Conflict between Religion and Science*, which was essentially an anti-Catholic screed.[53]

One such press decree in a December 1884 *New York Times* editorial argued that the university would fulfill no practical purpose, since Catholic opposition to scientific progress was normative. Targeting evolution, the piece stated "the hypothesis of evolution would find no countenance in a Roman Catholic university, and its pupils would feel that in many fields they must practically ignore much of the work of the most eminent scientific men of the century."[54] It was precisely the kind of reaction Catholic University's supporters might have expected, but its actualization stimulated a Catholic reaction combining insecurity with greater determination to prove the critics wrong.

Bishop John Lancaster Spalding's 1885 letter seeking financial support for the future school said one of the institution's prime goals was the reconciliation of science and religion.[55] Speaking at the 1888 cornerstone laying, Spalding promised the university would "teach the best that is known and encourage research; it will be at once a scientific institute, a school of culture, and a training ground for the business of life."[56]

From the start, the school featured a liberal Americanist atmosphere. Bishop John Keane, a cleric trained by Baltimore's Sulpician priests, served as the first rector and was described by a successor as "Fr. Hecker's spiritual child in everything."[57] An early trustee

53. See Draper, *History of the Conflict*. The other major work of the late nineteenth century that subsequently contributed to the same myth of longstanding warfare between scientific and religious concerns came from the pen of the aforementioned education reformer and founder-president of Cornell University, Andrew Dickson White, in his 1896 two-volume work *A History of the Warfare of Science with Theology in Christendom*.

54. Quoted in Ellis, *Formative Years*, 119. This was not a monolithic sentiment. One exception was the nonsectarian *New York Sun*'s complimentary piece on December 11, 1884: it argued that the proposed Catholic institution should be welcomed by Americans since it would lead to a more educated and informed Catholic clergy (Ellis, 117).

55. Spalding quoted in Ellis, *Formative Years*, 184.

56. Spalding quoted in Ellis, *Formative Years*, 289.

57. Quoted in C. Joseph Neusse, *The Catholic University of America: A Centennial History* (Washington, D.C.: The Catholic University of America Press, 1990), 34n127.

recalled a preoccupation with scientific prestige in both Keane and the school's second rector, the liberal Bishop Thomas Conaty (1896–1903): "The first two rectors looked with awe on 'science,' of which they knew very little.... The scientific people, rather sure that they would not be interfered with, managed to do as they pleased."[58] It was during Conaty's tenure that Fr. Ryan pursued his graduate work at Catholic University.

In selecting his inaugural faculty, Keane made clear his preference for hiring American-born professors who would garner the public's favor and further the school's goal of acquiring scientists of repute, including in the new social sciences.[59] Keane brought in Fr. Edward Pace, an American who trained in Rome, to teach divinity. Pace soon became one of the faculty's most vociferous advocates of the social sciences. Along with Thomas Shields, a Johns Hopkins-trained biologist, Pace codirected the education department for years.[60]

The school's 1893–94 yearbook reveals the role that science as a marker of progress would play in American Catholicism's complicated tap dance of boundary negotiation and status aspiration vis-à-vis non-Catholic America. The yearbook boasted: "Happily we can point, even now and in this country, to individual Catholics whose scientific attainments command a merited respect.... Let men of this stamp be formed into a body; and without weakening in the least their ardor of investigation, they will be palpable proof of our Catholic sympathy with progress."[61]

Ryan undertook his first year of graduate study at Catholic University before the papal condemnation of Americanism. Pope Leo XIII anathematized the movement in his letter to Cardinal Gibbons, *Testem Benevolentiae*, in 1899. To those across the ocean in Rome,

58. Neusse, *Catholic University of America*, 121.

59. Patrick Henry Ahern, *The Catholic University of America, 1887–1896: The Rectorship of John J. Keane* (Washington, D.C.: The Catholic University of America Press, 1948), 4. On the science faculty, see Ahern, 53.

60. Neusse, *Catholic University of America*, 129–30.

61. "The Work of the University," *Year-Book of the Catholic University of America, 1893–94*, quoted in Neusse, *Catholic University of America*, 65.

Americanism looked like a coherent movement that was closely related to a controversy within French Catholicism said to emphasize the *active virtues* at the expense of the *passive virtues*, often meaning social service over the pursuit of prayer devotions and
mystical efforts. As this could reasonably describe the progressive
Social Gospel in America and Ryan's own predilections, Ryan accli-
mated well to the Americanist milieu at the school, especially with
respect to the Americanist model of relations between church and
society.[62] After Americanism's condemnation, the chief Americanist bishops Gibbons and Ireland denied that any American Catholic had ever accepted the kind of Americanism that had been
characterized in *Testem Benevolentiae*. They did this somewhat
disingenuously.[63] Ryan's studies, formation, and hyper-social emphasis seem to have been little affected by this affair, especially giv-
en the fact that the papal letter could not erase the practical social
Christianity orientation of his most formative mentors there. Ryan
was wont over the years to deeply credit the influence of two liberals and firm believers in the crucial role of the social sciences at

62. This rebuke of Americanism was an 1899 encyclical letter titled *Testem Benevolentiae*
("A Discourse on Beneficial and Proper Teaching"). Pope Leo XIII was concerned that Catholicism in the American context not become akin to Social Gospel Protestantism veering
toward theological immanentism. On the pope's distinction between active and passive virtue,
see "*Testem Benevolentiae* (To James Cardinal Gibbons: True and False Americanism in Religion)" in *Papal Pronouncements: A Guide: 1740–1798*, vol. 1, ed. Claudia Carlen (Ann Arbor:
Pierian Press, 1990), 60.

63. Both bishops made sure to clarify that the condemned doctrine was never what they
meant when using the term *Americanism*. When Gibbons received *Testem Benevolentiae*, he
quickly moved to defend himself: "This extravagant and absurd doctrine as I would willingly
call it, this Americanism as they have chosen to call it, has nothing in common with the views,
the aspirations, the doctrines and the conduct of Americans. I do not think that there could
be found in the whole country a single bishop or priest or even a well-instructed layman, who
has ever put forward such extravagances. No this is not, never has been and will never be our
Americanism." Gibbons quoted in Thomas McAvoy, *The Great Crisis in American Catholic
Church History, 1895–1900* (Chicago: Henry Regnery, 1957), 286. Likewise, Ireland, upon receiving *Testem Benevolentiae*, wrote to the pope a letter clearly intended to strongly distance
himself from suspicion: "Today the light has been shed abroad and misunderstandings cease.
Now we can scotch the error which some have wished to cloak under the name of Americanism, and can define the truth.... Verily, with all the energy of my soul, I repudiate and I
condemn all the opinions which the Apostolic letter repudiates and condemns—all those false
and dangerous opinions to which, as the letter points out, certain persons have given the name
of Americanism" (Ireland quoted in McAvoy, 282).

Catholic University: Frs. William Kerby and Joseph Bouquillon.
Kerby had founded the school's Department of Sociology in
1897 and served as one of Ryan's graduate professors. He addressed
the church's ecclesiology from a sociological perspective, contending it was "subject ... to the action of social forces and limited in
natural powers.... The Church as a social group, rather than the
whole congregation of all the faithful [the Body of Christ], appeals
to our sense of loyalty and enlists our sympathies."[64] Advocating
intense study of the then professionalizing field of sociology by his
students, Kerby wrote in 1901, "We must study social science and fit
ourselves.... The age is drifting to the conviction that the last decisive test of any religion is its power to meet the social question."[65]
Ryan would take these lessons to heart.

Moral theology professor Fr. Bouquillon, Ryan's dissertation
adviser (and, a decade earlier, Kerby's), incorporated sociological
and economic analyses into his courses. These encouraged Ryan's
practical bent in approaching theological issues from the perspective of their concrete expression.[66] Ryan's earlier predilections were
thus nurtured under the influence of these men at Catholic University.[67]

64. Kerby quoted in R. Scott Appleby, *Church and Age Unite!*, 220.

65. Kerby quoted in Broderick, *Right Reverend New Dealer*, 33. Scholar Robert Preston
considered Kerby to be an early member of the new breed of American Catholic reformers
establishing themselves in the late 1890s who "analyze[d] society scientifically and ... use[d]
the social sciences in the determination of reform methodology." Robert M. Preston, "The
Christian Moralist as Scientific Reformer: John A. Ryan's Early Years," *Records of the American
Catholic Historical Society of Philadelphia* 81 (March 1970): 27. See also David O'Brien, *Public
Catholicism* (New York: Macmillan Publishing, 1989), 146; and Paula M. Kane, *Separatism
and Subculture: Boston Catholicism, 1900–1902* (Chapel Hill: University of North Carolina
Press, 1994), 25.

66. Broderick, *Right Reverend New Dealer*, 33. See also Ryan, *Social Doctrine*, 63–64. According to scholar Charles E. Curran, from the moment Bouquillon arrived at Catholic University in 1889, he insisted that "a highly scientific and living moral theology" should maintain
constant intercourse with practical science. Charles E. Curran, "Thomas Joseph Bouquillon:
Americanist, Neo-Scholastic, or Manualist?," in *The Catholic Theological Society of America:
Proceedings of the Fiftieth Annual Convention*, ed. Paul Crowley (Santa Clara, Calif.: Santa
Clara University, 1995), 162.

67. Ryan, *Social Doctrine*, 65–67. By his own assessment, his economics became somewhat Keynesian, and his proto-demography somewhat Malthusian, in orientation (Ryan, 65–
67). In 1906, Ryan published his completed PhD dissertation under the title *A Living Wage*.
Richard Ely wrote the introduction (Broderick, *Right Reverend New Dealer*, 45).

A few words on the early social sciences are in order. The Progressive Era's social sciences have been characterized as an arena where a quasi-secularized social gospel was transferred into the realm of positivist-conceived professional expertise. Although many of the newly-emerging social science disciplines of the late nineteenth and early twentieth century were predicated on forms of scientism, their appeal lay also in the promise of actualizing the social promises of modernity—including modernist religion—by utilizing the scientific method. This realm comprised a highly attractive union of reform interests.[68] In such a schema, that which was scientific was seen as the engine guiding a teleological trajectory of social progress. Social science afforded figures like economist Richard Ely and philosopher Lester Ward the hope of transferring their previous millennial hopes into progressive history. In Ely's case, for example, it would take the form of a millennial socialism in an equation engrafting evolutionary biology into economics.[69]

The influence of historicism was one of several factors encouraging nascent social scientists to conclude that positivist science was the key to unlocking humanity's increasing mastery of nature. This was the message of a number of works that guided the proto-social sciences, including those of Ward himself, of T. B. Wakeman, and of others who had reconfigured the positivism of Auguste Comte for the American milieu.[70] Likewise, the influence of John Stuart Mill's and Herbert Spencer's works was substantial in late nineteenth-century America, encouraging, among other things, a hyper-naturalism and developmentalist evolutionism in early American social science thought.[71] Books such as biometric

68. For more on this, see Dorothy Ross, *Origins of American Social Science*, 54.

69. Ross, *Origins of American Social Science*, 104–6.

70. On forms of Comtism disseminated in America, see Harp, *Positivist Republic*, esp. chap. 5 on Ward. As Don Meyer put it, the Victorian era saw two major trends in Western intellectual life, "a restrictive naturalism and ... an emphatic scientism" (Meyer quoted in Harp, *Positivist Republic*, 16).

71. Ross, *Origins of American Social Science*, 55, 93, 96. Spencer's ideas were widely disseminated by individuals like John Fiske in *Popular Science Monthly*. For a good discussion of Spencerian evolutionary positivism and its influence in the United States, see T. J. Jackson

eugenicist Karl Pearson's *Grammar of Science* (1892), Albion Small's *General Sociology* (1905), and Herbert Croly's *The Promise of American Life* (1909) brought updated, professionalized, and, ultimately, technocratic versions of such views firmly into the next century.[72] The optimistically conceived potential of the social sciences to improve American life exerted a powerful effect on the trajectory of professionalizing intellectual culture, with the social sciences themselves all the while draped in the image of objectivity.

John Dewey would be the apotheosis of this trajectory; that he refashioned what had been an older religious impulse was clear in his work. It was Dewey, after all, who contended that "religious doctrine and values" should be "restate[d] … in modern scientific, sociological terminology."[73] In his 1909 essay "The Influence of Darwinism on Philosophy," Dewey argued that Charles Darwin had helped philosophers get beyond their older defective Hegelian world-spirit, thus bequeathing the great gift of the evolutionary method to philosophy. Over time, Dewey increasingly clothed his philosophical ideas in the vocabulary of naturalistic science. His highly influential major works of the 1920s, especially *The Quest for Certainty* (1929), presented scientific truth as the instrument for moving humanity upward in its evolutionary ascent, and both his practical and applied philosophy centered on improving the world through forms of experimentalism. As one prominent historian put it, Dewey had abandoned his earlier faith in religion but not his *religious* faith. The latter was simply directed toward experimental scientific methods.[74] For the John

---

Lears, *No Place of Grace: Antimodernism and the Transformation of American Culture, 1880–1920* (New York: Pantheon Books, 1981), chap. 1, esp. 21–23.

72. Ross, *Origins of American Social Science*, 157–58. Such books tried to prove that social science could be just as scientific as natural science. See Harp, *Positivist Republic*, chap. 6 (on Albion Small and E. A. Ross) and chap. 7 (on Herbert Croly). Harp argues that "progressives conceived of the scientific expert in terms very similar to Comte's description of the 'Positive Priesthood' and as virtually identical to Ward's vision of the civil service technocrat" (194).

73. Dewey quoted in Bruce Kuklick, *Churchmen and Philosophers: From Jonathan Edwards to John Dewey* (New Haven: Yale University Press, 1985), 243.

74. Kuklick argues that before his abandonment of metaphysics, Dewey accepted the monistic immanentism fashionable in Protestant modernist circles in the late nineteenth century. The divine force immanent in the natural order meant that social science could grasp "the absolute" (Kuklick, *Churchmen and Philosophers*, 233).

Dewey of the interwar period, "the experimental method secured religious feeling."[75]

It was the early twentieth-century portion of this trajectory when John Ryan introduced his published dissertation as *Social Doctrine* (1906), its title hinting at his own religious feeling about social reform. Mainline economic and social thinkers praised it in reviews, but some Catholic experts claimed it revealed a surprisingly weak command of theology, even Catholic moral theology, the field in which Ryan had earned the degree. Much of the writing focused on practical social systems.[76] Archbishop Ireland required Ryan that same year to return to a teaching appointment at St. Paul's Seminary in Minnesota, although Ryan would have preferred to remain at Catholic University. Although he could not at that time remain in Washington, D.C., he was able to take with him the perspectives and approaches he had cultivated there.

Once back at St. Paul's, Ryan insisted priests' seminary training be "fundamental and scientific," and he devoted a large chunk of his courses in moral theology to what he termed "the aims and methods of monopoly; the aims and methods of the labor union."[77] Both at St. Paul's and when he was finally given leave to accept a faculty appointment at Catholic University in 1915, Ryan taught political science and sociology alongside moral theology. Like his mentors, he framed the latter in the terminology of inductive and practical social science. At Catholic University, Ryan admitted this was part of his attempt to counter what he saw as the excessive deductivism of his students.[78]

This concern about deductivism brings us to the Catholic movement that was connected to many of the liberal strands ad-

75. Kuklick, *Churchmen and Philosophers*, 252–53.
76. Broderick, *Right Reverend New Dealer*, 45.
77. Ryan, *Social Doctrine*, 107. At Catholic University, Ryan eventually became a professor of political science while simultaneously teaching economics at the all-women's Trinity College. Later, his professorship at Catholic University officially changed to moral theology until he joined the new School of Social Science as a professor of sociology in 1937. Ryan, *Social Doctrine*, 131.
78. Broderick, *Right Reverend New Dealer*, 53.

dressed here. Whether it was, in fact, a movement, per se, has been in dispute for some time among scholars. But one thing not in dispute is that those who swam in its currents targeted neoscholasticism for stunting theology or philosophy in the decades surrounding the turn of the twentieth century. Perhaps it can best be called an orientation. It was "modernism."

The 1907 papal encyclical *Pascendi Dominici Gregis* (On the Doctrine of the Modernists) of Pope Pius X (r. 1903–14) defined and condemned modernism as a heresy, reinforcing the propriety of neoscholastic deductivism.[79] The special relevance of modernism and the reaction to it is emblematized by something William Slattery wrote in 1909. A one-time Catholic University professor who was formally deposed from the priesthood for modernism, Slattery makes clear his identification of modernism with the newest practices and philosophy of science in his writing that the church's reaction to modernists demonstrated that it was, in fact, anti-scientific. Slattery called *Pascendi* "a formal declaration of war against modern science."[80] That assessment is debatable, but it does show how a modernist himself strongly identified his movement with science. At any rate, the encyclical letter codified modernism and then characterized it as "the synthesis of all heresies."[81]

79. Pius X, *Pascendi Dominici Gregis*, Encyclical Letter (September 8, 1907), http://www.vatican.va/content/pius-x/en/encyclicals/documents/hf_p-x_enc_19070908_pascendi-dominici-gregis.html. The official Vatican English translation of the encyclical includes subheadings such as: Vital Immanence; Deformation of Religious History the Consequence; Individual Experience and Religious Certitude; Religious Experience and Tradition; Faith and Science; Faith Subject to Science; The Methods of Modernists; Immanence and Symbolism; The Evolution of Doctrine; How the Bible is Dealt With; Subjective Arguments; Modernism and All the Heresies.

80. Slattery quoted in Portier, *Divided Friends*, 180.

81. Vidler argued that the most that can be said of Catholic modernism as a movement is that it comprised people (some lay scholars and some priests) who, in various ways and with different and sometimes contradictory emphases, shared "a desire to promote the adaptation of Catholicism, of the Church and its teaching, to new conditions." Alec R. Vidler, *A Variety of Catholic Modernists: The Sarum Lectures in the University of Oxford for the Year 1968–69* (Cambridge: Cambridge University Press, 1970), 16. A spate of subsequent scholarship in Catholic modernism has veered from what has been called the "phantom heresy" school of thought of John Tracy Ellis and Thomas McAvoy; to the continuity school of R. Scott Appleby (*Church and Age Unite!*) and others emphasizing the reality of modernism and its continuity with Americanism; to more recent works highlighting not only intellectual but geopolitical

The remedies ultimately prescribed by the pope in order to eliminate modernists' influence have been often criticized as severe and
as stunting Catholic intellectual life in America, although this is
something of an oversimplified assessment. Church institutions
were to root out suspected modernists from any official positions
they might occupy by using processes prescribed in 1910's *moto
proprio*. Despite this rigor, however, condemning modernism
was insufficient to stem the tide of modernist scholars' intellectual influence, the key ones being Catholic progressives residing
in departments other than formal theology departments.[82] Ryan,
Cooper, and O'Brien would all drink from this inchoate modernist font through Catholic University's social science faculty where
ideas connected to both European and American modernists had
been planted in the late nineteenth and early twentieth centuries.[83]
Those ideas lived on in more muted, subaltern forms in the hands
of some of the social scientists mentioned above as well as some
others—arguably eventually through Ryan and Cooper themselves
teaching there, and through O'Brien teaching elsewhere.

Whether or not modernism was a coherent, organized movement, the modernist spirit did depend upon some coherent and
consistent assumptions. Both Protestant and Catholic, modernists
framed religion in new ways so that educated people could find
meaning in teachings derived from the ancient past, with its foreign intellectual and cultural contexts. In this sense, those suspected of modernism were some of the most aware of the intimate connection between religion and other elements of culture because of
their emphasis on historicism. They were also self-conscious about
doing something new.

---

factors and arguing that individual modernists' arguments are the point more than a modernist paradigm is. For the latter, see Portier, *Divided Friends*, esp. 21–26, 60. See also Kauffman,
Tradition and Transformation, 160–77, 216–23.

82. Portier insightfully argues that "by conceding theology to Roman neo-Thomists such
as [Joseph] Fenton, Catholic University social scientists and historians between the modernist
crisis and Vatican II were able to sustain an Americanist tradition of a religiously informed
openness to the age" (*Divided Friends*, 30).

83. See Portier, *Divided Friends*, 79.

Influenced by intellectual trends of the nineteenth century, especially Kant's challenge to objectivism, many who were eventually termed modernists became preoccupied with the notion that religious expression was itself relative and, thus, had to coincide with the prevailing science and philosophy of each new age to be of use. Ironically, part of that attitude had its mirror image in the late medieval West's attempt to reconcile a newly rediscovered Aristotle with traditional elements of Catholic Christianity. From the later nineteenth century, neoscholastic thought came to symbolize for Catholic antimodernists a means of conserving traditional Christian truth while fully engaging modern culture, especially modern science.[84] To putative modernists, this approach was anathema for supposedly being dry and anachronistic.

Catholics imbibing the modernist spirit were not interested in merely responding to the new philosophical and scientific developments of the late eighteenth century and the nineteenth century by expressing old theologies in new terminology. Instead, they saw the new era as presenting a chance to wholly reconstruct the ideas of theology and dogma by synthesizing them with modern thought.[85] A key proviso in this was that evolutionary development of religion itself would allow fuller realization of truth than had been possible in past ages. The unfolding of truth was, in other words, progressive. This perspective was often called developmentalism.

American Catholic modernism was somewhat derivative in its foundations from both Americanism and European modernism but was, as one of its best scholars noted, unique both in its particular claims and in how its practitioners expressed them. Its uniqueness lay in its composite nature, mixing Protestant liberalism, progressivism, and European Catholic modernism. In the

84. On Aquinas's rapprochement with Aristotle and the intellectual context in which it took place, see Jean Leclercq, *The Love of Learning and the Desire for God: A Study of Monastic Culture* (New York: Longman, 1961), 73, 99, 226.

85. An excellent overview of theological modernism—centered on Protestantism but applicable in a number of ways to Catholicism near the turn of the twentieth century—is Kathryn Lofton's "The Methodology of the Modernists: Process in American Protestantism," *Church History* 75 (June 2006): 374–402.

latter respect, American modernists were especially influenced by George Tyrrell, Alfred Loisy, and St. George Jackson Mivart and by their opposition to neoscholasticism. As in Protestant modernism, American Catholic modernist affinities tended toward immanentism.[86]

The demand placed on Catholic intellectuals by Pope Leo XIII's enshrinement of neoscholasticism ultimately forced a sense of competing pulls on the community of Catholic scholars—on both their intellectual loyalties and their social ones. On the one hand, the modernist intellectual community saw the modern scientific method as the sine qua non of intellectual life itself, including theological work, and, on the other hand, the ecclesiastical institution to which they belonged held them to a radically different vision grounded also in a premodern philosophy of science.[87] This fractured inheritance—between the inductive and the deductive—is an important factor in our discussion of liberal Catholics in America.

Those imbibing the Americanist-modernist spirit naturally gravitated to connecting with modern intellectuals on the writers' own terms. Ryan enjoyed substantial success here, too. His tenure at Catholic University coincided with his pursuit of active social reform and intellectual exchange with non-Catholics. He noted in 1914 that only when Catholics joined secular groups in large numbers would they "command that measure of social and civic prestige which they ought to possess."[88] In the non-Catholic public square, Ryan himself achieved substantial renown. National atten-

86. R. Scott Appleby, *Church and Age Unite!*, 2. One of the ways in which American Catholic modernists, in particular, differed from "other liberals" was in "the level of self-awareness with which they appropriated the modern." Appleby pointed out that like the European Catholic modernists, Americans "resolutely opposed ... the neo-scholastic theological Orthodoxy which reasserted itself with a vengeance in America, as elsewhere, after 1907" (2). They also especially endorsed historical critical methods. Appleby has argued that Gibbons, Ireland, and the other Americanists "shared the conviction that Roman Catholicism was at a crucial point in its history, and that America would lead the way in transforming the relationship between the church and the age" (84). Catholic priests in the Sulpician order, prominent in Baltimore, were particularly enthusiastic modernists up until modernism's official condemnation in 1907. See also Portier, *Divided Friends*, 21, 31, 33.

87. Kurtz, *Politics of Heresy*, 54.

88. Ryan quoted in Broderick, *Right Reverend New Dealer*, 63.

tion attended the publication of his book *Distributive Justice* (1916), securing his reputation as a member of the broader progressive movement and the hitherto Protestant Social Gospel.[89] It earned him plaudits from liberals and some radicals.[90] His biographer pointed out that throughout it all, Ryan himself did not realize how much his language symbolically mirrored that of secular reformers.[91]

Ryan carried on widespread professional correspondence with some of the most influential figures in intellectual print media. Among these were Paul Hutchinson, longtime editor of the *Christian Century*; Lewis Gannett of *The Nation*; Bruce Bliven of the *New Republic*; and H. L. Mencken of the *American Mercury*. He also engaged to some extent with John Dewey, Walter Lippmann, Margaret Sanger, and other notables. Ryan was not infrequently called upon by the journalists among these figures to represent Catholic perspectives in their print forums. Viewed as one of the Catholic intellectuals most able to function in the realm of public discourse, he was also often consulted by secular intellectuals for comment on authoritative Catholic positions and for clarification of statements made by other Catholics.[92] Ryan and Walter Lippmann also

89. Slawson, *Foundation and First Decade*, 38. As discussed earlier, some of Ryan's inspiration actually came from a papal encyclical issued back in 1891, Leo XIII's *Rerum Novarum* (On the Rights and Duties of Capital and Labor). Nevertheless, as David O'Brien put it: "framing his arguments in pragmatic terms and utilizing a semi-populist rhetoric that was second nature since his youth, he always sounded like a typical American progressive." David J. O'Brien, *American Catholics and Social Reform: The New Deal Years* (New York: Oxford University Press, 1968), 124–25.

90. A reviewer in *The Nation* "found [his book] useful as a résumé of economic reforms" and another in the *New Republic* considered it remarkable that although Ryan represented the Catholic Church, his book was "worthy of adoption as a manual of radical economic reform." Both quoted in Broderick, *Right Reverend New Dealer*, 92.

91. Broderick, *Right Reverend New Dealer*, 153. Ryan's other books were also widely renowned in the same circles. *Questions of the Day* (1931) was feted in the *New Republic* and in many other magazines and newspapers.

92. On Hutchinson, see Ryan Papers, box 17, folder 7, ACUA. See also, for example, Lewis Gannett to Ryan (September [?], 1928), in Ryan Papers, box 17, folder 7, ACUA. Ryan wrote to Dewey on January 21, 1930, to congratulate him on an article the latter wrote in the current issue of the *New Republic*, with Dewey replying on January 27 (letters in Ryan Papers, box 10, folder 4, ACUA). Other private correspondence between the two occurred in 1933 and 1939. For her part, Margaret Sanger wrote to Ryan on February 6, 1929, to ask him for comments

corresponded about anti-Catholicism, Ryan having written to Lippmann in late 1928 to ask if the latter would say something against anti-Catholic statements being made in the *Christian Century* and quoted in Lippmann's *The Nation* magazine. Lippmann admitted that he was "shocked [that] there is so much [anti-Catholicism] that comes to this desk that I feel almost at a loss how wisely to deal with it."[93]

A series of letters passed between Bruce Bliven (one-time editor of the *New Republic*) and Ryan over social hygiene. Bliven initiated the correspondence by writing Ryan to ask if the statements of another Catholic (Fr. Francis Connell) about the marriage of those with venereal disease were authoritatively Catholic.[94] For many in the media, Ryan was seen as the voice of official Catholicism.[95]

Even before he had graduated from Catholic University himself, Ryan was being criticized by conservative intellectual priests in his church; his subsequent increasing prestige and personal prudence prevented these critiques from escalating into denunciation, but the early critiques give a flavor of how he was viewed by conservative Catholic moralists. For example, in response to an article Ryan had written in the modernist *New York Review* in early 1907 contending that arguments based on consequences were the best vehicle for asserting Catholic moral teachings, priest-professor Charles Plater complained that "Ryan's reasoning led directly to a Kantian empty form."[96] By the end of that same year, Ryan was also embroiled in a public debate with well-known English moral theologian Fr. Thomas Slater, who implied in print—in April 1909 (after

on her book *Motherhood and Bondage*. He replied that he "should be glad to have the book and send you some comments on it after I have read it." Ryan Papers, box 33, folder 18, ACUA.

93. Ryan to Lippmann (October 17, 1928); Lippmann to Ryan (October 22, 1928), in Ryan Papers, box 22, folder 3, ACUA.

94. Bliven to Ryan (March 1, 1941); Ryan to Bliven (April 1, 1941); Bliven to Ryan (April 8, 1941), in Ryan Papers, box 1, folder 16, ACUA.

95. H. L. Mencken to Ryan (June 3, 1929); Mencken to Ryan (June 8, 1929), in Ryan Papers, box 25, folder 40, ACUA.

96. Fr. Charles Plater quoted in Broderick, *Right Reverend New Dealer*, 71. Ryan's original argument appeared in John A. Ryan, "The Method of Teleology in Ethics," *New York Review* 2 (January–February 1907): 409–29.

the papal condemnation of modernism)—that Ryan's ideas "moved in the direction of evolutionary morality."[97] Somewhat protected by having signed the oath against modernism required of all priests after 1907 and by his increasing public influence, Ryan never saw his views condemned by his church.[98]

John Montgomery Cooper, Anthropologist Apologist

John Montgomery Cooper, consummate Catholic progressive, spent the majority of his career serving as a professor of anthropology and religion at Catholic University.[99] He died relatively early of a heart attack at age sixty-seven, but a serious coronary event even earlier, at age fifty-nine, had already slowed him down. Nevertheless, Cooper enjoyed a full career featuring a mix of research and fieldwork in anthropology, education, teaching, and cultural engagement. He did this while publishing works in anthropological (and other) academic journals, articles in popular periodicals, and even a seminal book series on how to teach religion to nonspecialist undergraduates.

Cooper successfully entered the American intellectual public square though his commitment to science-centered argument. His success is evidenced by developments such as his elections to the American Council of Learned Societies, to full fellow posi-

---

97. Broderick, *Right Reverend New Dealer*, 72.

98. The oath against modernism was required of all priests by Pius X (Broderick, *Right Reverend New Dealer*, 182, 188).

99. Secondary sources dealing with Cooper are scant. For material composed around his death, see W. H. Russell, "John M. Cooper, Pioneer," *Catholic Educational Review* 47 (September 1949): 435–41; Flannery, "John Montgomery Cooper"; Paul Hanly Furfey, "John Montgomery Cooper." For more recent works, see Slawson, *Foundation and First Decade*; McKeown, "From *Pascendi* to *Primitive Man*"; Sharon Leon, "'Hopelessly Entangled in Nordic Presuppositions': Catholic Participation in the American Eugenics Society in the 1920s," *Journal of the History of Medicine and Applied Sciences* 59 (2004): 3–49; Patrick W. Carey, "John Montgomery Cooper, Catholic Progressive," in *American Catholic Religious Thought*, 261–71; "Biographical Note" in *John Montgomery Cooper: An Inventory of the John Montgomery Cooper Papers: The American Catholic History Research Center and University Archives*, The Catholic University of America, https://libraries.catholic.edu/special-collections/archives/collections/finding-aids/finding-aids.html?file=cooper (accessed July 19, 2016).

tion in the American Association for the Advancement of Science (AAAS), and—unprecedented for a Catholic priest—to the presidency of the American Anthropological Association in 1940 (after serving as its secretary from 1931–37).[100] There were also his formal affiliations with both the ASHA and the AES, both of which attested to his role in bringing a Catholic presence to spaces hitherto hardly occupied by those of that faith. Ryan, too, was a member of the latter society for a time but withdrew. More visible than Ryan in such intellectual crossover movements, Cooper saw the sciences as the key connecting framework for himself and the church to engage secular culture. He, like Ryan, sought to be viewed both within the church and by non-Catholics as a scientist and progressive liberal.[101] His participation in mainline intellectual debates on their own ostensibly scientific terms sometimes led to his presence and arguments getting co-opted by opponents and used to support extra-scientific suppositions. On the other hand, as has been pointed out in the scholarship, Cooper was sometimes able to use his reputation as a progressive professional scientist to recontextualize positivist-framed data claims, especially in the ASHA and the AES.[102]

As a liberal Catholic operating first in the Progressive Era and then in the post–World War I milieu, he only half-heartedly covered his disdain for neoscholastic philosophy both in terms of Catholic college religion instruction and as a way of grounding Catholic moral arguments on social issues—even when addressing insider Catholic audiences; he instead preferred an approach that favored induction and scientific methodologies. Influenced by empirical biology, psychology, anthropology, and the progressive education movement, Cooper focused on the practical, results-oriented effects of religion.[103]

100. On his election as AAAS fellow, see Burton Livingston [permanent secretary of AAAS] to Cooper (January 31, 1931), in JMC Papers, box 7, folder 9, ACUA. For the other memberships, see McKeown, "From *Pascendi* to *Primitive Man*," 6n9.

101. Leon, *Image of God*, 41.

102. See Leon, *Image of God*, 41–44.

103. Carey, *American Catholic Religious Thought*, 261.

Hoping to create a cadre of Catholics interested and proficient in pursuing scientific research, Cooper pioneered the Catholic Roundtable of Science (CRTS) association in 1928. The group, loosely constituted, never completely crystallized in either its organization or goals, but it is clear that for Cooper, the point of it was to foster scientific training and, in particular, scientific publication by Catholics in standard science journals, thereby making contributions to bench research in order to accrue respectability and prestige for the Catholic Church in America. A major problem, however, was that Catholic scientists who *had* achieved success at schools like Harvard and MIT reported to Cooper that "it is suicide" to advertise personal Catholicism to secular colleagues.[104] Conservative Catholics, such as some associated with the Jesuit magazine *America*, were suspicious of the idea of Catholic scientists trying to blend in anyway because conservative Catholics' goal was a specifically Catholic science, one that was to be framed for public consumption in neoscholastic arguments. For Cooper, however, pursuing the CRTS effort was itself the way to overcoming both sets of problematic attitudes.[105]

After studying at the seminary of St. Charles in Ellicott City, Maryland, the talented Cooper moved on in 1899 to Rome, where he entered the renowned North American College. His achievements there included two doctorates, a PhD by 1902 and an STD degree in 1905. It was in Europe that Cooper's fire for archaeology and anthropology ignited. He read widely and voraciously in those subjects. Interestingly, however, none of his graduate degrees were taken in either field; the veneer of degree-holding professionalization seems to have successfully obfuscated that fact even for the purpose of his professional pursuits.[106] The year 1905 saw his

104. John Tobin to Cooper (December 2, 1933), in JMC Papers, box 22, folder "Catholic Research Roundtable 1933 meeting," ACUA.

105. See Artigas, Glick, and Martínez, *Negotiating Darwin*. See also Gleason, *Contending with Modernity*, 76, 108–23.

106. Paul Hanly Furfey points out that Cooper "had never taken a formal course in any of the anthropological sciences" (Furfey, "John Montgomery Cooper," 56). Indeed, one noteworthy fact about two of our central figures, Cooper and Ryan, is that neither possessed a

return to the United States and his ordination to the priesthood. His return to the United States brought him back to Baltimore, the mother see of the American church under its dean of bishops, the Americanist Cardinal James Gibbons. Gibbons assigned Cooper as assistant pastor of St. Matthew's parish in Washington, D.C., a fortuitous posting that led to Cooper's longstanding association with the Smithsonian Museum of Natural History's Bureau of American Ethnology and also with the Catholic University of America. His tutelage at the former came from the renowned anthropologist Aleš Hrdlička. Cooper began teaching part time at the Catholic University of America in 1909.[107]

In 1916, Cooper published his first anthropological volume, *Analytical and Critical Bibliography of the Tribes of Tierra del Fuego*; from that point on, Cooper wore the combined hats of, in his words, "anthropologist, sociologist, religious educator and sacred theologian."[108] By 1920, he assumed a full-time faculty position at Catholic University, remaining there until his death in 1949.[109] In 1926, attempting to wed scientific study to Catholic missionaries' work, he founded the Catholic Anthropological Conference. Interestingly, while Cooper held a doctorate in theology and acknowledged that title, when writing for secular audiences he made sure that he would be referred to as an anthropology professor, not a religion professor.[110] This emphasis was likely to accentuate the

---

graduate degree in the field in which he claimed specialization in the public sphere: anthropology and economics, respectively.

107. On the professionalizing anthropology field and its relationship to progressive evolution in the period, see Constance Clark, "Anthropology and Original Sin: Naturalizing Religion, Theorizing the Primitive," in *Science without God: Rethinking the History of Scientific Naturalism*, ed. Peter Harrison and Jon H. Roberts, 216–34 (Oxford: Oxford University Press, 2019).

108. "Biographical Note."

109. Cooper initially served as a religion instructor in the apologetics department. In 1920, he offered anthropological courses in the sociology department, becoming assistant professor in 1923. By 1928, he was made Professor of Anthropology, even though an independent anthropology department did not form until 1934. See Furfey, "John Montgomery Cooper," 58, 61.

110. See, for example, Cooper clarifying this point after his radio address against racism that was aired on CBS's "Church of the Air" program; his clarification is found in a letter from Cooper to the editor of *Crisis* (May 7, 1935) after the latter requested permission to print a

authority of his words via the prestige of scientific professionalism.

Cooper sought to form a division called "mission science" in the Catholic University history department. He conceived it as running what he termed mission institutes and roundtables. These were for professionals to discuss mission-science problems or scientific questions discerned while on mission work. As part of the mission-science program, he set up a five-step scientific method of hypothesis and observation that was to guide missionaries in the field. Cooper envisioned such missionaries as often being women who had been trained in social work. From the start of his time at Catholic University, Cooper also envisioned that the anthropology effort would include the publication of a scientific missionary periodical. That vision came to fruition with the debut of *Primitive Man*, which ultimately became the journal of the Catholic Anthropological Conference, edited by Cooper from its inception in 1928 until his death.[111]

Influenced by the discipline of comparative religion and by his fieldwork among native tribes in North America, Cooper incorporated anthropological perspectives into the undergraduate religion courses he began to teach at Catholic University; one contemporary noted that the religious practices of oral societies steadily influenced Cooper's presentations in theology and religion courses.[112] Cooper authored a four-volume series of religion textbooks for undergraduates in the 1910s partly because he did not like that texts in the Catholic scholastic manualist tradition were being used to teach undergraduates. His longstanding interest in practical religious education culminated with the formation of the Religious

---

transcript of the talk. JMC Papers, box 4, folder "Radio Address: Religion and the Race Problem: Corresp. May 5, 1935," ACUA. On Cooper's departmental affiliations, see above.

111. Cooper, "Plan for CUA Mission Center" (n.d.), in JMC Papers, box 54, folder 10, ACUA.

112. Furfey, "John Montgomery Cooper," 61. As McKeown put it, "Tierra del Fuego was a long way from Rome, but the issues of historical development, critical scholarship, and cultural pluralism 'crossed the wide ocean,' engaging John Cooper in his anthropological studies just as they had engaged the theologians of the pre-*Pascendi* period" ("From *Pascendi* to *Primitive Man*," 21).

Studies Department at Catholic University in 1929, a department that he chaired until 1938.

As was also true for our other central figures, Cooper involved himself with the NCWC and its precursor, the National Catholic War Council. He served in both as chair of the committee on laywomen's activities. Further, his connection to women's service groups tied him to the field of social work at the university. Social work was the one professionalized field by the early twentieth century associated more with women than men, and in 1920 Cooper forged a national link-up of women's societies for the NCWC.[113] At a meeting he arranged in March of that year, 123 national delegates from 57 different women's societies met in Washington, D.C.[114] It was there that the NCWC bureau known as the National Council of Catholic Women emerged as a clearinghouse for social-work information.[115]

Not long afterward, however, a politicized feud involving the seating of the New England delegate representing the diocese of Cardinal William O'Connell frustrated Cooper into resignation from the NCWC in a fit of irritation with both O'Connell and NCWC secretary John Burke.[116] At the root of this debate was the larger question of diocesan bishops' authority in relation to the national organizations, like the NCWC, that acted across diocesan boundaries. One major outcome of Cooper's NCWC efforts was an increase in his own national stature, Fr. Paul Hanly Furfey having noted that Cooper's work with the NCWC "had brought him into national prominence as a leader in social group work."[117]

113. Slawson, *Foundation and First Decade*, 76–77. For more on the women's social-service efforts and professionalization in the American Catholic context, see Brown and McKeown, *The Poor Belong to Us*.

114. Slawson, *Foundation and First Decade*, 77.

115. Slawson, *Foundation and First Decade*, 77.

116. Slawson, *Foundation and First Decade*, 79. The issue at the heart of this dispute was O'Connell's objection to a national organization having any influence whatsoever on his decisions as a local bishop.

117. Furfey, "John Montgomery Cooper," 59. Furfey himself passed through Catholic University's graduate school, studying under Fr. Thomas Verner Moore (who was trained by Edward Pace) and Fr. William Kerby. Furfey arrived for study in 1917, just as Cooper was

Cooper and Discursive Communities

Connections to the NCWC tended to legitimize the statements of Catholic figures connected to it in the eyes of the non-Catholic mainstream—and had exactly the reverse effect on die-hard Catholic conservatives. Cooper, however, did not really need the organization's help in getting such respect. He achieved esteem from non-Catholic thinkers through his own efforts. His technical research and specialized scholarship ingratiated him to non-Catholic anthropologists even as his active publishing in mainline intellectual magazines and journals connected to education, sociology, anthropology, eugenics, and social hygiene placed his name on the desks of many in the interwar republic of letters. Regina Flannery-Herzfeld, Cooper's secretary before herself training as a professional anthropologist, attested that he carried on "an enormous correspondence with scholars in all parts of the world."[118]

Cooper actively sought membership in every non-Catholic professional society that would have him, even those with which few Catholics dared associate. These latter included the AES, with which he remained officially connected until late spring 1931.[119] Cooper served in 1928 on the AES Board of Directors and sat for several years on its Birth Regulation Committee, finally resigning from the latter only in June 1930 when it openly endorsed the idea of physicians prescribing contraception. Interestingly, Cooper contended in his resignation letter that his decision centered not only on his ethical views but also on his particular unwillingness

becoming established at the university. Like Cooper and our other main figures, Furfey imbibed the Americanist vision for connecting Catholicism to the broader culture as a priest-social scientist, a task for which he saw NCWC as perfectly placed. See Nicholas K. Rademacher, *Paul Hanly Furfey: Priest, Scientist, Social Reformer* (New York: Fordham University Press, 2017), 37–38, 49, 58–61.

118. Flannery, "John Montgomery Cooper," 68.

119. The effect of Cooper's affiliations with sex education, social engineering, and other matters was that "his network of contacts with non-Catholics in these movements developed rapidly.... Throughout [World War I and the interwar era] ... a common set of questions about religion, reproduction, child and family, social control and education connected his contemporary preoccupations and his anthropological interests" (McKeown, "From *Pascendi* to *Primitive Man*," 5).

to associate with any movement that acted either for or against legal rules on birth control because "I do not believe in religion meddling in politics."[120] Cooper's claim certainly made awkward bedfellows with the political activism of his own Roman Catholic Church where contraception laws were concerned.

Cooper's resignation from the AES as a whole only came on April 9, 1931, even though Pope Pius XI (r. 1922–39) had already issued the encyclical *Casti Connubii* (On Chaste Marriage) in the end of December 1930, an encyclical expressly forbidding any Catholic participation in eugenics in no uncertain terms.[121] In Cooper's resignation letter, he gave an entirely science-centered rationale for his decision, saying the "official program of the AES" had become "antithetical in numerous ways" to his views—both "scientifically unsound" and "socially undesirable." He did add that he was "still interested in the international eugenics movement" whenever it operated "on a scientific basis."[122] Despite Cooper's resignation, he remained a good friend of eugenicist Paul Popenoe and told Guy Burch of the AES that his resignation in no way meant he was uninterested in the AES's continuing activities.

It was with reluctance that Cooper formally disassociated himself from the group; to him the benefits of such connections were

120. Cooper to Guy Irving Burch (June 4, 1930), in JMC Papers, box 19, folder 8, ACUA.
121. In the context of emphasizing the prime parental role of educating children properly and in contrast to the general emphasis both for married couples themselves and for others to be instructed by the state or non-church educational institutions in the ways of sexuality, *Casti Connubii* repudiates exaggerated physiological education "by means of which, in these times of ours, some reformers of married life make pretense of helping those joined in wedlock, laying much stress on these physiological matters, in which is learned rather the art of sinning in a subtle way than the virtue of living chastely." Pius XI, *Casti Connubii*, Encyclical Letter (December 31, 1930), http://www.vatican.va/content/pius-xi/en/encyclicals/documents/hf_p-xi_enc_19301231_casti-connubii.html.
122. Cooper to Leon Whitney (April 9, 1931), in JMC Papers, box 19, folder 8, ACUA. See also Cooper to Paul Popenoe (November 18, 1930), in JMC Papers, box 19, folder 8, ACUA. Cooper mentioned that he had talked over the issue with Ryan, whom he referred to as both a colleague and a friend (Cooper to Whitney). Whitney, in his reply, says that he "reads between the lines" of Cooper's resignation letter and that despite Cooper saying he resigned because eugenics is unscientific, Whitney believes the real reason for Cooper's resignation is his Roman Catholic religious views. Whitney to Cooper (April 21, 1931), in JMC Papers, box 19, folder 8, ACUA.

obvious such that he had remained for years in his position even when the organization had clearly been moving in the direction of classifying contraception as a desirable eugenic measure and of advocating other aspects of negative eugenics. He had stayed because of the discursive and networking connections with the scientific mainline his membership afforded him; the chance to possibly influence the AES's policies; and the example he was giving other Catholics on how to serve their church through serving science. John O'Brien's private congratulations to Cooper on his subsequent presidency of the American Anthropological Association shows the liberal Catholic cadre's pragmatic view of Catholics' involvement with broader professional communities: "You certainly are giving an inspiring example to our Catholic educators by going out and mingling with others," O'Brien wrote, "and thus winning prestige for the Church among the scientific scholars of our land."[123] In this vein, Cooper served on the National Research Council on the executive council and as a member of the Division of Anthropology and Psychology; on the Social Science Research Council, and other organizations. As noted above, Cooper was also elected to the ultimate tier of Fellow in the AAAS in January 1931.[124] In all of these organizations, Cooper was motivated in large part by a desire to make Catholicism—and himself as a Catholic in the sciences—visible in American scientific culture.

In dealing with other Catholics established in scientific fields, he sought connections with big names known in public culture, and he did not shy away from those who were controversial.[125]

123. O'Brien to Cooper (January 13, 1943), in JMC Papers, box 13, folder "O'Brien, Rev. John," ACUA.

124. JMC Papers, box 7, folder "American Association for the Advancement of Science," ACUA.

125. Cooper was largely responsible for getting the famous priest-physicist who developed the big bang theory, Fr. Georges LeMaître, to serve as a visiting professor at Catholic University in 1933. See Cooper to John A. Tobin (December 9, 1933), in JMC Papers, box 22, folder "Catholic Research Roundtable, 1934," ACUA. See also the letter from Cooper to Tobin (December 1, 1933). Cooper's correspondence with evolutionary anthropologist J. Franklin Ewing led to a connection with the controversial Jesuit Fr. Pierre Teilhard de Chardin, with whom Ewing was friend and colleague. See J. Franklin Ewing to Cooper (May 15, 1938), 2, in JMC Papers, box 9, folder "Ewing, J. Franklin," ACUA.

Regina Flannery Herzfeld, Cooper's former secretary turned professional anthropologist, was careful to point out in a memorial write-up that Cooper's activities with not-so-famous Catholics also kept an eye on the mainstream. Mainline, rather than specifically Catholic, anthropological organizations, she said, were always his primary focus as a professional anthropologist. The separate Catholic anthropology group he founded—the Catholic Anthropological Conference—was "to increase the scientific anthropological output, especially of missionaries, and in no way to duplicate the activities of secular anthropological organizations."[126] Contrary to the view held by more conservative Catholics involved in the sciences—that is, that the bench research, once framed and presented in holistic neoscholastic garb, would constitute a "Catholic science" or a "Catholic anthropology"—for Cooper and his cadre, there was no Catholic science, only science.

Wearing the variegated hats of professional anthropologist and expert on the family for non-Catholics and teacher of religion and encourager of scientific achievement for Catholics, Cooper's lengthy professional and private correspondence with religious and secular intellectuals ran the gamut. Non-Catholic public intellectual lights of the interwar era—including figures such as H. L. Mencken, sex investigator Alfred Kinsey, eugenicists Paul Popenoe and Leon Whitney, and Mary Ware Dennett of the Voluntary Parenthood league—sought out Cooper's intellectual and cultural critiques. Margaret Sanger invited Cooper to address the International Birth Control Conference in 1925.[127] Mencken and Kinsey separately contacted Cooper in 1931 and 1946, respectively, seeking what they called an authoritative Catholic explanation of particular aspects of the church's views on sexual morality.[128]

126. Flannery, "John Montgomery Cooper," 67.

127. McKeown, "From *Pascendi* to *Primitive Man*," 13.

128. See the letter from Michael Williams on a proposed article sought by H. L. Mencken —to be written by Cooper—that would appear in an anthology Mencken was preparing on the ethical questions of birth control. Williams to Cooper (November 17, 1931), in JMC Papers, box 17, folder "Miscellaneous-W," ACUA. Alfred Kinsey contacted Cooper for an "authoritative" explanation of the Catholic Church's ideas on sexual morality to assist his research,

Cooper's longstanding affiliation with the ASHA—founded in
1914 as part of the Progressive movement's crusade against prostitution and venereal disease during World War I—led to him playing a substantial role in the American sex education movement, as
will be further seen in chapter five. The ASHA brought sex into the
limelight garbed in technical, rational, and professionalized terms.
Cooper's own associated rhetoric framed marriage, family, and reproduction in scientific and pragmatic idioms, though it should be
noted that for several years his presence on ASHA's board led the
organization to table resolutions calling for contraception as a social hygiene cause, since Cooper had privately told them that such
resolutions would result in his resignation.[129]

As one-time chair of the ASHA's General Advisory Committee,
Cooper specifically encouraged eugenicist Paul Popenoe's *Modern
Marriage* as recommended reading for all ASHA members in a late
1933 mass mailing.[130] His letter accepting an invitation to join the
ASHA Advisory Committee on sexually transmitted diseases ac-
centuates Cooper's faith in scientific problem solving and his impulse to rationalize social and ethical problems, even sometimes at
the expense of previously acceptable religious approaches. In this
case, he contended it was crucial to "plac[e] at the disposal of re-

---

which Kinsey characterized as "an honest attempt to find out what people do sexually and . . .
analyses of the scientific aspect of the problem." Kinsey to Cooper (July 1, 1946), in JMC Papers, box 16, folder "Miscellaneous-K," ACUA. Cooper's reply, recommendations, and books
were acknowledged by Kinsey in a July 8 letter. Kinsey to Cooper (July 8, 1946), in JMC
Papers, box 16, folder "Miscellaneous-K," ACUA.

129. Board of Directors Meeting minutes (January 31, 1934, and April 13, 1934), in JMC
Papers, box 19, folder "American Social Hygiene Association," ACUA. The physician Robert Dickinson had asked that the ASHA board particularly consider endorsing "control of
conception" (indicated in the minutes of January 31). It should be noted that the Boards of
Directors of the ASHA and the AES saw substantial overlap, so Cooper continued working
alongside figures like Maurice Bigelow, Raymond Fosdick, Roscoe Pound, and others in the
former even after resigning from the latter. For more on the numerous personal and intellectual interconnections between America's top professional associations for social hygiene,
eugenics, genetics, and, by the 1930s, contraception, see Jonathan Peter Spiro, *Defending the
Master Race: Conservation, Eugenics, and the Legacy of Madison Grant* (Burlington, Vt.: University of Vermont Press, 2009), 129 and app. D, 395.

130. Cooper to Maurice Bigelow (December 19, 1933), in JMC Papers, box 19, folder
"American Social Hygiene Association 1933–1936," ACUA.

ligious groups the knowledge, experience, and methodologies of the ASHA."[131]

In 1931 in reply to a White House conference on sex education, Cooper argued that sex education must be justified as a rational goal of society-wide altruism.[132] Altruism was something of a loaded term; its origin was in social utilitarian arguments originating in Victorian British Comtist thought; it functioned as a secular psychological category and later found itself employed in positivist discourses of genetics and eugenics. While Christianity had largely accommodated itself to the term by the early twentieth century, altruism was still sometimes associated with reducing to biochemical evolutionary terms what Christianity had characterized as free-will expressions of love of neighbor for God.[133] The question here is the extent to which Cooper's rhetoric in the secular social science discourse acquired unexpected colorings or associations. At any rate, upon the recommendation of the ASHA, Cooper was asked as late as 1947 to pen a *Time* magazine piece as an "expert authority" on social hygiene and the family.[134]

What makes Cooper's longstanding formal involvement with the ASHA more noteworthy is the fact that in 1931 the Roman Sacred Congregation on the Holy Office answered the following in the negative: "If the method called 'sex education' or, also, 'sex initiation,' may be approved." They decreed,

In the education of youth the method must be strictly followed which up to now has been adopted by the Church and by holy men, and which was recommended by Our Holy Father in the Encyclical Letter on "The

131. Cooper to Ray Lymun Wilbur (March 29, 1940), in JMC Papers, box 8, folder 7, ACUA.

132. Cooper to M. J. Exner (March 10, 1931), in JMC Papers, box 19, folder "American Social Hygiene Assn 1928–1937," ACUA.

133. See Thomas Dixon, "The Invention of Altruism: Auguste Comte's *Positive Polity* and Respectable Unbelief in Victorian Britain," in *Science and Beliefs: From Natural Philosophy to Natural Science*, ed. David M. Knight and Matthew D. Eddy, 195–211 (Aldershot, UK: Ashgate, 2005); and Dixon, *The Invention of Altruism: Making Moral Meanings in Victorian Britain* (Oxford: Oxford University Press for the British Academy, 2008).

134. Walter Clarke [ASHA Director] to Cooper (March 12, 1947), in JMC Papers, box 8, folder 7, ACUA.

Christian Education of Youth," published December 31, 1929. ... Therefore, in no way can approval be given the writings and publications put forth, particularly in these times, to spread the new method, even by some Catholic authors.[135]

Cooper escaped censure partly by promoting his interest in the science involved. As noted above, maintaining multiple allegiances in such encounters was a marker of our figures.

One of Cooper's exchanges with John O'Brien, at the time preparing a book on evolution, illustrates his concern that Catholic thinkers writing in arenas where ambiguity was rife treaded a line serving the goals of advancing progressive scientific and religious interest. Cooper was particularly adept at furthering the progressive Catholic interest without drawing much negative attention from opponents within the church, and he wanted O'Brien to learn to do the same. It is evident that the two were involved in directed efforts to craft discourse designed to befriend the secular elite and to change the orientation of Catholic thinkers in the direction of scientific study and expression rather than in the direction of deductive philosophy. Archival correspondence shows Cooper cautioning O'Brien for tactical reasons not to be overtly critical of Catholic theologians who had challenged Darwin's ideas even on evolution of spirit so as not to stir up their opponents within the Catholic Church. Cooper warned O'Brien that the latter's strongly-worded criticisms of Catholic thinkers in "the preparation of Chapters ... on Copernicanism and the Theological Furore [*sic*] first raised against Darwinian Evolution ... as you point out ... may antagonize [the theologians] and accomplish nothing in bringing about the attitude we desire."[136] As a reward for his success in

135. Monsignor Enrico Pucci [Rome Correspondent, NCWC News Service], "Condemnation of 'Sex Education' and 'Eugenics' Theory by Holy Office" (April 13, 1931), JMC Papers, box 16, folder "Miscellaneous-K," ACUA.

136. O'Brien to Cooper (March 21, 1931), in JMC Papers, box 13, folder "O'Brien, Rev. John," ACUA. In 1949, another Catholic liberal, Paul Hanly Furfey, wrote of Cooper, "Being himself a scientist of note, he was able to discuss the relation between religion and science with an unusual degree of authority. Perhaps no part of Dr. Cooper's work proved to be more controversial than his work in this area. His methods have been many times attacked and

treading this line as a scientist who actively reconciled science and religion, Cooper was awarded the Mendel Medal in 1939.[137]

Cooper the Modernist?

While never disciplined by his church for crossing a line too far, Cooper's words and actions revealed him as tied to the older Catholic Americanist-modernist worldview. An essay published shortly after Cooper's death characterized him as a link in a chain wrought by those at Catholic University in the progressive tradition—a chain including Frs. Thomas Bouquillon, Thomas Shields, William Kerby, Thomas Verner Moore (psychiatrist), Ryan, and others— for integrating Catholic University into broader American life and progressive education. It particularly noted Cooper's pioneering work in shifting the way religion was taught to undergraduates.[138] Cooper's new approach is extolled precisely for moving far away

---

many times defended.... The least that can be said is that he developed a highly original method of presentation" ("John Montgomery Cooper," 54). Furfey was a graduate student at Catholic University and later became a colleague and friend of Cooper's in the sociology department (49). Back in 1931, he had approached Cooper about possibly co-authoring a volume on "the unrecognized or unconscious motives" in spiritual and ascetic practices with research from "psychology, social work and education." Furfey to Cooper (March 7, 1931), in JMC Papers, box 9, folder "Furfey, Dr. Paul H.," ACUA. Spirituality was to be explained in light of "recent developments [that] have shed new light on the phenomen[a]." Catholic conservatives saw his naturalistic approach to spirituality as redolent of condemned modernism. Cooper's reply centered on a program of moving the Catholic expression of religious issues to the language and frameworks of modern science. It is worth noting that Cooper's postscript suggests he was aware of being under suspicion of deviating from Catholic orthodoxy. Cooper to Furfey (June 30, 1931), in JMC Papers, box 9, folder "Furfey, Dr. Paul H.," ACUA.

137. A 1939 letter from leading Catholic evolutionist and anthropologist J. Franklin Ewing congratulated Cooper on the Mendel medal honor. In this letter Ewing remarked, "It is indeed fitting that an outstanding Catholic scientist and priest of our day should receive a medal named after his predecessor in the fields of science and religion of former times!" Ewing to Cooper (May 23, 1939), in JMC Papers, box 49, folder 9, ACUA. By 1945, however, even Ewing wondered, along with conservative American Jesuit Francis P. LeBuffe, SJ, of America magazine, whether Cooper had gone too far in his praise of a liberal Catholic's book on evolution. LeBuffe wrote: "May I say that both Fr. Ewing and I wonder whether your praise of [Fr. Ernest] Messenger's book is justified." LeBuffe to Cooper (August 9, 1945), in JMC Papers, box 11, folder 18, ACUA.

138. On Cooper's teaching methods in the religion department, Patrick Carey has said that he "initiated a new approach to theological education for undergraduates that was in tune with many marks of the progressive education movement" (American Catholic Religious Thought, 67).

from formal arguments to religion's sociological aspects.[139] A
Catholic scholarly analyst described Cooper's anthropology-tinted
intellectual model as one based in the evolution of dogma and centered in induction from ends to means.[140]

Catholic philosopher-theologians, some Catholic practicing
scientists, and others privately criticized Cooper on numerous occasions for what appeared to be scientism and naïve empiricism.
One noteworthy example is found in Cooper's longstanding correspondence—spanning from the later 1930s through much of the
1940s—with Fr. Thomas Hanley, OSB, of St. Martin's College in
Lacey, Washington. A member of the philosophy faculty, Hanley
conducted a detailed exchange with Cooper on the latter's philosophy of science, especially as related to sexuality and contraception.
Within the many letters passed back and forth, Lacey, an expert
in neoscholasticism, said that Cooper's argumentation proceeded
from "a conscious or unconscious Voluntaris[m]."[141] Voluntarism
had been characterized as part of the earlier modernism due to
framing morality's bounds in the relativistic perspective of individual will rather than in the absolute order of nature discerned by the
intellect. Associated particularly with Immanuel Kant in modern
philosophy, voluntarism was a serious problem for the neoscholastic because it apparently valued individual will over objective
reason. Hanley also complained that Cooper's arguments about
contraception revealed that "excessive [philosophical] pragmatism
[is] characteristic of Cooper's approach to the problem."[142]

J. E. Kempf, a lay Catholic professor of bacteriology at the University of Michigan School of Medicine, attributed a careless scientism to Cooper in his review of an address Cooper gave to the

139. W. H. Russell, "John M. Cooper, Pioneer," 440. Thomas E. Shields, in whose company
Cooper was included, was a Johns Hopkins PhD graduate who had studied biology and experimental psychology. "At the Catholic University [Shields] began to develop a Catholic philosophy of education that was clearly congruent with new developments in biology, the doctrine
of evolution, and experimental psychology" (Carey, *American Catholic Religious Thought*, 66).

140. McKeown, "From *Pascendi* to *Primitive Man*," 5.

141. Hanley to Cooper (February 10, 1948), in JMC Papers, box 9, folder "Hanley, Thomas," ACUA.

142. Hanley's review of Cooper's argument (n.d.), in JMC Papers, box 9, folder "Hanley,
Thomas," ACUA.

Catholic Teachers Association, an address reprinted in *Commonweal* magazine's May 25, 1945, issue. Kempf warned the priest of the danger inherent in letting unrestrained enthusiasm for scientific achievement cause one to forget how the dominant philosophy of science—naturalism—supposedly subtly tied itself to metaphysical materialism. He also cautioned Cooper not to forget the agenda of certain philosophically naturalist scientists, who, he said, tended to use science to propagandize against religious worldviews. As Kempf put it to Cooper: "You mention that science has aided the Church in the struggle against superstition.... However, there is a counterpart to this advance. In allaying superstition, the scientist has set himself up as the final judge on matters where he has not the slightest scientific knowledge." Kempf continued his rebuke by reminding Cooper that in such a scientist's view, "if his convictions disagree with revealed truths, he repudiates the revealed truths." Kempf included contraception in his litany, warning Cooper that "science has also encroached upon some moral problems, such as birth control, euthanasia, castration, abortion, and the hodge-podge of disconnected notions called psychotherapy."[143]

Kempf concluded by directly challenging a central pillar of Cooper's focus throughout his career: "While it might be desirable to develop research in Catholic schools in order to meet the approval of the world and give certain individuals security, the Catholic schools could do science the greatest service by combatting the threat."[144] Coming from a convert to Catholicism who spent his professional career in the realm of mainline science, this critique of Cooper's *modus operandi* highlights how some Catholic opponents saw his desire to fit himself—and Catholicism—into American public discourse as overlooking a key contest being waged over the philosophy of science and the proper application of scientific authority in American culture.

Fr. John O'Brien was not as prominent in public intellectual

143. Kempf to Cooper (June 21, 1945), 1, in JMC Papers, box 16, folder "Miscellaneous-K," ACUA.

144. Kempf to Cooper, 2.

circles as either Ryan or Cooper, nor could he match them in terms of creative intellect. But he was still a major player in our story, particularly due to two of his books that widely reached non-Catholic intellectuals and scientists in the interwar era. One treated of Catholicism and contraception; the other, of Catholicism and evolution.[145] In both volumes, O'Brien's arguments centered on social and biological science, employing ends-based argumentation that skated near to utilitarianism after giving perfunctory nods to natural law. Consistent with the approach of his fellow liberal-progressive Catholics, O'Brien allotted the neoscholasticism prescribed by *Aeterni Patris* basically no role in his reasonings.

Possessing a social science doctorate and stationed at major national universities throughout his career—the University of Illinois and later Notre Dame—O'Brien operated in many of the same institutional and intellectual networks as Ryan and Cooper. He also embodied their vision of outreach to American culture via the sciences, a vision emblematized by the NCWC, whose orientation strongly reflected their shared perspectives. As we have already seen, Ryan played an important role in the organization as head of the Social Action Committee and as ghostwriter of the seminal proto-NCWC Bishop's Program on Social Reconstruction in 1919.[146] Cooper, too, was at one time secretary of the National Catholic War Council's Department of Women's Activities and ultimately became chair of the NCWC's Department of Lay Activities consortium of women's societies.[147] O'Brien served for several years in the NCWC Education Department.[148]

---

145. O'Brien quoted in Romig, *Book of Catholic Authors*, 245. See also Morrison, "History of American Catholic Opinion," 344–45.

146. Catholic historian Joseph McShane, SJ, wrote that the publication of the Program permitted the Catholic Church to "enter into the American religious and social mainstreams ... as a progressive and Progressive force in American life." Joseph McShane, *Sufficiently Radical: Catholicism, Progressivism and the Bishops' Program of 1919* (Washington, D.C.: The Catholic University of America Press, 1986), 282.

147. Slawson, *Foundation and First Decade*, 77. A combined personality dispute and policy disagreement in the organization however, led Cooper to resign his post in a huff the same year he was appointed to it. He left the War Council at the same time (Slawson, 77).

148. Slawson, *Foundation and First Decade*, 266. O'Brien would eventually be dismissed from the organization in 1926 in the midst of controversy (Slawson, 266–74).

Connections to the National Catholic Welfare Conference

In a sense, the NCWC was the clearest institutional expression of the network that viewed science and scientific argumentation as the key to connecting Catholicism to broader American society. Seeking both practical prestige and a way to channel the Catholic tradition of service toward viable interface with mainline American culture, Catholic University's trustees had voted in November of 1917 to create an official organization for managing the church's efforts during World War I. Initially called the National Catholic War Council and centered on coordinating military chaplains, the NCWC gained momentum when it became clear that it could efficiently act as a Catholic liaison with official American institutions in postwar reconstruction.[149] Catholics seeking a bridge for connections with the broader culture, like O'Brien, Cooper, and Ryan, supported the idea of the NCWC with particular gusto.[150] So, too, did likeminded thinkers at Catholic University, such as Edward Pace and the Paulist Fr. John Burke. Ryan was recruited to draw up a Catholic roadmap for the NCWC that would work like the Protestant Federal Council of Church's program to meet postwar needs.[151]

149. Slawson, *Foundation and First Decade*, 30; David O'Brien, *Public Catholicism*, 153. Catholic journalist Michael Williams reveled in the progressive rhetoric of efficiency and organization as well as in Catholic triumphalism when he described the manner in which this pledge drive was conducted: "[The] immemorial machinery of the Church ... demonstrated its immortal youth ... [and] demonstrated its adaptability as well as its permanency by 'gearing in' with all the most approved and 'efficient' of the most up-to-date methods to supplement the pulpit appeals." Michael Williams, *American Catholics in the War: National Catholic War Council, 1917–1921* (New York: Macmillan, 1921), 179.

150. Slawson, *Foundation and First Decade*, 37. The Protestant Federal Council of Churches claimed it would monitor potential legislation in the interest of America's Christians, but many Catholics saw the need to create their own organization since the Federal Council would ostensibly protect only Protestant interests. Two examples of legislation that Protestants of many stripes favored but Catholics largely opposed were the Volstead Act (Prohibition) and the Smith-Towner Act (Federal Education Department). Protestant support for these acts spanned the Federal Council to the Freemasons and all the way to the Ku Klux Klan. See Slawson, *Foundation and First Decade*, 47, 87.

151. Ryan, *Social Doctrine*, 145. See also Broderick, *Right Reverend New Dealer*, 105.

The NCWC was divided into departments—including Education, Press, Social Action, Missions, and Lay Activities—and Social Action was itself split into two subdivisions, the National Council of Catholic Men and the National Council of Catholic Women.[152] Channeling the activist progressive Catholic impulse, the organization would grow to become the official voice of liberal American Catholicism by the mid-1920s and was recognized as such both in and outside the church.[153]

One of the NCWC's first postwar initiatives set the tone for its progressive image in the assimilationist culture of postwar America and de facto mirrored the earlier goals of the Catholic Americanization movement.[154] Its Social Action department linked up eleven national Catholic immigrant-orientation groups into a federation called "Loyal Americans" in 1919. Ryan drew up a plan in which social workers in the NCWC Social Action bureau would teach Americanization classes.[155] The bureau then published a pamphlet called *The Civics Catechism* in 1920 that focused on Americanizing urban immigrants. This pamphlet so seamlessly fit in with the assimilation message that underpinned much of the Protestant Social Gospel that it soon saw use by all manner of non-Catholic organizations, including Hull House and Chicago Commons.[156] A look at the pamphlet reveals that it was geared toward constructing an orderly, loyal, and law-abiding citizenry and

152. Technically, the NCWC and its oversight committee comprised of both laity and priests was only advisory to the bishops in their annual session, but in practice the committee was almost totally autonomous (Slawson, *Foundation and First Decade*, 61).

153. Slawson, *Foundation and First Decade*, 38. In Slawson's words, "it is safe to say that in the popular mind ... by 1928, the NCWC ... had established itself as the official voice of the [institutional] Catholic Church and was recognized as such by the government" (285). In issues like immigration or birth control, proclamations authorized by the NCWC (or made by its affiliated figures) were seen by outsiders as somewhat official because of the identity of the NCWC as "the authoritative representative of American Catholicism" (Slawson, 286).

154. John A. Lapp was co-director of the Social Action department, although he was headquartered in a Chicago branch of the department while Ryan manned the influential main office in Washington, D.C. (Broderick, *Right Reverend New Dealer*, 109).

155. Broderick, *Right Reverend New Dealer*, 108.

156. Slawson, *Foundation and First Decade*, 74. The pamphlet was translated into Italian, Polish, and Slovak (the latter two editions selling fifty thousand and forty thousand copies, respectively). It was also serialized in over fifty foreign-language newspapers (Slawson, 75).

middle-class values. It also reflected the Progressive Era concern with personal and public hygiene framed as civic duties to be dealt with scientifically.[157]

That framing highlights the NCWC's central vision on how to reach the American mainline and simultaneously counter the long-standing shibboleth of purported Catholic opposition to science. It emphasized the need for Catholic engagement with and usage of the dialect and idiom of science.

A decade later, an NCWC editorial illustrates the same concerns about scientific effort. Appearing in March 1929 and titled "Science and Religion" the NCWC editorial quoted a recent exchange in the popular press about the alleged "conflict between religion and science," decreeing, "from the Catholic standpoint, the best solution of the conflict will be attained ... not by writing books explaining away the conflict but by active entrance on the part of Catholics into the scientific field and by original contributions made to science."[158] In an averred criticism of Catholics using neoscholasticism in public debate, it argued that demonstrations rather than revelations or deductions were most appropriate for promoting religious ideas: "The apologetic of words carries much less conviction than the apologetic of facts."[159] In a somewhat perplexing turn, the editorial endorsed the possibility of achieving its goals as a byproduct of immigration. Admitting that the restriction policy did and would continue to reject a slew of immigrants from

157. On the concern with hygiene, for example, see lesson 2 in the pamphlet chapter entitled "Health." Question 4 asked "Why ought every one join in the 'swat the fly' campaign? A. Because it is for the benefit of all the people to kill these carriers of disease." Another question asked, "Is spitting harmful to others? A. Yes, when done in public places, in the street car or on the sidewalk it spreads disease." Lesson 1 included this exchange: "Has the Health Officer the right to quarantine anyone who has a contagious disease? A. Yes, this right is given him by law in order to protect the lives of greater numbers. [Question 6]: In what other way can the carelessness of one person endanger the health of others? A. If one man is careless about removing dirt or garbage from his premises he endangers the health of all." Committee on Special War Activities, *Civics Catechism on the Rights and Duties of American Citizens*, Reconstruction Pamphlets, no. 13 (Washington, D.C.: National Catholic War Council, 1920), 21, 19.

158. NCWC Editorial (March 1, 1929), in JMC Papers, box 21, folder "Catholic Research Roundtables Articles (1929–1930)," ACUA.

159. NCWC Editorial (March 1, 1929).

predominantly Catholic countries, the editorialist nevertheless emphasized how the increasing wealth and leisure among Catholics already living in the United States brought the chance for an educated middle-class cadre to engage in productive scientific scholarship. Building up a Catholic scientific elite was the most important of goals, for "if Catholic truth is to receive a sympathetic hearing from intellectual leaders today, one important approach is by way of the natural sciences."[160] Here we see the twin mandate to employ scientific framing when making arguments to non-Catholics and to cultivate Catholics themselves as professional scientists who would positively reflect on the American Catholic cohort's respectability writ large. Few emblematized either the NCWC vision or goals better than O'Brien, but before he was able to take up his role in the NCWC, he first had to complete his own education and receive ordination.

O'Brien the Controversialist

O'Brien graduated from St. Viator's College in Bourbonnais, Illinois, with a bachelor's degree in 1913; he added an MA in 1914. In 1916, Bishop Edmund Dunne of the diocese of Peoria laid his hands upon O'Brien's head, bringing him to what he called his "first great goal," the priesthood of the Roman Catholic Church.[161]

Like Cooper and Ryan, O'Brien also had ties to the Catholic University of America. He spent the 1916–17 academic year in graduate studies for education and psychology, studying—as he was proud to say—"under Drs. [Edward] Pace, [Thomas] Shields, and [William] Kerby."[162] O'Brien thus connected with the very pro-

160. NCWC Editorial (March 1, 1929).

161. O'Brien quoted in Romig, *Book of Catholic Authors*, 243. Three years later, the same Bishop Dunne conferred priestly ordination upon another Peorian and St. Viator alumnus, Fulton J. Sheen.

162. O'Brien quoted in Romig, *Book of Catholic Authors*, 244. See also Winton U. Solberg, "The Catholic Presence at the University of Illinois," *Catholic Historical Review* 76 (October 1990): 769. Solberg included sociology in the list of what O'Brien received in those years. Social science disciplines were fluid in the early twentieth century. All of those disciplines were,

fessors who had been veterans of the modernist and Americanist milieu on that campus and who, despite their professed antimodernist oath, contained within themselves the subaltern residuals of those intellectual currents. It was, however, at the University of Illinois, where he went on to earn a PhD in the School of Education, that O'Brien would make his biggest mark in our timeframe. He served as that university's Catholic chaplain from 1917 through 1939 and was at Illinois when publishing the works that concern us most here.

O'Brien characterized his time as the Newman chaplain at Illinois as extremely busy. After fulfilling grueling daily chaplaincy obligations, he resumed his night-owl tendencies, "doing my writing after the clock had struck twelve and the telephone had ceased to ring."[163] In 1924, Bishop Dunne appointed O'Brien diocesan superintendent of parochial schools, a post he held through 1930. On the whole, O'Brien was fortunate that Dunne sympathized with his outlook and methods; at one point the bishop lauded O'Brien's educational philosophy as "progressive mode[s] in the right direction."[164]

O'Brien showed that progressive orientation in his doctoral work, too, writing on the cutting-edge progressive education topic of silent reading. Graduate students in education received doses of multiple social science subfields by O'Brien's era. The professionalizing field of education was replete with psychological theory; graduate students of education usually had to take psychology courses as part of their normal studies. With this kind of cross-training and a PhD from a non-sectarian university, O'Brien garnered a measure of respect from progressives that he simply could not have enjoyed had his doctorate come from a Catholic-run university.[165]

at various points, part of Catholic University's larger social science department. Even after they became distinct departmental entities, there was considerable overlap and interrelationship. See C. Joseph Neusse, "The Introduction of the Social Sciences in the Catholic University of America 1895–1909," *Social Thought* 12 (Spring 1986): 30–41.

163. O'Brien quoted in Romig, *Book of Catholic Authors*, 244.

164. Quoted in Solberg, "Catholic Presence," 773.

165. See Elbridge C. Grover, "The Status of Education as an Academic Subject in American Colleges," *Educational Research Bulletin* 7 (January 11, 1928): 12–15. The overlap between fields

Dunne's successor in the diocese of Peoria in 1930, Bishop Joseph Schlarman, maintained no such enthusiasm for either O'Brien or his progressivism, notwithstanding O'Brien's claim that his work as director of the Newman Foundation at Illinois brought three-hundred converts.[166] It was precisely O'Brien's overall approach to ecumenism that fanned the flames of his new bishop's ire. That ire grew to such proportions that Schlarman would ultimately dismiss O'Brien from the diocese in 1939, forbidding him from serving the liturgy or even staying overnight in diocesan boundaries ever again.[167]

Outreach lay at the heart of O'Brien's whole approach, and this included a large dose of writing aimed at non-Catholics. He would ultimately write over forty books and hundreds of pamphlets, though it should be remembered that publishing standards of the time allowed much repetition in material from book to book. He also published essays and pamphlets. All the while, however, he made sure to keep in personal touch with regular people by spending his summers preaching in the streets of various Southern cities.[168]

O'Brien also published several collections of papers derived from symposia he had organized in the interwar years. The papers that he as editor chose to present in his most prominent interwar era collection, *Catholics and Scholarship* (1938), reflected his long-standing belief that Catholic respectability and cultural influence depended on prominence in social and biological science. Its es-

---

is revealed in the historical memory of O'Brien. At times, he has been referred to in print as a psychologist and as having "receiv[ed] the Ph.D. degree in psychology." Matthew Hoehn, ed., *Catholic Authors: Contemporary Biographical Sketches 1930–1947* (Newark, N.J.: St. Mary's Abbey, 1948), 582. Other sources described him as an educational theorist. His dissertation was published as John Anthony O'Brien, *Silent Reading, with Special Reference to Methods for Developing Speed: A Study in the Psychology and Pedagogy of Reading* (New York: Macmillan, 1921).

166. O'Brien quoted in Romig, *Book of Catholic Authors*, 244.

167. Solberg, "Catholic Presence," 796. O'Brien spent the 1939–40 academic year in residence at the University of Oxford and then settled at Notre Dame in the fall of 1940, where he remained for the rest of his long career.

168. "John A. O'Brien Papers," *Notre Dame Archives Index*, http://archives.nd.edu/find aids/ead/index/OBR001.htm (accessed February 2, 2021).

say titles are indicative, including his own "Catholics and Cultural Leadership," Karl Herzfeld's "Filling the Gap in Science," James Reyniers's "Ways and Means of Developing Catholic Scientists," David McCabe's "The Path to Eminence in Economics," Jerome Kerwin's "Enhancing Catholic Prestige," and others.[169]

O'Brien made his biggest name in writings dealing with Catholicism's relationship to the modern world, especially birth control, evolution, sex education, and population demography. After publishing a thirty-page pamphlet with the Paulist Press in 1930 titled *Evolution: Facing the Facts*, he expanded his discussion of evolution two years later in a full book, explaining that his interest in doing so stemmed from a sense at Illinois that "many ... religious difficulties of the students centered around the problem of evolution."[170] He was proud to announce that his book *Evolution and Religion* (1932) "received wide acclaim from scientists and philosophers," including famed paleontologist Henry Fairfield Osborn of the New York Museum of Natural History, Princeton biologist Edwin Grant Conklin, Nobel laureate physicist Robert Millikan, and others.[171]

On contraception, O'Brien had claimed that the Great Depres-

169. See John A. O'Brien, ed., *Catholics and Scholarship: A Symposium on the Development of Scholars* (Huntington, Ind.: Our Sunday Visitor Press, [1939]); O'Brien, "Catholics and Cultural Leadership," in *Catholics and Scholarship*, 27–37; Karl Herzfeld, "Filling the Gap in Science," in *Catholics and Scholarship*, 86–96; James Reyniers, "Ways and Means of Developing Catholic Scientists," in *Catholics and Scholarship*, 107–29; David McCabe, "The Path to Eminence in Economics," in *Catholics and Scholarship*, 146–52; Jerome Kerwin, "Enhancing Catholic Prestige," in *Catholics and Scholarship*, 154–64.

170. O'Brien quoted in Romig, *Book of Catholic Authors*, 245.

171. O'Brien quoted in Romig, *Book of Catholic Authors*, 245–46. For Osborn reference, see Morrison, "History of American Catholic Opinion," 45. While implying trickle-down effect through the attention of such prominent scientists, O'Brien simultaneously lamented his book's "disproportionately meagre sale—perhaps because of the limited number who have the background in philosophy and in science, as well as interest in the problem, to read it and to understand it" (O'Brien quoted in Romig, *Book of Catholic Authors*, 246). Dissertator John Morrison wrote: "*Evolution and Religion* ... was extensively noticed by leading non-Catholics. Conklin reviewed it [favorably] for the Scientific Book Club. Michael Pupin, a distinguished physicist, bestowed lavish praise on it.... J. Howard Beard, a Protestant and Chairman of the Illinois Board of Health, reported to Fr. O'Brien that his book was making a good impression upon rural Protestant clergymen and would do much to prevent a future repetition of the Dayton episode" (344–45).

sion "rendered more acute than ever the problem of birth control," leading him to write the long pamphlet *Legitimate Birth Control* (1934) at a time when the question of the rhythm method was a lively and much-discussed one in Catholic circles. O'Brien reissued it with some reworking—including new tables and charts for practical implementation of rhythm—in book form as *Natural Birth Control* in 1938. He did so despite the fact that the Apostolic Delegate had expressly told the American episcopate in a confidential letter that priests and others involved in rhythm method debates were not to openly recommend the method and that "no Catholic periodical or newspaper ... [should] advertise the theory in question, or discuss it."[172] Both this book and O'Brien's earlier one on evolution will be discussed in more detail in a subsequent chapter. Of this volume, O'Brien himself wrote elsewhere that in publishing on the rhythm method he was "seeking to afford guidance and relief for hard pressed parents" and was "show[ing] the harmony of Christian ethics with the findings of gynecological science."[173]

O'Brien characterized what became his best-selling book, *The Faith of Millions* (1938), in the same vein, purporting to offer Catholic teachings not only in terms of Biblical truths but also "in the light of modern thought and science."[174] O'Brien averred that the book "swept the country like wildfire," with success being "as instantaneous as it was phenomenal." His key boast for *The Faith of Millions* echoes the extent to which he was preoccupied with his reception outside merely Catholic circles. O'Brien called it "a consistent best seller among religious books each year since its appearance."[175]

172. "Archbishop of Laodicea/Apostolic Delegate letter 'Not to be Published'" (May 23, 1936), in NCWC papers, box 85, folder "Social Action: Family Life Bureau: Birth Control, 1931–1958," ACUA. The letter indicates that the NCWC had written to the Apostolic Delegate asking about the issue and that this reply was the official response.

173. O'Brien quoted in Romig, *Book of Catholic Authors*, 246.

174. O'Brien quoted in Romig, *Book of Catholic Authors*, 246.

175. O'Brien quoted in Romig, *Book of Catholic Authors*, 246. He went on to say that by 1942 its sales passed 130,000 and that German, Portuguese, and Hungarian translations were being prepared to supplement existing ones in French and Spanish (246).

O'Brien's commitment to such dialogue with representatives of other religions—especially Protestants and Jews, and even Freemasons, among other groups traditionally seen as incompatible with Catholicism—endeared him to some in those groups as well as to other liberal Catholics. But it earned him enemies among those who considered themselves more authentic representatives of the church's tradition, and this list extended beyond the above-mentioned Bishop Schlarman.

As with Cooper, O'Brien's direct connection to the NCWC led to his embroilment in conflict. His reputation for interfaith cooperation combined with his impolitic complaints about "the backwardness of Catholic intellectual life" while in the organization saw him chastened for indifferentism—a lack of concern on properly distinguishing between Catholicism and other religions—by some important conservative Catholic clergy.[176] Even in the 1920s the complaints already flowed. In 1926, for example, the Jesuit former president of Marquette University, Fr. Herbert Noonan, SJ, accused O'Brien of heterodoxy partly on the basis of his claim that Catholics could study secular subjects anywhere and only needed Catholic instructors and surroundings when they studied religion proper.[177]

A year earlier, O'Brien had drawn negative attention from conservatives when he addressed the Illinois state convention on the question of Catholic education. In a speech that subsequently saw wide distribution, O'Brien said that the Catholic Church was not interested in teaching secular subjects like agriculture but rather in imparting religion.[178] Three well-circulated pamphlets extended and elaborated on this stance.[179] The notion that Catholicism could be compartmentalized in religion courses struck a nerve with numerous American Catholics of the time although, as we have seen,

176. Solberg, "Catholic Presence," 778.
177. Solberg, "Catholic Presence," 785.
178. Slawson, *Foundation and First Decade*, 266.
179. The pamphlets were: *The Catholic Foundation at the University of Illinois* (1922); *The White Harvest* (1923); *A Ghost and Its Flight* (1925). The latter title, especially, reveals that part of O'Brien's plan was to respond to the active Ku Klux Klan in Illinois.

certainly not with Cooper.[180] O'Brien claimed of the Catholic educational apparatus that if one "takes ... [religion] out of a Catholic college ... only secular education remained. By inserting religion into a secular program, he argued, the essence of Catholic education was preserved."[181]

From the late nineteenth century, Catholics like Archbishop Ireland who were involved in the Americanist movement had strongly favored public education. Several argued that this stance showed not only Catholic patriotism but also acquiescence to the American cultural vision inculcated in public schools. Their opponents in the church viewed the public school system as having a nefarious combination of Protestant and secular biases. Some opponents of O'Brien's position charged him with encouraging a state monopoly on education, something that had long frightened Catholics who, not entirely without cause, worried about subtle Protestant proselytizing of their children in public schools. For such people, maintaining an entirely separate and thriving Catholic-run educational bloc was, in effect, a defensive posture against a Protestantism often seen as connected with the Ku Klux Klan.[182]

180. The popes had indicated that, just as with an ideal government, an ideal education would take place in a holistically integrated Catholic environment. There were provisions for religious supplementation when one couldn't have private Catholic education. One portion of Pope Pius X's *Acerbo Nimis* ("On the Teaching of Christian Doctrine") in 1905 stated, "In larger cities, and especially where universities, colleges and secondary schools are located, let classes in religion be organized to instruct youths who attend public schools from which all religious teaching is banned" (quoted in Solberg, "Catholic Presence," 766). The applicability of such a proviso in the case of Champaign, Illinois (where the University of Illinois's campus was located) is debatable.

181. Slawson, *Foundation and First Decade*, 266. Here, Americanist forerunners like Archbishop Ireland had anticipated later interwar stances. Regarding the school question, Ireland had made arrangements with Minnesota public school boards to have certain church-owned buildings used for state-run education during the day, followed by post-school day religion classes taught by Catholics in the evening. Ireland directly modeled his plan on that of the "Accademia" group connected to Americanist Isaac Hecker in the nineteenth century. Accademia was a salon of New York–centered priests fiercely opposed to separatist parochial school education (Slawson, *Foundation and First Decade*, 266).

182. Solberg, "Catholic Presence," 782. The conservative Jesuit-run *America* magazine published seven pieces in 1925 alone dealing with public schools and the Catholic philosophy of education. A common theme in these pieces was that an education in religion was not the same thing as a religious education, one writer bluntly stating, "Catholics ... should be in Catholic schools." Jesuit Paul Blakely, associate editor of *America*, addressed the Catholic

Like Cooper, but never with the same restraint, O'Brien argued that Catholic intellectual life crawled along in perpetual weakness. He argued that reaching out through religion courses to the many Catholics enrolled at the University of Illinois would be a way of both serving their needs and preparing them to reach out to non-Catholic America as part of a better educated laity.[183]

In certain ways, alignments in the fight over the philosophy of education were analogous to those in the cultural fight over the philosophy of science. By the interwar period, liberal-progressive Catholics sided with their non-Catholic progressive colleagues against the neoscholastic Catholics in both territories.

O'Brien's approach rankled Baltimore's powerful Archbishop Michael Curley. The former's strong statements as an education columnist for *Catholic School Interests* magazine did him no favors with such opponents in the church. In one column, O'Brien's claim that Protestant Bruce Barton's *The Man Nobody Knows* was "the only true picture of Christ that has appeared since the Gospel narrative itself" led Curley to reply that Barton's book was, in fact, "blasphemous and heretical."[184] The powerful Cardinal O'Connell of Boston also opposed O'Brien, having characterized both him and the NCWC as "Americanism reincarnate."[185]

Educational Association in the summer of 1926 and, in so doing, quoted—and harshly critiqued—statements from O'Brien's pamphlets as examples of what Catholic education was *not.* The association thus passed a resolution stating that every single Catholic student, from elementary to college age, should be in a Catholic school.

183. Solberg, "Catholic Presence," 777. O'Brien claimed that more of Illinois's college-attending Catholics were at the University of Illinois than all of the state's Catholic colleges (Solberg, 777). Engaging religiously unaffiliated and anti-Catholic perspectives, he said, was key, and "the great State Universities are the real battle grounds on which the fate of institutions and the battles of conflicting theories of belief and philosophies of life are fought out" (Solberg, 777).

184. Solberg, "Catholic Presence," 789. Curley said that O'Brien's original comment appeared in *Catholic School Interests*, a place where O'Brien, as book review editor, had recommended other "distinctly Protestant" books "totally devoid of Catholic tone" (Solberg, 789).

185. Slawson, *Foundation and First Decade*, 276. Boston's Cardinal O'Connell and others associated the nationally organized and bureaucratized vision of American Catholicism emblematized by the NCWC as redolent of the unwelcome American tendency to centralize American life and remove the power to determine certain matters from states or individuals to centralized (i.e., non-Catholic) government control (Slawson, 276).

In March of 1927, the NCWC education department director asked for O'Brien's resignation. This came shortly after O'Brien had agreed to endorse an ecumenical prayer composed by a Methodist minister imploring tolerance after a Ku Klux Klan incident in Illinois. The prayer was addressed solely to God the Father, in part to permit its use by local Jewish rabbis. The NCWC news service published a piece erroneously attributing co-authorship of the prayer to O'Brien. This (inaccurate) claim was repeated in the popular press. Curley fumed while liberal Protestant journal *Christian Century* congratulated O'Brien for his supposed joint authorship of the ecumenical prayer.[186]

By then, Curley had publicly and repeatedly questioned O'Brien's theological orthodoxy. In a thunderous speech in the same month, March 1927, Curley openly lambasted both the priest and the NCWC. He also personally denounced O'Brien in a letter to the leading Vatican representative in the United States, Cardinal Raphael Merry del Val, stating that O'Brien and the NCWC had created an atmosphere "redolent of unbelief and sheer materialism" and that O'Brien's attitudes were "liberalising and un-Catholic."[187] Although del Val instructed Curley to let the issue drop quietly, the NCWC was forced to cut official ties with O'Brien.

The details laid out in this chapter suggest the extent and contours of the liberal-progressive vision represented by Fr. O'Brien and our other two main figures. They also show the thin ice on which they all, to various degrees, were perceived to tread by more conservative American Catholics wedded to the official, ultramontane, and neoscholastic-oriented vision of the papacy and much of the American episcopate in the interwar era. Both the veins of intellectual diversity found within an American church sometimes painted with a more monolithic brush and the victories and alliances gained by the trio perhaps protected them from the

---

186. "Protestant, Catholic and Jew Formulate Common Prayer," *Christian Century* 44 (March 10, 1927): 310. The *American Hebrew* and the *Jewish Daily Bulletin* also reported positively on the incident (Solberg, "Catholic Presence," 789n56).

187. Slawson, *Foundation and First Decade*, 273–74.

antimodernist forces' ability to silence them. Their affiliation with social science departments rather than with theological faculties certainly did so. Although their priesthoods and public voices survived the formal antimodernist push, it is worth noting the specific nature of the criticisms leveled against the trio. The criticisms are thematic, citing them for embodying aspects of Americanism and modernism streams as condemned by the papacy and the church's high offices. The NCWC and our figures connected to it were construed as radical by more conservative American Catholics who not only disapproved of them but also particularly labeled them as intellectually tied to Americanism and modernism.

O'Brien himself was a less circumspect and savvy expression of what were nevertheless the same lineage and ties binding together Ryan and Cooper with respect to progressivism, Americanism, and modernism. Asking themselves how American Catholicism could reconcile with modern American public culture, their response was to reach out to the ecumenist and secular mainline, use the tools of science, and ignore—as well as provoke—those Catholics who believed the church in America must not try to blend in but rather to distinguish itself from non-Catholicism in all major arenas of culture.

nity, Leo XIII, ordered the Vatican to unseal and make available
its centuries-old archival collection connected to Galileo Galilei
and the church's 1633 proscription of his statements elaborating
on Nicolas Copernicus's heliocentric cosmology. Leo's impetus lay
in a hope to demystify church operations while bringing to light
the truth about the Galileo situation in the face of lurid accusations about those events from anticlericalists and their allies, who
claimed that the Roman Catholic Church had fought a centuries-
long battle to suppress scientific verities. Myths about a church
hostile to new scientific ideas went at least as far back as Voltaire in
the early modern West but had accelerated in the second half of the
nineteenth century for a complex of reasons. Pope Leo asserted,
and the archives confirmed, that Galileo was punished only lightly
and without suffering and, moreover, that this punishment derived
in no way from any anti-scientific attitudes by the church. Instead,
Galileo's reprimand derived firstly from his hasty assertions about
the cosmos in absence of defensible proof using the standard scientific methods of his age, a particular problem in the seventeenth
century since the church saw itself as responsible for ensuring the
accuracy of *all* truth claims. Secondly, the Inquisition censured his
having taught as authoritative his own personal scriptural interpretation—this in an era of ubiquitous Protestant challenges to
the church's interpretive prerogatives. By publishing these archival
sources, Leo sought to clarify the situation from the church's historical and judicial record and thereby to demonstrate that it had
not acted in an obstructionist, antiscientific spirit. Many readers
of the time, however, viewed the documents through the lens of
the conflict thesis famously promulgated in John William Draper's
popular anti-Catholic diatribe, *History of the Conflict between Religion and Science*. Draper's erroneous facts and myth-making about
the Galileo episode seemed to trump the archival information in
the public mind and, often, even in the scholarly mind, both then
and for decades afterward. A feeling of insecurity lingering from
this appropriation of the Galileo incident, combined with a deter-

mination to show that Catholicism itself was now much more welcoming to science, is evident in liberal Catholic interwar writings.

More recent evidence also suggests that the resurgence of myths about the Galileo situation led many turn-of-the-century church officials to embrace an extremely circumspect approach toward evolutionists—even toward those they considered extreme.[2] This caution extended to the highest-ranking Roman Jesuits in charge of Vatican committees on censorship, a number of whom were personally opposed to evolution. The most recent authoritative study concluded that the church had no formal position on evolution, including in the early decades of the twentieth century. Also, no official condemnation of any Catholic's book on evolution—no matter how far afield it may have strayed from what more conservative officials felt was warranted—was ever published.[3] Internal pressure applied to particular authors, however, did see some withdraw books that Italian Jesuits who exerted subaltern bureaucratic sway felt had crossed an acceptable line.[4]

Perhaps the most important such case involved an American physics and chemistry instructor at the University of Notre Dame in the fin de siècle, Fr. John Zahm. Zahm's story is already known in American Catholic historiography and has recently been revisited.[5] Zahm found himself on the receiving end of substantial behind-the-scenes pressure after certain Italian Jesuits decided that his popular books connecting science and religion should be removed from circulation. The books were *Bible, Science, and Faith* (1894) and the influential and internationally best-selling *Evolution and Dogma* (1896). The Jesuits and some others influential in Rome argued that these books, especially the latter, contained elements of

2. See Artigas, Glick, and Martínez, *Negotiating Darwin*, 1–3.

3. Artigas, Glick, and Martínez conclude that the archival sources do not show a churchwide official policy on evolution; rather, responses were meted out on an ad hoc basis (*Negotiating Darwin*, 4).

4. On internal church politicking by Italian Jesuits who influenced private pronouncements about evolution, see Barry Brundell, "Catholic Church Politics and Evolution Theory, 1894–1902," *British Journal for the History of Science* 34 (2001): 81–95.

5. See Slattery, *Faith and Science*.

theological modernism—not yet formally condemned but which they strongly disapproved of—and also of Americanism. In so doing, they contended that these concepts as present in his books were intimately tied to his defense of evolution.[6] The Congregation of the Index thus approached him.[7]

Catholic opponents of Zahm wishing to silence him, however, feared the effects of attempting to quash a Catholic author who was popular even outside of church circles; they loathed exposing the church to new Galileo-esque accusations of obscurantism. But to Zahm's opponents within the church bureaucracy, the praise his work received from figures ambivalent or hostile to Catholicism made him guilty by association. For example, Zahm's *Evolution and Dogma* received a flattering review in Edward Youmans's important magazine *Popular Science Monthly*.[8] By the 1890s, this periodical had been credited for advocating the positivist vision of the philosophy of science known as uniformity of nature. According to Youmans, careful adherence to uniformitarianism was the sine qua non of a professional scientist, whereas the appeal to non-naturalistic philosophies in public science marked an amateur dilettante. Moreover, Youmans's magazine had also popularized the anti-theological work of Herbert Spencer and Thomas Huxley in America, both anathema to most traditional Christians of the time.[9]

6. Don O'Leary has argued that officials in the Vatican curia went after Zahm for presenting Sts. Augustine and Aquinas as evolutionists. See O'Leary, *Roman Catholicism*, 99. In Slattery's description of Roman concerns about Zahm, he agrees that Zahm's co-opting of Augustine and Aquinas was important in the case against him. Noting the role such attributions also played in a similar condemnation of Dominican priest Fr. Marie-Dalmace Leroy, Slattery points to the particular role of these claims by Zahm in the case made against him by his chief Roman adversary—and author of his official condemnation—titular Archbishop Otto Zardetti, and in the report written by the Dominican consultor, Enrico Buonpensiere, in 1898 (*Faith and Science*, 53, 148).

7. This was after Zahm had been formally denounced to the Vatican in 1897 by Zardetti (Brundell, "Catholic Church Politics," 89).

8. See E. L. Youmans, "Scientific Literature: Popular Books," *Appleton's Popular Science Monthly* 49 (July 1896): 414–15.

9. O'Leary, *Roman Catholicism*, 99. Earlier in the nineteenth century, the uniformity of nature had enjoyed an extensive theistic or—in some cases, at least—deistic variant. One finds such uniformity in the works of famous British theistic naturalists John Herschel, James Maxwell, and others. However, later in the century, the anti-Anglican Thomas Huxley and

Seeing a Catholic's work embraced by such determined enemies of scientific neoscholasticism, yet at the same time fearing
accusations of repeating the church's imperious behavior of the
seventeenth century, the church's official teaching institutions
in Rome could not be persuaded to make a public decree on Fr.
Zahm's work. However, the Congregation of the Index privately
pushed him to remove his books from further sale.[10] As in other
cases of early Catholic evolutionists, like St. George Jackson Mivart
(who ended up censured), it is difficult to conclusively state whether it was a concern for theological modernism—ideas of natural
emergence and transformation of doctrine—or, instead, a concern
for scientific evolution as applied to the natural world that actually
spawned behind-the-scenes repudiations.

Ultimately, the only official public actions by the church in
any way relating to evolution came through decrees on biblical
interpretation.[11] In 1893, Pope Leo XIII issued the encyclical *Prov-
identissimus Deus* and, in 1902, created the official Pontifical Biblical Commission as a standing department to deal with biblical
hermeneutics. Both were formal attempts to confront challenges
to biblical integrity that derived from what were seen as extreme
applications of the historical-critical method of exegesis.[12] They
did, however, emerge just as the evolution question was heating up
in certain Catholic circles. While the encyclical declared the entire
canonical Scripture to have been written under inspiration of the
Holy Spirit and to be exclusively subject to the church's authoritative interpretation, it also cited the position of St. Augustine of

his coterie commandeered the concept of uniformity of nature for anticlerical purposes; they
successfully made it seem utterly antithetical to theism, not only for the methodology of science but often even in a full cosmological sense. In Huxley's case, this appropriation went
with his campaign against the notion of teleology in nature. See Stanley, *Huxley's Church and
Maxwell's Demon*, 34–37, 57, 61–68. By Zahm's time, uniformity was squarely connected with
Huxley's interpretation.

10. Brundell, "Catholic Church Politics," 90.

11. This conclusion holds true according to Slattery, too, though only in a technical sense
as he contends that the extant record as much as shows the condemnation of Zahm as a de
facto condemnation of evolution (*Faith and Science*, 151–52).

12. O'Leary, *Roman Catholicism*, 68.

Hippo that some materials in the Bible, while apparently contrary to human reason, either require closer study or are expressed in figurative language.[13]

The Biblical Commission's 1909 decree on the first several chapters of Genesis was immediately viewed in light of the evolution issue, but it never actually mentioned evolution. Its cautious wording should be understood partly in relation to the 1907 papal condemnation of theological modernism by Pope Pius X in *Pascendi Domenici Gregis*. By not mentioning evolution even in passing, the Commission's decree invited many subsequent claims and cross-claims by Catholics and others as to its relevance for evolution. By the 1920s, American Catholic conservatives like the Jesuit Fr. Francis LeBuffe had contended for some time that the 1909 Commission's decree on Genesis ruled out the possibility of accepting even the bodily evolution of humans. By contrast, liberals such as evolution enthusiast Fr. Ernest Messenger and his regular correspondents O'Brien and Cooper believed that the decree's wording had been crafted so as to purposely *not* rule out physical evolution. Ryan, too, though not a confidante of Messenger, presumed the same thing, as will be clear below in his Scopes Trial rhetoric.[14] At any rate, the decree was vague enough for Catholics on all sides of the evolution question to cite it in defense of their positions. Presumably, American Catholic bishops also had their own perspectives on evolution. They, however, were subject to the papacy and its commissions and could not make unilateral decrees on questions of official church policy on such matters anyway, either singularly or corporately.[15]

13. O'Leary, *Roman Catholicism*, 69–71.

14. LeBuffe insisted that the 1909 decree provided "at least a disciplinary prohibition regarding the teaching of the evolution of even Adam's body." Francis P. LeBuffe, letter to the editor, *Commonweal* 2 (June 17, 1925), 163. See also Morrison, "History of American Catholic Opinion," 281. On Cooper's and O'Brien's consistent communication with Messenger, see Morrison, "History of American Catholic Opinion," 342. More recently, historian Peter Bowler claimed that the decree officially removed all question of conflict between evolution and the biblical texts. Bowler, *Reconciling Science and Religion: The Debate in Early-Twentieth-Century Britain* (Chicago: University of Chicago Press, 2001), 324.

15. For specific bishops and their personal views on evolution, see R. Scott Appleby,

Our brief consideration of the institutional Catholic context in the 1920s for science, in general, and evolution, in particular, is complete with the pontificate of Pope Pius XI. Pius proceeded with what Leo XIII had envisioned as overtures to the modern sciences while remaining firmly within the neoscholastic mantra disdained by most science-minded liberal Catholics of the age. This institutional scaffolding was comprised of both the cautious American episcopate and the more mixed bag of European bishops, some of whom openly supported the evolutionism that had come from the pens of three European Catholic clergy-scientists whose scientific acumen accorded Catholicism significant international intellectual prestige. It is these three figures who most strongly influenced American Catholic discourse on science and evolution itself by the 1920s. They were Frenchman Fr. Henri de Dorlodot (1855–1929); Austrian priest Erich Wasmann, SJ (1859–1931); and English St. George Jackson Mivart (1827–1900).

Canon Dorlodot, a geology professor at the University of Louvain and an avowed Darwinist, had called Darwin "the interpreter of the organic world; just as Newton was the voice from heaven come to tell us of the glory of the Creator."[16] Beyond arguing the clear compatibility of evolution and Catholicism, Dorlodot's book *Darwinism and Catholic Thought* (1921) interpreted early Christian writers like St. Augustine through the lens of evolution "as Darwin understood it."[17] It was an anachronistic claim that would be repeated by a number of American Catholics in the 1920s. Jesuit entomologist Erich Wasmann also enthusiastically embraced descent with modification.[18] Conservatives, who derided what they saw

---

"Exposing Darwin's Hidden Agenda: Roman Catholic Responses to Evolution, 1875–1925," in *Disseminating Darwinism: The Role of Place, Race, Religion, and Gender*, ed. Ronald L. Numbers and John Stenhouse, 173–208 (Cambridge: Cambridge University Press, 1999).

16. Dorlodot quoted in O'Leary, *Roman Catholicism*, 126.

17. Francis J. Wenninger, review of *Darwinism and Catholic Thought*, by Canon Dorlodot, trans. Ernest Messenger, *American Midland Naturalist* 8 (March–May 1923): 213.

18. Bertram Windle (1858–1929), one-time anatomy professor at the University of Toronto and science editor of *Commonweal* magazine, said, "The great lesson which Fr. Wasmann taught … was the virtue of accepting, without question, whatever science had to offer" (quoted in Morrison, "History of American Catholic Opinion," 313–14).

as their liberal brethren's excessive enthusiasm for the evolution bandwagon, accused the liberals of making "Wasmannism" seem to be *the* Catholic position.[19] Wasmann had authored significant portions of the first *Catholic Encyclopedia*'s article on evolution, a series that found its way into almost every Catholic parish rectory in the early decades of the twentieth century.[20] Known on the Continent as a prolific opponent of the German Ernst Haeckel's monism, Wasmann's evolutionism emerged from his close entomological observations.[21] Finally, the work of St. George Jackson Mivart must also be accounted for when considering Catholic contexts by the 1920s. Mivart was excommunicated late in life, although the cause was not formally attributed to his writings on evolution. He published several books in the later nineteenth century endorsing descent with modification.[22] While he favored evolution by discontinuous steps over Darwin's thesis of evolution by gradual natural selection, he was a firm evolutionist who certainly antagonized Catholic authorities by counseling Catholic scientists not to let their search for truth be impeded by church officials and by relentlessly attacking the way the church had handled the Galileo episode.[23]

With the work of these European Catholic scientists on the table by the 1920s, new Catholic precedents had been established for our actors beyond what had existed in Zahm's era, although any broader openness to Catholic intellectual creativity was tempered by *Pascendi* and the aforementioned ultramontane mindset of

19. See, for example, Simon Fitzsimons, "Wasmann and Evolution," letter to the editor, *Commonweal* 2 (July 8, 1925), 228–29.

20. See Erich Wasmann, "Evolution," in *The Catholic Encyclopedia: An International Work of Reference on the Constitution, Doctrine, Discipline, and History of the Catholic Church*, ed. Charles G. Herbermann et al. (New York: Robert Appleton Co., 1909), 5:656.

21. Robert J. Richards, *The Tragic Sense of Life: Ernst Haeckel and the Struggle over Evolutionary Thought* (Chicago: University of Chicago Press, 2008), 366–67. Richards argues that Wasmann's views on evolutionary mechanism approximated an amalgamation of Hugo de Vries and Hans Driesch's views.

22. See Jacob W. Gruber, *A Conscience in Conflict: The Life of St. George Jackson Mivart* (New York: Columbia University Press for Temple University, 1960), 59.

23. O'Leary, *Roman Catholicism*, 86.

most American bishops in the 1920s.[24] Before turning to the 1920s and our actors' engagement with public science, prudence invites a sketch of major contours found in the discursive realm into which these Catholic sought entry in America. This means a brief look at Protestant clerical voices in public culture and at mainline scientific voices, most of which were themselves tied to modernist Protestantism. Part of the consideration is how science, particularly evolution, was seen to function in that realm both on its own merits and as a symbolically authoritative episteme.

Authoritative Protestant Voices

Given the schism of opinion in Protestantism between liberals and modernists on the one hand and conservative literalists on the other, any attempt to characterize interwar Protestant attitudes to evolution requires considerable nuance. One may consult the extensive literature on the Scopes Trial for views of the distinctions in the 1920s; only the most general sketch is possible here. Given the postmillennial hope in science among the modernists, it becomes difficult to separate their attitudes toward evolution from their worldview in toto; every such interwar voice of note, including the renowned liberal modernists Harry Emerson Fosdick of the Union Theological Seminary and Shailer Mathews of the University of Chicago Divinity school, championed evolution and tended to see it as the key factor in both biological and social development.[25]

24. For Pope Pius X's *Pascendi Domenici Gregis*, see the Vatican website. For the aftereffects and the requirement that priests and theologians take an oath against modernism, see Gleason, *Contending with Modernity*, 111–14.

25. Postmillennialism refers to a distinction in Protestant eschatology and biblical hermeneutics emerging in the nineteenth century and active well beyond that. The postmillennialists, associated with Protestant liberalism, and the premillennialists, associated with Protestant literalism, debated over the nature of a period referred to in Revelation (especially chapter 20). Originally, postmillennialism "represented a compromise between an apocalyptic and an evolutionary view of time.... The theory postponed history's cataclysmic end, ... allow[ing] the temporal interval necessary for the gradual evangelical conquest of the world and the triumph of secular progress." This progress to earthly utopia before the end of time was largely understood as needing science-centered intervention to fashion a moral and progressive social order. See James Morehead, "The Erosion of Postmillennialism in American

Fosdick, who asked "Shall the Fundamentalists Win?" in a heavily-publicized sermon in May 1922, worked concertedly to counter conservative Protestant anti-evolutionists. In one example, he penned a thoroughgoing defense of evolution for the American Institute of Sacred Literature to rebut conservative anti-evolutionist William Jennings Bryan.[26] Mathews, beyond regular endorsements of biological evolution and an intention to testify for the defense at the Scopes Trial, articulated an evolutionary episteme at the heart of religion itself. In the article "The Evolution of Religion," Mathews wrote, "Whatever may have been its origin, religion exhibits phenomena observable in social institutions to which the term 'evolution' may be legitimately applied.... There is a large measure of similarity between certain processes in social history and certain others in the building up of cellular organisms."[27]

It is no revelation to say that literalist and fundamentalist Protestants of the time opposed evolution. It is, however, important to note that neither around the Scopes Trial nor at other times could anti-evolutionism be summed up as the simple seven-day biblical literalism or young-earth creationism often mischaracterized as the soul of Protestant interwar opposition. Most educated Prot-

---

Religious Thought, 1865–1925," *Church History* 53 (1984): 61–62. Many modernists completely abandoned the idea of any literal return of Christ; instead, they were able to refashion postmillennialism into a metaphor for Christian-inspired social transformation in evolutionary history. Thus, while "the building of the Kingdom of God had become as much a matter of technique and program as it was of conversion and religious piety," the cult of efficiency and social engineering could be pursued with its own evangelical fervor by modernist postmillennialists (Morehead, 75–76). Premillennialists focused, by contrast, on personal moral perfection in preparation for a thousand-year reign of Jesus. Millennialism was de facto rejected as part of the error of "chiliasm" at the Second Ecumenical Council in the condemnation of Apollinaris's teachings, but in the Protestantism of our period, its acceptance in various forms had important implications for social thought. For connections between modernism and postmillennialism (and eugenics) in the United States, see Christine Rosen, *Preaching Eugenics: Religious Leaders and the American Eugenics Movement* (Oxford: Oxford University Press, 2004), 5–7, 16–18, 111–37.

26. Bradley J. Longfield, *The Presbyterian Controversy: Fundamentalists, Modernists, and Moderates* (New York: Oxford University Press, 2001), 9–11. See also Harry Emerson Fosdick, "Evolution and Mr. Bryan," in Fosdick and Sherwood Eddy, *Science and Religion: Evolution and the Bible*, 27–33 (New York: George H. Doran, 1924).

27. Shailer Mathews, "The Evolution of Religion," *American Journal of Theology* 15 (1911): 57–58.

estant conservatives espoused a form of the "day-age" theory or the "gap" theory hailing from later nineteenth-century Protestant thought.[28]

Publicly renowned fundamentalist ministers—such as William Bell Riley of First Baptist Church in Minneapolis (leader of the World's Christian Fundamentals Association) and John Roach Straton of New York's Calvary Baptist Church—spent their time in the 1920s describing not only their problem with evolution but also what they saw as the problematic public influence of figures like Fosdick and Mathews. Riley, Straton, and others of their ilk saw the latter as full-fledged agents of secularism and unbelief. In July 1925, the *New York Times* reported on a Straton sermon protecting biblical hermeneutics and "characteriz[ing] the teachings of Dr. Harry Emerson Fosdick as those of a 'social expert rather than the faith of a minister of the Gospel.'"[29] For his part, Riley said Mathews's and Fosdick's allegorical readings of the Bible in light of evolution prioritized science at all costs, barely making room for even the basics of Christianity: "Prof. Shailer Mathews pleads for the completion of the evolutionary theory by letting it 'include Jesus,' while Dr. Fosdick ... [tries] to save his evolutionary hypothesis from the collapse incident to believing in a Divine Christ" by averring that claims of non-naturalistic birth were simply common in pre-history.[30] On evolution and its mutating influence on Christianity, Riley

28. On subtleties in Protestant creationism in those decades, see Ronald Numbers, *Darwinism Comes to America* (Cambridge, Mass.: Harvard University Press, 1998), 51–53. The day-age theory rendered the "days" in chapter one of Genesis as vast epochs. The gap theory separated an original creation of the cosmos from a much later creation of Eden. Only the Seventh Day Adventist group argued in favor of biblical days of twenty-four hours for creation. Numbers, *The Creationists: From Scientific Creationism to Intelligent Design*, expanded ed. (Cambridge, Mass.: Harvard University Press, 2006), 51. The general tenor of this anti-evolutionism also involved disputes over the philosophy of science—i.e., distinctions between hypothesis and scientific fact and the nature of empiricism—as well as pragmatic concern about how belief in evolution affected society's moral distinctions between humans and animals. Each of these areas factored into Bryan's own view. See William Jennings Bryan, *In His Image* (New York: Fleming H. Revell, 1922), 119–35. See also Numbers, *The Creationists*, 65.

29. "Straton Says Fosdick Is a 'Social Expert'; Declares Ousted Pastor's Faith Is Not That of a Minister of the Gospel," *New York Times*, July 13, 1925, 15.

30. William B. Riley, *Inspiration or Evolution?* (Cleveland: Union Gospel Publishing, 1923), 72. For more on related ministers' opposition to evolution, see Numbers, *The Creationists*,

said as far back as 1909 that "the theory of evolution and false theology are indissolubly linked together."[31]

Theologically modernist Protestants' strong enthusiasm for contemporary science and evolutionary worldviews coincided with their near-universal support of eugenics—a movement that they exalted via pulpit and pen, partly as a corollary to the aforementioned postmillennial vision. The ideas behind the supposedly scientific eugenics, or "good birth," movement originated in Great Britain with research statistician Sir Francis Galton's ideas on heritability of genius. Galton constructed his ideas from then-current views of scientific heritability in evolution and statistical probabilities, analogizing to humans from animal husbandry. Although he coined the term *eugenics* in 1883, Galton had published a two-part article "Hereditary Character and Talent" that contained his early ideas on the subject in 1865. It was in the early twentieth-century United States that a full-fledged, science-garbed eugenics movement grew to its broadest ideological and institutional forms and that eugenic ideas on selective breeding saw themselves particularly embedded in categories of racialist biology.[32]

In 1904, the Carnegie Institute founded the major organization dedicated to scientific eugenics—the Station for the Study of Experimental Evolution—at Cold Spring Harbor, Long Island, under the direction of geneticist Charles Davenport. Davenport worked there to find ways of "improv[ing] the national protoplasm," encouraging the reproduction of the so-called "fit," a program later known as positive eugenics, and seeking how to prevent the reproduction of those categorized as biologically "unfit," a plan later

---

61–63, 65. Most opposition by such ministers either indirectly centered on the philosophy of science—i.e., distinction between hypothesis and scientific fact and the nature of empiricism—or on the practical effects of belief in evolution as it affected moral distinctions between humans and animals (Numbers, 65).

31. Riley, *The Finality of Higher Criticism; Or, The Theory of Evolution and False Theology* (1909), quoted in Jon H. Roberts, "Religious Reactions to Darwinism," in *The Cambridge Companion to Science and Religion*, ed. Peter Harrison (Cambridge: Cambridge University Press, 2010), 96–97.

32. Diane B. Paul, *Controlling Human Heredity: 1865 to the Present* (Highlands, N.J.: Humanities Press, 1995), 20.

known as negative eugenics.[33] The Eugenics Record Office was created in 1910 as the research department of the Station and was run by Davenport's assistant Harry Laughlin.[34] By the 1920s, the United States had become the major center of the eugenics movement via these two agencies and with the added founding of the AES in 1922 by Laughlin, Henry Fairfield Osborn, and lawyer Madison Grant.[35]

Galton claimed that he had conceived of eugenics while reading his cousin Charles Darwin's *On the Origin of Species*.[36] And Darwin himself cited the role Galton's ideas played in his own evolutionary thinking in *The Descent of Man* (1871).[37] Although Darwin himself never endorsed programs to deny charity to the poor or control reproduction, a number of subsequent eugenicists claimed their ideas extended from Darwin's. His own son, Leonard Darwin, made this claim as longtime president of the British Eugenics Research Society and as a supporter of the involuntary sterilization prong of the eugenics movement.[38]

33. Daniel J. Kevles, *In the Name of Eugenics: Genetics and the Uses of Human Heredity* (Cambridge, Mass.: Harvard University Press, 1995), 45–48.

34. Matthew Frye Jacobson, *Whiteness of a Different Color: European Immigrants and the Alchemy of Race* (Cambridge, Mass.: Harvard University Press, 1998), 78.

35. In 1921, the Station and the Eugenics Record Office combined as the Carnegie Institute's Department of Genetics to pursue both research and popularization. Davenport led it until 1934. See "Eugenics Record Office," Archives of Cold Spring Harbor Laboratory, accessed March 6, 2020, https://library.cshl.edu/special-collections/eugenics.

36. Kevles, *In the Name of Eugenics*, 8. For more on the Eugenics Record Office, see Garland Allen, "The Eugenics Record Office at Cold Spring Harbor, 1910–1940: An Essay in Institutional History," *Osiris* 2 (1986): 225–64. In addition to Carnegie, John D. Rockefeller, and philanthropist Mary Harriman, John Harvey Kellogg (founder of the Race Betterment Foundation in 1906) also contributed.

37. Darwin mused about human evolutionary heritability in analogies with animal breeding in *The Descent of Man*: "With savages, the weak in mind and body are soon eliminated...; We civilized men, on the other hand, do our utmost to check the progress of elimination. We build asylums for the imbecile, the maimed, the sick; we institute poor-laws." He went on, "thus the weak members of civilised societies propagate their kind. No one who has attended to the breeding of domestic animals will doubt that this has to be highly injurious to the race of man." Charles Darwin, *The Descent of Man and Selection in Relation to Sex* (Princeton: Princeton University Press, 1981), 168.

38. Leonard Darwin's arguments appeared in publications of the top American scientific associations. See, for example, Leonard Darwin, "The Aims and Methods of Eugenical Societies," *Science* 54 (October 1921): 313–23; Leonard Darwin, "The Field of Eugenic Reform," *Scientific Monthly* 13 (November 1921): 385–98. In the latter, Darwin justified mandated, state-sponsored sterilization. His work also appeared in popularized science magazines. See

Clergy endorsement of eugenics was not wholly coincidental. The eugenics movement both in the United States and in Britain made concerted efforts to obtain the approval of liberal clergy to help stimulate social support.[39] In the attempt to forge broad coalitions for extending eugenics, in 1923 the AES created an advisory council and a series of outreach committees, one of which was the Committee on Cooperation with Clergymen.[40] As a member of the AES Advisory Council and the Committee on Cooperation with Clergy, Harry Emerson Fosdick supported eugenics as part and parcel of a postmillennial social vision celebrating scientific improvement of society, once proclaiming "few matters are more pressingly important than the application to our social problems of such well-established information in the realm of eugenics as we actually possess."[41] Shailer Mathews, too, wrote in support of eugenics in the context of his enthusiasm for science's role in society. In one 1927 example, Mathews argued that even the lights of the ancient church would have agreed: "it is hard not to see how sympathetic Augustine might have been with our modern knowledge of evolution and eugenics."[42] Sermon contests were held to see who could most thoroughly champion eugenics as an apotheosis of the Gospel and Protestant eugenicist clergy did not hesitate to berate non-eugenicist colleagues as "stifl[ing] society's opportunity for progressive development." They blamed traditionalist clergy for re-

---

"Major Leonard Darwin's Address before the Eugenics Education Society," *Popular Science* 85 (1914): 205–8.

39. See Graham J. Baker, "Christianity and Eugenics: The Place of Religion in the British Eugenics Education Society and the American Eugenics Society, c. 1907–1940," *Social History of Medicine* 27 (2014): 281–302. On the United States in particular, see 294–301. The American Eugenics Society's "Eugenics Catechism," named with an obvious religious reference, overtly tied together evolution, eugenics, and control of births (Baker, "Christianity and Eugenics," 283–84).

40. The other two were Committee on Cooperation with Physicians and Committee on Cooperation with Social Workers. See "American Eugenics Committee Minutes" (August 9, 1922) and "Committee Minutes" (October 26, 1923), in AES Papers, box 5, folder "Committee Minutes, 1922–1925," American Philosophical Society, Philadelphia (henceforth APS).

41. Fosdick quoted in Kevles, *In the Name of Eugenics*, 68. See also Rosen, *Preaching Eugenics*, 116–17. Fosdick's support was clear but, at times, cautious.

42. Mathews quoted in Rosen, *Preaching Eugenics*, 133–34.

maining blind to supposedly clear evidence that Jesus Christ himself prescribed the eugenics movement in the New Testament.[43]

On the other hand, conservative Protestant anti-evolutionist
voices tended to eschew support for the eugenics movement along
with its associated scientific racialism. One reason was that Darwin
was used to justify the movement and its goals.[44] William Jennings
Bryan characterized the whole ideology of eugenics, especially its
tactic of sterilization, as a "brutal" consequence of the "malignant
philosophy of Darwinism."[45] Bryan wrote in his autobiography, *In
His Image* (1922), of ties he believed mutually bound eugenics and
evolution, leading him to reject both.[46]

Professional Scientists, Evolution, and Religion in the Wake of World War I

While progressive Catholics were preoccupied by the 1920s with
apologizing for alleged past sins against scientific naturalism while
themselves employing their own naturalist frameworks and language in public intellectual discourse, the same period saw some
of America's most prominent mainline scientists taking a different
tack by working to construct a public image of human evolution
that embraced, rather than avoided, philosophical and even theological language.[47]

43. Rosen, *Preaching Eugenics*, 122–23. In one eugenic sermon contest, a liberal Protestant
minister reinterpreted the parable of the Good Samaritan in a eugenic lens: "Once … the
Samaritan simply befriended the victim on the road to Jericho; in the early part of the twentieth century he would have provided 'better policing and lighting of the road' to discourage
… thieves; now, with eugenics, the Good Samaritan knew that his duty was to prevent those
thieves from ever being born in the first place" (Rosen, 123). To most figures in both sets of
Protestantism, Catholics were beyond the pale of redemption.

44. Numbers, *Darwinism Comes to America*, 67. See also Rosen, *Preaching Eugenics*, 17–18.

45. Baker, "Christianity and Eugenics," 295; Michael Kazin, *A Godly Hero: The Life of
William Jennings Bryan* (New York: Alfred A. Knopf, 2006), 275.

46. Bryan wrote that in books like *The Descent of Man* and elsewhere, Darwinism taught
"that Christianity impairs the race physically." Bryan noted that this "was the first implication
at which I revolted." He concluded that teaching evolution was not worth the cost to public
morals, altruism, and human dignity, all of which he saw as grounded in the cultural authority
of the Bible (*In His Image*, 107, 149–50).

47. For more on the question of boundaries and connections between these realms, see

The most prominent scientists who popularized evolution in the interwar period, especially paleontologist Henry Fairfield Osborn and embryologist Edwin Grant Conklin, were themselves Protestant modernists or strongly influenced by modernism. As has been argued elsewhere, these figures intertwined elements of Protestant modernist theology, especially divine immanence, into their popular works on evolution. They presented evolution as teleological and progressive in a way that could seem to deify the evolutionary process itself.[48]

At Princeton University alone, the religious and scientific views of modernist science faculty such as Arnold Guyot and James McCosh affected undergraduate students William Berryman Scott and Henry Fairfield Osborn, both future paleontologists. McCosh and Guyot directly influenced Osborn's religious idealism about evolution in ways that encouraged Osborn to later teach about evolution's perfecting tendency in both spiritual and physical senses.[49] This Princeton milieu on evolution and religion also encouraged figures like faculty member Edwin Grant Conklin to develop his affinity for connecting religious and scientific ideas as he espoused

Peter Harrison, "'Science' and 'Religion': Constructing the Boundaries," *Journal of Religion* 86 (January 2006): 81–106; and Harrison, *Territories of Science and Religion*. See also Thomas F. Gieryn, *Cultural Boundaries of Science: Credibility on the Line* (Chicago: University of Chicago Press, 1999). On such intertwining by Osborn and Conklin, see Alexander Pavuk, "The American Association for the Advancement of Science Committee of Evolution and the Scopes Trial: Race, Eugenics, and Public Science in the U.S.A.," *Historical Research* 91 (2018): 149–58.

48. See Ian Barbour, *Issues in Science and Religion* (Englewood Cliffs, N.J.: Prentice Hall, 1966), 102. On Osborn in this vein, see Osborn, "Evolution and Religion," *New York Times*, March 5, 1922, 91; and Brian Regal, *Henry Fairfield Osborn: Race and the Search for the Origins of Man* (Aldershot, UK: Ashgate, 2002), 158–59. On Conklin's teleological evolution, see Alexander Pavuk, "Biologist Edwin Grant Conklin and the Idea of the Religious Direction of Human Evolution in the 1920s," *Annals of Science* 74 (2017): 75–79. Another such example of a modernist Protestant scientist blending ideas from theological modernism into his discussions of evolution was Harvard geologist Kirtley Mather. See Edward B. Davis, "Altruism and the Administration of the Universe: Kirtley Fletcher Mather on Science and Values," *Zygon* 46 (September 2011): 517–35.

49. David N. Livingstone, *Dealing with Darwin: Place, Politics, and Rhetoric in Religious Engagements with Evolution* (Baltimore: Johns Hopkins University Press, 2014), 182–84. McCosh, along with Osborn's own mother (who read James McCosh's books), also cultivated Osborn's evolutionary idealism (Regal, *Henry Fairfield Osborn*, 31–33). So did the Romanticism and scientific claims of Edward Drinker Cope (Regal, 61–65). Regal also contends that the theosophy of Madame Helena Blavatsky further influenced Osborn's ideas on evolution (146–47).

various forms of teleological, immanentist evolution in his public writings.[50] Conklin, who once wrote Harry Emerson Fosdick to say his sermons were his favorite radio program, argued for a God as "present in natural laws" and for "the doctrine of divine immanence in all natural phenomena."[51]

Teleology and immanentist theology for evolution also related to Conklin's and Osborn's particular support for eugenics. In public writings, they rendered eugenics as an essential component of biosocial evolution, having its own spiritual implications. In Osborn's words, the "moral tendency" of "the hereditarian interpretation of history" is "in accord with the true spirit of the modern eugenics movement."[52] He counseled scientists to focus on the "conservation and multiplication for our country of the best spiritual, moral, intellectual, and physical forces of heredity."[53] Conklin, likewise, wrote in his widely circulated 1921 volume, *The Direction of Human Evolution*, that "the religion of evolution ... is the religion of the world's greatest leaders and teachers ... which strives to develop a better and nobler human race and to establish the kingdom of God on earth," and that "evolution has revealed a larger teleology than was ever dreamed of before."[54]

In accord with their teleological views, the models of evolution of Osborn, Conklin, and other like-minded scientists accorded natural selection only a subordinate role, in favor of models echoing

50. Livingstone, *Dealing with Darwin*, 181–84, and 155–96 for the broader picture at Princeton. See also Bradley J. Gundlach, *Process and Providence: The Evolution Question at Princeton, 1845–1929* (Grand Rapids, Mich.: Eerdmans, 2013), chaps. 5 and 9; Regal, *Henry Fairfield Osborn*, 31, 37–39. The Protestant Conklin sometimes called himself a "pantheist." See, for example, Conklin to Arthur Watham (February 28, 1924), quoted in Pavuk, "Biologist," 79.

51. Conklin to Fosdick (February 6, 1928), quoted in Pavuk, "Biologist," 70. Edwin Grant Conklin, *The Direction of Human Evolution* (New York: Charles Scribner's Sons, 1921), 212–13; Livingstone, *Dealing with Darwin*, 179–81.

52. Henry Fairfield Osborn, preface to *The Passing of the Great Race: Or, The Racial Basis of European History*, 2nd ed., by Madison Grant (New York: Charles Scribner's Sons, 1918), viii–ix.

53. Osborn, preface to *The Passing*, ix.

54. Conklin, *Direction of Human Evolution*, 246–47, 225. Racialism was also embedded in Conklin's eugenic vision. See, for example, Conklin, 80.

neo-Lamarckism and orthogenesis.[55] Throughout his life, Conklin held that natural selection could not solely have accounted for evolutionary adaptation and survival fitness.[56] Osborn constructed a progressive, quasi-Lamarckian evolution and consistently opposed those who denied his model.[57] These scientists also invoked well-worn anti-Catholic tropes and claims of the church being intolerant to science when it suited their need to counter critiques of their theologizing. They were not averse to invoking the bogey of a mythologized Galileo incident as a warning not to interfere. For example, in the same issue of the AAAS's *Science* journal, in which Osborn made subtly theological claims about evolution, Conklin contended that religion's—read Catholicism's—supposedly longstanding attack on science was being reenacted by Bryan in the Scopes Trial. He wrote, "Science now deals with the evolution of the elements ... of the body, mind, and society of man, of science, of art, government, education and religion.... In the face of all these facts, Mr. Bryan and his kind hurl their medieval theology, ... beating their gongs and firing their giant crackers against the ramparts of science."[58]

55. Gundlach, *Process and Providence*, 217. Another example of Protestant modernism's wide influence on public evolutionary science was aforementioned Harvard geologist Kirtley Mather. Mather, who had taken Bible courses directly from Shailer Mathews, articulated a teleological evolution directed by "a creative and administrative power operating within the natural order," a power "immanent, permeating all of nature." Over time, he said, "evolution has resulted in progress toward the attainment of the good, the true, and the beautiful" (Mather quoted in Edward Davis, "Altruism," 522). On Mather's connection to Shailer Mathews, see Edward Davis, "Altruism," 520. On other well-known American scientists supporting linear or quasi-linear teleology in evolution at the time, see Constance Areson Clark, *God or Gorilla? Images of Evolution in the Jazz Age* (Baltimore: Johns Hopkins University Press, 2008), 45, 58. This tendency to de-emphasize natural selection continued until the full integration of Mendelism and statistics brought the new-Darwinian synthesis in the 1930s. See Peter J. Bowler, "Revisiting the Eclipse of Darwinism," *Journal of the History of Biology* 38 (2005): 19–32.

56. See Edwin Grant Conklin, *Heredity and Environment in the Development of Man*, rev. 2nd ed. (Princeton: Princeton University Press, 1917), 187, 189. In his most important book of the 1920s, *The Direction of Human Evolution*, Conklin affirmed that Darwin's natural selection was the only sure mechanism of evolution, but certainly not the *only* mechanism (9–13).

57. See Henry Fairfield Osborn, "Orthogenesis as Observed from Palaeontological Evidence Beginning in the Year 1889," *American Naturalist* 56 (1922): 134–43. Orthogenesis was particularly popular with paleontologists in the 1920s. Peter J. Bowler, *The Eclipse of Darwinism: Anti-Darwinian Evolution Theories in the Decades around 1900* (Baltimore: Johns Hopkins University Press, 1983), 159–65.

58. Henry Fairfield Osborn and Edwin Grant Conklin, "The Proposed Suppression of the Teaching of Evolution," *Science* 55 (March 1922): 266.

In other instances, the modernist scientists co-opted liberal Catholics' naturalistic rhetoric as examples of intelligent, sophisticated Christianity in support of their own arguments and to deflect conservative Protestant accusations that their renderings of evolution were objectionable. In one *Forum* magazine article, Osborn quoted two Catholic scientist-evolutionists to denounce William Jennings Bryan as being not only scientifically incompetent but also religiously out of touch. In another example, Osborn employed liberal Catholic rhetoric to parry accusations of irreligion coming directly from conservative Protestants like John Roach Straton.[59]

Writing as experts whose knowledge transcended even their exalted scientific positions to arbitrate the moral and social teachings they believed were embedded in evolution, Osborn, Conklin, and other scientists of like mind helped comprise part of the movement seeking a *national science* by the 1920s. The Great War's lingering sting, combined with social-cultural dissonance resonating from the 1919 Red Scare, stimulated a renewed search for reliable principles of social order and progress based on common denominators. The movement echoed trends that had existed in Western Europe, too, from the nineteenth century, where a quest for the unity of the sciences—with scientific values as the unifying principle for moral and social norms—had seen substantial social, political, and ideological investment since the nineteenth century. Broad conversations about science and religion garnered substantial focus in the American public square by the 1920s partly in service to this goal.

The idea of new and science-derived ethics was itself, of course, not novel. New was the idea of a collective scientific effort to construct and coordinate such a schema for adoption into democratic society just when relativity theory had supposedly confounded tra-

59. See Osborn, "The Earth Speaks to Bryan," *The Forum* 73 (June 1925): 797. On the Straton situation, see also Raymond W. Murray, *Man's Unknown Ancestors* (Milwaukee: Bruce Publishing, 1948), 325. Murray specified that "Osborn defended himself and the museum by the rather clever device of citing the large number of Catholic authorities whose views concerning the practice of prehistory coincided with his own. He pointed out that if he were guilty of advancing un-Christian ideas ... then a part of the blame would have to be passed on to European Catholic priests ... who furnished him with much of his own knowledge concerning fossil man!" (325).

ditional ethics. Scientists, including Osborn, Conklin, the 1923 Nobel laureate in physics—Robert Millikan of Caltech—and others, worked for the cause. In Millikan's articulation, the model subtly strengthened connections between modern science and religious ideas deriving from Protestant modernist thought, especially the aforementioned divine immanence acting through evolution. Ultimately, evolution served as the program's epicenter and unifying concept.[60]

The evolutionary goals were particularly discernable in the famous 1923 *Joint Statement upon the Relations of Science and Religion*, co-authored by Millikan and Osborn and signed by many of the country's prominent scientists and a number of liberal religious officials.[61] Osborn wrote of his involvement: "I signed it because I am thoroughly convinced that the naturalist needs a credo or profession of faith," adding that evolution was both the process and guide for human progress, a "simple, direct, teaching of Nature ... full of moral and spiritual force."[62] Osborn and Millikan believed it was professional scientists who were best suited to discern the lessons of evolution to guide society as revealed through the spirit of evolution over time.

Catholics Who Said "Science Service ... Can Be Depended on for an Absolutely Scientific Statement"[63]

Spreading a vision of national, unified scientific morality was partly the point of the Washington, D.C.–based *Science Service*, a not-for-profit group connected to the AAAS and designed to disseminate

60. One motive imputed to Millikan was "the ideological necessity of providing a *unified perspective* on nature, science, society, and progress." Ronald C. Tobey, *The American Ideology of National Science: 1919–1930* (Pittsburgh: University of Pittsburgh Press, 1971), 148. For Millikan's own conclusions, see Robert A. Millikan, "The Present Status of Theory and Experiment as to Atomic Disintegration and Atomic Synthesis," *Nature* 127 (January 31, 1931): 167.

61. See Robert A. Millikan, "A Joint Statement upon the Relations of Science and Religion," *Science* 57 (June 1, 1923): 630–31.

62. H. F. Osborn, "Credo of a Naturalist," *The Forum* 73 (January 1925): 493, 486.

63. Michael Williams, "*Week by Week*," *Commonweal* 17 (March 1, 1933): 480.

scientific material and vision through the national press. Founded by newspaper publisher E. W. Scripps in 1921, it had been inspired by conversations between Scripps and University of California zoologist William Ritter. The group's first leader was Edward Slosson, a science journalist and one-time chemistry instructor. Slosson had written earlier that year of public science needing to be framed in a manner that would "persuade the public to accept scientists' values," producing a "consensus that would provide the cultural unity necessary for national science and ... preserve America's traditional framework and beliefs."[64] One historian of science argued that the agenda amounted to a science-directed social utopia within the scheme of progressive liberalism's vision for the future, a vision centered in concepts of unity, law, and progress echoing from the eighteenth century.[65]

As an example of the religious-theological elements of this brand of national science, in 1928, *Science Service*'s managing editor, Watson Davis, published an article in the *New York Times* magazine *Current History* entitled "The Evolution Theory Entering a New Phase."[66] It centered on the theory of emergent evolution, partly the brainchild of French philosopher Henri Bergson. The quasi-theological vision Davis articulated contained echoes of Osborn. He focused on a recent address by Ritter at that year's AAAS annual gathering, the same meeting in which Osborn was elected president.[67] Ritter contended that the idea of mind and body as fundamentally separable was "marked for extinction" since "there is no trace of such a thing as a body independent of a mind or a

64. Slosson quoted in Tobey, *American Ideology*, 74.

65. Tobey, *American Ideology*, 87–88, 170–72. See also Daniel Patrick Thurs, *Science Talk: Changing Notions of Science in American Culture* (New Brunswick: Rutgers University Press, 2008), 94–98. Kirtley Mather later served on the Board of Science Service. Edward Davis, "Science and Religious Fundamentalism in the 1920s," *American Scientist* 93 (2005): 258–59.

66. Ritter was the first president of *Science Service*'s board of trustees; among his successors in that capacity was Edwin Grant Conklin. In 1925, the organization had sent botanist Frank Thone and civil engineer-journalist Watson Davis to Tennessee in order to cover the Scopes Trial, which they presented in conflict thesis garb.

67. Watson Davis, "Recent Scientific Progress: The Evolution Theory Entering a New Phase," *Current History* 27 (February 1928): 709.

mind independent of a body."[68] This, he said, enabled a deliverance from the broader "materialistic-mechanistic philosophy" because it purported to explain more: "The order of nature is truly universal, limitless, ... self-adequate and unified.... There is neither place nor need anywhere for such a conception as that of the supernatural."[69]

Ritter presented science as a future-oriented system of ethical guidance. He contended that scientific interest in evolution would turn people away from looking into the past and instead gear them toward looking for "what [man] is and may become as a *through and through* natural being."[70] Ritter went on, "There is left no trace of doubt ... about the adequacy of the creative power of the natural order to produce man, not only with all his physical but with all his spiritual attributes.... The religious emotion is a response to the natural order. It does not depend on a supernatural order, or even a belief in such an order as has been so generally supposed."[71]

The depiction in the liberal Catholic press of *Science Service*'s natural science and its major figures suggests how the latter was willing to endorse entities questioning the perspective of institutional Catholicism in America in a seeming attempt to connect and interface with mainline public science in the interwar era. Michael Williams's *Commonweal* magazine, for example, did nothing to diminish the notion of *Science Service*'s scientific objectivity when reporting early in 1933 that the big bang theory developed by Catholic physicist Fr. Georges LeMaître had successfully solved a scientific puzzle that for some time had engaged Robert Millikan, a solution to which Albert Einstein himself ultimately added his endorsement of LeMaître. *Commonweal* declared: "As the *Science News Letter* is the organ of Science Service, the institution of the popularization of science organized under the National Academy of Science [and] ... the American Society for the Advancement of Science, it can be depended on for an absolutely scientific statement of the case."[72]

68. Davis, "Recent Scientific Progress," 709.
69. Davis, "Recent Scientific Progress," 707.
70. Davis, "Recent Scientific Progress," 707.
71. Davis, "Recent Scientific Progress," 707.
72. Michael Williams, "*Week by Week*," *Commonweal* 17 (March 1, 1933): 480.

Catholic journalist Michael Williams, a member of the NCWC Press Association since World War I, had founded *Commonweal* in 1924 as a weekly magazine designed to engage mainline intellectual conversations and engage educated non-Catholics who would listen to Catholic arguments provided that they were presented in a scholarly and dispassionate tone. It was read as the representative of intelligent Catholic opinion by the Walter Lippmanns and the H. L. Menckens.[73] Its reputation for liberalism spanned both outside and inside Catholicism. Jesuit priest Fr. John Wynne, SJ, one-time editor of the Jesuit-run *America* magazine, flatly complained that *Commonweal* was too liberal and too non-Catholic.[74] Overall, the magazine lay within the alignments of Frs. Ryan, Cooper, and O'Brien. All three of them appeared in its pages. Williams even asked Ryan to serve on the board at one point.

The Scopes Trial of Evolution and *Commonweal*[75]

The cultural centerpiece of evolution in the interwar public square was the Scopes Trial of 1925. An extensive literature analyzing the trial and its meaning is extant, though a good deal of it before recent years presents the trial within the historically debunked "warfare thesis" conflict metaphor of science-religion relations. The public construction of the trial has exerted an enormous influence—both at the time of the trial and in subsequent decades—on the public image of evolution.[76] At its base, the trial was a test

73. Rodger Van Allen, *The Commonweal and American Catholicism* (Philadelphia: Fortress Press, 1974), 27. See H. L. Mencken, letter to the editor, *Commonweal* 20 (November 2, 1934): 35. See also Robert B. Clements, "The Commonweal, 1924–1938: The Williams-Schuster Years" (PhD diss., University of Notre Dame, 1972), 118. See also Heinz Eulau, "Proselytizing in the Catholic Press," *Public Opinion Quarterly* 11 (Summer 1947): 191.

74. John Wynne to Francis Talbot (June 12, 1936), in John Wynne Papers, box 63, folder 16, GURBSC.

75. A portion of this section is a selected reprint from Alexander Pavuk, "Evolution and Voices of Progressive Catholicism in the Age of the Scopes Trial," *Religion and American Culture* 26 (2016): 101–37. Copyright © 2016 Center for the Study of Religion and American Culture. Reprinted by permission of Cambridge University Press.

76. The best scholarly analysis of the Scopes Trial is still Edward J. Larson's *Summer for the Gods*. The trial's memory and meaning continue to be misrepresented, misunderstood, and inaccurately analogized by many journalists in the same defunct warfare metaphor. See, for

case by the American Civil Liberties Union (ACLU) in conjunction with public officials in Dayton, Tennessee, over the legality of Tennessee's Butler Act (Tenn. H.B. 185), a 1925 law introduced by John Butler and signed by Governor Austin Peay that prohibited state-funded schools from teaching human evolution or any versions of human origins that contradicted the book of Genesis. While the law did not specify how to interpret Genesis and did not prohibit teaching the evolution of non-human life, its context was conservative Tennessee Protestantism. The case, broadcast nationally both through radio hook-ups and in print media, was widely discussed and became famous for pitting two prominent enemies against each other as attorneys arguing the case: Clarence Darrow defending science teacher John T. Scopes and former Secretary of State William Jennings Bryan for the prosecution. On a narrow reading of the case, the judge found Scopes guilty of violating the Butler Act (which he admitted likely having done) and fined him one hundred dollars, although the ACLU paid his fine (which was later voided on a technicality).[77]

While those are the facts, it should be noted that the construct of evolution at issue in the Scopes Trial was substantially intertwined with eugenics in public culture as well as by the defense (although the attitude of Darrow himself is not as clear). This was apparent from several angles. One was evolution's presentation in the framework of eugenic social engineering throughout the Tennessee-adopted textbook underpinning the trial, George W. Hunter's *A Civic Biology* (1914).[78] Another was the AAAS's Committee on Evo-

---

example, Max Boot, "Foes of Science Faced Ridicule at the Scopes Trial. We're Paying the Price 95 Years Later," *Washington Post*, July 8, 2020, https://www.washingtonpost.com/opinions/2020/07/08/foes-science-faced-ridicule-scopes-trial-were-paying-price-95-years-later/.

77. Darrow and the ACLU brought testimony from a number of scientific experts and religious modernists to the case to attest to the veracity of evolution and its inoffensiveness to religion, though these ended up not being employed in the trial due to the narrow reading of the case's meaning taken by the presiding judge James Raulston. Written statements were entered into the record. See *The World's Most Famous Court Trial: State of Tennessee v. John Thomas Scopes*, 3rd ed. (Cincinnati: National Book Co., 1925).

78. See George William Hunter, *A Civic Biology, Presented in Problems* (New York: American Book Co., 1914), 195–96, 261–63, 405. Among other contemporary textbooks, this

lution, created in April 1922 to defend the integrity of evolution. It was made up of three scientists, Osborn, Conklin, and Davenport, whose public constructions of evolution in that decade were, as stated above, intertwined with eugenics, and they were not alone among scientists in making that connection.[79] Still another was that when ACLU attorney Forrest Bailey wrote to committee members in June 1925 asking for "men who are competent ... to protect the interests of science," the committee was glad to contact Leonard Darwin, internationally known head of the British Eugenics Society, for that purpose.[80] Osborn, whom the AAAS's organ *Science* reported as "tak[ing] a very active part in the scientific side of the Tennessee trial," wrote in the same forum that Darwin had cabled him offering to help with the defense and saying that he and the British public were in strong support of the trial.[81]

The *Literary Digest*, the *New York Times*, and other respected print media frequently turned to and quoted from *Commonweal* on Catholic perspectives on evolution in general and the Scopes Trial in particular.[82] For the Scopes Trial, they could first of all go

was not atypical. For an example of biologized "civic sociology," see Willard W. Beatty, "A Normal-School Course in Sociology Introductory to Work in the Social Studies," *American Journal of Sociology* 26 (1921): 573–80. For an extensive survey of interwar biology textbooks showing these trends, see Anselm M. Keefe, "Biology Texts Used in Catholic Colleges," *Bulletin: National Catholic Education Association* 37 (1940): 219–20; and Paul L. Carroll, "A Survey of Textbooks in College Biology," *Bulletin: National Catholic Education Association* 37 (1940): 221–58.

79. See Pavuk, "Race, Eugenics, and Public Science." See also Clark, *God or Gorilla*; Gregory Michael Dorr, *Segregation's Science: Eugenics and Society in Virginia* (Charlottesville: University of Virginia Press, 2008), 70.

80. Forrest Bailey to Edwin Grant Conklin (June 4, 1925), in Conklin Papers, box 17, folder 31, Rare Books and Special Collections, Princeton University Library. On Darwin's role in British eugenics as more than merely a figurehead, see Norberto Serpente, "More than a Mentor: Leonard Darwin's Contribution to the Assimilation of Mendelism into Eugenics and Darwinism," *Journal of the History of Biology* 49 (2016): 461–94.

81. Henry Fairfield Osborn, "Evolution and Education in the Tennessee Trial," *Science* 62 (July 17, 1925): 43.

82. See, for example, "The Catholic View of Evolution," *Literary Digest* 86 (July 4, 1925): 34. In this article, not only were excerpts from *Commonweal* extensively quoted, but excerpts were also taken from the *New York Times*, citing the views of John Wynne, a co-editor of the *Catholic Encyclopedia*, as saying (during the Scopes Trial) that he "upholds the principle of teaching evolution as a scientific theory of human origin and disapproves of attempts to legislate against it" ("Catholic View of Evolution," 34).

to Michael Williams himself. Williams, present in Dayton for the length of the trial, characterized the motley bunch of alliances he found there as "Protestant fundamentalists [versus] ... a most bizarre and incongruous aggregation of 'liberal' Protestants, 'modernists,' 'scientists' (some of them genuinely deserving the title and heaps of them mere dabblers and pretenders) and of free speech champions, agnostics, cranks, and 'nuts.'"[83] Looking back, one might well add "Catholics" to this list.

One finds in *Commonweal* an extensive set of articles on the Scopes Trial and related issues. The majority of these articles presented pictures of Catholicism that obviated accusations of scientific obscurantism or conservatism. Williams's own pieces contained certain recurring, identifiable motifs. For one, Williams attempted to distance Catholics as far as possible from Galileo-inflected accusations of anti-scientific bias. Two, he expressed concern about putative plots by conservative Protestants to use the state to manipulate school curricula and to legislate so-called Protestant interpretations of Scripture in public schools. He cast Bryan as committing the same kind of mistake the church itself had committed three hundred years earlier in the case of Galileo. By pouring scorn on Bryan, the church was clearing its name. Three, Williams expressed fears that Tennessee's Protestants sought to quash the broader separation of church and state (another trope hitherto used against Catholics). Finally, his articles endorsed science broadly and evolution specifically, urging that all thinking Catholics should follow suit by emphasizing freedom of inquiry.

Less than two months before the Scopes Trial commenced, Williams published an editorial on the anti-evolution movement asserting that "freedom in scientific teaching is not merely in danger but actually under attack."[84] He brought up the singular example of a (Protestant-run) Illinois town that allegedly required teachers to instruct students that the earth is flat. The myth of the

---

83. Michael Williams, "At Dayton, Tennessee," *Commonweal* 2 (July 22, 1925): 262.
84. [Michael Williams], "On Teaching Evolution," *Commonweal* 1 (April 22, 1925): 647.

widespread belief in a flat earth in the Middle (or "Dark") Ages was a longstanding red herring. Critics of the Catholic Church cited it to contrast alleged Catholic obscurantism with modern enlightenment.[85] Here, Williams turned the tables and accused Bryan of operating like an obscurantist of the Dark Ages. At the same time, he rhetorically placed the Catholic Church far away from Bryan—and obscurantism. Contrasts to Bryan and his brand of Protestantism became a vehicle for advancing the openness of liberal Catholicism.[86] For Tennessee, Williams argued, the Scopes case was a case "against ... the expanse of modern learning, ... bidding science to remain outside its boundaries, ... defying the modern world, ... and seeking to ban the modern intellectual world from their hills."[87] Williams's contrast with Protestantism tied Catholicism both to modernity and to modernity's prime achievement, science.

On the eve of the Scopes Trial, Williams editorialized that the trial would "in no way" be about "the truth or falsity of the hypothesis of evolution"; rather, it was "an attempt to set up an established Protestant church in America."[88] Williams, a progressive New Yorker, viewed William Jennings Bryan not as heir to any legitimate nineteenth-century majoritarian political viewpoint but rather as a "menace to liberty."[89] He did, however, admit that Catholics were entitled to disagree with those who proposed to teach evolution as a proven fact *if* such people also proceeded to preach "philosophies and methods of thought which are socially dangerous," but he gave neither specifics nor suggestions of how such Catholics were to combat such a threat.[90]

Williams did not attempt to silence Catholics who dissented

85. [Williams], "On Teaching Evolution," 647. For more on the Illinois episode to which Williams referred, see Christine Garwood, *Flat Earth: The History of an Infamous Idea* (New York: Macmillan, 2008), chap. 6, esp. 210–12.

86. For more on the apocryphal character of the flat-earth myth in Catholic Christendom and its use as a straw man against Catholics starting in the Enlightenment, see Jeffrey Burton Russell, *Inventing the Flat Earth: Columbus and Modern Historians* (New York: Praeger, 1997).

87. [Michael Williams], "Concerning the Scopes Case," *Commonweal* 2 (June 3, 1925): 85.

88. [Williams], "Concerning the Scopes Case," 85.

89. [Williams], "Concerning the Scopes Case," 86.

90. [Williams], "Concerning the Scopes Case," 85.

from his views, staying true to his goals of making *Commonweal* an open forum for varied perspectives. But he did reserve the right to rebut such views, and he expressed distress if any Catholic seemed to indicate sympathy with Bryan. In the July 22, 1925, issue, for example, Williams wrung his hands over the embarrassing fact that "a large part of the press" reported the presence at the trial of a Catholic private citizen named P. H. Callahan who seemingly supported Bryan. Since Callahan was Catholic, some newspapers asked whether he, in any way, represented "official Catholic support of Mr. Bryan." This, lamented Williams, "was deplorable." Williams's concern was of sensational headlines about this scenario implying that "American Catholicism was taking its place with the Protestant Fundamentalists in the opening stages of a great struggle to capture the mechanism of state government for the propagation of religion." He assured readers that by no means had any Catholics responded to Bryan's call to assist him in the embarrassing trial, adding, "Surely, intelligent Catholics should concur in thinking that cold water of the chilliest sort should be thrown upon any such disastrous movement." [91]

Williams framed his arguments in *Commonweal* around the concept of pluralism, constructing the trial as part of a broader Protestant attempt to gain control of the public school system. His voice on this issue was augmented when the *New York Times* published an article centered on Williams as *Commonweal* editor during the Scopes Trial, "Bryan Aim Assailed by Catholic Editor."[92] And in Williams's *Commonweal* pieces, he duplicated the somewhat ironic nature of fellow Catholic John Ryan's pleas to the effect that in a religiously pluralistic society the school must offer a purely secular education. This idea challenged some other articles appearing in *Commonweal* on education, as well as the premise of

91. Williams, "At Dayton, Tennessee," 265. Anti-Catholics had often claimed that Catholic Americans secretly hoped to introduce the papal model of Catholic government; this probably encouraged Williams's vehement desire to separate all Catholics from even the slightest appearance of support for Bryan.

92. See "Bryan Aim Assailed by Catholic Editor," *New York Times*, July 13, 1925, 17.

numerous Catholic bishops and priests who believed that a young person's education could not properly be decoupled from a religious worldview. Although Williams himself did not go so far as opposing Catholic parochial schools, he argued that since Protestants did not have such schools, they should form them if they wished. That way, he said, each religious group could offer sectarian education suitable for its own communicants while the public school system could achieve the desired result of being completely nonreligious.[93]

Williams did express concern that science textbooks—even Tennessee's official biology text, George Hunter's *A Civic Biology*—themselves sometimes presented material in what he called a "slipshod" manner. But while Williams in other contexts decried the eugenic Nordicism touted widely in the 1920s, he did not comment on how *Civic Biology* tied eugenic racial rhetoric to evolution in various places throughout the book.[94] Williams's failure to highlight this connection was also apparent when *Commonweal* reported without critique that Major Leonard Darwin, president of the British Eugenics Education Society, had written to John Scopes in order to send a "word of warm encouragement" in his endeavors.[95] The implication of the notice was not the problematic intertwining of eugenics with evolution but rather the international unanimity of scientists' support for the defense.[96]

At the conclusion of the trial, Williams congratulated Catholics for being so "cautious in extending the hand of fellowship to the chief actors in the drama at Dayton, Tennessee," again suggesting ties between the defense and the Ku Klux Klan: "Given the men-

93. [Michael Williams], "The Scopes Dilemma," *Commonweal* 2 (July 15, 1925): 241–42.

94. [Michael Williams], "On the Freedom of the Teacher," *Commonweal* 2 (June 24, 1925): 169–70.

95. "Dayton and Great Britain," *Commonweal* 2 (August 5, 1925): 301.

96. Williams's own editorials and articles over the years that specifically focused on evolution supported its science legitimacy but not scientism or naïve scientific utopianism. See the following unsigned Williams editorials or notices: [Michael Williams], "Soundings in Mystery," *Commonweal* 7 (November 16, 1927): 379–80; [Williams], "Week by Week," *Commonweal* 7 (March 7, 1928): 1139; and [Williams], "The Conquering Cockroach," *Commonweal* 10 (September 11, 1929): 459.

tal caliber and temper of the leading fundamentalists ... the Klan, as might have been guessed, ... offers itself as a fighting phalanx and Thundering Legion of Fundamentalism."[97] To the end, Williams emphasized a relationship between the Klan and Tennessee Protestantism, a relationship echoed in the other major journals of opinion.

Williams published other Catholic authors in *Commonweal* on issues concerning Scopes and evolution. These articles, which continued to appear in the wake of the trial, fell into two main streams. One was the repudiation of Catholics—and non-Catholics—who dared to criticize evolution or interfere with the purview of expert science; the other bolstered the authority of non-Catholic scientists who commented on the positive religious implications of evolution, even if their theological visions were antithetical to Catholicism. Curiously, some Catholics had long complained that the trouble with perceptions of the science-religion conflict was that too many theologians left their field of competence to make embarrassingly false scientific contentions, and vice versa. One scholar who studied the Catholic press contended that the small liberal Catholic community had expressed significant embarrassment in the first few decades of the twentieth century about nineteenth-century Catholics untrained in the sciences making critical statements about evolution. These Catholic evolutionists "became their own worst critics, censuring those of their number" who ostensibly brought ridicule on Catholicism by offering untrained criticism.[98]

Some *Commonweal* authors took advantage of rare opportunities to criticize liberal Protestants for seeming insufficiently committed to science. D. W. Fisher's "In Defense of Science," published in January 1926, attempted to score points for Catholic enlightenment by chastising the liberal Protestant Harry Emerson Fosdick for his comment that scientists take numerous facts on faith. Fish-

97. [Michael Williams], "Week by Week," *Commonweal* 2 (September 9, 1925): 411.

98. Morrison, "History of American Catholic Opinion," 295. Morrison went on specifically to say of the 1920s, "Catholic writers have been at each other's throats over questions like human evolution, spontaneous generation and St. Augustine's theory of Genesis" (323).

er lectured against this position, defending science by referring to both Newton's and Darwin's unassailable mathematical evidence. He contended that for Fosdick to write such things was "a serious indictment to bring against science and great men of science. And I am led to suggest here some defense, not of reason in religion, but of reason in science."[99]

If a Catholic author published an article in *Commonweal* expressing any reservations about evolution, a firestorm of responses appeared criticizing Catholics who dissented from the enthusiastic party line. It was somewhat acceptable to disagree on the mechanism of evolution; it was unacceptable to question enthusiasm over evolution.[100] Doing so interfered with the goals advancing Catholic prestige in America. In the flow of the Scopes Trial, Bertram Windle, science popularizer on *Commonweal*'s editorial board, even-handedly reviewed Fr. Barry O'Toole's *The Case against Evolution*. O'Toole, a conservative with scientific inclinations, predicated his critique on the AAAS's 1924 decree that the proof for evolution should be compelling enough to convince all the world's scientists. O'Toole said it was not. Although Windle sharply disagreed with O'Toole's conclusions, he admitted that they were presented cogently and reasonably (albeit with poor science).[101] Windle was concerned that if a priest questioned evolution, anti-Catholic forces would argue that Catholics were being discouraged from thinking for themselves.

99. D. W. Fisher, "In Defense of Science," *Commonweal* 3 (January 20, 1926): 290.

100. During the 1920s, scientists were themselves in dispute about the extent to which natural selection drove evolution. See Bowler, "Revisiting the Eclipse of Darwinism." Some non-Darwinian evolutionary theories (i.e., those not assigning primacy to natural selection, per se) were popular in the first few decades of the twentieth century. These included theories based in orthogenesis and saltationism (Bowler, 24).

101. Bertram Windle, review of *The Case against Evolution*, by Barry O'Toole, *Commonweal* 2 (June 10, 1925): 124. Windle's articles and reviews dealing with aspects of science and religion appeared frequently in *Commonweal*. Morrison argued of Windle, "*The New York Times* considered Windle the spokesman of the [Catholic] Church in North America" ("History of American Catholic Opinion," 338). A few months after the Scopes Trial, Windle made another Galileo-trial-centered plea designed to distance modern Catholicism from previous Catholicisms: "Our way today is not the way of those days." Bertram Windle, "The Roman Catholic View of Evolution," *Current History* 23 (December 1925): 336. See Barry O'Toole, *The Case against Evolution* (New York: MacMillan, 1925).

Immediately after *Commonweal* published Windle's review, liberal Catholics thrashed O'Toole "vigorously," while priest-scientist
Stefan Richarz accused O'Toole of "repeating the idiotic assertions
of [so-called flood geologist George McCready] Price." Further, "a
Jesuit priest, Fr. A. F. Frumvellar, ... joined in the chorus of liberal
vituperation against Fr. O'Toole. [He] was shocked that a priest
[O'Toole] dared attack Fr. Wasmann and Canon Dorlodot." Frumvellar was quoted as saying O'Toole's ideas were "unworthy of serious scientific consideration."[102] Despite Richarz having lumped
O'Toole with infamous Protestant flood geologist Price, liberal
Catholics seemed less to suggest that O'Toole's book was an ignorant diatribe than that he deserved condemnation for having
dared to dissent from their obeisance to evolution, gateway to the
science-minded American intellectual mainstream.

Both Windle and Williams employed claims about evolution's
ability to be reconciled with religion from legitimate scientists who
nonetheless espoused extremely unorthodox religious views tied
to evolution. These opinion leaders included famous British physicist Oliver Lodge, who argued that the ether through which radio
waves traveled was a discernible substance inhabited by ghosts,
and Henry Fairfield Osborn, whose immanentism was inconsistent with Catholicism, a religion he had publicly attacked on numerous occasions.[103] *Commonweal* still seized on the opportunity
to invoke the opinions on evolution of any prestigious scientist
provided that he eschewed overt materialism.[104] The irony of pro-

102. Morrison, "History of American Catholic Opinion," 336.

103. In an unsigned article by Williams from February 1926, "Osborn on Religion," Henry
Fairfield Osborn is given "the fullest sympathy" for expressing the need for "certain aspects
of eternity" to be given attention in schools for the purposes of inculcating morals. Williams,
while arguing the need for current public education to remain totally secular, uses Osborn's
utterances as a springboard to advocate revamping the school system. See [Michael Williams],
"Osborn on Religion," *Commonweal* 3 (February 2, 1926): 343. See also [Williams], "Sir Oliver and Evolution," *Commonweal* 3 (February 10, 1926): 370–71; Windle, review of *Ether and
Reality*, by Sir Oliver Lodge, *Commonweal* 3 (February 17, 1926): 415–16; Windle, review of
Evolution and Creation, by Sir Oliver Lodge, *Commonweal* 4 (September 29, 1926): 508–9.

104. On Osborn's immense public scientific prestige in the 1920s, see Regal, *Henry Fairfield Osborn*, xii.

gressive Catholic involvement in the public discourse was demonstrated in Osborn's *Forum* magazine article of 1925. There he quoted a progressive Catholic to attack William Jennings Bryan and religion-centered questions about the way evolution was framed during the trial.[105]

Fr. Ryan and the Scopes Trial

John Ryan's response to the Scopes Trial was consistent with the progressive, social science-oriented tenor of his public engagement. It revealed assumptions characteristic of Catholicism's Americanist-modernist continuum on secular public education and the positivist approach to science and expert authority. It also reflected his distrust of the majoritarian strand in the American political tradition that Bryan represented in the trial. And it manifested Ryan's particular concern with protecting Catholic minorities in public schools from what he depicted as a creeping Protestant plan to use the power of the state to influence how science was being taught and to inculcate Protestant denominationalism into the schools. Ryan's rhetoric on Scopes, science, and legislative prerogatives was also noteworthy for the care he took to distance himself and his church from movements that were associated with intolerance of any kind in the public sphere.

To the pleasure of its radical and liberal members, the ACLU sponsoring the Scopes defense included Ryan in its ranks. He had joined the organization in 1921, at the time the only Catholic priest ever to serve on the ACLU national board. His membership in the ACLU while a leader of American Catholic intellectual life was of both symbolic and practical importance. As his biographer observes, reformers outside the church were more than willing to advertise American Catholic approval, even in indirect forms.[106]

105. The quote was from Henri Dorlodot (Osborn, "Earth Speaks to Bryan," 797). Later in the article, he invoked the Jesuit paleontologist, Pierre Teilhard de Chardin, to do more of the same.

106. Broderick, *Right Reverend New Dealer*, 115.

Ryan was often less concerned that his name be associated with radical causes than with achieving his goal of pulling American Catholicism squarely into the reform arena.[107] If a group with which he was affiliated championed a cause he rejected, he would accuse it of being either economically irrational or unscientific, or both.[108] As noted above, his critiques were rarely expressed in religious language in the broad public square.

The day after Tennessee's legal system indicted John Scopes for violating the state's Butler Act, Ryan joined the rest of the ACLU board's assembly in New York City. He offered no dissent when the board accepted the aggressively agnostic and anti-Catholic Clarence Darrow's offer to assume the lead in defending Scopes against the State of Tennessee.[109] According to ACLU president Roger Baldwin, a personal friend of Ryan, the latter privately told him, "I can't object to your going into a case like this. I don't care where the body comes from as long as the soul is recognized as the creation of God."[110] If Ryan had missed the fact that Darrow long propagandized against there being any such thing as a "soul" to protect, he would be able to read about it by the end of 1928 in *Commonweal*. M. W. Weston's article, "Is the Soul a Myth?," surveyed Darrow's recent piece in *Forum* magazine that called belief in a soul or immortality "a delusion" on the basis that science had not proved the existence of souls.[111]

Ryan's focus lay in combating the dangers of Protestant major-

107. Broderick, *Right Reverend New Dealer*, 67.

108. Broderick, *Right Reverend New Dealer*, 143.

109. Darrow was an intellectual disciple of the so-called Great Agnostic, Robert Ingersoll. Darrow characterized the Scopes case "as innocent, truth-seeking scientists versus an oppressive, fundamentalist huckster" (Larson, *Summer for the Gods*, 71, 100–1). He was certainly no friend of Catholicism. *Commonweal* printed an article during the Scopes Trial summer pointing out a strange statement Darrow had made impugning the Catholic Church with the erroneous claim that "The Pope issued a bull against a comet once upon a time. But the comet kept on coming just the same. Apparently it had not heard anything of the bull.... Does not every schoolboy know that Catholicism is the religion of the dark ages?" G. R. Garrett, "A Pope, a Comet, and Mr. Darrow," *Commonweal* 2 (June 24, 1925): 181.

110. John Ryan, interview with Roger Baldwin, May 8, 1958, quoted in Broderick, *Right Reverend New Dealer*, 141.

111. M. W. Weston, "Is the Soul a Myth?," *Commonweal* 8 (December 26, 1928): 230–33.

itarianism, not scientism. The ACLU's precursor organization, the Civil Liberties Bureau, founded in 1917, had focused on protecting general civil liberties, hazily defined. This vision saw itself transformed during World War I into a defense of individual liberty against powerful majorities, a shift partly spurred by the Wilson administration's wartime crackdown on free speech. The organization itself transformed into the ACLU. A notable historian of the Scopes Trial has argued that this shift deeply affected the ACLU's response to the anti-evolution movement.[112] The ACLU's emerging view of rights was of self-determined and scientifically informed rights.

In 1925, the *New York Times* christened the Scopes Trial "the greatest debate on science and religion in recent years."[113] The newspaper reinforced that framing during the trial by publishing in July Maynard Shipley's *Science League of America* contest seeking the best essay on "the Superiority of Evolution over Genesis."[114] This reinforced the problematic warfare thesis science-religion model framing the trial and perhaps helped determine that trial's symbolic meaning. Within that dubious binary framework, Ryan's rhetoric would best be placed on the science side. His contributions to the public discourse in New York newspapers contained nothing to counter the *Times*'s framing. For example, in a June 1925 letter to the editor of New York's *World*, Ryan outlined his approach to the anti-evolution question. He claimed the most important ramification of both the Scopes Trial and the broader attempt to legislate against the teaching of evolution was a violation "of the neutrality of the public schools in matters of religion."[115] Fearing Protestant sectarian influence in the schools greatly and saying "Let me say that I detest quite as heartily as you do the spirit of intolerance which is at least in part responsible for the Tennessee Anti-

112. Samuel Walker quoted in Larson, *Summer for the Gods*, 63.
113. *New York Times*, July 3, 1925, 6, quoted in Larson, *Summer for the Gods*, 180.
114. *New York Times*, July 3, 1925, 6.
115. Ryan, "The Anti-Evolution Trial," *(New York) World*, June 5, 1925, in Ryan Papers, box 51, folder 6, ACUA.

Evolution law," he argued the need for the total secularization of the public schools.[116] As with other liberal Catholics, Ryan advertised his suspicion of Protestant motives from the start. Also like other liberal Catholics, Ryan in this sense seemed to agree with Darrow and those of post-Social Gospel, science-centered progressivism that religion was best left a private affair. Darrow went on to say that science was the only "public activity that is the cause of progress ... and everything that makes civilization today."[117]

In the period following the Scopes Trial, Ryan worked to further the positions he had articulated during the trial. His comments appeared alongside a broad array of non-Catholic public figures in the 1927 ACLU pamphlet *Anti-Evolution Laws*. Those other figures included the renowned eugenicist zoologist David Starr Jordan; Protestant modernists such as Ralph Sockman and Shailer Mathews; liberal rabbi Louis Mann; and *Christian Century* editor Paul Hutchinson. The pamphlet's stated purpose was to fight the "attack upon the freedom of teaching."[118] Ryan's essay echoed many of his previous arguments, including his concern that conservative Protestants would attempt to insert denominationalism into the public schools. "Indeed," Ryan warned, "there are many indications that precisely this is among the ulterior objects of those groups that are urging the enactment of anti-evolutionary legislation."[119]

Ryan articulated only one concern about the teaching of evolution: that of individual teachers adding overtly materialist com-

116. Ryan, "The Anti-Evolution Trial." Later, in 1929, *Commonweal* reported that in a South Dakota public school, it was a Catholic student's parents who protested against their child having to listen to a Bible reading (even, according to state law, "without sectarian comment"), and that this protest led the state Supreme Court to disallow the Bible from being read. Mark O. Shriver, "Reading the Bible in Public School," *Commonweal* 11 (November 27, 1929): 108–9.

117. Larson, *Summer for the Gods*, 218.

118. Ryan's words show that he did not agree with the idea that a public teacher could teach absolutely anything he or she wanted, but that he believed that the problem when one did needed to be dealt with "administratively." John A. Ryan et al., *Anti-Evolution Laws* (New York: American Civil Liberties Union, 1927), 28, in Ryan Papers, box 51, folder 7, ACUA. Ryan argued his case using legal and constitutional lenses.

119. Ryan et al., *Anti-Evolution Laws*, 28.

mentary in an ad hoc manner in the classroom. He viewed this possibility as the real cause for the extreme responses of the anti-evolutionists, although, as we have seen, there was little of that. Consonant with progressives' trust in the authority of professional experts, Ryan argued that "the only competent authorities" to decide what was to be taught were state boards of education. These boards were not elected but were constituted of appointed experts. For Ryan, this was precisely their advantage. Possessing expertise through training in education theory, they would naturally seek, and comprehend, the best technical solution to given problems. By contrast, he argued, "the average state legislature is [not] competent" to judge between various evolutionary theories, just as it would not be able "to choose between conflicting economic theories or . . . any other technical question of the curriculum."[120]

Ryan argued further that absent expertise, denominational Protestants in legislatures would "be tempted to go further and prescribe the positive teaching of religious and even denominational tenets in the public schools."[121] Here Ryan essentially echoed the suspicion expressed in the highbrow press around the Scopes Trial: Tennessee was scheming to pass a law whereby a literal interpretation of the book of Genesis would be taught in public schools.[122]

Ryan seemed unattuned to the way that contemporary textbooks—particularly Tennessee's adoption, the above-mentioned *Civic Biology*—presented a blend of natural science and mechanistic philosophy embedded in race hierarchies and eugenics.[123] Ryan wrote, "all that is certainly known about evolution can be set forth

120. Ryan et al., *Anti-Evolution Laws*, 28.

121. Ryan et al., *Anti-Evolution Laws*, 28.

122. See, for example, a 1925 article in *The Nation* with the claim: "side by side with the effort to prohibit the teaching of evolution goes the parallel movement to teach the creation story of the Book of Genesis." Quoted in Miriam De Ford, "The War against Evolution," *The Nation* 120 (May 20, 1925): 566.

123. For more on the holistic vision presented in textbooks of that era, see Adam Shapiro, "Civic Biology and the Origin of the School Antievolution Movement," *Journal of the History of Biology* 41 (2008): 409–33, esp. 416–23 and 427–30; and Shapiro, *Trying Biology: The Scopes Trial, Textbooks, and the Antievolution Movement in American Schools* (Chicago: University of Chicago Press, 2013), esp. 65–80.

without denying or endangering the religious faith of any pupil."[124] This is particularly notable since back in 1915 the book's author, George Hunter, had dismissed what he was sure was the Boston Catholic hierarchy's opposition to certain phrasing and content in the parts of his book discussing eugenics and elements of human sexuality.[125]

Catholic participation in public debates about evolution and the Scopes Trial influenced the discourse on the trial, evolution, and American scientific authority that reached beyond Catholic audiences. The materials addressed above suggest that one must look beyond more obvious blocs of secular thinkers, including scientists, to discern the full range of voices that played a part in how these topics were constructed in intellectual forums aimed at wide public consumption.

Training and experiences in the science-centered Progressive Era, paired with hopes to engage the broader intellectual community by using science-centered discourse in the 1920s, led liberal Catholic figures like Fr. Ryan and others in *Commonweal* to blur the alleged boundaries between science supporters and religious figures that conservative Protestants seemed to reinforce in that period. Ironically, however, by embedding their public rhetoric on evolution and other questions surrounding the Scopes Trial almost exclusively in naturalistic categories of social and biological science while overlooking the tendency of ostensibly secular opponents to employ the language of religion, they unintentionally fostered trends they had hoped to redirect while seeing some of their own rhetoric co-opted and used against their interests. By extension, their own efforts to fit in seamlessly with a mainline culture placing such a premium on science helped obscure the fact that the construct of evolution ostensibly at stake in the Scopes Trial carried with it subtexts of eugenics and anti-immigrant and anti-Catholic discourse that figured importantly in the shaping of evolution's

124. Ryan et al., *Anti-Evolution Laws*, 27.
125. On the Boston scenario, see Shapiro, *Trying Biology*, 62.

symbolic cultural meaning between the wars. Having crossed the boundary marker of the Scopes Trial, we are now ready to hear from our other two main figures, Frs. Cooper and O'Brien, and their most important output on these same issues of science, religion, evolution, and scientism in the public square.

～ 3

Conceiving the Macrocosm, Part 2

Evolving into the 1930s

The reader may dismiss the foregoing heuristic
interpretation as the stuff of which dreams are made.
But sometimes even in speculation and dream there
may be a touch of truth and reality.

—Fr. John Montgomery Cooper (1928)

Not long after the ripples of the Scopes Trial had begun to spread
out, Cooper's series of four radio addresses, titled *Religion and Science*, aired on New York's Paulist station WLWL, beginning February 4, 1926. The talks, which are extant in Cooper's manuscripts,
provide a window into his vision for redirecting Catholic science
in America and replacing the theory of science-religion conflict
with one of interdependency. Religion's relationship with science,
he argued, was not merely one of mutual peace; it was one in which
two equally necessary pursuits traveled specific, overlapping roads
toward mutually reinforcing goals. Perhaps noteworthy given the
fact that his addresses were aired on a Catholic-sponsored radio

Epigraph is from John Montgomery Cooper, "Biological Evolution and the Catholic Social Ideal" (1928), in JMC Papers, box 42, folder "Unpublished Manuscripts," ACUA.

station, Cooper hardly ever uttered the word "Catholic." It was "religion" of which he spoke; this indicated an intended audience beyond merely Catholics. His reading of both religion and science proved expansive.

Cooper's first talk proposed that religion had to be viewed in light of modern science. As to the past, he contended an equivalent guilt by both religion and science over the ages in espousing "worthless" ideas that subsequently and thankfully disappeared in the face of progress. Both realms had engaged in a grand progression over time "onward" and "upward"—a progression that resulted in creative advances for both.[1] When they first appeared on the scene, he said, the new ideas frightened some people. Science's theory of human bodily descent from lower life forms was a prime example. People who have opposed this idea, he said, did so either because of antiscientific prejudice, blind biblical literalism, or hyperemotionalism. In a note of positivism, he asserted that these negative reactions were not premised on anything having to do with the idea per se. Somewhat akin to John Ryan's view that teachers' extempore comments in the classroom were what caused some to view evolution as problematic in relation to religion, Cooper argued that continued suspicions about human evolution were precipitated by "a few scientists of the extreme left wing and a few theologians of the extreme right wing."[2]

Cooper maintained that the Bible had to be examined and understood through modern scientific eyes. The question of human origin and, thus, how to approach the "sublime hymn" of the Genesis creation accounts, concerned science far more than religion.[3] Catholicism, of course, did not offer a literalistic reading of Genesis, but Cooper spoke of the scripture as though its modest significance for moderns lay in its poetry rather than in particular theological truths conveyed in that poetry. All that one had to glean

1. Cooper, "Religion and Science – A, February 4, 1926," 2, in JMC Papers, box 42, folder "Religion and Science," ACUA.

2. Cooper, "Religion and Science – A," 5.

3. Cooper, "Religion and Science – A," 7.

from the Old Testament was the fact that God created the universe; after that, one entered science's turf. What Cooper said was an acceptable approach to the Hebrew Bible for the historical-critical school of thought. However, without saying that the alternative was simple literalism, *Pascendi* condemned modernism, thus calling into question the historical-critical school's application. At any rate, in contrast to his reading of the Genesis story, Cooper did appear to see more theological value in modern science.

Cooper told his radio audience that whenever he was asked to sermonize about creation to a modern, educated congregation, he invariably regaled them with details from current scientific theories such as astronomers' and physicists' notions of galaxies. He maintained that if someone were to come to him a few years later and say that some of the theories about which he sermonized had been disproven, he would have the perfect right to retort as follows: "You moron, can't you understand that speaking as I was from the pulpit I was not delivering a technical lecture on science? I was teaching religion and illustrating religious truth from current science."[4] Science seemed the best language with which to talk about human origins and other theological ideas.

Cooper concluded that first radio talk by encouraging his listeners to go to the aforementioned Millikan- and Osborn-authored *Joint Statement* on science and religion to discern the perspective that everyone, including all Catholics, should adopt on these matters. Quoting from this document, Cooper laid out the plan for his remaining talks: he would not merely show that religion and science existed without conflict; he would illustrate how they, in fact, advanced each other's causes.[5]

Cooper returned to the airwaves the following week, focusing on the reasonableness of religion. Rather than hearkening to a neo-Thomist model of reason and faith, he employed an empiricist, historicist epistemology. For example, Cooper opposed the claim

4. Cooper, "Religion and Science – A," 8.
5. Cooper, "Religion and Science – A," 9.

that religion relied merely on faith for its truth claims by saying instead that "religion is based on a vast amount of carefully criticized and tested scientific evidence" and that "the historic fact of the resurrection of Jesus Christ rests on contemporary documentary evidence as convincing as the historical evidence for the Black Death in Europe or the conquest of Mexico by Cortez."[6] Cooper added that present-day theology itself was constructed partially out of modern science's building blocks since theologians in their formal work had to regularly draw upon both natural and social science in their technical work.[7]

Cooper's third talk, airing February 18, focused on medicine and psychology. It contained some of his most revealing language on the purpose of religion, a purpose consonant with not only the Progressive Social Gospel but also the emerging therapeutic Christianity characteristic of liberal Protestantism in the interwar years.[8] His central point included the anthropocentric view that both religion and science worked to serve man, and he presented a litany of science's practical achievements, especially in medicine. Cooper went on to characterize scientific researchers as quasi-monastic heroes of laboratory discipline and martyrs to the quests of reason. Applying this religious rhetoric to scientific investigators was more than a casual metaphor. Cooper explained, for example, how Walter Reed's ascetic labors in mapping disease put him in the category of hero while one of Reed's researchers, who contracted yellow fever while attempting to understand its workings, became "a martyr to science, to duty, and to humanity."[9]

6. Cooper, "Religion and Science – B, February 11, 1926," 2, in JMC Papers, box 42, folder "Religion and Science," ACUA.

7. Cooper, "Religion and Science – B," 3. This is one of the positions overt modernists had considered a key premise. See, for example, Briggs, "Modernism Mediating." Briggs there asserted "Modernists accept without hesitation the results of modern science ... [and] advocate a reform of the Church ... in accordance ... with scientific, social and economic principles" (880).

8. On the therapeutic strand in mainline Protestantism by the interwar years, see Eugene McCarraher, *Christian Critics: Religion and the Impasse in Modern American Social Thought* (Ithaca: Cornell University Press, 2000), chap. 5.

9. Cooper, "Religion and Science – C, February 18, 1926," 1, in JMC Papers, box 42, folder "Religion and Science," ACUA.

Cooper's lineage in the Progressive gospel of efficiency also emerged in the radio talks. Science's pursuit in the laboratory "provides religion with the technical knowledge that enables religion to accomplish its work efficiently."[10] Cooper reframed Christianity's larger spiritual tradition in physicochemical terms. It was, thus, the force of religion, or the religious impulse, that drove people to struggle in the labors of medical research. Further, scientific techniques would eventually disclose the true nature of the human mechanism, both physical and mental, rendering much more effective religion's treatment of what he referred to not as sin but as "moral disease."[11]

In commending psychological science, Cooper reimagined his church's relationship to the human person. Although psychology between the wars leaned toward mechanistic models, Cooper embraced rather than excused that so as to use it for his rhetorical advantage. Psychology's physicochemical approach, he said, revealed the empirically true understanding of human nature. This understanding would finally permit religion to see where it had gone wrong in its past attempts to foist its morality on human beings. Analogizing between bodily and moral disease, Cooper argued that authoritative knowledge of a problem's source was halfway toward winning the struggle against it.[12] His language, at times, went beyond openness to the ideas and methods psychology could offer for treating mental maladies and sometimes seemed to reconceptualize the theology of sin into a stance on psychological disease—as though one had become the other rather than both coexisting as alternate experiences or states.

One historian of science studying the history of psychology has highlighted two propositions about early to mid-twentieth century psychology of religion that are relevant for assessing Cooper's language. The first was its human-centeredness rather than God-

---

10. Cooper, "Religion and Science – C," 3.
11. Cooper, "Religion and Science – C," 5.
12. Cooper, "Religion and Science – C," 5.

centeredness. The second was a prevalent tendency, influenced by behaviorism, to write about the mind-body relationship in ways that promoted not only naturalism but also determinism in the name of science.[13] Cooper did admit certain missteps "here and there" by psychology in the "lustiness of [the emerging discipline's] youth," but suggested that those days had passed and medical psychology could eventually repair man's moral problems. Seeming to blend what Catholics traditionally called sin into a schema of evolutionary medical progress, Cooper contended that "the newer psychology has already put into religion's hands a great mass of invaluable new information ... upon the technique of soul-moulding."[14]

Cooper's anthropocentric rhetoric on the origins and development of the human person also saw the Catholic confessional reduced to humanity's "psychological clinic ... soften[ing] people's sorrows."[15] Cooper reinforced the idea that psychology had, thankfully, almost taken over the older, more primitive "clinics" of religion; its insights and methods would coordinate what he rendered as religion and psychology's selfsame goal: improving *conduct*. Humanity's moral problems—which were themselves essentially social problems—would be solved clinically.[16] Thus did Cooper seem to replace the Catholic sacramental idea of confession with therapeutic naturalism.

As with the other sciences, Cooper implicitly denied that the alleged theological problems within professional psychology were related to any broader issues in the philosophy of this science. Instead—as he privately wrote but did not state on air—they were brought on by "the occasional trivial misunderstandings that arise between individual religionists and scientists... [and are fomented]

---

13. Jon H. Roberts, "The Science of the Soul: Naturalizing the Mind in Great Britain and North America," in *Science without God? Rethinking the History of Scientific Naturalism*, ed. Peter Harrison and Jon H. Roberts (Oxford: Oxford University Press, 2019), 174–81.

14. Cooper, "Religion and Science – C," 5.

15. Cooper, "Religion and Science – C," 6.

16. Cooper, "Religion and Science – C," 5.

through ignorance or malice."[17] Cooper concluded his talk with a call to both religion's and science's workers of goodwill not to waste any more time attempting to prove that religion and science do not conflict. He instead called for a future where "the twain" embraced the common goal for which they were "commissioned by God and man." That goal? "To serve human welfare."[18]

Cooper concluded the series of talks on February 25 with a lecture focusing on technology's value to humanity as a prime form of applied science. In his closing remarks, Cooper reminded listeners that any conflict between religion and science had been a "childish quarrel." Both needed to be seen as mutual correctives: "religion needs science and science needs religion."[19] In fact, religious people needed science in order to communicate in a realm where the intellectual, too, would be at ease.

Cooper's arguments about evolution were accorded both a hearing and a response, often approving of his manner of argumentation, by intellectual lights in the public square. As averred earlier, Cooper garnered respect for himself from non-Catholic intellectuals in a few main ways. He did so first by publishing myriad articles, including technical contributions to specialized journals and public magazines of opinion; pieces on comparative primitive religion for mainline anthropological journals; studies of youth and sex education for social hygiene journals; and commentaries on birth control for eugenics and other journals.[20] Second, he involved himself in every possible professional association of anthropologists and general scientists he could join. Third, he penned objectively framed articles popularizing science, especially evolution.

Cooper concurred with Catholic journalist Michael Williams of *Commonweal* that Catholics should welcome conservative Prot-

17. Cooper, "Religion and Science – C," 4 (sentence in manuscript is crossed out by hand).
18. Cooper, "Religion and Science – C," 7.
19. Cooper, "Religion and Science – D, February 25, 1926," 2, in JMC Papers, box 42, folder "Religion and Science," ACUA.
20. For a complete, chronological list of Cooper's publications in English covering 1910 through 1949, see "Bibliography of John Montgomery Cooper," *Primitive Man* 23 (July 3, 1950): 66–84.

estants' willingness to be publicly persecuted for their impassioned opposition to those who challenged religious or biblical authority within American culture. He wrote to the like-minded Fr. O'Brien that Catholics should gladly allow fundamentalists to take heat for religious obscurantism, even saying that the fundamentalists "should be encouraged to do so."[21] Catholics could meanwhile build credibility in the public sphere by writing in an objective tone and, thus, be seen taking the high road—both the rational and scientific high road.

It was to *Commonweal*'s pages that Austrian-migrant and Catholic physicist Karl Herzfeld of Johns Hopkins University turned in 1929, at Fr. Cooper's behest, to advocate forcefully the vision of our liberal figures that Catholics could and should best involve themselves in American public life through the sciences. Herzfeld's article, "Scientific Research and Religion," argued that Catholics could best influence American culture by producing trained scientists whose research and teaching would impact both generations of students and other scientific researchers for the greater good.[22] Catholics needed to stop making excuses for why they were not perceived as friendly to science and to instead start making original contributions to research that would prove the falsity of the premise. In other words, talking about science was one thing; doing it was another. Herzfeld contended that Catholic scientists who pursued this path would "by their mere presence and fame combat the argument often put forward that all scientific men are enemies of religion, and especially of Catholicism."[23]

Herzfeld sharply criticized Catholics who were ostensibly

21. Cooper to O'Brien (November 18, 1931), in JMC Papers, box 13, folder "Rev. John O'Brien," ACUA.

22. Herzfeld moved to the physics department at the Catholic University of America in 1936. "An Inventory of the Karl F. Herzfeld Papers at The American Catholic History Research Center and University Archives," *The Catholic University of America Finding Aids*, https://libraries.catholic.edu/special-collections/archives/collections/finding-aids/finding-aids.html?file=herzfeld (accessed March 11, 2018).

23. Karl F. Herzfeld, "Scientific Research and Religion," *Commonweal* 9 (March 20, 1929): 560.

friendly to science but spent their time penning defensive articles based on centuries-old Catholic scientific achievements. As
a way of opposing contemporary books painting Catholicism as
an enemy of progress, such an approach, he said, was futile. Even
more soundly did Herzfeld berate theologians who commented on
matters such as physical evolution. He insisted that only scientists
were qualified to address such topics in any meaningful way. As
a lure for following on his suggestions, he reminded readers that
Catholics will be qualified to comment intelligently on such matters when they themselves have been trained adequately through
graduate work in the sciences in numbers commensurate with
non-Catholics. Such training he characterized as "an extremely
important part of the lay apostolate."[24]

At the same time, Herzfeld insisted that experimental research
had nothing to do with religion. Topics like evolution, which many
viewed as religiously or philosophically centered, were, in fact, exclusively matters of science. Herzfeld asserted, "even if we consider evolution, what does it matter, so far as religion is concerned,
whether the horse had ancestors with three toes or one, or if Ar-
chaeopteryx, the first bird, is descended from reptiles?"[25] On the
one hand, Herzfeld's approach challenged *Commonweal*'s Catholic theologians to stay within their boundaries; its lay readers to
re-evaluate their educational priorities; and its non-Catholic readers to remember that Catholicism took no part in the Biblical literalism of fundamentalist Protestants. On the other hand, we have

24. Herzfeld, "Scientific Research," 562. For an earlier piece claiming that training in
scientific research was a matter for a lay apostolate, see the following unsigned editorial:
[Michael Williams], "Recruiting the Layman," *Commonweal* 9 (December 5, 1928): 118. After Herzfeld's article appeared, *Commonweal* subsequently reported that Jesuit Francis Power
published a response article in a May 1929 issue of the more conservative *America* magazine.
While Powers agreed that more Catholics needed to become "first-rate research workers," he
dissented from Herzfeld's "tonic" argument that the situation as it stood was so bad. Powers
contended that "reports on difficult original research in organic and inorganic chemistry have
been contributed, literally in scores, by the laboratories of Fordham and Notre Dame to such
authoritative organs as the *Journal of Biological Chemistry* and the *Journal of the American
Chemical Society*." See *Commonweal* 9 (May 29, 1929): 88.

25. Herzfeld, "Scientific Research," 561.

seen non-Catholic scientists like Osborn, Mather, Conklin, and others articulating a science-religion blended discourse for some time by the time Herzfeld wrote this. Despite lacking formal religious or theological training, these scientists regularly pronounced on theological matters and Biblical interpretation while advocating social plans predicated on their models.

Any assessment of Herzfeld's *Commonweal* article must account for the fact that this "lay apostolate of science" he advocated centered on outreach beyond Catholicism's borders.[26] Its goal involved inculcating into Catholics the importance of professional science so that they could practice and endorse it after training in it; the goal was *not* to inculcate a "Catholic science" in America but to inculcate science into Catholics and Catholic scientists into the professional scientific community. Cooper himself expressed this sentiment in December 1929 at the second meeting of his club created for those purposes, the Catholic Round Table of Science (CRTS), meeting every year at the AAAS annual conference. In that address, Cooper said his greatest hope was to avoid the notion of a separate Catholic science "inasmuch as science in general and scientific research in particular are, as such, neutral as regards religious belief."[27] It should be noted that this was a pointedly different view and approach than that undertaken by another Catholic scientific organization created a few years later in the interwar period, the *Institutum Divi Thomae*, at the University of Cincinnati. Even its name suggests that the institute's goal was not only to practice

26. Philip Gleason has discussed interwar era Catholic attempts to produce more academic research and research on a broader scale, especially at Cooper's Catholic University. See Gleason, *Contending with Modernity*, 176.

27. "Report of the Second Round Table" (1929), in JMC Papers, box 23, folder "Catholic Scientific Research, 1927–1933," ACUA. This ending phrase was often repeated verbatim in CRTS publications over the years. Father Anselm Keefe, secretary of CRTS, included an exact quote of this policy in an article he authored for the AAAS's *Science* magazine. See Anselm M. Keefe, "Fourth Round Table of Catholic Scientists Held in New Orleans," *Science* 75 (February 26, 1932): 245. See also, for example, "Report of the Third Round Table," (1929), 1, in JMC Papers, box 23, folder "Catholic Scientific Research, 1927–1933," ACUA; "Catholic Round Table of Science Here," *Catholic News* [NY], March 30, 1935, 19; "What Is the CRTS?," *Tabloid Scientist*, December 20, 1936, 2.

the sciences but also, when framing the results and implications for public consumption, to do so within the philosophy of neo-Thomism.[28]

The question of presentation and framing science for both the Catholic and non-Catholic public greatly preoccupied Fr. Cooper and his allies. Important efforts in this area centered on engagement with the press. The intent was to put the word out to Catholic media agencies and, ultimately, secular media agencies about increased Catholic commitment to science with the goal of fostering a science-minded American Catholic community.[29] In service to the first goal, Cooper and other CRTS leaders approached Justin McGrath, head of the NCWC News Service, asking him to print pieces "stressing the natural relations between religion and science ... [and] endeavoring to introduce a more irenic attitude on the part of the Catholic press towards science."[30]

In early February of 1929, Cooper sent out a series of letters to Catholic scientists in various disciplines asking that they serve as expert consultants to the NCWC's press bureau when it issued columns in their respective fields. One such correspondence, between Cooper and his geologist-friend Stefan Richarz, reveals their shared dissatisfaction with the way the American Catholic press was treating Catholics' scientific achievements. In this case, they particularly bemoaned the NCWC's recent report on the death of famous European Catholic evolutionist Henri Dorlodot. Both Cooper and Richarz believed that the American Catholic press had failed to properly celebrate Dorlodot and his achievements. They referred to the fact that the NCWC got its story from Fr. Francis LeBuffe, SJ,

28. On the *Institutum*, see John A. Heitmann, "Doing 'True Science.'" In various senses, this was the broader approach to Catholic public science endorsed by the renowned Catholic philosopher, Jacques Maritain.

29. Correlated with this effort were attempts to recruit future Catholic researchers from the best students in Catholic schools. Some CRTS members argued that this should be done in high school, envisioning high school CRTS club branches. Others argued that the shaping process should begin as early as grade school. "Meeting, December 28, 1928, Hotel Endicott, New York City, for the Promotion of Catholic Research," 2, in JMC Papers, box 23, folder "Catholic Research Roundtable—Meeting notes (1928)," ACUA.

30. "Meeting, December 28, 1928," 2.

the neoscholastic science writer at *America* magazine who scoffed at Dorlodot's celebratory attitude toward Darwinism. They were determined that a conservative Catholic like LeBuffe not be allowed to frame science-related stories for the Catholic reading public.[31]

A subsequent CRTS memorandum from Cooper addressed ways for CRTS to assume control of the Catholic press's presentation of science. It shows a plan in place by 1933 for Cooper to study E. W. Scripps's *Science News-Letter* every week and to send whatever articles he thought would be beneficial for Catholic readers to Catholic scientist-consultants. The latter, in turn, were to write up comments on the particular news item's significance, discern its importance for religion, and then send the report to the NCWC for printing.[32] Interestingly, while Cooper specifically insisted these interpreters be specialists in related scientific disciplines, he did not require that they have any theological training to assist them in showing the scientific matter's implications for religion.[33]

Ever since the NCWC press service's inception in 1917, some supporters had wanted its religiously sound science stories picked up by the national secular press. The same was now true of technical scientific research produced by Catholics. At the behest of CRTS, Catholics' research would be specifically framed in the idiom of *Science Service* by the latter's editors without any reference to religion. CRTS leaders brought Frank Thone of *Science Service* to address the 1934 CRTS meeting. There, Thone promised to widely publicize scientific research performed by Catholics by telling his listeners if they "would only furnish the material, the Science Service workers would act as the intestinal amoebae to help digest it for the termites of the public mind!"[34] The presentation of both

31. Richarz to Cooper (February 4, 1929), in JMC Papers, box 23, folder "Catholic Scientific Research, 1927–1933," ACUA.

32. "Memorandum on Project for Interpretation of Science and Scientific Discovery to Catholic Reading Public" (ca. 1933), in JMC Papers, box 23, folder "Catholic Research Roundtable Specialists Committee, 1933," ACUA.

33. "Memorandum on Project."

34. Frank Thone quoted in the *Tabloid Scientist* (February 1, 1935), 2, in JMC Papers, box 23, folder "Catholic Roundtable Meeting (1934)," ACUA.

science and religion were certainly key to the public reporting—both in the Catholic press and in the entire American press—of the most symbolically significant episode of the 1920s, the Scopes Trial, dealing with the key scientific concept of that age: evolution.

Cooper on Evolution in 1925 and 1928

Over a span of ten years—in 1925, 1928, and 1935—Cooper penned three pieces that focused on evolution and were aimed at three different forums. A comparison of these three pieces reveals his assumptions, his views on the philosophy of science, and his tactics in trying to popularize his perspectives, especially as his assumptions, views, and tactics developed over time. The first one was a short article written for a middlebrow magazine of mostly Catholic readership, the Paulist periodical *Catholic World*. The second was a chapter intended as a contribution to a compendium of essays for publication in Italy. The third was an expansive treatment on the evolution of the human body and mind published for his technical anthropological journal, *Primitive Man*, but of a length that could be considered a short book or very long booklet.

Cooper began the 1925 piece by arguing that scientific naturalism was a "fundamental heuristic principle" that could not be blamed when people took it too far.[35] Cooper's rhetorical exaltation of professional expertise in the article reached an almost absurd level when he insisted that in scientifically evaluating the then-popular claim by spiritualists to act as mediums for supernatural contact during séances, "the only group really qualified to evaluate and study the question scientifically" was "professional magicians."[36]

In this 1925 article, Cooper crafted a hypothesis about mental evolution, stating that if this type of evolution were eventually prov-

35. John Montgomery Cooper, "If Evolution Were a Fact?," *Catholic World* 121 (September 1925): 722.

36. Cooper, "If Evolution Were a Fact?," 722.

en empirically true, it might have made possible the human trait of *altruism* through purely natural processes. This, he said, meant that when a theistic being later infused a soul into the altruist-leaning hominid, the evolutionary mechanism would have served a greater and glorious cosmological purpose.[37] Cooper anticipated and sought to lay to rest a fear that his idea called into question an essential part of Catholic teaching: original sin. He maintained that the discrediting of Louis Agassiz's phylogeny thesis of human origins freed the Christian doctrine of original sin from refutation on evolutionary terms; the universal descent of humans from a single pair—monogenism—guaranteed that.[38] It is hard to see how Cooper could view his own argument as legitimate with respect to his contemporary Catholic Church, since figures like the famous and controversial paleontologist Fr. Pierre Teilhard de Chardin, SJ, whom Cooper would later publish in his own anthropology journal, forcefully claimed that the teaching on original sin could not coexist with evolution.[39] Of primary importance for our purposes, however, is Cooper's tendency to make arguments about human origins without appealing to religious authority other than to claim it did not disagree with what science was proving. He sounded at times a bit more like Teilhard in the next piece, from 1928.

Late in 1928, Cooper had prepared a piece he titled "Biological Evolution and the Catholic Social Ideal" for inclusion in a set of commemorative essays edited by Italian psychologist Fr. Agostino Gemelli.[40] On the surface, the 3,300-word manuscript was framed

37. See Cooper "If Evolution Were a Fact?," 727. Cooper's expansion of this argument (in the 1928 piece) will be addressed below.

38. Cooper, "If Evolution Were a Fact?," 725. Regarding Cooper's assurance on the idea of sin, see historian of science Thomas Dixon's "Invention of Altruism," 195–211. Dixon argues that Victorian British naturalists and scientists invented and framed this concept of altruism with an eye toward debunking theological notions of sin.

39. Teilhard, in his manuscript from 1933, *Christianity and Evolution*, opined that "original sin, imagined as the manner [*sic*] accepted today, is the straight jacket that suffocates at the same time our hearts and thoughts.... It represents a survival of the static view of the world which is not in accord with our new evolutionist thought." Pierre Teilhard de Chardin, *Christianity and Evolution* typescript (1933), 3, in Lucile Swan Papers, box 3, folder 27, GURBSC.

40. Cooper to Gemelli, (September 28 and October 3, 1928), in JMC Papers, box 42, folder "Unpublished Manuscripts," ACUA. It appears that Cooper's essay never made it into print.

in a manner reminiscent of his *Catholic World* article from 1925. However, in some key ways it went further than the earlier work. Cooper was careful to say that his argument was based on science but that his conclusions were not absolute. He asserted they were logical, yet speculative, extensions based in evolution as a "heuristic principle."[41] In this Gemelli essay, Cooper drew connections between contemporary scientists' views on evolution and the Catholic teaching about the role of God's grace in what he framed as simply a special form of human altruism. Making the science-religion connection, Cooper contended that he was simply trying to see whether the current understanding of bodily human evolution conflicted in any way at all with the Catholic Church's idea of "Christian altruism."[42] He saw no reason why the Catholic view could not be expressed in the scientific language.

From the start, however, Cooper's work suffered from eliding and conflation of terminology. For example, he never made clear where and when his frequent use of the term *altruism* was to be construed, on the one hand, in its technical scientific dressing as a naturalistic evolutionary instinct and, on the other hand, in the loose sense of a conscious choice to act selflessly.[43] It seems that he used it in both ways at different points. Also, Cooper overtly stated at one point that the article would avoid dealing with the evolution of "man's higher mentality," but in the following sentence, he said that his analysis did consider "assumed evolution of those cognitive, affective, and instinctive processes that are intimately dependent upon bodily structure and function."[44] Whether a soul was to be included in these categories is also unclear.

Despite ambiguity, the article did discuss the naturalistic development of altruism as instinct. According to Cooper, when it

41. Cooper, "Biological Evolution," 2.
42. Cooper, "Biological Evolution," 2.
43. On the Victorian scientific construction of altruism as a secular evolutionary-psychological category, see Dixon, "Invention of Altruism." For the historical development of the word *altruism* from its mid-nineteenth-century origins, see "altruism," in *The Compact Oxford English Dictionary*, new ed. (Oxford: Oxford University Press, 2004), 371.
44. Cooper, "Biological Evolution," 1.

reached a certain evolutionary level, altruism could be termed *love*.[45] This fourth and highest biological stage of altruism—out of which, he said, monogamy developed—was what kept some animal parents together to raise their young. He then speculated that this might be the end stage of a God-directed physical preparation for the future possibility of Christian altruism.[46] Cooper argued that this view of God using evolution to prepare the human race for subsequent purposes would make the theory not just palatable but also necessary and even majestic. The evolutionary development of altruistic love would thus have been intended to prepare prehistoric hominids for the subsequent role of divine grace and, therefore, for *"the innate, natural unselfish* trends that are the very heart of revealed religion."[47] In the main, this approach matched mainline anthropological and psychological professional theories about evolution of religion in the interwar era.

Throughout this work, Cooper appears to have been struggling to reconcile a theological immanentism with a Catholic view of a transcendent God. Cooper, of course, wrote the chapter assuming it would be published, even though it appears the volume of collected essays never appeared. It is evident that Cooper anticipated—and hoped to preempt—any negative responses by his conclusion of the piece with a classic rhetorical device allowing plausible denial of serious intent: "The foregoing is all hypothesis, of course, or, if the reader prefers, even speculation or dream." He cleverly added, "speculation within bounds is at its worst mental recreation [and thus] the reader may dismiss the foregoing heuristic interpretation as the stuff of which dreams are made. But," he concluded slyly, "sometimes even in speculation and dream there may be a touch of truth and reality."[48]

45. Cooper, "Biological Evolution," 8.
46. Cooper, "Biological Evolution," 7.
47. Cooper, "Biological Evolution," 10.
48. Cooper, "Biological Evolution," 10.

Cooper on Evolution in 1935

Cooper's extensive essay "The Scientific Evidence Bearing upon Human Evolution" (1935) expanded on his previous works on evolution but also differed significantly in that its rhetoric was exclusively empiricist and neutral in tone, rhetoric reflecting its status as an article in his professional anthropological journal *Primitive Man*, organ of the Catholic Anthropological Conference. Cooper had formed the Catholic Anthropological Conference himself in 1926 as a forum through which to recruit and train Catholics interested in science and anthropology—and particularly missionaries, who traveled through remote regions of foreign countries— to collect anthropological field data.[49] His goal with the Catholic Anthropological Conference was twofold: (1) to collect raw data on primitive societies; and (2) to reorient the missionary approach itself so that it was literally made a science. On the former, Cooper argued that this data collection would serve as material for published research, which was crucial because "Catholic standing in the world today depends and will continue to depend upon one thing and upon nothing else. It depends upon our contributions to scientific research.... To get this vast potential output onto the scientific market, all that would be needed is a little assistance."[50] Cooper sought to create a formal school of mission science at the Catholic University of America, or, at least, a division of mission science in the school's history department.[51]

Cooper's article in *Primitive Man* exemplifies a number of the tactical principles Cooper had been articulating for some time, especially his concern about presenting his writings to other scientists as objective and methodologically unimpeachable. The article opened by saying: "The purpose of the present paper is to review,

49. *The Catholic Anthropological Conference*, Washington, D.C. (1926), 2, in JMC Papers, box 57, folder "Catholic Anthropological Conference Publications," ACUA.

50. *The Catholic Anthropological Conference*, 4.

51. "Plan for CUA Mission Center" (n.d.), in JMC Papers, box 5, folder "Mission Science Project," ACUA.

as objectively as possible, the main lines of empirical evidence, pro and con" related to the whole of the human person, especially the mind, "from the anthropological standpoint," although psychology too "has to be drawn on heavily."[52] Cooper promised to sample the most up-to-date evidence on mental evolution from several disciplines: "cultural anthropology and primitive linguistics"; "comparative psychology," defined as the study of nonhuman animals' mentality; and "human psychology."[53] Cooper admitted the lack of physical evidence for human mental evolution from lower forms since the time of Darwin's *Descent of Man*, as no one had yet discovered an "antecedent structure," or vestigial form, from which the mind had clearly evolved. Cooper noted, however, that the only definitive thing about the question was the need for more research.[54]

What Cooper concluded was perhaps less significant than *how* he went about concluding it. He dismissed the idea of "emergent evolution" because it was unempirical according to naturalism. Perhaps more importantly, he employed the existence of the biological race category as evidence demonstrating the reality of human evolution.[55]

In this work, unlike in his 1928 piece, Cooper tried to clearly delineate what he meant by the *mind* and how it differed from what was usually meant by the term *soul*, the latter term not considered part of the professional anthropologist's purview. In using that term along with *mind*, however, his definitions were ambiguous, even overlapping, and left unanswered what he saw as their relationship, if any. It is not clear if he meant both could be approached naturalistically. Cooper defined the *human mind* loosely as "conceptual thought" in one place and as the origin of "the power of

52. John Montgomery Cooper, "The Scientific Evidence Bearing upon Human Evolution," *Primitive Man* 8 (January and April, 1935): 1–52.

53. Cooper, "Scientific Evidence," 1, 28.

54. On the lack of scientific evidence for antecedent structures, see Cooper, "Scientific Evidence," 51.

55. On emergent evolution, see Cooper, "Scientific Evidence," 52.

conceptual and rational thought" in another.[56] He went to lengths to address the term *soul*, calling it "the ultimate internal principle by which we think, feel and will."[57] Seeking a naturalistic definition, he argued that while the soul cannot be considered empirically, the question of "evolution of the free will" is under "exceptional and incidental" discussion by the empirical sciences—a rather obscure statement.[58] In attempting to write naturalistically in the context of a journal article, he was working within the anti-metaphysical cosmologies of anthropology and psychology. At the same time, he tried to allow for some space unreadable by those fields: a place for metaphysics. The elided problem, however, was that the positivist philosophy of those social-biological science fields lay claim to the ability to pronounce on the full aspects of human life from a perspective of empirical scientism. This was particularly true of physical anthropology, still dominant in that period over slowly ascending cultural anthropology.

A sign of the anthropological scientism surrounding Cooper and his discourse can be found in his comments about the legitimacy of the category known as scientific race or biological race. While Cooper argued that there was no empirical evidence for racial hierarchies of superiority and inferiority, he did appear to accept race as a genuine biological reality.[59] Professional physical

56. Cooper, "Scientific Evidence," 1, 22.

57. Cooper, "Scientific Evidence," 3. Cooper also contended that the soul was the body's animating principle as well as "the source of rationality, free will and immortality" (3). While it is not possible to judge conclusively about Cooper's full intended meanings in these instances, for the three different quotes, one could argue either way about whether his views were admissible for neo-Thomists. For Aristotle, the soul "covered all the functions of the person from the organic to the spiritual." Thomas Dixon, *From Passions to Emotions: The Creation of a Secular Psychological Category* (Cambridge: Cambridge University Press, 2003), 30. The discursive mind was the uniquely human aspect of souls, but neo-Thomists generally saw the matter, though not the form, as approachable through empirical techniques. I leave it to others to sort this out vis-à-vis Cooper's thinking here.

58. Cooper, "Scientific Evidence," 3.

59. On Cooper's rejection of scientific claims for particular race hierarchies (which set him apart from a field of physical anthropologists that had been insisting on their reality), see Cooper, "Scientific Evidence," 26. On the racialism still present in physical anthropology of the 1930s, see, for example, Michael Yudell, *Race Unmasked: Biology and Race in the 20th Century* (New York: Columbia University Press, 2014), esp. chaps. 5–8.

anthropology's acceptance of race was ubiquitous in the 1930s.[60] In an early section discussing bodily evolution, Cooper referred to a "white race" and its subdivisions deriving from a "common white race stock."[61] Later, he elaborated: "Within the human race there has certainly been bodily evolution; else we should have to ascribe such sub-races as the Caucasoid, Mongoloid, and the Negroid to three distinct origins … [or human stocks]." He added that "We know practically nothing about the missing links that connect up the three sub-races with the earliest human stock."[62]

Without delving more deeply into Cooper's work, a picture emerges from this and the other pieces of Cooper's role in liberal Catholics' participation in the interwar discourse on science and evolution. Cooper aligned the central elements of his writings to the presuppositions of the professional anthropological community's philosophy of science even while aiming each of the pieces, at least in part, to Catholics in addition to those professionals. Cooper's ambassadorship of naturalistic science extended to all parties. He translated his limited discussions of religious concepts into naturalistic-empirical terms in these works. How much did the frameworks and strategies underpinning Cooper's public discourse on evolution, and science in general, resemble or diverge from those of our other figures? On that note, we turn to look at our final Catholic apostle of science, Fr. O'Brien.

John A. O'Brien and Human Origins: Apostle of Scientism?

Many of the characteristics associated with Cooper and his publications apply also to O'Brien. The two were strategic allies and

---

60. Only in the early 1940s did Ashley Montagu's movement that denied the existence of race as a scientific reality in anthropology—following Franz Boas's earlier challenge to the concept in cultural anthropology—begin to substantially catch on. See his bestseller *Man's Most Dangerous Myth: The Fallacy of Race* (New York: Columbia University Press, 1942).

61. Cooper, "Scientific Evidence," 17.

62. Cooper, "Scientific Evidence," 21.

correspondents and, in certain cases, Cooper directly influenced O'Brien's manuscripts. The effects of their respective contributions to public origins debates were largely homologous. Both men rejected any notion of a particular Catholic philosophy of science or, indeed, the desirability of one. O'Brien likewise rejected the idea of a holistic philosophy of Catholic education. As discussed earlier, O'Brien was the first Catholic chaplain at the University of Illinois and held a PhD in educational psychology from that same school.[63] O'Brien's receipt of a doctorate from a public institution came amidst simmering debates in the American Catholic community about Catholics studying in non-Catholic schools. Conservative Catholics had insisted on holistic Catholic education embedded in neoscholastic philosophy. Since the late nineteenth century, Americanist Catholics had endorsed the practice of attending public schools, but their focus was on pre-college instruction and also on fostering American assimilation for Catholic immigrants. O'Brien's secular university credentials and methods invited criticism by more conservative Catholics; at the same time, they garnered him added respect among influential non-Catholic intellectuals who distrusted Catholic philosophical and cultural influences in separate schools. O'Brien's mainline professional colleagues appreciated the fact that his published arguments reflected the parameters of the education and psychology professions' prevailing philosophies of science. The coalescing professional disciplines of psychology and education, as social sciences, tied themselves to positivist naturalism and Spencerian stage development social theories. Education as a particular field was, of course, tied most closely to the pragmatism of John Dewey.[64]

63. See chapter 1 on O'Brien's PhD, awarded in 1920. His dissertation studied learning via silent reading, a topic that relied on arguments from both education and psychology. Each of these two fields developed its own professional apparatus but had substantial ties to each other. See Robert L. Church, "Educational Psychology and Social Reform in the Progressive Era," *History of Education Quarterly* 11 (Winter 1971): 390–405. Church said that contemporary "educational psychologists feel that their subspecialty emerged as a science about 1905.... Binet published his first intelligence scale in 1905" (390).

64. The focus in doctoral programs was on mapping individuals' internal learning

In 1932, O'Brien published a book titled *Evolution and Religion* as a major liberal Catholic contribution to the public debates about human origins and development. A scholar writing in the early post–World War II period argued that after initial slow sales, it achieved the largest non-Catholic readership of any Catholic work of the interwar era. It was widely quoted by prominent non-Catholic scientists and thinkers like Edwin Grant Conklin, Michael Pupin, and others.[65] Even Henry Fairfield Osborn lauded the book and also praised O'Brien himself "for his liberalism."[66] O'Brien was subsequently wont to express satisfaction that the book "received wide acclaim from scientists and philosophers," by which he actually meant both non-Catholics and liberal Catholics.[67]

O'Brien's stated purpose of the book appeared on the first page: "to interpret the bearing of evolution upon the philosophy of religion."[68] He proceeded to take the traditional Catholic view of the philosopher and reverse it. Rather than start with natural law or revelation and deduce the implications of evolution, the philosopher of religion "is to interpret the larger meaning of the data reported by the scientist, to trace their bearing upon the rational complexion of the universe, and to point out their implications

processes, hence the close connection with psychology. Arthur G. Powell, "University Schools of Education in the Twentieth Century," *Peabody Journal of Education* 54 (October 1976): 7. Powell pointed out that "most young educators in the 1890s agreed" that to obtain specialized expertise and its concomitant social prestige, "traditional sources of knowledge about education—practical experience and deductive philosophy—were inadequate" (10).

65. Conklin assessed it positively for *Scientific Book Club*. J. Howard Beard, chair of the Illinois Board of Health and a Protestant, "reported to O'Brien that his book was making a good impression upon rural Protestant clergymen and would do much to prevent a future repetition of the Dayton episode" (Morrison, "History of American Catholic Opinion," 344–45). According to Morrison, a fair number of Catholics were critical, "feeling that Fr. O'Brien had catered overmuch to popular tastes, but on the whole they were … complimentary towards his abilities" (345). Morrison went on to call Fr. Teilhard de Chardin, the French modernist scientist and not infrequent visitor to America, a "supporter" of O'Brien's (346).

66. On Osborn's commendatory letter to O'Brien, see Morrison, "History of American Catholic Opinion," 344.

67. See O'Brien quoted in Romig, *Book of Catholic Authors*, 245–46.

68. John A. O'Brien, *Evolution and Religion: A Study of the Bearing of Evolution upon the Philosophy of Religion* (New York: Century Co., 1932), 1.

upon the problem of ultimate causes."[69] O'Brien had replaced the scholastic approach with empiricism both for the philosophy of science and for the philosophy of religion, a pattern that earned accusations of modernism from the earliest twentieth century in Catholicism. O'Brien tacitly appealed to his own authority as a professional social scientist to legitimize his approach. At any rate, he himself did not teach in a theology department. It was likely on those grounds that he managed to avoid sanctions for his unorthodox philosophy of religion despite the antimodernist oath he, like all priests, had signed at ordination in the post-*Pascendi* era. O'Brien's opening concessions rhetorically cast his lot with the professional experts who read his book: they could recognize him as one of their own, something he himself intended.

O'Brien invoked various scientific disciplines, including "comparative anatomy, genetics, embryology, taxonomy, serology, and paleontology" to assert that all life from the "lowest and simplest forms ... [came] from a single protoplasmic cell."[70] Tracing human origins to a single cell reflected O'Brien's penchant for rhetoric designed to shock. For other Catholic evolution popularizers, asserting human and primate descent from a common hominid ancestor usually sufficed to make the point. For O'Brien, whether those of his Catholic readers would or would not blanch at the direct and absolute presentation of this point was not the issue. They had to accept the most far-reaching implications of the sciences. He reminded them that for the authoritative professional scientific establishment writ large, evolution was "universally recognized."[71] He summoned Edwin Conklin to confirm that there no longer remained any "missing links" between modern humans and anthropoids.[72]

69. O'Brien, *Evolution and Religion*, 1.

70. O'Brien, *Evolution and Religion*, 5, 7. I have not seen any of his contemporary Catholic authors point to this far-reaching extrapolation. It was also beyond some of the popular claims about evolution that often went no further than claiming that humans descended from a common hominid ancestor.

71. O'Brien, *Evolution and Religion*, 13, 15.

72. O'Brien, *Evolution and Religion*, 13.

On the science-religion front, O'Brien pointed out early on that he would avoid discussing the evolution of the soul, a choice that seems unexpected in the context of the larger book and his career at that time in general, especially his willingness to address delicate topics confrontationally. In this case, he merely said, "interesting and fascinating as they are ... the problem of mental evolution, the emergence of consciousness, and the metaphysical problem of the human soul ... will not be raised here."[73] Further investigation shows, however, that he had prepared a chapter on precisely those topics but was persuaded by Cooper to cut it from the draft stage for strategic reasons; the latter judged O'Brien's particular claims likely to scandalize more conservative Catholics. It was better to sacrifice the chapter to avoid inflaming the Catholic authorities at this stage in their efforts to create a science-friendly mindset and to spread acceptance of evolution. Given that Cooper himself had broached the topic of the soul in some of his own evolution writings—and not in a particularly uncontroversial way from the viewpoint of the conservative Catholic—one can infer that what O'Brien had written on the topic had gone beyond what even a liberal Catholic could get away with saying at that point. O'Brien agreed that in light of the tactical consideration, he ought to remove that material.[74]

Even without addressing evolution of the soul, O'Brien hardly avoided controversial argumentation in the book. For example, he acknowledged the widespread popular conflation of the general term *evolution* with the particular term *Darwinism*. By the early 1930s when O'Brien was writing the book, professional scientists usually used the latter term to mean evolution through the specific mechanism of natural selection. By noting the popular tendency to mix the ideas together, however, and then adding that nothing disturbs any matter of the Christian faith regardless of what infer-

73. O'Brien, *Evolution and Religion*, 6.
74. See O'Brien to Cooper (March 21, 1931), in JMC Papers, box 13, folder "O'Brien, Rev. John," ACUA.

ences one draws even particularly from Darwinism, O'Brien intentionally or unintentionally opened the question of just what kind of God the Christian faith implied. Catholic theistic evolutionists usually took pains to leave room for the direct infusion of a soul by a transcendent God. But Protestant modernist evolutionists, who were the large majority of evolutionary scientists in the interwar period willing to advertise some kind of belief in God, adduced an immanent, potentially impersonal God acting in evolution. Such was the case with both Conklin and Osborn, for example.[75] After invoking Conklin earlier, O'Brien turned for corroboration of his religious claim about Darwinism and evolution not to Catholic thinkers but rather to Shailer Mathews of the University of Chicago, the most renowned modernist Protestant theologian of the era. Perhaps unwittingly, O'Brien left open the possibility that readers might assume that he was implying that Mathews's quasi-pantheist God immanently guided evolution when O'Brien spoke of Darwinism having no effect on Christian teaching.[76] The potential for misunderstanding was particularly acute given the context of the early 1930s' emergence of the neo-Darwinian synthesis.

It is not possible to say whether O'Brien was fully aware that his rhetoric had opened up this possible interpretation. But more conservative Catholic opponents, who saw him as consistently blurring the lines with Protestantism, were less likely to miss that point and could add another line to their résumé of opposition to him. Some important conservative Catholic clergy had for some time accused O'Brien of indifferentism, by which they meant lack of concern to properly distinguish between Catholicism and other religions. It was no small matter that O'Brien's own diocesan bish-

75. It should be noted that neither Osborn nor Conklin would fit the strict label "Darwinian" after the neo-Darwinian synthesis. Both argued that natural selection was not necessarily the primary factor driving evolution. On Osborn's immanentist God, see, for example, Osborn, "Evolution and Religion," *New York Times*, March 5, 1922, 91. On Conklin's immanentist God, see, for example, Conklin, *Direction of Human Evolution*, 72.

76. O'Brien, *Evolution and Religion*, 149. The specific book to which he referred was Mathews's *Contributions of Science to Religion* (New York: Appleton, 1927).

op, Joseph Schlarman, opposed him for the same reasons, eventually expelling him from the diocese.[77]

Things took a more unexpected turn in *Evolution and Religion* when O'Brien called on the scientist Conklin for particular support on *biblical* interpretation.[78] Conklin was a curious choice, not least for the fact that he was a scientist, not a biblical scholar. Secondly, there was Conklin's heterodoxy from the official Catholic perspective. Finally, on a number of previous occasions Conklin had shown an anti-Catholic religious attitude such that it was one thing to appeal to him for scientific conclusions, but it was another thing, especially for a Catholic priest, to appeal to him for particular religious understanding or scriptural interpretation.

Even without Conklin, O'Brien's own arguments about Catholicism, science-religion authority, and the Bible vis-à-vis nature were not just fairly radical but were at times self-contradictory. Early on, O'Brien made what was by this point liberal-progressive Catholics' standard mea culpa about the Galileo incident. He then equated those who had opposed Galileo with all who currently opposed any aspects of the absolute fact of evolution. He also invoked, then surpassed, the standard Mivart-Wasmann-Dorlodot model of arguing that Augustine was actually an evolutionist by adding that Augustine had actually been a more radical evolutionist than Darwin.[79]

In other parts of the book, O'Brien emphasized the Catholic Church's own history of relations with science in the warfare model redaction. Characterizing Protestant fundamentalists in the Scopes Trial as having simply presented a grotesque version of "the view that dominated ... religious thinking up until the last few centuries," he implied the truth of a then-widespread, yet inaccurate, contention characteristic of anti-Catholics who said that the Catholic Church had used Genesis as a literal blueprint of human

77. See Solberg, "Catholic Presence," 777–78.
78. O'Brien, *Evolution and Religion*, 19–20.
79. O'Brien, *Evolution and Religion*, 34, 35, 81, 217.

origins just as conservative Protestants did now.[80] In O'Brien's confused history, that view had been "frequently adopted by Christian
writers from the early days of the third and fourth centuries."[81]
A reader of O'Brien's work may wonder how it is that if Patristic
teachers—a category into which Western Christianity's dominant
figure, Augustine, himself fell—were much more sophisticated
than contemporary fundamentalists in their biblical hermeneutics,
their same church has been as backward on that topic as the fundamentalists of O'Brien's own day.

O'Brien's narrative reflected the continual-progress presumptions characteristic of both progressive thought and positivist science of that era. As such, O'Brien's narrative tended to contrast
the backwardness of the past with the enlightened nature of the
present. This model also led O'Brien on more than one occasion in
the volume to present variations on the theme that previous views
of the Bible and nature were "now obsolete with the progressive
scholarship of the present day."[82]

Proponents of the warfare thesis tied to John William Draper's
anti-Catholic volume discussed earlier had laid significant blame
on organized religion for the supposed warfare of religion and science. O'Brien admitted the truth of the warfare model's view of
the history, his only difference from its staunch proponents being
a claim that at least now the church was finally emerging from the
darkness. O'Brien employed his own metaphor to describe how
for several centuries the church had been manning the rear guard
and was now an army "beating a retreat to a safer and more remote
terrain," a shift shown in the final removal of Galileo's text from the
church's Index of Forbidden books and the continued quest to fully
clear his name and admit error.[83]

Near the end of *Evolution and Religion*, O'Brien espoused what

80. O'Brien, *Evolution and Religion*, 56.
81. O'Brien, *Evolution and Religion*, 56.
82. O'Brien, *Evolution and Religion*, 56.
83. O'Brien, *Evolution and Religion*, 85.

seemed the particular modernist view of contemporary science gradually offering a more advanced connection to God. Although he began by legitimately averring that the "naïve pseudoscience of Bryan" would and should not carry the day in these decades after the Scopes Trial, he then employed that extremism as a red herring to contrast with the only reasonable alternate view for a progressively sophisticated era. As he put it, "the free and untrammeled prosecution of scientific research [would become] the most effective stimulus to a growing knowledge of God."[84] Reiterating the "great indebtedness of both philosophy and religion to the findings of science," O'Brien maintained that science—not religious institutions, or tradition, or even revelation—would be the chief source of human beings' future encounters with divinity.[85]

It is worth mentioning that another of O'Brien's books in the 1930s built on these themes and extended the latter point. *Religion in a Changing World* extended his claims about the sacrality of science. Early in that volume, O'Brien declared: "Science ... will aid us in securing a better vision of God.... In this sense there is something priestly in the labors of the scientist in his laboring.... For [he] too [seeks] to clarify the application of ethical and eternal truth to the changing social and economic conditions of modern life."[86] O'Brien's image of the scientist transformed him into a high priest of sorts.

As noted above O'Brien had shared drafts of *Evolution and Religion* with Cooper. The latter advised him to tone down his more hyperbolic rhetoric and, especially, not to try discrediting his opponents within the Catholic Church, as had been his wont. Cooper

84. O'Brien, *Evolution and Religion*, 120. For more on this view albeit in a different context, see David Hollinger's classic essay "Justification by Verification: The Scientific Challenge to the Moral Authority of Christianity in Modern America," in *After Cloven Tongues of Fire: Protestant Liberalism in Modern American History*, ed. Hollinger, 82–102 (Princeton: Princeton University Press, 2013).

85. O'Brien, *Evolution and Religion*, 243.

86. John A. O'Brien, *Religion in a Changing World: Christianity and Modern Thought* (Huntington, Ind.: Our Sunday Visitor Press, 1938), 20.

particularly warned O'Brien off "tak[ing] [a] barking and snapping attitude" saying, "I believe that a perfectly objective attitude toward the evidence, and emphasis on the evidence itself, regardless of what 'the [Catholic theological] authorities' say ... is the only scientific and Catholic attitude we can take."[87] Cooper contended that this posture of objectivity was a good rhetorical measure, and that any other course might raise the ire of conservatives and, thus, retard their common hope to advance evolutionism.[88]

Upon receiving Cooper's comments and edits, O'Brien wrote back to admit that Cooper's approach was wiser than his own had been and also to express pleasure that the two agreed on the main goals. O'Brien enthused: "I am more than delighted to learn of your agreement with the viewpoint presented.... I hope it may be the beginning of a liberalizing of [the Catholic] viewpoint."[89] After completing his revised manuscript for *Evolution and Religion*, O'Brien wrote again to thank Cooper for his cautious counsel and professed his debt to Cooper for the shape the book ultimately took. O'Brien took pains to point out his "radical modifications in the treatment, ... modifying every reference to theologians which might be construed as critical."[90]

Throughout all of this, Cooper and O'Brien together advanced their common goal: advocating for changes in Catholic thought and trying to open Catholics up to American intellectual life. Both ultimately agreed that anything other than a strategic caution in the book "may antagonize [Catholic moderates and conservatives]." Such would be disastrous, "accomplish[ing] nothing

87. Cooper to O'Brien (November 18, 1930), in JMC Papers, box 13, folder "O'Brien, Rev. John," ACUA.

88. A long handwritten letter from Cooper to O'Brien went into much greater detail about how assuming an objective air would have the greatest influence in changing the minds of "Catholic authorities" about evolutionary discourse. Cooper to O'Brien (March 15, 1931), in JMC Papers, box 13, folder "O'Brien, Rev. John," ACUA.

89. O'Brien to Cooper (November 22, 1930), in JMC Papers, box 13, folder "O'Brien, Rev. John," ACUA.

90. O'Brien to Cooper (October 22, 1931), in JMC Papers, box 13, folder "O'Brien, Rev. John," ACUA.

in bringing about the attitude we desire."[91] One wonders what the original drafts looked like if the toned-down version was the one eventually published.

A Cord Helping Tie Together European and American Modernism: Pierre Teilhard de Chardin

"Man is nothing else but evolution become conscious of itself.... [My] deepest conviction is that we are on the eve of a spiritualistic evolution."[92] Thus did the *New York Times* quote the French paleontologist-anthropologist Teilhard in a speech he delivered in Philadelphia during the spring of 1937. Teilhard, the famous yet controversial Jesuit priest scientist, had come to the City of Brotherly Love to participate in the International Symposium of Early Man held at the Philadelphia Academy of the Natural Sciences and also to receive the seventh annual Mendel medal for reconciling science and religion, awarded at nearby Villanova University. Teilhard's French Jesuit colleagues had hoped the internationally known figure would bring some positive recognition to the Catholic Church by offering technical presentations in his scientific field, but Teilhard used these forums to articulate some of his particularly unorthodox assertions about theology and evolution.

Teilhard's remarks, covered widely in both the Catholic and mainline press, created such scandal that Boston College's Jesuit president had to tell Teilhard that the college could not go through with the ceremony awarding the honorary doctorate he had been slated to receive there a few days later.[93] The president feared that

91. O'Brien to Cooper (March 21, 1931), in JMC Papers, box 13, folder "O'Brien, Rev. John," ACUA.

92. "De Chardin Is Honored," *New York Times*, March 23, 1937, 9. The *Times* feted Teilhard as the "discoverer of Peking Man" (9).

93. En route from Philadelphia to Boston, Teilhard traveled to New York to meet with his friends in the Museum of Natural History; these friends included Henry Fairfield Osborn, whom Teilhard referred to as "the great Osborn." Pierre Teilhard de Chardin, *Letters from a Traveller* (New York: Harper and Brothers, 1962): 3, 167–69.

doing so would create too many problems for the school with Catholic authorities and others.[94]

Teilhard, the paleontologist and speculative modernist theologian, seems to have exerted more than a little influence on the thought and rhetoric of Cooper, O'Brien, and other American Catholic science-religion reconcilers. As O'Brien had put the Teilhardian sentiment in *Religion and a Changing World*, "the onward sweep of the sciences ... profoundly altered the framework of many traditional conceptions."[95] Aside from what can be gleaned from rhetorical and logical affinities between Teilhard's works and the Americans' discourse, there is evidence of direct, behind-the-scenes influence. According to a well-placed Catholic scholar, certain liberal Catholics in America in the 1920s started to meet regularly to strategize on how to publicly advance the evolutionary views of Messenger and Dorlodot. Gathering together often in the 1920s and 1930s and led by O'Brien, this group included Fr. Ulrich Hauber, biologist and president of St. Ambrose College in Iowa; Cooper; Fr. Joseph Murray; and Fr. J. Franklin Ewing, an American Jesuit evolutionist. This cadre maintained direct communication with Teilhard in France.[96]

After the public debacles in Philadelphia, the Jesuit order rarely permitted Teilhard to speak publicly on anything but technical science and continued its policy of never permitting Teilhard to publish his theological speculations in his lifetime. In retrospect,

94. Thomas M. King and Mary Wood Gilbert, *The Letters of Teilhard de Chardin and Lucile Swan* (Washington, D.C.: Georgetown University Press, 1993), 78. Although denied his degree, Teilhard wrote to a friend that while in Boston and Washington, D.C., he "had several private talks, perfectly frank, with [his] younger colleagues" and that he met with Catholic anthropologists (King and Gilbert, 78).

95. O'Brien, *Religion in a Changing World*, vii.

96. Morrison, "History of American Catholic Opinion," 342. Morrison's personal interview with O'Brien included the latter's statement that their small clique actively sought to gain control of the Catholic media's presentation of evolution (342). Besides O'Brien's direct confirmation in the interview, Morrison's evidence for the Teilhard connection included letters between O'Brien and a Roman cardinal, Achille Liénart, who supported the American group and communicated regularly with them. These letters were in the O'Brien papers at the University of Notre Dame (342). Morrison added that the group also communicated regularly with Ernest Messenger at the University of Louvain (342).

this is not terribly surprising, given some of what Teilhard argued. For example, he wrote in 1933 in material that was prohibited from publication that the Catholic and other Christian churches were obsolete at this point in evolution. In his words, "[We must] admit therefore that Christianity has now reached as has Humanity the limit of a natural cycle of its existence." He added that when theology is adjusted for evolution, "Evil ceases in this new perspective to be an incomprehensible element and becomes a natural feature in the structure of ... [an evolving world]."[97] And he firmly contended that in view of evolution, the biblical figure of Lucifer—the "light-bearer"—had to be seen as a positive force in history. This beneficent Lucifer was a naturally evolving entity, he said, who would aid human generations in a mental-spiritual ascent. With bodies transformed through evolution, they would unite with a newly conscious aspect of the earth itself in an ascent farther and farther upward to eventual convergence into what he called "the Omega Point" of the universe.[98]

In Conclusion

As we have seen, interwar Catholic participation in mainline origins and evolution debates was more complicated than often presumed and also not without influence in American public culture. The examples from a larger whole in these chapters on science in general, and evolution in particular, add to the contours of not only the history of Catholic intellectual life but also the story of science's shifting authority in interwar American public life. Liberal Catholic thinkers participated in conversations with mainline thinkers and in discourses involving intersecting streams of both science and scientism. In their enthusiasm to repudiate and distance themselves from anti-modernist Protestants, and from the legacy

97. Teilhard, *Christianity and Evolution*.
98. On Lucifer/Satan as a natural, positive figure for Teilhard, see Teilhard de Chardin, *Christianity and Evolution*, 3. The Omega Point and his main ideas are described in *The Human Phenomenon* and several other of his works.

of accusations that Catholicism had been antithetical to science, they contributed to various degrees in both the science and the scientism of public culture. As they did so, they showed themselves as having drunk from their own cups of science-centered theological modernism and positivist social science.

～ 4

Microcosmic Conception and Contraception

The 1920s

> They exercise genital acts, yet prevent the conceiving of children. Not in order to produce offspring, but to satisfy lust, are they eager for corruption.
>
> —St. Epiphanios of Salamis (375)

All major and most minor Judeo-Christian religious institutions in America strongly opposed artificial birth control in the early decades of the twentieth century. But so, too, did the medical and public health professions and the American legal apparatus. This belies the subsequent impression that Catholics alone represented the major threat against birth control. Nevertheless, in this mix, some of the most influential public rhetoric in the birth control debates either came from Catholics or was drafted in response to Catholics' statements. There was, however, a spectrum of Catholic discourse with more complex effects on those broader debates than is usually acknowledged. General histories commenting on

Epigraph is from St. Epiphanios of Salamis, *Medicine Chest against Heresies* (*Panariou*) 26:5:2 (375), https://archive.org/stream/PanarionEpiphaniusCOMPLETE_201905/Panarion%20Epiphanius%20COMPLETE_djvu.txt.

the birth control movement have tended to presume some Catholic Augustinian monolith or traditionalist formalism. Yet liberal Catholics made their particular cases by calling on the same authority of modern science as did their ostensibly secular opponents when the latter defended artificial contraception. While some argued that this was mere expediency or practicality on the part of the Catholics, it also reflected liberal Catholics' dissent from institutional Catholicism's neoscholastic focus of that era in favor of a theological quasi-modernism—and even scientism—derived from intellectual connections to Progressive Era social sciences.[1] The liberal-progressive Catholics we discuss may have underestimated the secularizing effect this could have on the broader discourse.

Neither the birth control discourse itself nor liberal Catholic involvement with it constitutes simple, direct lines. The turn of decade from the 1920s to the 1930s saw developments—both without and within Catholicism—of a magnitude that influenced multiple levels of the debate and resulted in genuine differences over time. Among these developments were the Great Depression's acceleration in 1930 and the papal encyclical *Casti Connubii* (On Chaste Marriage), which addressed contraception and was issued at the end of 1930 partly in response to the Anglican Lambeth Conference's shift in position on artificial birth control earlier that year.

Mainline Protestants' Public Approaches to Contraception

As with American Protestant and Jewish approaches to evolution and eugenics, their approaches to contraception in the early decades of the twentieth century are best understood with an eye on distinctions between theologically conservative and liberal blocks. A general enthusiasm for science and technology, and for modernity's putatively scientific value system, carried through for modernists and liberals within both Protestantism and Judaism such that

1. On secular language as a conscious choice, see Tentler, *Catholics and Contraception*, 50.

they eventually supported artificial contraception within scientific schema. The theological conservatives in both groups likewise retained traditional approaches to the subject while, at times, employing their own scientific justifications for doing so. Denominational distinctions were clear enough in official pronouncements, though those denominations themselves largely conformed to either a liberal-modernist or conservative block. The added factor of section, or region, also figured substantively in the issue. Northern and Southern wings of the Methodist and Baptist churches, for example, largely diverged on this topic by section. The patterns of traditionalism and reform also held true for Jews, especially as Reform Judaism increased in public prominence by the interwar period through figures like Rabbi Steven Wise of New York.[2]

The ascendance of a pro-contraception lobby around World War I saw some slight foray by religious figures into the public debate on the topic, although this remained rare until late in the 1920s.[3] The shift toward more discussion—and for liberals, changed views—came for Protestants with the activity of the Federal Council of Churches of Christ (FCCC) and for Jews with the Central Conference of American Rabbis. Both of those groups ramped up discussion in the late 1920s and officially endorsed contraception as a legitimate part of marriage by 1930 (the Rabbis' Central Conference) and 1931 (the FCCC).[4] Although the details of various Jewish responses are of significance and have their own complexities, for want of space and given both Protestantism's paramount cultural influence and the fact of Jewish leaders' pronouncements largely paralleling Protestants' on the same modernist-traditional axis, a

2. Setting aside the important influence of secular Jews like Horace Kallen and others in the era's social sciences, R. Laurence Moore contended that the Reform branch of Judaism "constituted a rapid program of Americanization [leaving it] ... looking much more like a form of liberal Protestantism than what had been practiced in the shtetl" (*Religious Outsiders*, 78).

3. Multiple Protestant groups avoided the contraception topic as part of their general opposition to the public circulation of what they considered obscene topics, and as such, grafted the question of discussing contraception in with opposition to eliminating obscenity laws (Tobin, *American Religious Debate*, 100–1).

4. On the Reform Jewish position culminating in the Conference of Rabbis' proclamation, see Tobin, *American Religious Debate*, 106, 153–54.

brief look at the Protestant discourse can provide the necessary context for our purposes.[5]

Mainline Protestants, such as Episcopalians, saw their official contraception line substantively influenced by developments overseas, particularly in London. It did not appear that the influence would be for change in the early postwar era. The 1920 Lambeth Conference of the Anglican communion essentially echoed the 1908 Conference's stance on marriage and reproduction, decreeing: "The Conference ... regards with grave concern the spread in modern society of theories and practices hostile to the family. We utter an emphatic warning against the use of unnatural means for the avoidance of conception, together with the grave dangers—physical, moral and religious—thereby incurred." The confreres also "urge[d] the importance of enlisting the help of all high-principled men and women ... in bringing pressure to bear upon authorities, both national and local, for removing such incentives to vice as indecent literature ... [and] the open or secret sale of contraceptives."[6] Yet by 1930, the Lambeth Conference saw a seismic shift to guarded, yet open, support for contraception by married couples. This significantly spurred the 1931 Federal Council's endorsement of artificial contraception in the United States, saying "the careful and restrained use of contraceptives by married people is valid and moral."[7] Nevertheless, a number of individual Protestants and

---

5. Kathleen Tobin has noted that Orthodox Jewish positions on contraception paralleled those of fundamentalist Protestants; Conservatives resembled Protestant moderates; and Reform rhetoric and decisions echoed the Protestant modernists and were rife with social science arguments. On Reform, in particular, Tobin pointed out that "Reform rabbis, and the liberal Jewish leadership in general, resembled many Protestant social gospellers, as they took their humanitarian role very seriously, using Scripture and science to improve society" (*American Religious Debate*, 26).

6. "Resolution 68 and 70, Problems of Marriage and Sexual Morality," in *The Lambeth Conference: Resolutions Archive from 1920* (published by Anglican Consultative Council of the Anglican Communion Office, 2005), 20–21, https://www.anglicancommunion.org/media/127731/1920.pdf. See also Peter Sedgwick, "The Lambeth Conferences on Contraception, 1908–68," *Theology* 123 (2020): 96–98; Tobin, *American Religious Debate*, 54, 99.

7. The Federal Council listed its committee's justifications thusly: "It is important to provide for the proper spacing of children, the control of the size of the family, and the protection of mothers and children; and because intercourse between the mates, when an expression of their spiritual union and affection, is right in itself." Federal Council of the Churches of Christ

denominations both within and without the Council's affiliation refused to accept the FCCC's decision. The post-1930 changes will be addressed further in a subsequent chapter; here we emphasize the distance traversed to that point.

The 1916 General Convention of the Protestant Episcopal Church in America defined marriage as "intended for the mutual companionship ... for the procreation of children and for their nurture and training," adding "to ignore or defeat any of these purposes is a sinful violation of God's institution."[8] Even the liberal mainline Protestant *Christian Century* in 1921 still emphasized the importance of procreation in an article "The Glory of Fatherhood," although by mid-century, while the liberal Northern Baptist and Methodist churches' statements on marriage deplored the divorce rate generally, they did not mention contraception.[9] The Methodists' General Conference of 1928 did not place contraception anywhere on the agenda. But behind the silence, changes were afoot through the auspices of the Federal Council.

Any Northern Methodist who had even privately wanted to discuss a shift on contraception would have had to deal with New York's most famous Methodist, Anthony Comstock of the long-standing anti-obscenity laws bearing his name, at least until his death in 1915.[10] By 1929, it was actually a Northern Methodist pas-

in America, "Moral Aspects of Birth Control" (New York: FCCC Committee on Marriage and the Home, 1938). See also "The Churches and Birth Control," *Federal Council Bulletin* 14 (1931): 19. On the Protestants in the Council rejecting the majority view, see E. T. Plopper, "Protestants and the Acceptance of Contraceptives in Britain and the U.S.A." (PhD diss., University of Notre Dame, 2015), 392n62.

8. Quoted in Tobin, *American Religious Debate*, 58. It did not hurt Episcopalian chances for shifting that Margaret Sanger made good on her promise from 1931 to indirectly contribute money from her organization to the Federal Council of Churches' Rev. Worth Tippy in order to help repel fundamentalist Protestants opposing the Council's contraception initiatives. Upon Sanger's earlier request, Tippy had himself provided her with a list of Episcopalian bishops he knew to be sympathetic to contraception (Plopper, "Protestants," 424–25). Plopper details the workings of the unorthodox funding arrangements, noting that Sanger's monetary and other support of the Federal Council continued into the 1940s (420–24).

9. Tobin, *American Religious Debate*, 49.

10. On the Comstock laws, see Ashley Boggan, "A God-Sent Movement: Methodism, Contraception, and the Protection of the Methodist Family, 1870–1968," *Methodist History* 53 (2015): 69–70; Noonan, *Contraception*, 412.

tor, Rev. Worth Tippy, who led the FCCC's Commission on the Church and Social Service and wrote its *Ideals of Love and Marriage* pamphlet issued that year. This pamphlet reoriented the framing of marriage while emphasizing sociological models of education. Tippy also authored the dramatic 1931 FCCC statement titled *Moral Aspects of Birth Control*, which endorsed birth control as a practical good in marriage.[11]

On the shift, the writing was already on the public wall by 1929 when modernist Baptist Harry Emerson Fosdick published "Religion and Birth Control" in the *Outlook and Independent* magazine. There he wrote: "It is high time for those whose dominant interests lie in the realms of ethics and religion to be outspoken about the vexatious and highly controversial subject of birth control," arguing that "to encourage ... a sane, scientific control over this most important part of human life ... is the ideal."[12]

By contrast, conservatives in Southern Baptist and Methodist communions substantially differed from those groups' Northern wings.[13] In 1920, the Southern Baptist Rev. E. W. Stone published an article arguing that the burden of having a number of children was actually an overall positive, one that helped prevent divorce by providing another layer of the spousal bond.[14] Region also saw itself reflected in the largely immigrant Missouri Synod Lutherans' strong opposition to contraception, even as the United Lutherans of the North moved in the liberal-modernist currents by framing the matter in social service and reform terms.[15]

11. On Tippy, see Plopper, "Protestants," 346. *Ideals of Love and Marriage* was also issued under the name *Protestant View of Sex, Love, and Marriage*.

12. Harry Emerson Fosdick, "Religion and Birth Control," *Outlook and Independent* 8 (June 1929): 301. Fosdick demonstrated his science-minded progressive instincts, saying "The day will come when the old haphazard spawning of many children ... will be looked upon as utter barbarism" (314).

13. For example, Southern Methodists officially rejected contraception in the interwar years. It was only in 1940, after a merger of the three major Southern Methodist denominations, that a shift to de facto endorsement of contraception appeared. The new science-centered arguments were made in the new united church's *Social Creed* document. See Boggan, "God-Sent Movement," 78–79.

14. Stone quoted in Tobin, *American Religious Debate*, 60.

15. Tobin, *American Religious Debate*, 43–44. And Alan Graebner noted "From the

The Catholic Church and Birth Control

Despite a different rhetorical emphasis centered in neoscholastic philosophy by the early twentieth century, the Roman Catholic Church's standard position on contraception had for centuries been anchored to Western Christianity's most popular and educated Church Father St. Augustine, although it should be noted that the Christian East did not generally share Augustine's rendering of "original sin" nor, therefore, sexuality's role in ostensibly transmitting it. In the nineteenth century, responding to a noticeable decrease in the French birth rate and, later, in that of other European countries, both the Vatican and Catholic seminaries began paying closer attention to increasingly widespread (although mostly furtive) contraceptive practice.[16]

In the mid- to late nineteenth century, official Catholic Church entities pronounced several times on questions put to them about what was termed *onanism*, questions coming chiefly from French clergy.[17] A decree by the Roman Holy Office of the Inquisition in 1853 contrasted onanism, which it conceived as *coitus interruptus*, with "artificial means" of avoiding insemination. In this, it echoed a response by the Roman Penitentiary of 1822.[18] The question of artificial contraception was not as prevalent at that point and, therefore, onanism was the focus of the condemnations. Of note

nineteenth century through the 1930's, Missouri Synod [Lutherans] ... were consistently and flatly opposed to all forms of contraception." Graebner, "Birth Control and the Lutherans: The Missouri Synod as a Case Study," *Journal of Social History* 2 (1969): 304.

16. On the simultaneous decline of the birth rate and stabilization of the death rate in Western Europe at the time, see Noonan, *Contraception*, 394. Noonan argued that the pattern coincided with the point when European Catholic theology was at its virtual nadir (395–96). Lacking both creativity and fidelity to even the traditional texts, seminaries relied on formulaic and legalistic manuals; the most widely used on sexuality was Jesuit John Gury's *Compendium of Moral Theology*, itself based on the Scholastic theologian Alphonsus Liguori's *Moral Theology* of 1748 (Noonan, 320, 396).

17. The word *onanism*, in the sense of achieving orgasm for reasons other than procreation—ostensibly deriving from the book of Genesis, chapter 38—first appeared in European sources in the mid-eighteenth century (Noonan, *Contraception*, 397). During that period, the word was also seen as linked with masturbation, both vices involving the use of seminal emission for other than procreative purposes.

18. Noonan, *Contraception*, 397.

in that period is one other decree: an 1842 Penitentiary response to a bishop's question about whether a priest hearing confession should question the penitent if he suspected any of these behaviors, or should rather permit "good faith ignorance" to continue (the exception being if the penitent him- or herself brought up an example and asked whether it was sinful).[19] The answer given was that, in normal circumstances, the priest should refrain from asking. Part of the rationale was to avoid suggesting the idea if the person had not thought of it on his or her own.[20]

In 1843, the process known as cold vulcanization was perfected and applied to rubber; this would lead to an increase in the use of rubber condoms for prophylaxis. When asked about condoms, the Congregation explicitly declared their use to be in violation of natural law in a decree of 1853.[21] That, however, was as far as things went in the nineteenth century. Many look to the Inquisition's decree of May 21, 1851, under Pope Pius IX (r. 1846–78) as the nineteenth century's most definitive statement on these various issues until the late period of Leo XIII's pontificate. In the 1851 decree, onanism was declared "scandalous, erroneous, and contrary to the natural law of marriage" but not "heretical."[22]

In America, institutional Catholic pronouncements on the topic of contraception also initially treated contraception in light of onanism as elaborated by the nineteenth-century neoscholastic manuals. The term's use was later abandoned. Ryan was the American Catholic most responsible for influencing both the church's in-

19. This position was articulated by the Sacred Penitentiary, which itself cited the section titled "The Practice of the Confessor" in Liguori's work (Noonan, *Contraception*, 401).

20. Noonan, *Contraception*, 402–3.

21. Noonan, *Contraception*, 400.

22. On the nuances therein, Noonan argues that the 1851 decree "was firm, but comparatively restrained." The strongest note of censure applied was "erroneous" rather than "heretical." On the implications therein, Noonan says that "the propositions were thereby characterized as untrue in terms of Christian theology, but not formally contrary to the faith" (*Contraception*, 403). Noonan's larger contention is that these decrees were relatively mild and that the rapid increase in contraceptive practice and the internationalization of its propaganda during the next seventy-five years led to the Catholic Church becoming increasingly strict and proactive on this topic (406).

ternally directed pastoral policy and its outwardly directed rhetoric away from the "don't ask, don't tell policy" that had prevailed in the mid-nineteenth century to an overt and proactive condemnation of contraception. In America, as in Europe, the shift was related to a perceived increase in the breadth and influence of the organized movement favoring contraception.

Ryan began to work toward a reorientation of internal church practice regarding contraception as well as toward making the church's position more visible to non-Catholics. However, the manner in which he did so in his outward-directed rhetoric will be of particular note here. After writing the article on the history of marriage in the *Catholic Encyclopedia* (1910) making no mention of contraception, Ryan penned a piece directed at other Catholic priests in *Ecclesiastical Review* titled "Family Limitation" (1916). There, he argued with frankness that the proliferation of contraceptive advocates meant that priests must henceforth "overcome their inhibitions to publicly address the problem of contraception."[23] The following year, 1917, the Catholic Church issued a new codification of its canon law that defined marital sexuality quite legalistically. Although conceding that there were secondary benefits to marriage, the state of matrimony itself was defined almost wholly in terms of procreation, a state the code described contractually as "the exclusive and perpetual right over the body of the partner as regards the acts capable in themselves of generating offspring."[24] This definition added grist to the mill whereby priests were to make sure that marital intercourse was procreative in intent.

Ryan influenced American Catholic bishops' discussion of contraception in their joint pastoral addresses from the early twentieth century; the bishops' 1919 pronouncement used Ryan's arguments

23. McGreevy, *Catholicism and American Freedom*, 158. This meant both in sermons and in the confessional.

24. "Haec ignorantia post pubertatem non praesumitur." *Codex Iuris Canonici*, canon 1081, §2 (1917), http://www.jgray.org/codes/cic17lat.html. Marriage fell short of its own definition if no such exchange occurred. It should be noted that the 1917 definition was not new but rather a reemphasis on the legal model first articulated under Pope Alexander III (r. 1159–81).

as a baseline in their discussion.[25] After this decree was issued and
read in all American Catholic parishes on February 22, 1920, the
Catholic hierarchy became associated with strong opposition to
the birth control movement.[26] With contraception now openly
addressed from the pulpit, in the confession box, and in bishops'
newspaper articles, the American Catholic Church's official stance
was set for the interwar period. Ryan would contribute more to that
official stance as director of the NCWC's Social Action department
throughout the 1920s, but his noteworthy pronouncements from
that corner were more tentative than his individual contributions
to the birth control discourse.[27] The significant internal role Ryan
played in the institutional Catholic Church's rigorous opposition to
birth control by the end of World War I rendered the influence of
his own later rhetoric, seen below, all the more ironic.

Soon after the onset of the world's economic depression, the
institutional church made its most official and binding proclamation ever on contraception. It came in the form of Pope Pius XI's
December 1930 encyclical letter, *Casti Connubii*. Framed in a broad
discussion of marriage and family, this decree marked the first instance of the papacy itself directly addressing birth control and
sterilization. Its timing was important, too, since the scientific understanding of women's ovulation had advanced significantly right
around that time, bringing into consideration the new, ostensibly
scientific, rhythm method of birth prevention. The encyclical and
its influence are considered in chapter six. Here, it is simply noted
that *Casti Connubii*, objecting to both contraception and sterilization, was of such public significance that it played a noteworthy
role in the development of American birth control discourse itself.

As averred above, it is a given that Ryan was the major archi-
tect of American Catholic rhetoric on contraception. Ryan's op-

25. Noonan, *Contraception*, 423–24.
26. Noonan, *Contraception*, 424.
27. For an explanation of this difference, see Paula Viterbo, "The Promise of Rhythm: The
Determination of the Woman's Time of Ovulation and Its Social Impact in the United States,
1920–1940" (PhD diss., SUNY Stony Brook, 2000), 281.

positional verbiage is seen through his publications, his political activism, and his directorship of the NCWC's Social Action department. Given the scale of Ryan's involvement in the American birth control story, the intent here is not comprehensive coverage but rather consideration of Ryan's main rhetorical themes. These are approached through the lens of several key pieces to discern continuity and change in his approach, particularly toward the end of the 1920s. Ryan brought American Catholicism squarely into the American birth control debate in a manner that ultimately helped shift the ground rules of that debate.

Although Ryan's rhetoric eventually came to focus on social science proofs, it was also rooted in what had been traditional American tropes of rugged individualism and self-sacrifice. Ryan saw himself as representing both genuine American and genuine Christian values. He also saw himself as an exemplar of traditional American liberalism. In 1926, he wrote a letter to Paul Hutchinson, editor of the liberal Protestant *Christian Century* magazine, beginning with "As a Catholic and an American liberal." His sense of what the second half of this identity meant was becoming increasingly discordant for the left, especially as postwar assumptions about what constituted a healthy psyche jettisoned older Protestant-influenced values, which centered on self-control and delay of gratification. At the same time, an emphasis on individualism eclipsed an older faith in political majoritarianism.[28] Some of Ryan's stances as a liberal would ultimately sound discordant to the interwar left.[29] But it was the obscuring of the first half of that aforementioned identity—of whatever was uniquely Catholic in his birth control rhetoric—that concerns us here. Ryan's expressed

28. Ryan to Hutchinson (September 2, 1926), in Ryan Papers, box 14, folder 7, ACUA.

29. Thomas Haskell characterized these changes as a shift "from a formalist understanding of the human self in which self-denial, temperance and education were the solutions to economic [and social] stress toward an antiformalist understanding that stressed social explanations for individual crises" (Haskell quoted in McGreevy, *Catholicism and American Freedom*, 130). On the shift in currents as concerned birth control, see Gordon, *Woman's Body, Woman's Right*, 179.

ideas on contraception often tied in to his notions on economics, both international and domestic.

Ryan rigorously argued in numerous public statements that poverty had to be compassionately, aggressively, and progressively dealt with, although never by means that defied the divine order. Even when Ryan wrote for Catholic readers, it was not in biblical revelation or in tradition but rather in natural law where this order was to be discerned. When writing for non-Catholics, he characterized the outcome for a society that turned against that natural order not in terms of sin and its consequences but rather in terms of a failure of national survival on the world stage, where "flabbiness of will," "laziness," and "mediocrity of intellect" would lead to "an inefficient character" and, thus, national disaster.[30] Ryan's rhetoric essentially constituted a Catholic gospel of efficiency expressed in the language of social consequences rather than of religiosity or spiritual efforts. When he addressed the public arena, it was in the role of a sociologist or industrial ethicist, not of a theologian.

Ryan's social science discourse was inseparably tied to his domestic push for aggressive economic restructuring. As a result, his rhetoric became that much more pointed with the depression of the 1930s.[31] As Pope Leo had put it, even capitalism was expendable if it led a state to defy the natural law.[32] Ryan's language of reform, increasingly secular over time, included admonitions to avoid social degeneration triggered by abandoning the traditional use of marital sexuality for what he characterized as selfish pleasure-seeking.[33]

30. John A. Ryan, *Questions of the Day* (Boston: Stratford Co., 1931), 269.

31. The parts of Ryan's economic thinking in the 1920s discernibly derived from Catholic sources were usually drawn from Pope Leo XIII's socioeconomic encyclical of 1891, *Rerum Novarum*, or The Condition of Labor, itself the best articulation of the living wage idea subsequently championed by Ryan himself.

32. It was no coincidence that only four months after *Casti Connubii*, Pope Pius XI issued another encyclical treating of the world's economic order titled *Quadragesimo Anno*, or Forty Years Having Passed (since *Rerum Novarum*). *Quadragesimo Anno*'s subtitle indicated its ambition: "Reconstruction and Perfection of the Social Order." For a solid overview, see Thomas C. Kohler, "*Quadragesimo Anno*," in *A Century of Catholic Social Thought*, ed. George Weigel and Robert Royal, 27–44 (Washington, D.C.: Ethics and Public Policy Center, 1991).

33. Tobin, *American Religious Debate*, 69.

Ryan and Birth Control in the Public Square of the 1910s

John Ryan's first influential statement on birth control came in his entry on Malthusianism and neo-Malthusianism (1913) in the original *Catholic Encyclopedia*. There he characterized contraception as rotten fruit from a rotten neo-Malthusian tree that warped one's sense of social and personal obligations. At the same time, he offered a neoscholastic critique of it. In his words, contraception led to "varying degrees of egotism, materialism and self indulgence."[34] Ryan insisted on the practical superiority of systemic economic reorientation over any scheme of birth control, saying that from the industrial perspective, "Neo-Malthusianism soon defeats its own end.... If the restriction of offspring were confined to the poorer classes, their labour would indeed become scarce relatively to the higher kinds of labour, and their wages would rise, provided that their productivity were not diminished through deterioration of character." He added a "however," saying "the comfortable classes adopt the method much more generally than do the poor, with the result that the excessive supply of unskilled labour is increased rather than diminished.[35] Again, however, Ryan did not ground his argument in this early piece *exclusively* on negative social consequences; he also offered a natural-law-based critique, even employing the tell-tale "intrinsic immorality" claim about contraception so characteristic of neoscholastic argumentation at the time.[36]

In the summer of 1915, the United States was edging ever closer to entering the Great War raging in Europe amidst Germany's

34. Tobin, *American Religious Debate*, 67.

35. John A. Ryan, "Theories of Population," in *Catholic Encyclopedia* (New York: The Encyclopedia Press, 1913). http://en.wikisource.org/wiki/Catholic_Encyclopedia_(1913)/Theories_of_Population.

36. Ryan, "Theories of Population." His words in this early source, avowedly aimed at Catholic readers, were: "The practices [and consequences of neo-Malthusianism] are intrinsically immoral, implying as they do either foeticide, or the perversion of natural faculties and functions, to say nothing of their injurious effect upon physical health" (Ryan, "Theories of Population").

pronouncements about superior biology as a causal constituent of a stronger body politic. Ryan was simultaneously launching his major campaigns in a birth control war then heating up in the domestic public square. In August 1915, he penned a response to Mary Alden Hopkins's article "The Catholic Church and Birth Control" for *Harper's Weekly*. Ryan opposed Hopkins partly on the basis of biblical interpretation, a rare practice for him. In this case, it was elicited by Hopkins's own use of biblical arguments. Ryan used the Bible sparingly, however, clearly stating that it was not the best place to look for moral arguments refuting contraception. While Hopkins went to the "St. James Bible [*sic*]" in her search for "God's Law," Ryan preferred appealing to philosophy.[37]

Hopkins claimed that Christianity was open to contraception since the Bible offered no overt opposition. Ryan's counterargument centered on anachronism: the Bible, he said, could not be expected to explicitly condemn things impossible until many centuries after it was composed. Making this case, however, he seemed to ignore the fact that the ancient world employed numerous tactics that sought—sometimes successfully—to separate sexual intercourse from pregnancy.[38] Ryan countered Hopkins's biblical arguments with one of his own that revolved around the then-popular Catholic interpretation of the story of Onan in Genesis chapter 38.

In this story, a personage named Onan was bound by Jewish law to have sexual congress with his widowed sister-in-law in order to continue the family's progeny. Contemporary Catholic interpretation suggested the fault lay in Onan's manner of avoiding impregnation. Ryan thus contended: "The description of the punishment of Onan certainly involves an *implicit* condemnation of *all* preventive devices, of the *principle* of artificial prevention, not merely of the particular artifice used by Onan."[39]

37. Mary Alden Hopkins, "The Catholic Church and Birth Control," *Harper's Weekly* 60 (June 26, 1915): 609.

38. See Noonan, for example, on practices in the Roman Empire in *Contraception*, 10–20.

39. John A. Ryan, "The Catholic Church and Birth Control," letter to the editor, *Harper's Weekly* 61 (August 7, 1915): 144.

One problem with Ryan's argument lay in its apodictic tone, evident, for instance, in the following statement: "Such has been the interpretation of this passage invariably given by Christian authorities."[40] Certainly, variant arguments had been made by individual Protestants, as well as by Orthodox, and even by Catholics, over time.[41] Even when Ryan might have profited by introducing his own biblically based claim, he preferred to invoke Cicero rather than the Bible's book of Jeremiah to make his point about the importance of God having implanted a law in nature and in the human heart. As he put it, "The Scriptures do not even profess to furnish such full and satisfactory ethical instruction. Hence we Catholics seek both the principles and doctrines, not only in the Bible but ... in the natural moral law, 'that unwritten law,' to quote the words of Cicero, 'which is inborn, which we have derived from nature herself, and from which is the highest reason.'"[42]

Later in his response, Ryan expressed confidence that the Catholic teaching about birth control's illicit nature would never change: "The Church condemns, and ten thousand years hence will condemn, the artificial prevention of conception as something unnatural and essentially contrary to the moral law."[43] This absolute confidence was buttressed with a threat of sorts based on the consequences of abandoning that nineteenth-century American tradition of self-denial: "[The Catholic Church] will forever forbid

40. Ryan, "Catholic Church," 144.

41. Although certain Patristic figures, such as St. Clement of Alexandria, may be argued to have referred to Onan in this way (see Clement of Alexandria, *The Instructor of Children* 2:10:91:2), the connection was not clear in the second millennium Roman Catholic Church. In the sixteenth century, the *Catechism* did not appeal to the story of Onan in its condemnation of attempts to avoid impregnation. It used instead the example of Jacob and Rachel (Gn 28–30) to discuss the positive purposes of marriage (Noonan, *Contraception*, 359–60). The story of Onan became more associated with masturbation. The use of Onan's name to describe *coitus interruptus* seems to have re-emerged in Roman Catholic sources in the nineteenth century. Mary Alden Hopkins's article against Ryan, at any rate, treated withdrawal as scientifically inferior to the rational birth control she would advocate: "In passing it should be mentioned that this somewhat crude method of limiting families [withdrawal] is as severely censured by modern neurologists today as it was by the ancient prophet" (Hopkins, "Catholic Church," 609).

42. Ryan, "Catholic Church," 144.

43. Ryan, "Catholic Church," 144.

the Sacraments to those of its members who weakly yield to the temptation to indulge in this perverse and debasing practice."[44]

After joining to this a line of argument that must have sent shivers up the spines of those anti-Catholic Progressives who feared American "race suicide" (i.e., promising birth controllers that "the more extensively their recommendations were followed, the sooner the Catholic element will become predominant in our population"), Ryan then added a clever spin on co-opted Darwinian language.[45] The resulting rhetoric would surely have resonated with a *Harper's* pre–World War I readership, imbued with the assumptions of Herbert Spencer's notion of survival of the fittest. Ryan joined together all the factors previously listed: "The Catholic element will survive because it is the fittest to survive, because it will conserve those moral qualities of self-control, self-sacrifice, endurance, and loyalty to God and the soul which are the principal conditions of survival in the competitive struggle for survival among human beings."[46] Continuing in the virile, masculine-inflected language of the day—favored by the likes of Theodore Roosevelt—Ryan triumphantly concluded by vowing that "We [Catholics] shall protect ourselves against ... rotten hearts and flabby intellects.... In the nurture of human beings, quantity cannot be had without quality, [so] we shall rejoice that our view of the moral aspect of birth control compels us to provide for both the quantity and the quality."[47] This Catholic triumphalism on birth control would recede as the anti-Catholic 1920s followed in the wake of events such as A. Mitchell Palmer's crusade against the immigrants, whom many associated with the first Red Scare, and would increase during the

44. Ryan, "Catholic Church," 144.
45. Ryan, "Catholic Church," 144.
46. Ryan, "Catholic Church," 144.
47. Ryan, "Catholic Church," 144. As contemporary surveys from the interwar years reveal, Ryan's optimism on the extent to which Catholics would actually heed the prohibition on birth control was itself rather unwarranted. See, for example, Joseph J. Spengler, "The Decline in Birth-Rate of the Foreign Born," *Scientific Monthly* 32 (January 1931): 54–59; and Samuel A. Stouffer, "Trends in Fertility of Catholics and Non-Catholics," *American Journal of Sociology* 41 (September 1935): 143–66.

social struggles that came with the Great Depression. But in 1915, those were not the clouds on the horizon.

Ryan's two initial attempts to put a natural-law-based argument into the language of inductivism and practical science—and even to mix deductive and inductive reasoning—led to a pattern whereby he would move toward argumentation garbed almost wholly in inductive science. As critics pointed out, the prescriptions he would make eventually became inconsistent. Other legitimate critiques against Ryan's broader inconsistency would come when his birth control rhetoric was compared with his rhetoric on state enforcement of Prohibition and sterilization. Ryan eventually did a public about-face on both of these. In some cases, the rhetorical fracture would lead Ryan to proffer overtly inconsistent social prescriptions; other times, his conclusions seemed neoscholastic and thoroughly Catholic but were veiled behind a rhetoric of scientific, utilitarian pragmatism. In both scenarios, he de facto contributed to the rise of social scientific, efficiency-grounded arguments' hegemony in the public sphere. About areas other than contraception, scholar Joseph Chinnici, OFM, has suggested that Ryan's fracturing of spirituality from social justice—and the world of the church from his church in the world—ended up contributing to both the secularization of social discourse and the accommodation of his church to values not its own.[48]

Ryan in the 1920s

As a sample of Ryan's shifting public discourse in contraception in the 1920s, we consider the major themes of three pieces, from 1925, 1927, and 1930.[49] Five major lines of argument characterize the

48. Joseph Chinnici, *Living Stones: The History and Structure of Catholic Spiritual Life in the United States* (New York: MacMillan Publishing, 1989), 145.

49. The first of the three pieces was Ryan's "Social Questions: 'Arguments' for Birth Control," *Catholic Charities Review* 9 (May 1925): 175–78. This article critiqued the published material from the Sixth Annual Birth Control Conference held in New York City earlier in 1925. The second was Ryan's debate with a Protestant minister, G. A. Studdert Kennedy, who was more sympathetic to birth control than Ryan was: John A. Ryan, "Is Birth Control Right?—A

pieces, allowing for some verbatim overlap.[50] Ryan's most prevalent tack was to claim that those who refrained from birth control retained the practical virtues of "self-control," "hard work," and "sacrifice," which he presented as being the bases of individual and social "efficiency."[51] In other words, a society composed of families possessing these virtues—families of a kind that were lost when home environments were characterized by the self-aggrandizing attitudes of those who practiced contraception—would be "fitter," and thus have more of the moral fiber needed to build up a robust society and economy. Essentially, Ryan fused these qualities together into a formula for efficiency; abandoning such a formula would, by contrast, bring about individual and social dissolution.[52] Ryan promised that Catholics would not practice birth control and thus would become more fit and thus dominate the rest of the population should the latter fall into the contraceptive morass.[53] His wording in the 1925

Debate II—The Wrong of It," *The Forum* 78 (July 1927): 15–19. Ryan indicated that he had been asked to "make his case in terms of the health and happiness of the human race" in this piece (15). The third was composed in 1930 but before the December 31 issuing of the papal encyclical *Casti Connubii*. It was a chapter in Ryan's book *Questions of the Day* (268–73). This book was widely reviewed both inside and outside the American Catholic community. Several of the reviews highlighted the birth control chapter as one of the most significant. For a spectrum of clippings from its journal and newspaper writeups, see Ryan Papers, box 73, folder 16, ACUA.

50. Also worth considering is a fourth article found in Ryan's papers but, in part because it was undated and in part because its presentation was very similar to the 1925 piece already included, I did not include the fourth article in the analyzed set here. On the basis of the dates referenced within, I would estimate that it originated around 1925, the same year as Ryan's "The Sociological Aspect of Birth Control," *Trained Nurse and Hospital Review* (ca. 1925), 734–39, in Ryan Papers, box 48, folder 11, ACUA. Both this piece and the published one critiqued the 1925 Birth Control Conference, although the article in the *Trained Nurse and Hospital Review* focused more closely on Henry Pratt Fairchild's warnings about overpopulation as a goad to birth control—population claims which Ryan dismissed as "unscientific" (Ryan, "Sociological Aspect of Birth Control," 738).

51. Ryan, "Social Questions," 177; Ryan, "Is Birth Control Right?"; Ryan, *Questions of the Day*, 269, 273.

52. Back in 1915, Ryan had presented this same set of qualities in the language of masculinity via a letter declining an invitation to join the Birth Control League: "I am invited to send two dollars for membership in the Birth Control League. I must respectfully decline, with the observation that I had much rather give the money to an organization for the training of prize fighters. It would aid in the development of at least *some* manly and human qualities" (Ryan quoted in Hopkins, "Catholic Church," 610).

53. Hopkins, "Catholic Church," 610.

piece was most succinct (and pragmatic) in the claim that living in line with the Catholic moral code was the only way that was "practically consistent with national welfare, social justice, and a morally efficient race of human beings."[54]

Ryan's second most emphasized argument in these articles from the 1920s focused on demographics and statistics. His main contention in these arenas was that birth control advocates' use of demographic evidence to substantiate their positions was "flagrantly unscientific," especially when they claimed that the declining birth rate was being offset by a declining death rate.[55] Once birth control became the norm, he said, the population would inevitably decline, something he referred to as an argument of "social psychology."[56] Along with his demographic assertions, Ryan more than once approvingly cited the conclusions of Louis Dublin of the Metropolitan Life Insurance Company, a very visible but somewhat iconoclastic statistician active in interwar population debates. Ryan contrasted Dublin's warnings about population decline via dropping birth rates with the impending threat of overpopulation cautioned by demographers that had been cited by prominent proponents of both eugenics and birth control.[57]

Ryan's three remaining major themes can be classified as operating in the realm of the economic and the psychological, often combining appeals to both. Ryan critiqued birth control proponents as elites who demanded the poor do something they would not expect from their own kind: purposely depriving oneself of "normal" family life when economically challenged. They demanded this, he said, "instead of putting the responsibility for low wages

54. Ryan, "Social Questions," 178.
55. Ryan, "Is Birth Control Right?," 17.
56. Ryan, "Social Questions," 176; Ryan, "Is Birth Control Right?," 17; Ryan, *Questions of the Day*, 270–71.
57. Ryan, "Social Questions," 175–76. Dublin played a major role in the public sphere's demographics debates in both the 1920s and the 1930s; he was president of the American Statistical Association. In articles featuring a dizzying array of statistics and projections of the birth rate into the future, Dublin cited the expanding practice of birth control as a major cause of what he saw as a dangerous pattern, population decline. Louis Dublin, "Birth Control: What It Is Doing to America's Population?," *The Forum* 96 (November 1931): 270, 272.

and the evil industrial conditions upon the industrial system ...
and seeking industrial justice."[58] Ryan's alternative to this model
was based on his aforementioned premise that all workers had an
innate right both to a family and to a "living wage" paid to support
them. In arguing that it would make far more sense to adjust industrial relations, Ryan accused those who disagreed with him of
"blaming the victim[s]" of poverty and punishing them for what
they were suffering as the result of the elites' transparent greed.[59]

Ryan analogized between contemporary birth control advocates'
demographic and economic arguments and the nineteenth-century
British upper class's espousal of Malthusianism in order to shift the
blame for working-class misery from off their shoulders. He said
contraception advocates were using the same logic to comfort their
own consciences when, in reality, they were themselves "exploiters"
and "oppressors."[60] Extending this aspect of his critique—almost indistinguishable from its Marxist sibling—Ryan employed the Marxist epithet "bourgeois" to characterize birth control advocates (and
those advocating state-sponsored sterilization for the same reasons)
in two of the articles.[61]

Ryan also employed what can be called a slippery slope argument. He contended it was a basic truth of human nature—as evidenced by social science studies—that people who became habit-
uated to a lenitive practice that they would not otherwise resort to
except under duress would subsequently make such expedients the
norm. In this way, he argued, they would lose both the strength and
the will to endure similar hardships, thus resulting in an overall
steady weakening of character. As Ryan put it, "all our knowledge
of psychology" indicates that people who resort to birth control
from a sense of not being able to afford children surely would not
stop the practice simply because their economic lot improved.[62]

58. Ryan, "Social Questions," 176.
59. Ryan, "Social Questions," 176; Ryan, "Is Birth Control Right?," 18.
60. Ryan, "Social Questions," 177.
61. Ryan, "Social Questions," 177; Ryan, "Is Birth Control Right?," 18.
62. Ryan, "Is Birth Control Right?," 19; Ryan, Questions of the Day, 270.

The last of Ryan's main claims was that birth control advocates and eugenicists who thought they could encourage putatively "fit" parents to reproduce in greater numbers by appealing to their sense of duty to the nation and the human race were both naïve and ignorant of human psychology. This argument was the positive eugenics antitype to directed birth control, although both were part of a similar race hierarchy model of bettering society. Certain "race" groups were directly encouraged to either procreate—if scientists classified their group as being of good stock—or refrain from doing so—if instead they were classified as being of poor stock.

By contrast, Ryan contended that contracepting parents and children raised in small families—themselves naturally less driven to competition, hard work, or study—would not look beyond their own desires and needs. Such were by temperament the last sorts of people who would respond to a call to fulfill their obligations to the larger human race.[63] He argued that it was the pursuit of luxury and ease over the duties of child-rearing that generally led such people to practice contraception in the first place.[64]

It should be noted that interspersed throughout these arguments about human psychology in his 1925 and 1927 pieces, Ryan did mention the neoscholastic expression *intrinsic immorality*, although he no longer attempted to justify why or how contraception fell into this category. Its deductive rationale, best exemplified by Fr. Thomas Mahoney's August 1928 article in the Catholic *Ecclesiastical Review*, was that contraception was inherently "gravely sinful" since it not only assailed the obvious prime purpose of sex—procreation—but also involved *perverting a faculty*. In neoscholastic terms, the "generative faculty," expressed in the sex act, would be employed for a purpose other than that for which it was first created: procreation.[65]

---

63. Ryan, "Social Questions," 177.
64. Ryan, "Is Birth Control Right?," 16; Ryan, "Social Questions," 178.
65. Mahoney's was the classic 1920s' Catholic argument against contraception on the basis of deductive neoscholasticism. See Thomas Mahoney, "The 'Perverted Faculty' Argument against Birth Prevention," *Ecclesiastical Review* 74 (August 1928): 133–45; see also the

Mahoney argued that Catholics who participated in mainline birth control discourse needed to make their deductive philosophical premises *more* obvious, not less, by defining the word *unnatural* in its technical, philosophical sense, meaning that the word referred to formal, rather than material, results of human acts. If they did so, he believed, non-Catholic listeners would stop assuming the word was meant in the mere physiological sense of doing something not found elsewhere in nature. Mahoney grounded this call for more overt neoscholastic explanations by pointing out that a reader who doesn't accept natural law Catholic argumentation against contraception—and believes merely that the latter decry birth control because "unnatural"—could easily refute that argument by appealing to what is natural in the animal kingdom, such as observed homosexual activity.[66] Mahoney added that if Catholic writers followed his advice, they could effectively demonstrate that contraception was intrinsically unnatural and could adhere to the "perverted faculty" argument as to *why* it was unnatural.[67]

Instead, Ryan consistently argued that it was the ends, demonstrated by empirical evidence of human beings' mental, physical, and intellectual failures resulting from abandoning moral order, that best demonstrated why artificial contraception was a mistake.[68] It some ways, this manner of arguing undermined what Ryan actually contended and encouraged his opponents to simply retort that his psychology claims and demographic statistics were wrong or not the majority view in those professions.

As alluded to earlier, Ryan argued the way he did because he

summation and commentary on this article in a review of "The 'Perverted Faculty' Argument against Birth Prevention," by Thomas Mahoney, *Fortnightly Review* (August 15, 1928): 320. (This latter piece was printed without an author's name but was labeled in Ryan's papers as having been authored by noted Catholic moral theologian Arthur Preuss [Ryan Papers, box 33, folder "Preuss, Dr. Arthur," ACUA].)

66. Mahoney, "'Perverted Faculty' Argument," 136–37.

67. Mahoney, "'Perverted Faculty' Argument," 134–35, 137.

68. Ryan, "Is Birth Control Right?," 19. In *Questions of the Day*, Ryan's assertions about the naturally negative consequences of violating the moral law are backed up by an odd appeal to none other than Henry George from his socialist economic treatise *Progress and Poverty* (Ryan, *Questions of the Day*, 272).

himself did not fully *believe* the Catholic neoscholastic argument against contraception. Therefore—and not merely for tactical reasons—instead of shoring up the natural law explanation for why contraception was wrong, his corpus of public discourse laid the groundwork for both Catholics and non-Catholics to dismantle it in the 1930s. In setting up this unintended consequence, Ryan would have special help from John Montgomery Cooper. This will become clearer below in the examination of their pronouncements in the latter half of 1928.

A "Perversion of Faculties"?

Two and three months after Thomas Mahoney's article had appeared in the Catholic clergy monthly *Ecclesiastical Review*, Ryan and Cooper both wrote long letters to the editor critiquing it. Cooper's letter built upon Ryan's and extended it, but Ryan's was the one that broke new ground. His criticism centered on Mahoney's use of a certain phrase to describe why contraception was inherently wrong. The phrase was: "opposed to the good of [humans'] rational nature."[69] Ryan asked, "How shall this phrase be interpreted? In the sense of consequences? Or in the sense of intrinsic badness?"[70] He pointed out that Mahoney had argued the latter, and that "all the writers of treatises on moral theology" agree.[71] What Ryan said next, however, implied not only that he doubted the neoscholastic stance in the matter but also that he himself had long defended it while doubting its logical implications: "while I have consistently accepted and defended this view myself, I have never found it entirely free from difficulty."[72]

A rather extensive critique followed. It rested partially on a scenario that would explode into the open two years later with the

---

69. Mahoney quoted in John A. Ryan, "The Immorality of Contraception," letter to the editor, *Ecclesiastical Review* 74 (October 1928): 408.

70. Ryan, "Immorality of Contraception," 408.

71. Ryan, "Immorality of Contraception," 408.

72. Ryan, "Immorality of Contraception," 408.

promulgation of *Casti Connubii*: that of having intercourse when it was known that no conception was possible. Here, Ryan gave several common examples of situations where natural law, and thus the Catholic Church, allowed for just such a thing to occur: "that portion of the intramenstrual period when conception is improbable, or during pregnancy, when it is impossible, or in case one or both parties are sterile."[73] These cases were, he said, not "grievously sinful," as contraception was said to be; in fact, they were not sinful at all. The fact that the parties knew that conception was not possible did not forbid them from rationally using their generative organs—going through all the usual motions, so to speak. Ryan correctly pointed out that whether one purposely contrived or incidentally timed intercourse so that no pregnancy was possible, the basic fact was that sex for purposes entirely separate from the primary purpose of procreation was sometimes considered morally faultless. He went on to say that if there were any case scenarios in which it was "morally blameless" to have sex without any possibility of producing a baby, then it could not be said that having intercourse in absence of "the primary end" of sexuality was always inherently wrong. That is, purposely nonprocreative sex was not always a "perversion" of the "faculty" of sexual congress. And if it was not always wrong, then it was not *inherently* wrong.[74] Ryan admitted that this opening left a vast chasm that could logically apply to any use of the genitalia in the absence of the possibility of conception and that there was no way to argue when, on the basis of neoscholastic primary and secondary ends reasoning, it was unacceptable.

73. Ryan, "Immorality of Contraception," 409. It should be noted that neoscholastic philosophy did leave room within the moral sphere for the secondary ends of an act. In the case of marital intercourse, these would be things such as "relief from concupiscence or promotion of mutual love" (Ryan, 409). Key, however, was that these secondary ends were never to be pursued without an openness to the act's primary purpose. In the case of sex, this would be procreation. One was not forbidden to take pleasure in the secondary ends—for example, in the act of eating itself. All elements in the human experience of sexuality—primary and secondary—were licit, to use the technical term, albeit hierarchically ranked, with one being the universal, primary end.

74. Ryan, "Immorality of Contraception," 409.

In the course of his presentation, Ryan confessed that his doubts about these aspects of the neoscholastic argument had been growing for many years. He mentioned publishing an article back in 1907 that tried to prove the "intrinsic immorality" of cases when there was subjection "of man's lower to his higher nature," as in the case of seeking "'sexual satisfaction [before] he has undertaken the burdens of self-control and self-denial involved in the marital union.'" He now admitted that "as an 'intrinsic' argument this consideration does not seem to me now to have as much cogency as I attached to it in 1907."[75]

Ryan restated that the "inherently illicit" argument failed to adequately cover all cases of having sex while aware its primary end could not be fulfilled. It also did not cover certain cases where one *purposely tried to avoid* its primary end: "The couple that deliberately restricts intercourse to a certain time in the intramenstrual period also attempts to defeat the primary end; yet this aim is not condemned by the [Catholic] moralists. Nor is its attainment construed as a moral defect."[76] After poking fatal holes in certain aspects of the neoscholastic argument against contraception, Ryan proposed what he saw as a better way to make the case: the wedge theory practicality argument. Although he did not say so, what he did was to propose an inductive argument in place of what he said was the failed attempt of deductive reasoning.[77] Ryan claimed

75. Ryan, "Immorality of Contraception," 410. The earlier article he referred to appeared in the modernist journal of Dunwoodie seminary, the *New York Review*, when he was a professor at St. Paul's Seminary in Minnesota. See John A. Ryan, "Method of Teleology."

76. Ryan, "Immorality of Contraception," 410.

77. Ryan never admits he is doing this, nor is it certain that he was even conscious of substituting one for the other. He himself closed up one neoscholastic loophole in which he might have otherwise taken refuge by calling his proposal deductivist. Neoscholastic argumentation permitted one to argue not only in terms of intent but also in terms of consequences. The consequences were rational deductions about the bad things that would necessarily happen—especially to other innocent parties—as a result of one's morally illicit behavior. Ryan invoked the case of a man fathering an illegitimate child and abandoning it, a case that had been brought up by Aquinas, to say that this deductive-consequences reasoning did *not* apply to contraception. Aquinas had pointed out that an innocent child suffered the consequences of the original sex act and, thus, that the sexual immorality had this additional aspect, but Ryan pointed out that this consequences argument could not be used as an absolute criterion in setting standards for sex since "many actions are morally lawful, even though they fall under the category of [venial]

that this approach was in full accord with deductive logic provided that one took into account the fact that he was not arguing on the grounds of direct consequences but, instead, was emphasizing the principle of indirect consequences.[78] Ryan's stated reason for employing this slippery slope argument was, in short, that it was based on evidence he brought from psychology, demography, and other social sciences. It should be emphasized that when he argued publicly in those terms, he was not just using the sort of framings most acceptable to non-Catholics for convenience's sake or to persuade non-Catholic elites who were dismissive of deductivism. He was basing his own case on induction. That is what left his arguments open to co-opting or rejection on his own terms by his opponents. All they had to do was to purport to have disproven his social science statistics or to have undermined his other empirical evidence.

Ryan as much as admitted he was skating on thin ice but averred that no other course was available. He said that if the Catholic Church admitted that the ban on contraception was not morally or logically justified in every case, then people would hasten to practice contraception. Notwithstanding the fact that this article appeared in a Catholic magazine specifically targeted to other priests, he actually said nothing in religious language about a fallen human nature, only that he knew his contentions to be true based on what psychology had demonstrated. As Ryan put it, "in certain rarely occurring situations contraception can probably take place without any direct evil results to the individuals or to society," but the indirect consequences of permitting these exceptions were too dangerous to countenance.[79]

Ryan's final claims in this article rested on a combination of

---

sins. They are given a special classification in conformity with their special nature or circumstances. It would seem that the same treatment should be accorded to the irregular sexual intercourse which involves no evil consequences to children, as in the case of sterility; and likewise to birth prevention in certain restricted cases, say, when the life or health of the wife would be endangered by pregnancy" (Ryan, "Immorality of Contraception," 410). In other words, by ruling out the neoscholastic version of argument by consequences, Ryan de facto made it impossible to conclude that his own arguments by consequence were anything other than inductive.

78. Ryan, "Immorality of Contraception," 410.

79. Ryan, "Immorality of Contraception," 410.

social and individual psychology: "no community which accepts [contraception] in exceptional conditions will long restrict it to those conditions, no matter how carefully the latter may be defined by persons assuming to speak authoritatively."[80] He admitted that physicians who suggested contraception for cases where standard intercourse would endanger health made a good point—and one that was even morally sound from all angles. However, this stance, he said, could never be sanctioned because if it were, "it would receive wider extension from all persons who believed their situations to be equally urgent" and would legitimate contraception, for example, "on account of domestic friction, poverty, the desire to improve the standard of living, ... the inconveniences of childbearing and the disagreeable consequences when the parties are unmarried."[81]

Ryan's conclusion drove the point of his inductivism home: "Hence, there is no socially safe middle ground between complete prohibition of birth prevention and such general addiction to the practice as will inevitably bring about a declining population and a profound deterioration of social and individual character and competence."[82] If one theoretically questioned this utilitarian goal—which, he claimed, was a rational consequent—he had an answer for that as well: "The individual whose case is exceptional may plead that if birth prevention were restricted to situations such as his there would be no evil results, but he must recognize that he is supposing an impossibility. *Therefore he must forego [sic] the practice in the interest of the human race.*"[83]

Cooper's "Devastating Broadside"

The issue of the *Ecclesiastical Review* following Ryan's piece featured Cooper's letter to the editor piggybacking on Ryan's critique and extending it in new directions. Cooper began by saying that

80. Ryan, "Immorality of Contraception," 410–11.
81. Ryan, "Immorality of Contraception," 411.
82. Ryan, "Immorality of Contraception," 411.
83. Ryan, "Immorality of Contraception," 411 (my emphasis).

Thomas Mahoney's original argument was "the clearest and most thorough statement of the argument against birth control drawn from its 'unnaturalness' that has ... appeared in English."[84] He immediately followed that up by saying that the point itself—contraception as "grave intrinsic sinfulness"—was neither persuasive nor even correct.[85] Unlike Ryan's argument, Cooper's was partially made using religious language; reading that argument, however, one seriously wonders why any Catholic would be told to avoid contraception or would obey that injunction when faced with anything but the most ideal circumstances. After indicating that he "concur[red] heartily" with the reasons Ryan gave for his own dissent from Mahoney, Cooper said he wished to add a few "further observations."[86]

Cooper observed that even if contraception took place in a manner *not* falling into the exceptional circumstances Ryan had outlined, the most that could be said was that a *venial* sin had occurred.[87] In Catholic moral theology's hierarchy of sin as it stood, he said, "sins against rational nature" were of a type classified in a category called venial (as were "perversions of faculties") but were nothing more serious than that. Contraception was obviously defiance of the way nature would operate if unregulated, and pregnancy was clearly connected with the design of both human and animal sex organs. Thus, contraception was clearly a subversion of the natural order. No argument there, he said. But why did Catholic teaching explicitly supersede the usual assignment of *venial* for violations of the natural order in the particular case of contraception, and only in that case? The church classified contraception as always a *mortal sin*.

84. John Montgomery Cooper, "Birth Control and the 'Perverted Faculty' Argument," *Ecclesiastical Review* 79 (November 1928): 527.

85. Cooper, "Birth Control and the 'Perverted Faculty,'" 527.

86. Cooper, "Birth Control and the 'Perverted Faculty,'" 527.

87. In scholastic terminology, *veniality* indicates a sin "minor in nature," warranting a punishment of only short duration. By contrast, a *mortal sin* is one "entailing or causing spiritual death." William Morris, ed., *The American Heritage Dictionary of the English Language* (Boston: Houghton Mifflin, 1980), s.vv. "mortal sin," "veniality." For Thomas Aquinas on the distinction between the two types of sin, see *Summa Theologiae* I-II, q. 88.

How, he wondered, was that stand to be justified? Cooper pointed out that eating "for pleasure alone" was simply a venial sin.[88] Why not sex as the expression of a couple's love, or for pleasure alone, and so on?[89] He admitted that he himself could see no impediment at all—at least no philosophical or theological impediment.

Cooper attacked the perverted faculty argument by saying that Catholic authorities have offered "facile assumptions" in place of "objective evidence" as to "what precisely is the natural function of the faculty under consideration." Who is to say, for example, that the *primary* purpose of speaking is to express one's thoughts rather than to *influence* other people's thoughts?[90] Consequently, if one wanted to stick to natural law argumentation, "a more detailed formulation of the function of the reproductive faculty is imperative." Such a formulation would bar contraception in all cases but permit sex in cases like sterility. But even then, he said, the point would hardly have been made correctly: "After we have succeeded—if we succeed—in so formulating this function, just precisely what concrete evidence are we going to muster to show that our formulation, and no other, represents the true function [of sex]?"[91] All of this amounted to Cooper essentially arguing that the neoscholastic argument should be thrown overboard—not simply because it was impractical to use with non-Catholic audiences but because it itself was not correct even in its internal logic.

Cooper pointed out—more forcefully than had Ryan—what he saw as flaws with the Catholic neo-Thomist argument against contraception, flaws which he viewed as deeper than Ryan had viewed them. Given this position, one wonders why he would think that the stance against artificial contraception should be kept at all.[92]

88. Cooper, "Birth Control and the 'Perverted Faculty,'" 527.
89. Cooper, "Birth Control and the 'Perverted Faculty,'" 527.
90. Cooper, "Birth Control and the 'Perverted Faculty,'" 528–29.
91. Cooper, "Birth Control and the 'Perverted Faculty,'" 529.
92. Cooper, "Birth Control and the 'Perverted Faculty,'" 530. Cooper pointed out that in areas of ethics that concern relations between human beings, rather than relations between humans and God, "we draw our ethical conclusions from the good or evil effects that any given line of conduct has upon the individual or his neighbor or both.... It does seem a little

Cooper's own answer was that it should be kept simply so that the church would not look bad: "Were the Church to give in one inch on her adamantine stand against contraception, she would soon be impaled on one or another horn of the dilemma of stultifying and contradicting herself or of abandoning her ethics of sex all along the line."[93]

The road to intellectual respectability for Catholic contraception arguments was a road that must necessarily bypass neoscholasticism. As things stood, "it looks very much," Cooper worried, "as if we were trying a short cut to establish grave intrinsic malice in a field where the evidence ... does not lie close to the surface, and where short cuts lead, not to our destination, but up blind alleys."[94] Instead of pursuing the direction of blind alleys, Cooper offered his own map for the future; like Ryan, he believed Catholics should frame their anti-birth control arguments on an ends-based slippery slope model. The religious basis Cooper offered for this position was not tied to Catholic moral philosophy but rather to a simple biblical precept: the command to "love God and love thy neighbor as thyself."[95] Cooper's unstated assumption was that one had to rely on inductive social science evidence to justify even that—in particular, on sociological and psychological evidence about sexuality. Only in this way could one hope to prove that "all forms of unchastity ... tend to thwart the accomplishment of an objective good that is of grave importance to the individual and the race, and to undermine and corrode the spirit of subjective love."[96]

Cooper used the last several pages of his letter to elaborate on this contention. His case can be consolidated into three related contentions, two of which I will classify as psychology- and sociology-

anomalous that only or chiefly in two fields, those of speech and sex, we suddenly switch our criterion from effects of conduct or effects of misuse of human faculties to misuse of the faculty in itself" (530).

93. Cooper, "Birth Control and the 'Perverted Faculty,'" 532.

94. Cooper, "Birth Control and the 'Perverted Faculty,'" 530.

95. Cooper, "Birth Control and the 'Perverted Faculty,'" 532. This is one of the few instances where we see any appeal to the Bible in either Cooper's or Ryan's birth control discourses.

96. Cooper, "Birth Control and the 'Perverted Faculty,'" 532.

related and the other one as demographics- and statistics-based. Contraception is bad because: (1) it can be shown by observation and psychology to weaken the subjective feeling of love in tête-à-tête romantic relationships (how he "proved," or intended to prove, this is not indicated); (2) in practicing birth control, couples might not have any children, and children are known to make couples feel less self-centered (i.e., they would have to care for helpless off-spring); and finally, (3) if people practice contraception, the population will decline and the human race will eventually die out.[97] Cooper concluded by saying that all of this proved the "intrinsic immorality" of contraception.[98] How he could discredit both the premise and the proofs of Catholic deductive arguments about contraception, substitute obviously inductive proofs, and then finish by saying that they were acceptable justifications for the original deductively derived claim would be difficult to understand without some of the background on Cooper already presented in this study. At center, however, these intellectual acrobatics did not mean Cooper was supplementing the natural law argument; rather, they constituted his replacement of the natural law argument with an argument based on the consensus of social science.

Some of Cooper's contemporaries observed this very characteristic in his reasoning. One example of an extensive critique in this light appears in a long exchange of letters from the late 1920s into the 1940s between Cooper and philosophy professor Fr. Thomas Hanley, a specialist in neoscholastic philosophy at St. Martin's College in Washington, mentioned earlier. Hanley characterized Cooper's arguments on birth control as deriving from "excessive pragmatism" and "unconscious philosophical voluntarism."[99] Hanley suggested that the voluntarism was just a shade differentiated from the full-blown expostulations of Kant and Nietzsche. He actually

97. Cooper, "Birth Control and the 'Perverted Faculty,'" 532–33.
98. Cooper, "Birth Control and the 'Perverted Faculty,'" 533.
99. Thomas Hanley, untitled typescript on St. Martin's College letterhead, point 13 (n.d.), 2, in JMC Papers, box 9, folder "Hanley, Thomas," ACUA. Hanley's accusations of voluntarism appear several times sprinkled throughout the long correspondence.

characterized Cooper's analogies and examples used to justify his stance on the Catholic anti-birth control argument as "diabolically" clever.[100]

Hanley was not some simple reactionary. In correspondence with Cooper, he admitted that neoscholasticism was not monolithic, that it had its own subschools of thought, and that it would profit from much-needed scholarly vetting. He did, however, see the valuable varieties of neoscholasticism as having certain basic orientations in common. With these premises in mind, Hanley actually characterized Cooper as disingenuously using neoscholastic language to express notions antithetical to neoscholasticism on those occasions when Cooper wrote for Catholic audiences.[101] In a jab with ponderous implications, Hanley told Cooper that his analogies revealed that Cooper believed "there would be nothing fundamentally unreasonable and immoral in the practice of [artificial] contraception by some hypothetical race on another planet which would not use contraception except for due child-spacing, ill-health, or danger of the wife, and optimum population control."[102]

"Would That the Neo Scholastics Might … Re-check Their Generalizations by Scientific Data": John Montgomery Cooper and Birth Control in the 1920s' Public Forum

By the mid-1920s, John Montgomery Cooper's other pieces on birth control, whether prior or subsequent to the one in *Eccle-*

---

100. Hanley, untitled typescript, 1. Although extrinsic to the time frame of this book, a letter from Hanley in the spring of 1944 repeated the same critique of Cooper from a decade earlier, showing that Cooper's engaged interlocutor did not find Cooper's defenses persuasive: "It is a source of amazement to learn, as I have since learned from others beside yourself, that your devastating broadside against the perverted faculty argument has gone unanswered." Hanley to Cooper (May 18, 1944), 2, in JMC Papers, box 9, folder "Hanley, Thomas," ACUA. Why, if he believed this, Hanley himself did not publish such an answer to his pen-pal is unclear.

101. Hanley, untitled typescript, 1.

102. Hanley, untitled typescript, 2.

siastical Review—and whether directed both at Catholics and at a broader audience—are quite similar to each other in tone and content.[103] By then, his tendency was to abandon his earlier habit of briefly detailing the standard Catholic natural law argument at the start before proceeding to make his case entirely on empirical, psychological bases which he substantiated with the contentions of scientific experts.[104] Even by the mid-1920s, one discerns the shift. As an example, Cooper's address to the eleventh annual meeting of the National Conference of Catholic Charities on September 11, 1925, mostly ignored the natural law argument.[105] Many of the pieces featured turns of phrase and even chunks of text repeated verbatim. Sections of the above-surveyed 1928 article were themselves lifted from his own work already published elsewhere.[106] The only exceptional things about that 1928 piece were the additional sections debating the fine intricacies of neoscholasticism vis-à-vis

103. Quotation in heading is from Cooper to Karl Herzfeld (November 17, 1934), in JMC Papers, box 9, folder "Herzfeld, Dr. K. F.," ACUA. This letter was Cooper's response to a letter from his like-minded friend, who had sent him a clipping from *Science* magazine. Cooper made the cited comment in passing in such a way that it is clear the two had previously discussed their displeasure with the neoscholastic lens through which many Catholics viewed scientific issues.

104. An example from the early 1920s where Cooper still uses overt neoscholasticism to a point is his well-circulated 1923 NCWC pamphlet *Birth Control*. The first of its eight chapters was "Catholic Principles and Teaching," in which he said "Having marital relations while at the same time using physiological, mechanical or other means to prevent conception is, in accordance with Catholic ethics, ever and always immoral, sinful and grievously sinful.... Her standard is not merely a matter of church law. It is a matter of divine law over which the Church has no authority.... Artificial prevention of conception is ever and always gravely sinful, just as adultery is." John Montgomery Cooper, *Birth Control* (Washington, D.C.: NCWC, 1923), 8.

105. See the transcription of that address in John Montgomery Cooper, "Family Limitation and Human Welfare," *Salesianum* (n.d.): 22–26, in JMC Papers, box 41, folder unlabeled, ACUA. Both this and the 1923 pamphlet mentioned above were directed primarily at internal Catholic audiences, yet Cooper's discussion of the natural law argument was already almost nonexistent by the 1925 article. For an example of a piece directed at a much broader, primarily non-Catholic audience in which he made no mention at all of the standard Catholic framing, see John Montgomery Cooper, "Birth Control," letter to the editor, *The Forum* 77 (January–June 1927): 150. For another such case, see "Birth Control," (1928), in JMC Papers, box 42, folder "American Sociological Society: Speeches," ACUA (typescript indicates it was sent for inclusion in the encyclopedia series *Universal Knowledge*).

106. Compare the final paragraph on the first page of Cooper's argument in "Family Limitation," 22, with the final paragraph in Cooper, "Birth Control and the 'Perverted Faculty,'" 531. There are also other examples of verbatim duplication in these two articles.

contraception. Cooper would by no means discuss neoscholastic notions in an article on birth control written for a non-technical audience (no matter how erudite). He likely used that approach in the *Ecclesiastical Review* piece because it was the Catholic priests' trade journal of sorts. Thus, it was a forum where Cooper's detailed refutation of arguments favoring natural law and "intrinsic evil" could hope to convince the largest number of Catholic priests to stop using such persuasion, since these arguments had been inculcated into them through seminary training.

Since nearly all of Cooper's works in this arena are quite similar and even repetitive, it will not be difficult to summarize his arguments in a relatively small space. His first significant piece was the pamphlet he published for the NCWC, *Birth Control* (1923). Beyond what was already remarked about this work, it can be said that the pamphlet argued its case "not in terms of the natural law but on a social ethic of love," as a recent history of Catholicism and contraception put it.[107] After the initial chapter, the arguments were essentially psychological, eugenic, demographic, and economic, as follows:

- *Psychological*, in terms of his claims about the detrimental effects of contraception on both individual and family psyches;[108]
- *Eugenic*, as Cooper put it: "contraception has been dysgenic" and it was the so-called "fit" who actually practiced contraception. Birth control directed at "the feebleminded" was inferior to segregation and gender separation anyway; as an ideal example of the latter, Cooper pointed to the Catholic Colony in Ursberg, Germany, which featured "permanent custodial care in farming colonies ... with strict segregation of the sexes";[109]

107. Tentler, *Catholics and Contraception*, 50. The author admiringly called this publication "far and away the most sophisticated Catholic production [on birth control] of the decade" (Tentler, 50).

108. Cooper, *Birth Control*, 25–29.

109. Cooper, *Birth Control*, 50–51.

- *Demographic*, since an underpopulated nation, he said, would be "exterminated or swamped out by hardier contiguous [*sic*] or immigrant groups";[110] and
- *Economic*, with bad effects on national production.[111]

On the move toward birth control as a scientifically grounded, increasingly respectable movement, *Eugenics* magazine had published a piece by the renowned physician and contraception advocate Hannah M. Stone titled "The Birth Control Clinic" in the spring of 1929. There, Stone argued that birth control was increasingly considered a legitimate research subject for scientific scrutiny and suggested that the next decade might finally feature truly scientific birth control. In her words, "The birth control movement in America has grown very rapidly. Birth control is increasingly being recognized as a vital public problem, and no comprehensive outline for social or human betterment can leave this question out of its program." Stone went on, "Lately ... serious attention [is] being given to contraception by biologists, physicians, and scientific workers generally, and we may very well expect that much will be accomplished in the next decade or so towards the promotion of scientific birth control."[112] *Eugenics* soon after published the Marxist political advocate Mary Louise Inman's review of the National Birth Control Conference meeting in New York. It had opened by declaring that the birth control movement had finally arrived at respectability. Inman noted that five of the six officers of the American Birth Control League were listed in the *Social Register*.[113] Inman's overall case also appeared substantially augmented—and the public role of Catholics in birth control and eugenics discourse made further complicated—by her appeal to a speech made at the conference by a man named E. Boyd Barrett, formerly Fr. E. Boyd Barrett, SJ.

110. Cooper, *Birth Control*, 52.
111. Cooper, *Birth Control*, 57, 66.
112. Hannah M. Stone, "The Birth Control Clinic," *Eugenics* 2 (May 1929): 9.
113. Mary Louise Inman, "The National Birth Control Conference, Reviewed," *Eugenics* 3 (January 1930): 12.

The Catholic [Loose] Canon at the 1929 National Birth Control Conference

Edward Boyd Barrett was a Catholic liberal and former Jesuit professor on the psychology faculty at Georgetown University who had enjoyed some significant prestige and notoriety in the American Catholic intellectual community up until the mid-1920s.[114] But his interest in the New Psychology and his increasing criticism of Catholicism led him to leave the priesthood in 1925 to engage more fully in the day's progressive debates. In 1929, Mary Louise Inman reported to her readers in *Eugenics* magazine about Barrett's speech at the recent National Birth Control Conference that showed him citing statistics suggesting that many Catholics already employed contraception. A few months earlier in the same magazine, she had also noted Barrett's claim that there was real division of opinion between Catholics in Rome and Catholics in America.[115] Inman pointed to Barrett's contention in his speech that the Roman Catholic Church would "eventually align itself [in favor of birth control] with the most progressive thought of the day instead of clinging to the traditions which even its own members are ceasing to respect or follow."[116]

Barrett was doubtless an unusual case, but it was lost on no one at the time that this very visible advocate of artificial contraception was himself a former Catholic priest. Having been published several times over the years in important Catholic periodicals, including *Commonweal* as late as 1925 (June 17 and 24), the once-respected liberal psychologist left the Jesuit priesthood after serving in it for

114. *America* magazine, operated by what had been Barrett's own Jesuit order, contributed to his rise and notoriety. During the editorial reign of Richard Tierney, SJ (1914–25), the magazine published six of Barrett's articles on various topics. See E. Boyd Barrett to Wilfred Parsons (September 2, 1925), in *America* Magazine Archive, box 9, folder "E. Boyd Barrett (1925–1931)," GURBSC.

115. Inman, "National Birth Control Conference," 12. On the claim by Barrett about the America-Rome division, see Mary Louise Inman, "In What Field?," *Eugenics* 2 (October 1929): 37.

116. Inman, "National Birth Control Conference," 13.

twenty years, married, and subsequently published unflattering popular books on the Jesuit order and Catholic policies, such as *The Jesuit Enigma* (1927) and *While Peter Sleeps* (1929).[117]

Oddly, even after Barrett left the priesthood and began issuing books criticizing aspects of Catholicism, *America* did not come out with a clear statement about what he had done, seemingly hoping instead that the controversy would go away on its own. This only increased the ambiguity about him and left birth control and eugenics activists freer to imply that he was little more than a progressive educated Catholic leading a charge within his own church that other reasonable Catholics would eventually come to embrace.[118]

Barrett was clear at the start of his 1929 conference speech that although he was no longer an active priest, he was still a Catholic: "I speak," he emphasized, "as one inside the Catholic Church."[119] Barrett also told the audience in his talk that "every priest knows that the Catholic people are practicing birth control."[120] Barrett also attacked compulsory clerical celibacy as "far worse than Birth Control" in eugenic terms, as "truly race suicide."[121] He also tried to emphasize that in many ways the birth control movement and the Catholic Church were already of one mind, saying, for example, that "both condemn abortion: It cannot be told in Catholic

117. Barrett did all of this only to repent and be permitted to return to the priesthood in 1948 even though married. See Donald Hayne, "Edward Boyd Barrett: Shepherd in the Midst" *America* (September 3, 1966): 230. In the same year in which Michael Williams published Barrett's articles (1925), the new editor of *America* magazine, Fr. Wilfred Parsons, SJ, put in place an official policy of censorship for anything Barrett submitted for publication going forward. See *America* Magazine Archive, box 48, folder 23, GURBSC. See also James Colgan to Parsons (January 29, 1928), in *America* Magazine Archive, box 9, folder 36, GURBSC.

118. In one instance, a communication written to *America*'s Parsons on Loyola University letterhead asked the editor to print a clear statement on Barrett since "many outsiders" had told him that it appeared like *America* was afraid to respond. Anonymous to Parsons (February 1, 1928), in *America* Magazine Archive, box 9, folder 36, GURBSC. Letters exchanged between Michael Williams and Parsons about how to deal with the Barrett situation also appear in this file. Unlike *America*, *Commonweal* did print a piece in the later 1920s criticizing Barrett, but only on the basis of him having defied the church and left the priesthood.

119. E. Boyd Barrett, "Address by Dr. E. Boyd Barrett, Hotel Astor, New York City, Tuesday, November 19, 1929. Rita C. McGoedrich (stenographic report)" (November 19, 1929), 1, in *America* Magazine Archives, box 9, folder 36, GURBSC.

120. Barrett, "Address," 2.

121. Barrett, "Address," 3.

schools that abortion is condemned in any stronger terms by the Church than by Birth Control protagonists."[122] Indeed, the *Birth Control Review* had just published a piece in November quoting its leading lights—including Margaret Sanger, Hannah Stone, Alice Hamilton, and others—strongly condemning abortion.[123]

Perhaps the most significant part of Barrett's speech at the Birth Control Conference was his statement on why the Catholic Church was wrong to prohibit birth control, a statement that likely took into account the critique discussed above by both Ryan and Cooper and published the previous year in *Ecclesiastical Review*: "I have clear proof that the Church does not regard contraception as against the natural law." He went on, "intrinsically wrong ... contraception is not."[124] One woman who wrote to the editors after reading *Eugenics*'s coverage of Barrett's talk expressed pleasure in the fact that Catholics maintained such a heterogeneity of views on birth control.[125]

Regarding the closing gap between birth control and eugenics, John Montgomery Cooper did not do anything as overt or brazen as Barrett. But his science-centered discourse, too, was open to co-option for various uses. As was his wont, Cooper maintained a tone of extreme objectivity in his publicly directed writings on the matter at hand. Contributing to a forum in the May 1929 issue of *Eugenics* on the question of whether birth control reduced the number of geniuses in society, he first called for a more careful definition of the term "genius" as opposed to "talent," saying the latter could be augmented through eugenics even as the latter also gave hope for "reduc[ing] a little the incidence of such mental

122. Barrett, "Address," 4.

123. "The Curse of Abortion," *Birth Control Review* 13 (November 1929): 307. See also Barrett's rejoinder to the Catholic bishop of Buffalo, who repudiated Barrett's claim at the Birth Control Conference that the church would eventually come around to endorse artificial contraception. E. Boyd Barrett, "Roman Catholicism and Birth Control," *Birth Control Review* 14 (January 1930): 11–12.

124. Barrett, "Address," 4.

125. Anna Garlin Spencer, "What Readers Write: Eugenics and Catholicism," *Eugenics* 3 (October 1930): 429.

defectiveness as is hereditary."[126] Providing no moral or religious critique, Cooper concluded his argument with a call for more and better science to solve the broader issue of the relationship existing among birth control, eugenics, and genius: "A few more facts, scientifically established, will help much more than all our wordy views and inconclusive guesses—including this one."[127]

The singularly secular nature of Cooper's arguments—and the interconnections he posited as potentially justifiable given more scientific research—did not go unnoticed by his associates in the AES, including Leon Whitney.[128] Later in the same issue where Cooper's essay appeared, a piece by noted eugenicist Albert Edward Wiggam drew together the supposedly related social reform movements by emphasizing their shared basis in evolution as then constructed: "The biological theory of thought is that evolution has given the organism a capacity of its own to 'hit back at the environment'—as Dewey pointed out long ago—and utilize it for its own good."[129] On such connections, Sanger's *Birth Control Review* published the sociologist and AES President Henry Pratt Fairchild's speech given at the National Birth Control conference that same year, a speech in which he argued that for managing future population improvement, "Eugenics and Birth control are inseparably linked together in a lasting relationship."[130]

Barrett's willingness to step into a light where the Roman Catholic Church could not fail to see him—including at birth control conferences—and to wholly dissent from one of its most definitive positions, while still claiming to be a good Catholic, can perhaps be said to represent a more extreme version of what Cooper,

126. John Montgomery Cooper, "The Birth Rate of Genius: Does Contraception Curb It?," *Eugenics* 2 (May 1929): 18.

127. John Montgomery Cooper, "Birth Rate of Genius," 18.

128. See, for example, Leon Whitney to Cooper, (April 21, 1931), in JMC Papers, box 19, folder "American Eugenics Society 1929–1931," ACUA.

129. Albert Edward Wiggam, "Eugenics and Evolution," *Eugenics* 2 (May 1929): 19. Evolution, he said, "proved" that the eugenic approach is superior to the euthenic approach (an approach emphasizing environmental over hereditary factors).

130. Henry Pratt Fairchild, "Birth Control and Race Improvement," *Birth Control Review* 13 (December 12, 1929): 343.

Ryan, and—as we shall see in chapter six—O'Brien did more subtly and to a lesser extent. Barrett's rhetoric was sure to be used by the church's opponents. But Barrett's hope was that the reason of modern science and rational social reform, as non-Catholics conceived of them, could eventually form a bridge between that church and progressive modernity. While Barrett's utterances sounded much like that of mainline birth control and eugenic advocates, there were ways in which they foreshadowed less shrill and overt utterances made in the 1930s by our three Catholic priests, who shared the full good graces of Barrett's church. Their utterances would operate in ways that bridged their liberal-progressive Catholicism with mainline debate even while unintentionally shearing away the bridge between sexual intercourse and pregnancy.

~ 5

In the Interest of Eugenics

Evolution and Birth Control
Come Together

Sexual Reproduction is the keystone of the whole
evolutionary structure.

—Edward Murray East (1927)

Interwar birth control debates operated within the larger social
reform ambit deriving from the Progressive movement and its organizational outgrowths. The discourse came to include and en-
compass social hygiene, the control of evolution through eugenics,
and demography. The birth control movement's interlocking organizational connections extended the progressive impetus toward
technical control of human heredity and the environment. In this
model, efficient, science-centered interventions would ostensibly
solve longstanding human ills, ending everything from sickness
and crime to, by the 1930s, economic depression.[1] It was the birth
control movement's social and intellectual proponents, led by Margaret Sanger and her professional scientist allies, who succeeded
in reconfiguring birth control after World War I into a technical,

Epigraph is from Edward Murray East, *Heredity and Human Affairs* (New York: Charles
Scribner's Sons, 1927), 70.
1. Viterbo, "Promise of Rhythm," 216.

scientific concept in eugenic framing even as they redefined periodic continence in marriage as a road to physical and psychological pathology. Shifts over the course of the 1920s culminated in the 1930 organizational link-up of the birth control and eugenics movements after what had been several years of the AES's repudiation of birth control as potentially dysgenic. This chapter examines how liberal-progressive Catholics John Montgomery Cooper and John Ryan engaged with, and influenced, debates both outside and inside the Catholic Church, debates that saw an intertwining of multiple science-centered reform discourses spanning birth control, eugenics, and social hygiene within the broader social schema of controlling heredity and evolution. The nature of this liberal-progressive Catholic engagement with such movements produced a series of unintended consequences that helped facilitate a broader belief in controlling evolution by controlling who conceived children. Likewise, in this period, artificial birth control saw itself transformed into one more technical tool in a tool chest of research and policymaking alongside measures like immigration restriction, sterilization, and eugenic marriage that were designed to rationally engineer American society and could, by the brink of the 1930s, help meet the challenges of the Depression.

Contraception and evolution had already been linked together from the nineteenth century in human origins science centered on ontogeny-phylogeny recapitulation. The recapitulationist school propounded the idea that each growing human fetus mirrored adult stage evolution through past forms. The gestating embryo's various developmental stages thereby recapitulated, in microcosm, longue durée macrocosmic human evolution. The most well-known version of recapitulation came to be known as the biogenetic law, associated with German Romantic zoologist Ernst Haeckel, although other forms of recapitulation were independently asserted in the United States by paleontologists Edward Drinker Cope, Alpheus Hyatt and Alpheus Packard.[2] Indeed, Charles Dar-

2. For a short overview of Haeckel's idea and his close connection with Darwin, see Ulrich Kutschera, Georgy S. Levit, and Uwe Hossfeld, "Ernst Haeckel (1834–1919): The German

win himself had linked large-scale origins and evolution with individual human origins and development in his volume *The Descent
of Man* (1871). Thus, despite recapitulation's debated status by the
1920s, schools of thought linking evolution and development from
conception enjoyed a prestigious pedigree, and the conclusions
themselves retained significant cultural-scientific resonance.[3]

Genetics as the Meeting Point for Evolution and Birth Control

The emergence of genetics as the research field centered on heredity, following Hugo de Vries's rediscovery of Dominican monk
Gregor Mendel's work at the turn of the twentieth century, created
a new and sure path on which evolution and birth control could
come together in the future. During the first decade of the twentieth century, scientists in various biological subfields in the United
States held to oversimplified models of human trait inheritance.
In that era, words like *breeding* and *generation*, adopted to human
sciences from animal husbandry, saw increasingly common use by
scientists as both they and others sought ways to apply insights
from genetics to influence human populations.[4]

In the 1920s, the foundation of applied genetics laid earlier in

---

Darwin and His Impact on Modern Biology," *Theory in Biosciences* 138 (2019): 1–7. Edward
Drinker Cope exerted a significant influence on Henry Fairfield Osborn, who lauded Cope as
"one of the greatest palaeontologists and anatomists America has produced" in the National
Academy of Science's biographical memoir he wrote for Cope. See Henry Fairfield Osborn,
"Biographical Memoir of Edward Drinker Cope, 1840–1897," in *National Academy of Sciences
Biographical Memoirs: Third Memoir*, vol. 13 (Washington, D.C.: National Academy of Sci-
ences, 1929), 127, 168, http://www.nasonline.org/publications/biographical-memoirs/mem-
oir-pdfs/cope-edward.pdf.

3. On Darwin making the connection, see, for example, *The Descent of Man*, 168. Recapitulation in Darwin's time was associated with the German anatomist Karl von Baer. For the
long history and scientific discussion of recapitulation, see Stephen Jay Gould, *Ontogeny and
Phylogeny* (Cambridge, Mass.: Belknap Press of Harvard University Press, 1977), esp. chaps.
3 and 4. See also Edward Larson, *Evolution: The Remarkable History of a Scientific Theory*
(New York: The Modern Library, 2004), 113–14; Bowler, *Eclipse of Darwinism*, 35–36. For a full
treatment of the orthogenesis model of evolution in the early twentieth century, encapsulating
recapitulation in various permutations, see Bowler, *Eclipse of Darwinism*, chap. 7, esp. 159–65.

4. Paul A. Lombardo, "The Power of Heredity and the Relevance of Eugenic History,"
Genetics in Medicine 20 (2018): 1307.

the century by geneticists, including the renowned Charles Davenport, acted as the impetus for broadscale biosocial reform plans designed to manage evolution. These plans built on problematic inferences from Mendelism, such as the inference that all traits are determined by single genes acting independently.[5] While some geneticists had abandoned these inferences after World War I, there were still those of influence, including Davenport himself, who further built on them to present eugenics efforts in the 1920s as "applied genetics."[6] In ostensibly taking control of future human evolution, these eugenics programs would supposedly prevent what scientists such as Harvard's eminent plant geneticist Edward Murray East called the threat of "biosocial retrogression."[7]

One of Sanger's achievements would be to make contraception respectable and researchable, even though at the dawn of the twentieth century it was stigmatized as a remnant of nineteenth-century agitation for free love, anarchism, and other radical movements lacking social and scientific legitimacy.[8] When Sanger was in Europe during the war, British birth control and eugenics leaders convinced her to shift away from what had been her previous socially controversial arguments prior to America's entry into the war. As a result, Sanger wholly reoriented birth control rhetoric after World War I.[9] Sanger had previously defended artificial contraception

5. Kenneth M. Ludmerer, *Genetics and American Society: A Historical Appraisal* (Baltimore: Johns Hopkins University Press, 1972), 39. Contributing, too, was an error of interpretation that took August Weismann's assertion about inherited traits lying in the germ plasm to mean that all traits are inherited that way.

6. Other public scientists and advocates called genetics itself "pure eugenics" (Ludmerer, *Genetics and American Society*, 50–51). Scholar Merriley Borell contends that "by the 1920s many biologists felt that one could and should accelerate the evolutionary process ... by the application of principles being developed in the emerging science of genetics." See Borell, "Biologists and the Promotion of Birth Control Research, 1918–1938," *Journal of the History of Biology* 20 (1987): 56.

7. East, *Heredity and Human Affairs*, 201.

8. Margaret Sanger had been tied to various radical movements prior to the 1920s; she even published a little-remembered newspaper in 1913 featuring on its masthead the customary anarchist slogan "No God, No Masters!" (Reed, *From Private Vice to Public Virtue*, 70–86). Sanger's known sexual relationships with married associates Havelock Ellis, H. G. Wells, and others seemed to embody the norms of the late nineteenth-century free love movement.

9. Sanger lived in Europe for part of 1914—spending most of her time in Britain—after prosecution under the Comstock obscenity law for publishing her book *Family Limitation*.

in places like her *Woman Rebel* newspaper in 1914, for example, by echoing a seeming Marxian analysis of family: "marriage laws abrogate the freedom of woman by enforcing upon her a continuous sexual slavery and a compulsory motherhood."[10] In 1916, Sanger's radical economics-based defense of contraception dubbed the Christian church—particularly Catholicism—a "market[er] on souls" that "has made breeding its main source of revenue."[11] By 1919, however, she struck a very different posture, medicalizing her arguments in eugenic terms: "Eugenics and advocates of Birth Control … are seeking a single end … [by] different methods.… Eugenists imply or insist that a woman's first duty is to the state; we contend that her duty to herself is her duty to the state." She went on: "The mother's health is more than likely to be wrecked [after early unspaced childbirths] and the later children are almost sure to fall short of that nervous and muscular health which might otherwise have been theirs."[12] This vision of social engineering is suggested by the term *birth control* itself. Sanger is credited with first publicly employing the phrase in lieu of the more traditional term *contraception.*[13]

By the end of World War I, the organized American birth control movement thus reoriented its discursive emphasis to rendering contraception a crucial, eugenic manager of human evolution, one that would simultaneously deal with heritable disease and population issues that facilitated poverty. But the effort by Sanger and affiliated scientists to get support from the eugenics establishment took considerable time to overcome substantial resistance. Many mainline public eugenics advocates, including those who founded

10. Margaret Sanger, "Marriage," *Woman Rebel* 1 (April 1914): 16, in Published Writings and Speeches, 1911–1959, microfilm C16:0530, Margaret Sanger Papers Project.

11. Margaret Sanger, "Birth Control," *Melting Pot* (July 1916): 5, in Collected Documents, microfilm C16:90, Sanger Papers Project.

12. Margaret Sanger, "Birth Control and Racial Betterment," *Birth Control Review* 3 (February 1919): 11.

13. Sanger wrote the article using the term *birth control* upon returning from a 1914 trip in France to study contraceptive methods (Tobin, *American Religious Debate*, 9). Mary D. Lagerway contends that Sanger's friend Otto Bobsein first privately used the term in 1914. See Mary D. Lagerway, "Nursing, Social Contexts, and Ideologies in the Early United States Birth Control Movement," *Nursing Inquiry* 6 (1999): 250–58.

the AES in 1922, expressed opposition to any connections with the birth control movement and retained these views for some years. Reasons given spanned claims that birth control was counterproductive in terms of scientific eugenics—those whose reproduction was most desirable from a eugenic perspective would be the ones most likely to employ contraception—to claims that contraception was bad for the emotional, physical, and moral constitution of individuals, families, and societies.[14] Many saw it as simply disreputable, especially given the contraception movement's roots.

As late as 1928, Charles Davenport himself had written to Leon Whitney, executive secretary of the AES, saying that the attempts of birth control advocates to join up with the eugenics movement were examples of mere opportunism, since "birth control does not taste in the mouth as well as eugenics."[15] Whereas Davenport saw his own organization, the Eugenics Record Office, as fully scientific, he saw birth control as "a quagmire out of which eugenics should keep."[16] He added a thinly veiled threat that should the AES ever involve itself with the Birth Control League, "it would be necessary for the Eugenics Record Office of the Carnegie Institution of Washington to withdraw its Moral Support."[17] But there were other eminent geneticists not nearly so averse to organized birth con-

14. The AES committee complained among themselves in 1925 that birth control advocates increasingly framed their arguments in the parlance of eugenics, something the AES did not view positively for the gamut of reasons noted above. "Committee Minutes" (March 28, 1925), in AES Papers, box 5, folder 4, APS. Contraceptive advocates were well aware of the hesitancy. For example, in 1926, New York physician S. A. Knopf had written a book titled *The Medical, Social, Economic, Moral, and Religious Aspects of Birth Control*, reviewed in the April 1928 issue of *Eugenical News*. Knopf pointed out "the fear that haunts many that contraceptive teachings will be practiced principally by the well-endowed.... Until that fear can be relieved, some eugenicists will hesitate before entering enthusiastically upon anti-conceptual propaganda." S. A. Knopf, quoted in *Eugenical News* 13 (April 1928): 46–47.

15. Davenport to Whitney (April 5, 1928), in AES Papers, box 1, folder 2, APS.

16. Davenport to Whitney.

17. Davenport to Whitney. Responding to the consistent appeals of Sanger, Whitney had baited Davenport, known for opposition to the contraception movement, by writing that Sanger had recently visited and told him she "felt very strongly about eugenics and seemed to see the whole problem of birth control as a eugenical problem." Whitney to Davenport (April 3, 1928) in AES Papers, box 1, folder 2, APS. In his history of the AES, Frederick Osborn claimed that the organization already had "close contacts" with the American Birth Control League by 1931 (Osborn quoted in Rosen, *Preaching Eugenics*, 157).

trol as Davenport. In fact, several of those geneticists—along with other scientists—would play key roles from early in the decade to build scientific and reform coalitions with Sanger and, ultimately, to bring together the two reform movements by the end of the decade. By the turn of the decade, artificial birth control had come to be seen as one of the centerpieces of eugenics reform plans. Control of conception meant control of evolution. As one scholar of that era described the building affinities, key researchers in the 1920s "foresaw the potential genetic and eugenic consequences of birth control and were eager to manage human evolution."[18]

Sanger was tapping into the enormous authority of professionalized science when she created the Birth Control Clinical Research Bureau in 1923, as a department of the American Birth Control League that she had founded in 1921.[19] The Clinical Bureau's four-person panel of advisory board scientists, with whom Sanger worked very closely, featured four eugenics enthusiasts, all of whom were tied to genetics. The board included geneticist Leon Cole of the University of Wisconsin; population biometrician Raymond Pearl of Johns Hopkins University, who had spent a year studying under eugenicist Karl Pearson in Britain; experimental biologist Clarence C. Little of the University of Maine, who had been Executive Committee chair at the Second International Congress of Eugenics in 1921, and the aforementioned eminent plant geneticist from Harvard, Edward Murray East.[20] Geneticist East illustrates in his person the particular networks Sanger and her asso-

18. Borell, "Biologists," 58.

19. Borell, "Biologists," 53, 67. Borell added, "It was the eugenic arguments that first urged the attention of prominent biologists and that accounted for their interest in birth control as a scientific problem" (57).

20. Besides affiliation with this committee, East, Cole, Little, and Pearl were also all on the National Council of the American Birth Control League (see, for example, the list in *Birth Control Review* 13 [January 1929]: 2); they each also held membership in the AES; Pearl and Little were members the Galton Society; and Little was in the Immigration Restriction League (Spiro, *Defending the Master Race*, app. D, 395). On Pearl's study with Pearson, see H. S. Jennings, "Biographical Memoir of Raymond Pearl, 1879–1940," in *National Academy of Sciences Biographical Memoirs: Third Memoir*, vol. 22 (Washington, D.C.: National Academy of Sciences, 1942), 297–98, 303, http://www.nasonline.org/publications/biographical-memoirs/memoir-pdfs/pearl-raymond.pdf.

ciates publicly established. He had been vice president at that 1921 Eugenics Congress and went on to co-plan, with Sanger, the Sixth Annual Neo-Malthusian and Birth Control Conference in 1925.[21] The people listed above were just a few of those embodying the intellectual and practical connections emerging in the 1920s between evolutionary genetics-eugenics and birth control.[22]

East spelled out in positivist form the connections between evolution, birth control, and genetics-eugenics in his widely-circulated book *Mankind at the Crossroads* (1923): "We are ... entering upon a new epoch of civilization—with our social problems ... defined and with [awareness of] the natural laws controlling our destiny. Proper direction of human evolution," he adjured, "is a worthy objective ... [and] in the eugenic sense ... this corrective is found in the control of human reproduction." East added, "I believe that if this remedial prescription is not generally accepted and put into practice, man's troubles will speedily multiply as they never have before."[23] East penned a book with very similar themes in 1927, *Heredity and Human Affairs*. On the particular role of artificial birth control in his schema, East concluded his 1927 book by referring to Sanger's closest associate: "The wisest humanitarian of our time [Havelock Ellis] holds contraception to be the greatest discovery of the nineteenth

21. Borell, "Biologists," 59. As Borell put it on Sanger's approach, "With the help of her scientific advisors, she then lobbied extensively for the creation of a laboratory program of contraceptive research to complement and advance her program of clinical services" (57). The Second International Congress of Eugenics, under the presidency of Henry Fairfield Osborn, gave birth to the Eugenics Society of the United States of America (ESUSA). The ESUSA was technically the precursor to the AES, but all assets, key figures, and plans were transferred from one to the other when the AES formally reincorporated with the new name in 1926. B. A. Mehler, "A History of the American Eugenics Society, 1921–1940" (PhD diss., University of Illinois, 1988), 66. Because of the continuities and to avoid confusion since the AES name is much better known than ESUSA, I follow what has become the convention of using only the AES name.

22. At Irving Fisher's behest, the original Committee of the AES decided to "cooperate with the American Genetics Association" and "subscribe to the Journal of Heredity" such that "many active members of the AGA also joined the AES" (Mehler, "History of the American Eugenics Society," 62). Besides geneticists East and Cole, other geneticists ultimately serving on the important Advisory Council of the AES were Harvard's William Castle; Johns Hopkins's Herbert Spencer Jennings; University of Chicago's Sewall W. Wright; and University of Michigan's Aaron F. Shull (Spiro, *Defending the Master Race*, app. D, 395).

23. East, *Mankind at the Crossroads* (New York: Charles Scribner's Sons, 1923), vi–vii.

century. He is obviously correct."[24] East's representation effectively captures the interwar progressive scientism that helped bring these movements closer together.[25]

Funding and Research Interconnections

Research funding patterns in the 1920s, too, began to draw together evolution and birth control through eugenics, demography, and public health as a result of concerted efforts by Sanger and others in the organized birth control movement. Monies from John D. Rockefeller and Andrew Carnegie backed Sanger's Clinical Research Bureau, the ASHA, and the Eugenics Record Office at the Center for the Study of Evolution in Cold Spring Harbor, Long Island.[26] The Rockefeller Foundation, having funded a series of social science efforts from the end of the war, was a substantial donor to the 1927 World Population Conference in Geneva, itself designed by Sanger with her advisory board in order to facilitate a more objectively framed construct for encouraging further research by biologists, statisticians, and sociologists for birth control goals.[27] The conference, in turn, helped stimulate laboratory studies of contraception by researchers sympathetic to the birth control

24. East, *Heredity and Human Affairs*, 310.

25. In Borell's words, "Reformers assumed that safe and effective contraception for the masses could be developed through scientific research. Eugenic arguments, as presented by geneticists (such as Sanger's advisers) had focused attention on the desirability of managing human evolution to eliminate poverty and disease" ("Biologists," 67). East campaigned for this idea not only in books but also in popular magazine forums. See, for example, Edward M. East, "Heredity—The Master Riddle of Science," *Scribner's Magazine* 78 (July 1925): 1–7, and East, "Heredity and Sex," *Scribner's Magazine* 78 (August 1925): 144–51. As an aside, it is worth noting that the former claim about managing evolution appeared amid the evolution discussion surrounding the Scopes Trial. See also East, "Tabu—A Defense of Birth Control," *The Forum* 77 (May 1927): 669–77.

26. Richard Soloway, "The 'Perfect Contraceptive': Eugenics and Birth Control Research in Britain and America in the Interwar Years," *Journal of Contemporary History* 30 (October 1995): 648. These overlaps suggest a contemporaneous perception of the movements as related to each other and perhaps tied to an overarching goal or vision.

27. Borell, "Biologists," 59–60. Borell argued that an added appearance of objectivity was created by "intentionally stripp[ing] the anticipated conference of explicit propaganda" and "eliminating its visible affiliations with neo-Malthusianism and with the birth control movement ... as a 'solely scientific' conference" (59–60).

movement's goals and "conscious of their implications for human evolution."[28] Scientists affiliated with the Birth Control League's Clinical Research Bureau were also able to secure funding for birth control research from the National Research Council, the Bureau of Social Hygiene, and other national and international organizations.[29]

One such example was the Crew study on chemical contraceptives from 1929 to 1931, directed by F. A. E. Crew of the Department of Animal Breeding at the University of Edinburgh and linked to Sanger's Committee on Maternal Health and Medical Advisory Board. Partial results and guidelines that directed this work appeared in Robert Dickinson and Louise Bryant's book, *Control of Conception* (1932).

Connections to Sex, Social Hygiene, and Cooper

The organized movement for social hygiene also saw board members overlapping between birth control and eugenics associations by the early 1920s.[30] At various points, Cooper, Edwin Conklin, Paul Popenoe, Guy Irving Burch, Maurice Bigelow, Leon Whitney, and others shared committee memberships in both the ASHA and the AES. And Burch and Bigelow served concurrently on the AES "Committee on Birth Regulation."[31]

An important thread tying what was known as positive eugenics to the reform skein of the ASHA existed in the latter's focus on sex education and the avoidance of venereal disease. This focus did not initially include artificial contraception since the ASHA did not

28. Borell, "Biologists," 63.

29. Borell, "Biologists," 63.

30. Spiro, *Defending the Master Race*, app. D, 395.

31. See, for example, letterheads from the AES in the late 1920s and early 1930s. JMC Papers, box 19, folder "American Eugenics Society 1929–1931," ACUA. See also JMC Papers, box 8, folder "American Social Hygiene Association," ACUA, for records of Cooper's involvement on the ASHA "Education Committee" through 1948. Burch also worked for Sanger in the 1930s on the National Committee for Federal Legislation for Birth Control. See also Gordon, *Woman's Body, Woman's Right*, 161.

officially back artificial contraception until after the 1920s. Cooper's commitment to the ASHA was deep-seated and longstanding; he belonged to the organization from the late 1910s up until his death in 1949. His rhetoric in connection with social hygiene—in dialogue with others in the movement—gives an insight into the intellectual currents, scientific language, and shared presumptions that helped gird the interlocking matrix of evolution- and conception-related movements that shared a basis in sexual questions—both controlling and directing sex. The marriage and venereal disease focus of social hygiene was broadly intended to have positive eugenic effects and prevent what sociologist E. A. Ross first called putative "race suicide" that would result from dysgenic marriage. Laboratory tests to detect venereal disease supplemented state statutes prohibiting the marriage of the infected, statutes referred to as "eugenic marriage laws."[32] Before looking at Cooper's ASHA-related language, a brief consideration of early twentieth-century discourse on continence and abstinence in relation to marital sexuality is useful for understanding the nature of the intellectual constructs and movements at play.

While emphasizing the importance of marriage's role in replenishing the earth with children in its long history, Christianity, and other religions, nevertheless also taught the legitimacy and even positive spiritual good of periodic restraint and continence within marriage, if employed discerningly.[33] And periodic conti-

---

32. See Paul A. Lombardo, "A Child's Right to Be Well Born: Venereal Disease and the Eugenic Marriage Laws, 1913–1935," *Perspectives in Biology and Medicine* 60 (2017): 211–32. A sample of the rhetoric includes dangers of "defective" women spreading bad heredity to children (and thus to society), a child's "right to be well-born," as eugenic enthusiast Jane Addams put it, and other angles (Lombardo, 218).

33. On marriage and procreation highlighted as one of the roads to sanctity in Christianity, an excellent and renowned example is found in the fourth-century Cappadocians St. Basil the Elder and his wife, St. Emelia, among whose ten children were counted brothers St. Basil the Great, St. Gregory of Nyssa, St. Naukratios, and their sister, St. Makrina the Younger, "the teacher." See St. Gregory Nazianzus's funeral oration for his good friend St. Basil: Gregory Nazianzan, "The Panegyric on St. Basil," in *Cyril of Jerusalem; Gregory Nazianzan*, vol. 7 of Nicene and Post-Nicene Fathers, 2nd ser., ed. Philip Schaff and Henry Wace, 395–422 (Peabody, Mass.: Hendrickson Publishers, 2004). On the role of continence in marriage, see for example, Gregory of Nyssa, "On Virginity," in *Gregory of Nyssa: Dogmatic Treatises, Etc.*, vol. 5

nence in marriage took on increasingly prominent rhetoric in the Anglo-American world after the debut of Anglican cleric Thomas Malthus's prescribed remedies in his famous 1798 volume *An Essay on the Principle of Population*, a treatise warning about the impending dangers of excess population. A corresponding exaltation of abstinence and purity in later nineteenth-century Protestantism, combined with the broader cultural value placed on self-mastery as a road to improvement, contributed to the uniting of several preexisting American purity groups in 1895 to form the American Purity Alliance.[34] This purity movement connected with efforts to curb venereal disease designed to go beyond merely targeting prostitution.[35]

The notion of adjuring not only females but also males to practice sexual restraint constituted a part of transatlantic Victorian activism driven by both clergy and feminists. One Church of England organization, making a cause out of manly self-control, saw a parallel emerge in the American Protestant White Cross Army.[36] Embedded in White Cross rhetoric was a sense that uncontrolled lust, even in marriage, was unhealthy and generally destructive on both physical and mental levels.[37]

While such social purity organizations did not wholly refrain from incorporating physiological or psychological language into their moral arguments, it took the formation of the ASHA in

---

of Nicene and Post-Nicene Fathers, 2nd ser., ed. Philip Schaff and Henry Wace (Peabody, Mass.: Hendrickson Publishers, 2004), chap. 8, 353.

34. On the purity movement and valuing of self-restraint, see Plopper, "Protestants," 312. Plopper noted that the American Purity Alliance "united many streams of social purity work emerging from the Women's Christian Temperance Union, the White Cross Society (a Protestant organization devoted to personal sexual purity), and the Y.M.C.A.'s and Y.W.C.A.'s, which published much of the literature devoted to establishing the importance of self-control among young men and women" (312).

35. Plopper "Protestants," 7.

36. Plopper "Protestants," 33.

37. For the social purity activists, "neither prophylactics nor regulation of prostitution removed what they viewed as the root problem: men (and possibly women) who lacked self-control. The bishops, clergy, and social purity advocates argued that the Christian answer to these social problems remained chastity, continence, self-restraint, or, in other words, sexual abstinence" (Plopper, "Protestants," 36).

1914—and its incorporation of the American Purity Alliance via the American Vigilance Association in 1915—to bring about a marked cultural and rhetorical shift whereby continence arguments came to be thoroughly framed in lenses of social and biological science.[38] The technical language of *hygiene* in the ASHA quickly replaced the American Purity Alliance's rhetoric of *purity*, though the ASHA retained its emphasis on abstinence and self-control, focusing especially on the young, while simultaneously decrying contraception until the Depression years. This was the combination of emphases that appealed to Cooper, who joined the ASHA shortly after its inception. It should be pointed out that another social hygiene organization, the research- and philanthropy-oriented Bureau of Social Hygiene, had actually appeared earlier, in 1911, under the auspices of John D. Rockefeller. But the Bureau of Social Hygiene—initially focused on investigations of criminality, sex, and venereal disease—incorporated and funded population and contraception studies by the mid-to-late 1920s and was connected in various ways to Sanger before that.[39]

38. The ASHA formed by combining the American Vigilance Association (which had incorporated the American Purity Alliance) with the physician-led American Federation for Sex Hygiene, created in 1907. The initial impetus for union was a joint meeting of the two groups in 1913 at the Fourth International Congress on School Hygiene in Buffalo, New York. See [Livingston Farrand], "The Social Hygiene Movement," *American Journal of Public Health* 3 (1913): 1154–55. For early articulated ASHA goals and intended methods, see the first honorary presidential address of Charles W. Eliot. Eliot, "The American Social Hygiene Association," *Journal of Social Hygiene* 1 (December 1914): 1–5. See also Kristin Luker, "Sex, Social Hygiene, and the State: The Double-Edged Sword of Social Reform," *Theory and Society* 27 (1998): 610–11. Along with Eliot, the former president of Harvard, and the ASHA director physician-eugenicist William F. Snow, initial ASHA board members included eugenicists David Starr Jordan, Roscoe Pound, Maurice Bigelow, the Rockefeller Foundation's Raymond Fosdick, and others. Americanist Cardinal James Gibbons of Baltimore was an honorary vice president. See the circa 1919 document "A History and Forecast," American Social Hygiene Association, n.d., https://socialwelfare.library.vcu.edu/programs/health-nutrition/american-social-hygiene-association-history-and-a-forecast/. Original in American Social Health Association Records, University of Minnesota, https://www.lib.umn.edu/swha. For a look at Gibbons's involvement with the cause, see Kristi L. Slominski, "Cardinal Gibbons as a Symbol for Early Sex Education," *U.S. Catholic Historian* 34 (2016): 1–25.

39. On the foundation of the Bureau of Social Hygiene, see Barry Mehler, "Sources in the History of Eugenics #2," *Mendel Newsletter* 16 (1978), http://www.ferris-pages.org/ISAR/archives2/sources/bsh.htm. On the various intellectual and funding connections between the Bureau of Social Hygiene and Sanger, see Borell, "Biologists," 63–66. Borell argues that in the

Cooper's connection with social hygiene, which he described as "medical and sanitary propaganda to arouse public and professional interest in and check the alarming growth of 'social' or venereal disease," reflected the moralizing expectations of expertise emerging from the Progressive movement. Cooper was not only formally affiliated as a member but also repeatedly re-elected to a position on the ASHA's Board of Directors, each reappointment bringing a three-year term.[40] Cooper worked energetically in this movement until his death in 1949 with his customary hope to professionalize Catholic efforts in social work while simultaneously trying—often unsuccessfully—to mediate what we may call the scientism endemic in numerous social hygiene efforts. His own rhetoric there, however, not infrequently lent itself to that same scientism.

Addressing Catholic would-be social workers in a *Catholic Charities Review* article in 1921, Cooper was willing to mention a few terms from Catholic moral theology and appeal to the authority of select Catholic moral theologians, but he primarily argued on the basis of contemporary social and psychological science, as advocated by figures like the eugenicist-psychologist and advocate of "genetic *psychology*," G. Stanley Hall.[41] Cooper argued that the pendulum toward the sense of modesty "swung in recent decades somewhat too far towards prudishness.... Moral sex education should [rely on grace but also] capitalize the desirable natural instinctive and quasi-instinctive impulses and instinct-habit consolidations."[42] Social hygiene, he told readers, "should begin with the

---

1920s the bureau gradually incorporated birth control into their program. Sanger and Robert Dickinson devised projects that appealed to Rockefeller's interest in population study. Borell, "Biologists," 65.

40. John Montgomery Cooper, "Some Recent Trends in Social Hygiene," *Catholic Charities Review* 5 (January 1921): 3. Cooper served on the ASHA board from the 1920s into the 1940s.

41. On Hall's early racialist-eugenic ideas, see G. Stanley Hall, "Eugenics: Its Ideals and What It Is Going to Do," *Religious Education* 6 (1911): 152–59. On genetic psychology, see John D. Hogan, "G. Stanley Hall and The Journal of Genetic Psychology: A Note," *Journal of Genetic Psychology* 177 (2016): 191–94.

42. See John Montgomery Cooper, "Sex Teaching in the Home," *Catholic Charities Review* 5 (September 1921): 218.

hygiene of the imagination" cultivated by outdoor activities over the "sex-stimulating commercial and 'passive' amusements, such as the theatre and the movies." Parents, Cooper said, were not living up to their obligations in cultivating the right instincts.[43] His solution was, in part, a turn to expertise.

Cooper de facto argued for a professionalized sex educator role in the church itself. For church sex educators, relying on writings in sex psychology and sex education that "owe a heavy debt to the Freudian school" would be acceptable because those presumably steeped in Catholic ideas of the psyche, such as Cooper himself, knew how to separate the wheat from the chaff. But, he said, general sex psychology writings should not be read by the average person.[44] Cooper envisioned a mediating role for these trained Catholic experts who would predigest the writings of mainline figures for parents. Yet although he may have removed the Freudian sexuality hierarchy from notions of the psyche, he retained the social hygienist's model of teaching sex education to Catholic youth, what he called "an approach by the affective and volitional route."[45] Cooper sounded the design in metaphors like "the inherited human instincts are the raw material from which the educational loom weaves its finished products." Cooper believed that in order to prevent misguided sexual outlets, the "parental instinct" in children had to be cultivated by targeting the "race preservation complex."[46]

Practically speaking, Cooper recommended "physical sex education" that not merely "repress[ed] and control[ed]" but also "develop[ed] the good constructive forces in the [race preservative] complex."[47] This included encouraging the child to sleep on a bed that is "fairly hard without too many blankets ... on his side rather than on his back [while wearing] clothing [that is] loose."[48]

43. Cooper, "Some Recent Trends," 4.
44. Cooper, "Sex Teaching," 218.
45. Cooper, "Sex Teaching," 218.
46. John Montgomery Cooper, "Sex Training in the Home," *Catholic Charities Review* 5 (December 1921): 321–22.
47. Cooper, "Sex Training," 323.
48. Cooper, "Sex Training," 323.

In what Cooper called "psychical sex education," he recommended inhibition and substitution. How? Here and elsewhere, Cooper demonstrated an affinity for recommending cold showers, as their "moral effects are good."[49] Cooper's preeminent emphasis was on keeping busy since, he argued, "solitary play or solitude in general is not good and may readily lead to sex aberrations."[50]

Cooper made sure his students at the Catholic University of America, and at the affiliated Trinity College for women, were taught about all of these aspects of social hygiene in his religion courses. In a 1930 letter to the director of the ASHA, he specified that social hygiene was a focus in the "family" portion of his courses, attesting that he discussed it with the "utmost frankness."[51] In 1934, Cooper reiterated his urging that sex education be taught in schools even as, thereafter, he continued on teaching and writing on the subject. He also maintained his position on the ASHA board long after NCWC member Edward Heffron had been prompted to write to NCWC General Secretary Msgr. Michael Ready in 1938 asking whether he himself should continue serving there alongside Cooper given his disquiet at how the ASHA's published output had become entirely "naturalistic" and given the ASHA's many recommendations of readings by eugenicists and birth control promoters.[52] Ultimately, the movements themselves shared a matrix of reform discourse derived from a common ground in the attempt to control the evolutionary process.

49. Cooper, "Sex Training," 323–24.

50. Cooper, "Sex Training," 324.

51. Cooper to William Snow (February 21, 1930), in JMC Papers, box 19, folder "American Social Hygiene Association: Part II, 1928–1937," ACUA.

52. Cooper to Snow (June 23, 1934), in JMC Papers, box 19, folder "American Social Hygiene Association: Part II, 1928–1937, ACUA; Heffron to Ready, "National Catholic Welfare Conference interoffice memo" (February 23, 1938), in NCWC Papers, box 117, folder "Social Action: Venereal Disease (VD) Control, 1930–1939," ACUA. Bibliographies issued by ASHA contained pamphlets by eugenicist Havelock Ellis, contraceptive advocate Hannah Stone, etc. "NCWC interoffice memo" (March 9, 1938), in NCWC Papers, box 117, folder "Social Action: Venereal Disease (VD) Control, 1930–1939," ACUA.

Margaret Sanger, Liberal Catholics, and Social Engineering

At the end of World War I, birth control advocates in Britain and America began emphasizing arguments centering on physiology and evolutionary psychology, arguments that directly challenged the assertions of ASHA social hygienists—as well as a cadre of Progressive Era physicians—about the healthfulness and social benefits of abstinence, including for men.[53] British paleontologist and birth control advocate Marie Stopes argued in 1918, for example, that continence caused not only nervous disorders but also "fibroid tumors."[54] Margaret Sanger and close associate Havelock Ellis mirrored Stopes's approach in the United States as Sigmund Freud's ideas on sexual repression further entered the American milieu with the 1915 English translation of his lengthy 1908 pamphlet, *Sexual Morality and Modern Nervousness*.[55] They concertedly reversed the ASHA argument through what one researcher has termed "pathologizing continence."[56]

Physiological and psychological arguments against continence constituted a full chapter in Sanger's well-circulated volume

53. On the social-hygiene-affiliated "Progressive-era doctors [who had] sought to prove what seemed to many men an outlandish idea, that sex was not necessary for health or efficiency," and on nineteenth century medical precursors, see Timothy Verhoeven, "'Apostles of Continence': Doctors and the Doctrine of Sexual Necessity in Progressive-Era America," *Medical History* 61 (2017): 89–106. Quotation from 90.

54. Stopes quoted in Plopper, "Protestants," 65.

55. Physician William J. Robinson, who translated Freud's pamphlet into English, publicized it in a series of lectures challenging the social hygiene movement's ideas on sexuality (Plopper, "Protestants," 331–32). Robinson also wrote about these ideas in his *Sexual Truths Versus Sexual Lies, Misconceptions, and Exaggerations* (Hoboken, N.J.: Critic and Guide, 1919). The perception of Freud's pamphlet's importance and relationship to eugenic ideals by the interwar era is suggested in its republication by the Eugenics Publishing Company of New York City. See Sigmund Freud, *Modern Sexual Morality and Modern Nervousness* (New York: Eugenics Publishing, 1931).

56. The phrase is Plopper's ("Protestants," 330). Birth control advocates were also not averse to supplementing science framings with the language of romanticism and religion. Stopes said in 1919: "On physiological, moral, and religious grounds, therefore, I advocate the restrained and sacramental rhythmic performance of the marriage rite of physical union" (Stopes quoted in Plopper, "Protestants," 66).

Woman and the New Race (1920).[57] Over the years, she frequently echoed the substance of her claim that "according to medical science, continence in marriage is positively harmful to health" and, if practiced for a length of time, "brings on serious nervous derangement."[58] Centering on what was normal and natural for human beings, an archival draft of a 1923 Sanger speech shows her employing nature-centered argumentation to counter both the ASHA's and religious groups' depictions of what was natural: "Self control or the denial of sex expression in a normal adult man and woman is ... much more against the laws of nature than the use of knowledge of Birth Control can be."[59] Sanger conjoined the accusation of unnaturalness with a parallel accusation of backwardness and opposition to the positive good of society's ability to engineer itself. In her words, "the control of natural forces for human ends is now generally accepted as a mark of enlightened humanity."[60]

Ellis likewise worked to reverse the common equation of unrestrained desire with animal lust, employing evolution-centered arguments to do so. In 1922, he wrote, "there is something pathetic in those among us who are still only able to recognize the animal end of marriage," adding "it has taken God—or Nature, if we will—unknown millions of years of painful struggle to evolve man ... above that helpless bondage to reproduction which marks the lower animals." He lamented that for those who oppose contraception, "it has all been wasted. They are at animal stage still."[61] The claim that his opponents possessed an insufficiently evolved moral

57. Arguing that Christianity was responsible for setting up the failed ideal of continence, she wrote that science knows better: "Virtually all of the dangers to health involved in absolute continence are involved also in the practice of continence broken only when it is desired to bring a child into the world. In the opinion of some medical authorities, it is even worse, because of the almost constant excitation of unsatisfied sex desire by the presence of the mate." Margaret Sanger, *Woman and the New Race* (New York: Brentano's Publishers, 1920), http://www.gutenberg.org/cache/epub/8660/pg8660-images.html.

58. Margaret Sanger, "The Pope's Position on Birth Control," *The Nation* 134 (January 27, 1932): 103.

59. Margaret Sanger "Notes on Eugenics and Birth Control," typescript (n.d.), in Sophia Smith Collection, microfilm S73:0091, Sanger Papers Project.

60. Sanger, "Notes on Eugenics and Birth Control."

61. Havelock Ellis, *Little Essays of Love and Virtue* (London: A&C Black, 1922), 71.

sensibility accorded with Sanger's rhetoric inverting the categories of prostitution and purposeful parenthood: "We call it prostitution when one sacrifices personal choices and love in the sexual relation for monetary gain; why should it be less prostitution when the end is the propagation of the species?"[62] It also corresponded with her advocacy of new eugenic morals, as she espoused in the same paragraph Nietzsche's "eloquent den[unciation]" of "slave morality" that favors "the preservation and propagation of the unfit."[63]

The shift to discursive common ground between the birth control movement and the eugenics movement—itself conceived as evolution control—had been facilitated with the help of liberal clergy.[64] In tandem with extending an invitation to liberal Protestant minister Harry Emerson Fosdick in the summer of 1922, the AES—located at that point at Cold Spring Harbor in loose affiliation with the Carnegie-endowed Eugenics Record Office—also invited Cooper and Ryan to join the society's Advisory Council, which they did.[65]

While Cooper and Ryan definitely did not endorse artificial birth control themselves, they were both officially in the AES on that council when it did in 1930, each resigning some months afterward. They also both held to scientized discursive norms even in their opposition to elements of the AES that they opposed. As a result, they often came across as simply inconsistent.

Part of the AES's stated reason for inviting clergy as advisors in the early 1920s was that they would provide increased legitimacy for the AES while making sure people did not associate eugenics with irreligion or with socially disreputable movements.[66] In that

62. Sanger, "Notes on Eugenics and Birth Control."
63. Sanger, "Notes on Eugenics and Birth Control."
64. The best work on these connections in terms of eugenics is Rosen, *Preaching Eugenics.*
65. While many American Catholics were cautious about the organized eugenics movement, especially the AES, Cooper and Ryan saw themselves as mediating between extreme elements of both Sangerian social engineering and conservative Catholicism. See Leon, *Image of God,* chap. 2, and Rosen, *Preaching Eugenics,* chap. 5.
66. "American Eugenics Committee Minutes" (August 9, 1922, and March 28, 1925), in AES Papers, box 5, folder "Committee Minutes, 1922–1925," APS. The committee sought out

goal, the AES succeeded. The Clergy Advisory Council was no mere ornamental committee of the AES; rather, it was the elected body that advised members of the Eugenics Committee, which, in turn, set the society's official policies on all matters. Whereas simple membership in the AES granted no authoritative voice in its work, serving on the Clergy Advisory Council signaled more significant influence.[67] In 1922, the committee was comprised of significant eugenicist scientists and activists, among whom were Charles Davenport, Henry Fairfield Osborn and Yale population statistician Irving Fisher.[68]

In the American Eugenics Society: Swimming in a Murky Pool of Social Reform Scientism

We can now move to a consideration of how Ryan's and Cooper's formal membership and involvement in the AES further defined their public roles in the interlocking matrices of social engineering and scientific reform.[69] Cooper's membership was ultimately in apparent defiance of the Catholic Church Holy Office's decree of March 1931 disqualifying Catholics from belonging to organized sex education and eugenics groups.[70]

---

clergy who already had a reputation for liberalism and enjoyed some measure of respect within mainline culture. By the turn of the calendar year, both Fosdick and Cooper appeared on the organization's letterhead. "AES Committee minutes" (April 28, 1923), in AES Papers, box 5, folder "Committee Minutes, 1922–1925," APS.

67. "Committee Minutes" (August 9, 1922, and September 6, 1922), in AES Papers, box 5, folder "Committee Minutes, 1922–1925," APS. This hierarchical ordering of the AES had grown out of decisions made at the Second International Congress of Eugenics.

68. For an annotated intellectual biography approach (termed by Mehler as *prosopography*) to the AES leadership and important affiliates in the 1920s, see Mehler, "History of the American Eugenics Society," 129–79.

69. On the way Cooper's and Ryan's involvement in the AES put them in conversation with a cluster of related issues beyond birth control, including immigration restriction, sterilization, and feminism, see Leon, *Image of God*, 38. By contrast, their connections to other related movements, such as social hygiene, preceded that direct involvement, most particularly for Cooper.

70. The Holy Office, as it was then titled, published a decree on March 21, 1931, prohibiting Catholics from participating in sex education programs. See the official English translation by Msgr. Enrico Pucci, Rome Correspondent of the NCWC, titled "Condemnation of 'Sex Education' and 'Eugenics' Theory by Holy Office" (April 13, 1931), in NCWC Papers,

At its September 1922 meeting, the AES Committee established several goals for the AES, one of which was to pick the right people to represent its outreach. At the time, its members were also determined to "emphasize the importance of *intelligence tests* and the *restriction of immigration*" and to "try to steer clear of the Birth Control Movement and the Venereal Disease Movement," that is, social hygiene.[71] Further, it was decided that the committee should focus itself on securing monies for scientific study in service to the movement and on shaping propaganda for "education and the application of research and opinion."[72] For the latter, the committee established the *Eugenical News* as the official organ of the AES. The actual scientific research on eugenics was to be performed by the Eugenics Research Association, which would employ both social and biological science methodologies or, as they expressed it in the record, "research by statistical, experimental, or other methods."[73]

By 1923, the Committee appointed three new oversight and consultation subcommittees: the Committee on Cooperation with Physicians; the Committee on Cooperation with Social Workers; and the above-mentioned Committee on Cooperation with Clergymen.[74] Cooper would take a much more active role in the various

Office of the General Secretary records, box 117, folder "Social Action: Venereal Disease (VD) Control, 1930–1939," ACUA. This decree had fleshed out what several months earlier had been announced by Pius XI in the encyclical letter *Casti Connubii*: "Now it is certain that both by the law of nature and of God this right and duty of educating their offspring belongs in the first place to those who began the work of nature by giving them birth, and they are indeed forbidden to leave unfinished this work and so expose it to certain ruin" (*CC*, par. 16). For the full encyclical text, see the Vatican website at http://www.vatican.va/content/pius-xi/en/encyclicals/documents/hf_p-xi_enc_19301231_casti-connubii.html.

71. "Committee Minutes" (September 6, 1922). On the AES and immigration, see Mehler, "History of the American Eugenics Society," 75.

72. "Committee Minutes" (June 9, 1922), in AES Papers, box 5, folder "Committee Minutes, 1922–1925," APS.

73. "Committee Minutes" (June 9, 1922). Roswell Johnson was appointed permanent editor of *Eugenical News* in October 1923. "Committee Minutes" (October 26, 1923), in AES Papers, box 5, folder "Committee Minutes, 1922–1925," APS.

74. "Committee Minutes" (June 9, 1922). By March of 1925, the central committee's minutes made known the group's attitude toward the importance of the Committee on Cooperation with Clergymen: too many clergy-at-large, they said, associated eugenics with birth control. They claimed that birth control advocates increasingly framed their arguments in the parlance of eugenics. "Committee Minutes" (March 28, 1925), in AES Papers, box 5, folder "Committee Minutes, 1922–1925," APS.

workings of the AES than Ryan would over the remainder of the decade. However, the ironies and unintended consequences of both of their names publicly appearing on the organization's masthead were numerous. One was that *Eugenical News* sometimes expressed attitudes pointedly rejecting any who employed religious arguments to question AES's perspectives. Such rejections at times denigrated the very premises of religion and presented them as opposed to science, as happened in a review of H. H. Newman's book *The Gist of Evolution* (1926). The reviewer of this volume opined that "a few Priests, in conspiracy with Mr. Bryan, have sought to distract attention from their own feebleness and ignorance by attributing the decline of interest in Man-made religion to the progress of knowledge and of science."[75]

Another irony of Cooper's and Ryan's names being associated with the AES was the consistent advertisement that Madison Grant and Charles Davenport were both closely connected with the AES when each of them testified before Congressional subcommittees in 1923 to endorse the supposedly unassailable scientific basis of race-based quota restrictions. These quotas would soon be applied in the 1924 Johnson Act against the "new immigrants" who hailed overwhelmingly from Catholic-dominant countries. For mainline eugenicists like Harry Laughlin and others, this bad stock was often presumed to be Catholic. Laughlin claimed in the early 1920s to have found a biological line directly connecting Southern and Eastern European immigrants, mostly Catholic, with mental deficiency.[76] The supposed associations between these places of origin and mental deficiency were claimed throughout the decade.[77] By

75. Review of *The Gist of Evolution*, by H. H. Newman, *Eugenical News* 11 (November 1926): 11.

76. See Leon, *Image of God*, 48.

77. See, for example, Adamantios Polyzoides, "Personal Factors in Immigration." *Eugenics* 2 (July 1929): 18. At the end of 1928, the AES split its publishing arm into two separate journals, reflecting the expanding and more technical notion of the eugenics movement's work. One bore the new title *Eugenics: An Illustrated Journal of Race Betterment* and was intended to cover all aspects of the eugenics movement. The other, *Eugenical News: Current Record of Race Hygiene*, was retooled into a more narrowly focused, research-oriented publication whose subtitle was changed to *Current Record of Human Genetics and Race Hygiene*.

February 1929, the AES reaffirmed its position by voting to send an
official resolution to then president-elect Herbert Hoover to again
"endorse the National Origins Provision of the Immigration Act."
In addition, at this same February board meeting, the crucial decision was made for the AES to officially cooperate with Sanger's
American Birth Control League.[78]

It was only at the start of 1931 that Ryan wrote to Leon Whitney
of the AES to resign and complain that his name had been associated with an organization endorsing cooperation with the birth
control movement. Ryan said he had forgotten that he was an official part of the AES since he was a member of many organizations
and had lost track. Ryan's stated reason for resigning was that he
originally had been assured that the group would operate "scientifically" but that it did not.[79] Other evidence from 1928 shown below
suggests Ryan might have acted sooner had he really been fully
concerned not to have his name associated with the AES before
Casti Connubii made it impossible to leave it there.[80]

The AES had long sought to establish the unimpeachably scientific nature of its positions. In his 1928 AES presidential address,
Harry Laughlin regaled his listeners with "The Progress of American Eugenics." Laughlin referred to the pivotal importance of the
1921 International Congress of Eugenics, which "established [eu-
genics'] relationship with the other sciences." He added that the
establishment of the Eugenics Record Office "marked the sound
organization of eugenics as a biological science."[81] As for the pedigree and promise of the movement for putting eugenic science into
practice, Laughlin assured his listeners: "American eugenicists, led

78. AES Minutes, Board of Directors Meeting (February 14, 1929), in AES Papers, box 7,
folder "1927–1929," APS.

79. Ryan quoted in *Catholic Bulletin* newspaper (n.d.), in Ryan Papers, box 51, folder 4,
ACUA.

80. Discussed in chapter 6 of this book, Pius XI's *Casti Connubii,* or "On Chaste Marriage," was a papal encyclical whose provisions included prohibiting clergy to associate with
organizations affiliated with eugenics and sex education.

81. Harry Laughlin, "Presidential Address of the American Eugenics Society: The Progress of American Eugenics," *Eugenical News* 13 (1928): 89.

by Davenport, are developing eugenical studies along the lines laid down by Charles Darwin and Sir Francis Galton." Eugenicists not infrequently appealed to the cultural authority of Darwin's name, tying it to the birth of eugenics as a method of self-legitimization even into the 1930s.[82]

In late 1928, John Ryan was asked to debate Rabbi David de Sola Pool in the point-counterpoint section of the *Eugenics* magazine. In his presentation, Ryan contended that the eugenics movement was actually resurrecting Thomas Huxley's notion that societies were too charitable to the so-called unfit. This marked an early lurch in a long retreat Ryan would make from his official tie to the AES. Ryan strongly argued against the notion that some groups should be de facto sacrificed for the supposed good of society, since there was no such thing as an abstract *society* apart from the individual people who comprised it. This abstraction of a nebulous and nameless society, he contended, was too often used as a screen behind which salvos were launched against the poor. This included telling such people to remain childless for the supposed betterment of the whole. It was political-economic formulation that grounded Ryan's critique.[83] Coming at a time when the birth control movement was close to its eventual rapprochement with organized eugenics, Ryan's piece shone light on what were the two movements' increasingly similar goals and rationales, yet Ryan remained a member of the AES, his name appearing on its letterhead of its endorsements refuting his own positions, at least until his above-noted resignation finally came.

Ryan presented in the public sphere a contradictory image on

82. Laughlin, "Presidential Address," 89. Eugenicists repeatedly expressed indebtedness to Darwin. The following appeared in *Eugenical News* in 1935: "Eugenics as a science, both pure and applied, owes a great debt to Charles Darwin. In his *Origin of Species* and *Plants and Animals under Domestication* Darwin laid the foundation stones on which other builders erected the structure of eugenics." *Eugenical News* 20 (June 1935): 98.

83. John Ryan, "Overcharitable to the Unfit?," *Eugenics* 1 (December 1928): 21. In an issue of *Eugenics* that followed soon thereafter, the editor attempted to demonstrate the compatibility and friendliness between eugenics and religion by saying that throughout its pages *Eugenics* offered abundant proof that eugenics was an ally, not a foe, of religion. Note from the editor, *Eugenics* 2 (February 1929): 33.

such matters. And the AES leadership continued to take advantage of his association with the organization and, by extension, of any possible connection to Catholicism during that period. In a February 1929 issue of *Eugenics*, for example, Harry Laughlin waxed enthusiastically about the movement's indebtedness to Catholic Gregor Mendel: "Mendelian Units, Mendelism, Mendel's Law—for all these concepts eugenicists are indebted to this monk and his experiments with peas."[84]

Ryan's public position looked further fraught with inconsistency when German Catholic priest Joseph Mayer's article "Eugenics in Roman Catholic Literature" was translated by Cooper's close friend Paul Popenoe for *Eugenics* in February 1930. That article brought to eugenicists' attention the fact that in 1927 the NCWC had published a pamphlet authored by Ryan with the title *Human Sterilization*; in it, he had expressed openness to the possibility of state-sponsored sterilization, although he preferred segregation of the unfit.[85] After *Casti Connubii* came out, Ryan suddenly reversed his position.

John Montgomery Cooper embodied an even more ambiguous presence in the public movement for eugenics than did Ryan. He frequently wrote about what was positive in the movement, although he privately expressed some reservations about whether it was doing much good on the whole. Cooper did criticize specific claims the AES sponsored about the scientific nature of race hierarchies and its focus on Nordicism, in particular.[86] His critique in

84. Harry Laughlin, "The Progress of American Eugenics," *Eugenics* 2 (February 1929): 7.

85. See quote of Ryan by Popenoe in footnote 11 to the latter's translation from the 1929 German article by Mayer published in *Eugenics* as Joseph Mayer, "Eugenics in Roman Catholic Literature," *Eugenics* 3 (February 1930), 47.

86. Leon's *An Image of God* and her earlier "Hopelessly Entangled" thoroughly document Cooper's critiques in these realms. See also Rosen, *Preaching Eugenics*, 143. On the other hand, Cooper's critiques suggest some acceptance of the very racial ontologies and even hierarchies he criticized; it was the specific ordering of "races" by race scientists, for which he found insufficiently credible evidence, that troubled him the most. His words reveal at least a tacit acceptance of some elements of biological race, likely as a consequence of professional inculcation into the heavily race-based theories of contemporary physical anthropology. This would not have come from his training in Rome; since the 1860s, Rome had insisted on the legitimacy of interracial marriage in refuting strict segregation laws (McGreevy, *Catholicism and American Freedom*, 55).

this realm, however, was of a different nature than Ryan's. Whereas Ryan's public arguments were based on economic justice, Cooper always framed both his assessments and critiques as disinterestedly objective science. Whenever Cooper argued against the particular idea of Nordic racial supremacy or the ordering of racial hierarchies, his dispassionate complaint was that they were as yet not scientifically proven. He wrote in early 1929, for example: "That differences in racial level may exist seems not improbable. If they do exist, some day we may refine our present technique as to be able to discover and demonstrate them. But neither the cultural nor the psychological evidence, as it stands today, is ... sufficient ... to establish with any scientific probability the superiority of Nordics or of any other racial group."[87] Cooper only resigned from the AES in April 1931, many months after the AES had already publicly endorsed birth control. And even then, his stated grounds for resigning were that the AES "had become scientifically unsound" and "socially undesirable."[88]

Physicians and Contraception in the 1920s

Birth control critiques coming from certain physicians who employed common anti-contraception themes revealed a gap still existing in the late 1920s between the organized birth control movement and medicine. For example, in prominent physician Halliday Sutherland's "The Fallacies of Birth Control," appearing in *The Forum* in the spring of 1927, Sutherland employed arguments that could as easily have come from the rhetorical pens of Ryan or Cooper when they wrote for mainline audiences.[89] His opening

87. John Montgomery Cooper, "Is Eugenics Racial Snobbery?," *Eugenics* 2 (February 1929): 20. Sharon Leon's aforementioned article, "Hopelessly Entangled in Nordic Presuppositions," and, especially, *Image of God* are the most thorough in their analysis of the way Cooper dealt with the element on Nordic supremacy in the eugenics movement. On his critiques of his opponents' insufficient empirical evidence and generally "unscientific" arguments, see Leon, "Hopelessly Entangled," 25, 47, and *Image of God*, 49, 57, 63.

88. Cooper to Leon Whitney (April 9, 1931), in JMC Papers, box 19, folder 8, ACUA.

89. See Halliday Sutherland, "The Fallacies of Birth Control," *The Forum* 77 (April 1927): 840–47.

sentence is just such an example: "The practice of contraception or birth prevention is unnatural in terms of ethics and unphysiological in terms of biology, ... unnatural ... in the same category as murder and sexual perversion."[90] Sutherland also contended that couples employing contraception were disinclined to self-sacrifice, leading to society-wide "moral weariness," and, further, that nations with higher contraception rates were steadily weakened and, thus, subject to assault by "more virile" neighbors, since "a nation whose numbers are dwindling offers a temptation to the declaration of war by a more robust and aggressive neighbor."[91]

Moving to a medical argument against *coitus interruptus*, Sutherland cited studies with rabbits purportedly showing that "when the female is subjected to truncated intercourse there are certain pathological changes in the organs of generation."[92] Likewise, he said, when human females were denied the intake of semen for any period of time, pathological changes—not only physiological but also psychological in nature—resulted.[93] Such arguments were by no means peculiar to Halliday at the time. Physicians and psychologists made similar claims going back to the nineteenth century.[94]

Evidence of the further closing gap between the organized birth control and eugenics movements by the late 1920s was that each issue of *Eugenics* magazine featured a column called "Birth Regulation" penned by physician Robert L. Dickinson, secretary of public health for New York City's Committee on Maternal Health and cooperator with Sanger. Dickinson represented a small but growing set of doctors warming up to birth control. Dickinson's column of February 1929 complimented the work of researchers in contraception, saying of one physician's book, for example, that "the first presentation of the technique of contraception ... marks

90. Sutherland, "Fallacies of Birth Control," 841.
91. Sutherland, "Fallacies of Birth Control," 842, 846–47.
92. Sutherland, "Fallacies of Birth Control," 847.
93. Sutherland, "Fallacies of Birth Control," 847.
94. See also Gordon, *Woman's Body, Woman's Right*, 161.

a long step forward."[95] Dickinson followed that up by reporting
approvingly that the previous five years had seen the federal postal
service somewhat more lax in its confiscation of birth control materials sent to clinics.[96]

The research grounding provided by projects like the aforementioned Crew study and other published research would also be
appealed to by Dickinson to help persuade the American Medical
Association to endorse contraception in 1937 as a medical matter
lying in physicians' purview.[97] Thus, even when certain geneticists
began to doubt the specific genetic and eugenic justifications for
contraception research in the 1930s, the AES had already endorsed
contraception in 1930 and begun actively cooperating with the organized contraception movement. The groundwork was already
laid and the connections between evolution, genetics-eugenics,
and birth control cemented in both public discourse and institutional connections.

The Line into the 1930s

As the prosperous 1920s gave way to the depressed 1930s, an interlocking matrix of evolution, eugenics, and birth control grounded
in interrelated organizational sponsors encountered a period of
social and cultural acceptance. Liberal-progressive Catholics like
Cooper, Ryan, and O'Brien had injected air into the unifying bal-
loon even as they, at times, tried to persuade their interlocutors
in the public square that certain streams in this matrix were pure
while others were polluted. As they trod along in the late 1920s using their hard-won influence, they frequently spoke the language of

95. Robert L. Dickinson, "Birth Regulation," *Eugenics* 2 (February 1929): 34–35. The physician James F. Cooper, whose book Dickinson lauded, contributed to a symposium in the
May issue on the link between eugenics and birth control. In it, the physician said: "Without
birth control ... there can be no eugenics or intentional betterment of the race." James F.
Cooper, "The Birth Rate of Genius: Does Contraception Curb It?," *Eugenics* 2 (May 1929): 19.
    96. Dickinson, "Birth Regulation," 35.
    97. Borell, "Biologists," 61, 70–72.

a social or biological science insider; at other times, they attempt-ed to offer science-plus-Catholic modes of moral reasoning. The former method of argument, however, increasingly replaced the latter, particularly as the Great Depression took hold, and, by then, often even in instances when their rhetoric was directed primarily at Catholics. They continued to seek public legitimacy, authority, and influence for themselves and their messages in a mainline cul-ture ever more centered in scientific language's public authority. They thus had to engage in a discourse that had steadily shifted into economic-demographic defenses of expert-endorsed contra-ception as a eugenically necessary measure intended to establish control over human evolution in the face of imminent social decay and economic collapse.

While Catholics and conservative Protestants shared the same positions on artificial contraception, Catholics maintained a refus-al to cooperate with conservative Protestants. Catholics ignored conservative Protestants' efforts to temper evolution's framing as a foundation upon which eugenic birth control efforts were append-ed as vehicles for social, economic, and so-called racial uplift in service of the rational direction of future evolution.[98] The linger-ing fear of rural Protestant anti-Catholic efforts from the 1920s—especially virulent in Al Smith's failed presidential venture in 1928—renewed Catholic aversion to any cultural efforts emerging from conservative Protestant blocs. At the same time, however, the liberal Catholics' viewpoint appeared inconsistent to many of those progressive elites whose favor they courted and who had been re-placing the splintering mainline liberal Protestant bloc's cultural authority in American letters. For one thing, the Catholics' often

98. Beyond the more familiar advocacy of eugenic contraception as an *inter*-racial boon, the spectrum of advocates of contraception as an *intra*-racial eugenic measure was wide in-deed by the mid-1920s and early 1930s. See, for example, African-American thinker W. E. B. Dubois in "Black Folk and Birth Control"; Fiske University social scientist Charles S. Johnson in "A Question of Negro Health"; and journalist Elmer Carter in "Eugenics for the Negro" in the American Birth Control League's *Birth Control Review* 16 (June 1932): 166–70. For more on connections between contraception, eugenics, evolution, and "race" in that period, see Yudell, *Race Unmasked*, esp. chap. 3; and Gregory Michael Dorr, *Segregation's Science*, 96–99.

anti-individualistic, science-centered rhetoric against certain types of birth control did not jibe with their simultaneous individualist rhetoric opposing state-sponsored sterilization and prohibition of alcohol. Critiques the Catholics faced for these inconsistencies could not be easily dismissed. The Great Depression further complicated the picture.

At the Brink of the Great Depression: Birth Control, Eugenics, and Demography

It would be difficult to overstate the significance of the Great Depression at the dawn of the 1930s. Its effects certainly extended to reform-minded discourse related to birth control and eugenics, further actuating both the cooperation and, ultimately, union of what had hitherto been two formally distinct movements. It did so by providing common conditions for large-scale efforts aimed at dealing rationally with the widespread suffering instigated by the economic collapse and its concomitant social reverberations. Economic and demographic birth control arguments centering on the need to conserve scarce resources were received more positively and widely by the public in the face of what might otherwise be the strain of population increase in the midst of economic depression. Contraception advocates had already made headway getting support for their movement by tying it to scientific authority and by converting the right people to the idea that birth control was a legitimate arm of eugenic science. The advent of economic freefall cleared a path for more persuasive population-based arguments for artificial contraception.[99] Such arguments tapped into the increased reliance on the social sciences by federal government plans to combat the Depression as connections between eugenics and

99. While not speaking exclusively about this period, scholar Lara Marks does identify presumed logic in these connections: "One of the basic assumptions … was that science had caused the problem of population growth by reducing mortality rates, and it was therefore up to science to solve the problem." Lara V. Marks, *Sexual Chemistry: A History of the Contraceptive Pill* (New Haven: Yale University Press, 2001), 37.

birth control were themselves becoming more prevalent in social science fields.[100]

The recognition in North America of professional demography, as a combination of biological and social science, crystallized in 1931 with the formation of the Population Association of America, patterned after the International Union for the Scientific Study of Population and Demography. Demography assumed an important role in supporting and promulgating eugenics.[101] Sanger's leadership cadre sought to prove the organized birth control case numerically. It was a way of rationalizing what had been, earlier in her career, openly neo-Malthusian arguments.[102]

These population-based arguments from the 1920s urged that if population were not checked in a rational manner, the world would suffer social upheaval, disease, and even war. More precise social planning, thus, required more precise population measurement. After the initial repugnance of many eugenicists to birth control was overcome via Sanger, population-based neo-Malthusian birth control was incorporated into the official American eugenics movement platform in the early 1930s. Indeed, neo-Malthusianism had itself long included a utopian strain that made it readily adaptable as one of several prongs of eugenics, provided it was properly framed as birth control selectively aimed at undesirables.[103] In this rendering, birth control easily transmogrified into an important part of the negative eugenics plan, implemented alongside policies like state-sponsored sterilization and racialist quota-based immigration laws to limit the spread of what was termed "bad stock" that weakened the country's physical and economic health.

One of *Eugenics* magazine's early efforts to tie together birth control, eugenics, and neo-Malthusian-underpinned population

100. See, for example, Norman E. Himes, "Robert Dale Owen, The Pioneer of American Neo-Malthusianism," *American Journal of Sociology* 35 (January 1930): 529–47.

101. Edmund Ramsden, "Social Demography and Eugenics in the Interwar United States," *Population and Development Review* 29 (December 2003): 548.

102. See Ramsden, "Social Demography and Eugenics."

103. Tobin, *American Religious Debate*, 11.

studies was a May 1929 piece constructing a shared history for the movements. It reified the birth control–eugenics–population connection in the United States back to the birth control efforts of radical pioneers Robert Dale Owen and Charles Knowlton.[104] What made this point of view especially interesting was the concurrent attempt by *Eugenics* to connect appeals of Catholics supporting state-sponsored sterilization with proposals to apply demographic-population control solutions to the Depression. That magazine drew special attention to international Catholic voices who could reinforce the claims of the AES that social policy in economically troubled times was best formulated by committees of scientific experts. In the magazine's May 1930 issue, Samuel Holmes reviewed the book *Eugenics: Aims and Methods* by the British Jesuit Fr. Henry Davis, SJ. Davis had argued that the church should accept the state's power to mandate sterilization as recommended by the British Mental Deficiency Committee of 1929. Holmes, in turn, urged Catholics to read and accept Davis's book, noting "the recommendations given in the Report for dealing with defectives are those of a body of experts, and it is gratifying to find that Catholics can agree with this body of competent and broad-minded specialists."[105]

Likewise, Kenneth MacArthur argued in the magazine's December 1930 issue that "numerous American religious leaders are

104. Norman E. Himes, "Eugenic Thought in the American Birth Control Movement 100 Years Ago," *Eugenics* 2 (May 1929): 5. Himes complained at the start that neither eugenicists nor demographers had sufficiently appreciated the extent to which "Robert Dale Owen had used as one of his strongest arguments for birth control 'the possibility it opened up for racial improvement'" (5). By early 1938, the American Birth Control League's medical director, speaking at the Conference on Eugenics and Birth Control, declared that the goals of the eugenics movement and "medically controlled" contraception efforts were almost identical. Eric Matsner, "Birth Control Future Policies Evidenced by Present-Day Trends," typescript, in AES Papers, box 2, folder "Conference on Eugenics and Birth Control," APS. Matsner also served as Executive Secretary of the National Medical Council on Birth Control. When the AMA endorsed birth control in 1937, the mainstreaming of eugenics, birth control, and demography as overlapping and mutually reinforcing movements with interconnected organizational infrastructures was largely complete.

105. Henry Davis, *Eugenics: Aims and Methods* (London: Burns, Oates and Washbourne, 1930), 39, quoted in Samuel J. Holmes, "Books and Bibliography: The Catholic View," review of *Eugenics: Aims and Methods*, by H. Davis, *Eugenics* 3 (May 1930): 200.

backing the program of the Eugenics Society."[106] In support of that contention, he printed an ecumenical list of fourteen names from the AES's Committee on Cooperation with Clergymen, among whom were Protestant modernists S. Parkes Cadman and Harry Emerson Fosdick, Rabbi Louis Mann, and John M. Cooper "of the Roman Catholic Church."[107] Cooper's and the others' backing, said MacArthur, showed that "progressive Christians" realized that the control of human heredity "offers a very powerful weapon for fighting the battle of the Lord to destroy the strongholds of evil."[108] Cooper's name was thereby co-opted into an argument that eugenics was a "holy" cause.

Co-opting the role of theologian, MacArthur criticized those who questioned or doubted the notion that "many Biblical phrases ... have a distinct eugenical significance" or those who expressed reticence over the idea of using eugenics to create "the Kingdom of God among men, the new social order in which the divine will is to be done on earth as it is in heaven."[109] In short, a social scientist invoked biblical-religious discourse and de facto claimed expert authority to interpret the Bible.

Also appearing in the December 1930 issue, Margaret Sanger's birth control lieutenant Guy Irving Burch, recently elected secretary of three AES committees, was pleased to co-opt Ryan's name when informing readers of the *Boston Herald*'s recent quote from Ryan, which said "compulsory legal sterilization for the prevention of the birth of feeble-minded persons is not necessarily contrary to the natural rights of the individual. Therefore, it is not necessarily immoral.... Up to the present, no official pronouncement on the question has come from any authority of the church."[110] Although

---

106. Kenneth C. MacArthur, "Eugenics and the Church: Answering Questions," *Eugenics* 3 (December 1930): 469.

107. MacArthur, "Eugenics and the Church," 469.

108. MacArthur, "Eugenics and the Church," 469.

109. MacArthur, "Eugenics and the Church," 469.

110. Ryan quoted in Guy Irving Burch, "Population: Public Health," *Eugenics* 3 (December 1930): 474.

much of this appropriation of Ryan and Cooper was rendered disingenuous by failing to include other qualifications on the matter they had made over the years, none of what was quoted had to be falsified. There was more to this susceptibility to co-optation than taking words out of context. In some cases, their words simply lent themselves to scientism. That their public discourse could be used this way serves as more evidence of the paradoxical and unintended consequences that obtained when liberal-progressive Catholics got the public hearing they sought in these areas.

In short, Sanger's public efforts in the 1920s cultivated the impression that birth control advocacy and implementation were the fruits of disinterested social engineers working for the betterment of society. Learning to control through scientific means what humanity had previously been powerless to deal with in a wide, coordinated manner, birth control would thereby improve the quality, while regulating the quantity, of the population. A union of interests tying together organizations predicated on the progressive goal of controlling nature through science and technology created a mutually reinforcing matrix of evolution, genetics-eugenics, birth control, social hygiene, and population studies. Liberal Catholics helped reinforce the matrix without intending to do so.

⌒ 6

Rhythm and Reverberation

The 1930s

> The question is not, therefore: Birth control or no birth
> control? The real question is Lawful birth control or
> unlawful birth control? Modern Science discloses the
> method by which parents may space their offspring in a
> natural, rational, ethical manner.
>
> — Fr. John A. O'Brien (1934)

Casti Connubii

On December 31, 1930, Pope Pius XI issued his worldwide encyclical letter *Casti Connubii* (*CC*).[1] It was only the second time in the modern era that a pope had issued a binding encyclical dealing specifically with marriage and sexuality. The first had been Leo XIII's *Arcanum Divinae Sapientiae* ("The Mystery of Divine Wisdom" or "On Christian Marriage"), on February 10, 1880. While decreeing that marriage was partly designed to make husbands and wives "better

---

Epigraph is from John A. O'Brien, *Lawful Birth Control: According to Nature's Law, in Harmony with Catholic Morality* (Fort Wayne, Ind.: Courtney Co., 1934), 96; also O'Brien, *Natural Birth Control without Contraceptives according to Nature's Law in Harmony with Catholic Morality* (Champaign, Ill.: Newman Co., 1938), 96.

1. Pius XI (Achille Ratti), elected pope in 1922, had been a compromise candidate and hailed from a blue-collar family in the foothills of Lombardy. See Frank Coppa, *The Modern Papacy, since 1789* (London: Longman, 1998), esp. 182–83.

and happier," *Arcanum*'s foregone conclusion was that marriage and sexuality were first and foremost intended for procreation. It did not mention contraception.[2]

CC, by contrast, presented a very different tone than *Arcanum* did. It deemphasized the emotional component of marriage and instead reiterated its primary procreative function while admitting to its acceptable secondary companionate aspects. The social and cultural environment had changed since 1880; *CC* was issued amid a vastly more assertive, respectable, and influential worldwide movement for birth control than had existed in 1880, a movement that now claimed additional credence in the face of the international Depression. Also, when *CC* was issued, the major secular journals of opinion had for some time been presenting birth control as a legitimate, rational correlative to other social restructuring.[3] One survey of birth control material in American magazines and journals of opinion remarked on what it considered the irony that the Great Depression acted as a tremendous boost to public interest in birth control and that even "many of the more conservative journals devoted room to the issue for the first time."[4] Soon after the stock market crash, what had been a mostly solid wall of religious opposition to contraception would also crumble.

CC was intended in part as a direct response to the Anglican Church's Lambeth Conference declaration in August 1930, which

2. Leo XIII, *Arcanum Divinae Sapentiae*, Encyclical Letter (February 10, 1880), http://www.vatican.va/content/leo-xiii/en/encyclicals/documents/hf_l-xiii_enc_10021880_arcanum.html. There had actually been one other papal issuance on marriage in this era, but it was not a worldwide binding decree. This was Leo XIII's *Dum Multa* of December 24, 1902. That text exclusively addressed the bishops of Ecuador, who were at the time engaged in a church-state dispute with a civil government attempting to assume some of the church's authority over the legal marriage contract.

3. The *New Republic*, *Harper's Weekly*, and *Survey* had been running pieces on birth control since 1915; *Harper's* serialized an eight-part series on the topic in October of that year. Rosanna L. Barnes, "Birth Control in Popular Twentieth-Century Periodicals," *Family Coordinator* 19 (April 1970): 160. As more evidence of its increasing coverage, *The Reader's Guide to Periodical Literature* indexed 23 articles on birth control from 1920 through 1924; 45 articles from 1925 to 1929; and 131 from 1930 to 1934. The *New Republic* and *The Nation* "continued to keep the issue alive during the prosperous twenties" (Barnes, 160–61).

4. Barnes, "Birth Control," 162.

had reversed that church body's absolute prohibition of contraception.[5] Although the Anglicans did stipulate that contraception was to be an exception, not the rule, for normal marital relations, the archbishop of Canterbury endeared himself to the science-minded by explaining that "complete abstinence may induce nervous disorders and injury to the body and mind."[6]

Lambeth's 1930 declaration on birth control, and its relation to science in general, was widely discussed in the American press. The *Literary Digest* printed a selection of American newspapers' responses to Lambeth, all of them positive. The *New York World* remarked of the British hierarchs' endorsements as a whole: "Next to the bishops' decisions on sex education and birth control, this one [on evolution] ... throws fundamentalism overboard altogether." The *Digest* also cited Memphis, Tennessee's *Commercial Appeal*, revealing that newspaper's warfare metaphor–based assumptions about prior relations between religion and science: "[Lambeth] is a summons to the church to make its peace with science. Since the warfare began, many have cried 'peace' when there was no peace."[7]

As noted in chapter 4, Lambeth turned out to be the harbinger of a seismic shift in the positions of mainline Christian and Jewish bodies.[8] It certainly stimulated the mainline Protestant Fed-

5. The 1930 Conference's Resolution 15 noted: "Where there is clearly felt moral obligation to limit or avoid parenthood, the method must be decided on Christian principles.... In those cases where there is such a clearly felt moral obligation to limit or avoid parenthood ... the Conference agrees that other methods [besides complete abstinence] may be used, provided that this is done in the light of the same Christian principles." See "Resolution 15 – The Life and Witness of the Christian Community – Marriage," *Index of Resolutions from 1930*, https://www .anglicancommunion.org/resources/document-library/lambeth-conference/1930/resolution-15 -the-life-and-witness-of-the-christian-community-marriage.aspx (accessed December 18, 2019).

6. The *New York Times*'s coverage of the Lambeth Conference, quoted in Guy Irving Burch, "Larithmics," *Eugenics* 4 (January 1931): 35. Burch explained that *larithmics* was a term coined by Henry Pratt Fairchild meaning "the scientific study of quantitative aspects of population control" (35).

7. "Anglicans Accept Evolution," *Literary Digest* 106 (September 6, 1930): 24.

8. By 1936, Margaret Sanger was able to take advantage of numerous such shifts to argue that intelligent religious organizations supported her position: "Outstanding among those who ... suppor[t] the principles of birth control [are]" the Episcopal Church; the Federal Council of Churches Committee on the Marriage and the Home; "the Unitarian Associations, the Universalist General Convention; Regional Conferences of the Methodist Church, a Special Committee of the Women's Problems Group of Philadelphia Yearly Meeting of

eral Council of Churches of Christ in the United States—though already on a trajectory to accept birth control—to endorse it the following year even less guardedly than did Lambeth.[9] Realizing early on the ripple effect Lambeth's decree would have, both Pope Pius XI and key European moral theologians believed a declaration of official Catholic position was in order, and sooner rather than later.[10] Indeed Rev. Worth Tippy, a leader at the FCCC, spurred by the Lambeth move, had established a behind-the-scenes dynamic of mutual organizational support with Sanger to promulgate birth control. This mutual support both preceded, and would extend for years following, the FCCC's birth control endorsement in 1931. The Vatican was right to believe the Catholic position was facing new and unprecedented levels of challenge.[11] *CC* appeared a little over four months after the Lambeth decree. It stipulated that a marriage, though a compact freely entered into by two individuals, was not "subject to any contrary pact even of the spouses themselves."[12] The encyclical went on: "No reason, however grave, may be put forward by which anything intrinsically against nature may become conformable to nature and morally good."[13] *CC* defined procreation as essential to sexuality because ordained in natural law: "Since, therefore, the conjugal act is designed primarily by nature for the

---

Friends," the Rabbinical Assembly of America, the Central Conference of American Rabbis, the General Council of Congregationalist and Christian Churches, and others. She also noted that "lay groups affiliated with the church, such as Y.W.C.A., Y.M.C.A., National Council of Jewish Women, and other women's church organizations, bring up reinforcements." What, she rhetorically asked, "is the reason behind this support? Birth Control, it is felt, will make for earlier marriages and happier marriages." Margaret Sanger, "Birth Control and Religion," unpublished typescript (February 4, 1936), in "Published Writings and Speeches, 1911–1959," microfilm 128:0454, Sanger Papers Project.

9. On the path to acceptance at the FCCC, see Plopper, "Protestants," 346–57, 360–99.

10. Noonan argues that multiple currents led to the promulgation of *CC*. It was purportedly crafted in response not only to the Lambeth decree but also to some European Catholic theologians who had been calling for a revision of the Catholic teaching on sexuality. See Noonan, *Contraception*, 424–27.

11. On Tippy and Sanger's correspondence and mutual assistance for the birth control cause, see Plopper, "Protestants," 425.

12. *CC*, par. 5. Later in this chapter, we see Ryan himself seizing on this line as opening the way for the rhythm method.

13. *CC*, par. 54.

begetting of children, those who in exercising it deliberately frustrate its natural power and purpose sin against nature and commit a deed which is intrinsically shameful and vicious."[14] The intrinsic sin concept embedded in neoscholastic terminology had entered the room and up to this point, little seems open to interpretation. To all appearances, CC reasserted the standard neoscholastic position that both Ryan and Cooper had publicly questioned back in 1928. Its orientation is not surprising given that one of its chief drafters was the internationally known Belgian moral theologian and rigorist Fr. Arthur Vermeersch, SJ, professor at the Gregorian University in Rome.[15]

Despite the severity of CC's language, one portion soon became the focal point for some respected Catholics' attempts to argue for sundering a seemingly unbreakable connection between intercourse and procreation.[16] The passage in question read: "Nor are those considered as acting against nature who in the married state use their right in the proper manner, although on account of natural reasons either of time or of certain defects, new life cannot be brought forth."[17]

A Peaceful Interlude

Both the Catholic press and the broader American press gave extensive coverage to CC. One historian of Catholicism and contraception has pointed out that no encyclical had ever seen such wide publicity, much of it respectful.[18] For Catholics, the language of CC reinforced their attempts to urge economic restructuring instead of birth control to confront the worsening global economic depression. So did a second papal encyclical aimed at the crisis and

14. CC, par. 54.
15. Noonan, *Contraception*, 424–25. Noonan said that Vermeersch, trained in both law and theology, had such influence at the Vatican that "from 1918 to 1934 he dominated Roman moral theology" (425).
16. Noonan, *Contraception*, 447.
17. CC, par. 59.
18. Tentler, *Catholics and Contraception*, 73–74.

issued a mere four months after *CC*: this was *Quadragesimo Anno*, subtitled "Reconstruction and Perfection of the Social Order," a title hearkening to a previous important encyclical on the social order, *Rerum Novarum*, issued forty years earlier with the subtitle "On the Rights and Duties of Capital and Labor."[19] Of course, not everyone was impressed. The *New Republic* showed its displeasure over an extended series of months. In late 1931, its editor went out of his way to complain about the papal position on contraception in an article that otherwise had nothing to do with Catholics.[20] The *Nation*, too, published a series of criticisms.[21]

American liberal Catholic contraception rhetoric actually featured a visible swing to population and demography arguments in the 1930s not long after *CC*. *Commonweal* was a noted locus of this rhetoric on contraception, particularly for liberal Catholics. At first, it had seemed things would remain *status quo ante en-cyclicum*. Michael Williams's editorial of January 21, 1931, ardently defended *CC*, framing it as a clear, unambiguous pronouncement that would require serious economic restructuring to fully enact.[22] Even here, however, a subtle dislocation is evident to the careful

19. See Leo XIII, *Rerum Novarum*, Encyclical Letter (May 15, 1891), http://www.vatican.va/content/leo-xiii/en/encyclicals/documents/hf_l-xiii_enc_15051891_rerum-novarum.html. As McGreevy put it: "Each document [*CC* and *Quadragesimo Anno*], the one on marriage and the other on the economy, called for wages to match needs" (*Catholicism and American Freedom*, 162–63). Whereas through the centuries, the wheels of the papacy had sometimes been criticized for moving too slowly in response to crises, in this instance there was no such delay. The response to the Depression was quick and far-reaching.

20. In refuting a reader who wrote to the *New Republic* saying that the flat tax would fix China's economic population problems in a more efficient manner than birth control, the editor suddenly brought Catholics into a discussion in which they had played no part: "Nothing is more painful than to watch the lucubrations of an intelligent Catholic social scientist [presumably John Ryan], whose thinking is rigidly confined by a medieval philosophy which has no possible validity under present conditions, and who uses the ingenuity of a hypnotic subject to justify his impossible position." "Too Many People?," *New Republic* 69 (December 1931): 85.

21. See, for example, George Lake, "The Spiritual Aspect of Birth Control," *The Nation* 134 (January 27, 1932): 110; and William Allen Pusey, "Birth Control and Sex Morality," *The Nation* 134 (1932): 112.

22. Williams argued that the present day's economic—and thus, contraceptive—ills were "the fulfillment of what [Pope] Leo XIII declared [in 1892's *Rerum Novarum*] must happen if the moral laws of justice and charity were not applied to the economic struggle." [Michael Williams], "Rome Has Spoken," *Commonweal* 13 (January 21, 1931): 310.

observer. Although Williams mentioned the natural law perspective in which the encyclical was explicitly framed, he did not overtly call it a natural law argument, nor did he say anything about contraception as intrinsically immoral.

Williams's editorial defended moral law, but more prominent in it was a sociological evaluation of the world's population and economy. It also evinced less of a need to make it seem that Catholics alone stood in defense of truth. Instead, the truth Williams was presenting was available to anyone who appreciated sound science and moral economic reasoning. Here, and in the letters to the editor he subsequently published, Williams seemed concerned to demonstrate that the clarity and self-evident truth of *CC* was, in fact, appreciated by many thoughtful people of good will. For example, a letter in the February 18 issue of *Commonweal* lauded the pope and his encyclical for force of expression and clarity. The writer claimed that *CC* applied universally to all good Christians and citizens: "I think that on that document alone I should want to look into the Catholic religion, and the Church of which the author of this document is the head, for it is so clearly an honest man's church."[23] Another letter Williams published called modern sexual mores "unscientific and immoral," while the Catholic Church's rendering of the moral law was an example of "her divinely scientific principles."[24] Science-centered arguments on birth control in *Commonweal* were to take center stage as Williams began to publish some new voices.

On April 1, 1931, *Commonweal* advertised a series of articles to debut on April 8 written by Dr. Edward Roberts Moore, chair of the Committee on Population Decline and Related Problems of the National Conference of Catholic Charities and a former social work professor at Fordham. The ad promised that Moore would "offer a series of articles about the problem of population and birth

23. William Franklin Sands, "*Casti Connubii*," letter to the editor, *Commonweal* 13 (February 18, 1931): 439.

24. William E. Kerrish, "Companionate Marriage," letter to the editor, *Commonweal* 13 (February 13, 1931): 438.

control.... Every phase of the subject has been carefully investigated; every conclusion reached will stand the test of scientific analysis.... You will not want to miss any of these articles and there are a number of your friends who will wish to know the Catholic position on this vital problem."[25]

The "Catholic position," as Moore proffered it, seemed to be based in population studies. Indeed, in the second installment of the series, titled "The Contraception of Prosperity," Moore presented the Catholic position on birth control as a series of demographic and economic theories, concluding with: "The primary explanation loosely described as the prosperity of the United States lies in the constant expansion of its consuming market."[26] To a reader of this series, the Catholic position seemed to be that birth control was in a practical sense dangerous because the American economic system as it stood needed a constant stream of consumption to remain stable. An unstable market, in contrast, put people out of work and thus inclined them to resort to birth control. The solution to both ills, therefore, was structural economic reform.[27]

By the end of September, Century Publishing turned Moore's work into a book, *The Case against Birth Control* (1931). *Commonweal* subsequently ran regular advertisements of the book that included its own endorsement promising "the weary Catholic apologist formidable facts and figures" and another by the *Philadelphia Public Ledger* calling it "a necessary book ... because for the first time in recent years it offers to its opponents an argument upon grounds that the opponents recognize as debatable." Later in the ad, the book is said to be a result of an investigation commissioned

25. "Birth Control" [advertisement], *Commonweal* 14 (April 1, 1931): iv. Moore was also a priest, but he was not referred to as such in the printed materials (in a small photo in the *Commonweal* ad, he did wear what appeared to be a clerical collar).

26. Edward Roberts Moore, "The Contraception of Prosperity," *Commonweal* 13 (April 15, 1931): 654.

27. Moore's final installment of May 20, 1931, announced that the preceding five articles in his series had been framed in public policy and medical science. That last article was a powerful natural law-centered defense of the church's view, although clearly amateur from a philosophical perspective. See Moore, "The Malice of Contraception," *Commonweal* 14 (May 20, 1931): 68–71.

by the National Conference of Catholic Charities carried out by Moore "and a trained corps of assistants." It concluded by promising that "the book presents the official Catholic attitude toward the practice of contraception and it presents FACTS not just theories, based on the findings of this extensive survey."[28]

By June of 1931, Fr. John Burke of the NCWC had received an internal memorandum complaining that too much emphasis was being placed on economic and scientific frameworks in Catholic birth control rhetoric. Ryan, in fact, was singled out as being particularly guilty. It is little wonder, however, that liberal Catholics schooled in the terms of the Progressive Era would move in this direction.[29] *Commonweal*, nevertheless, continued on its same line. A letter to the editor of *Commonweal* from November 18, 1931, featured neoscholastic aficionado Fr. Walter Farrell, OP, asking, "Have we Catholics, like the cigarette makers, gone in for catch-words instead of thinking?"[30] Farrell criticized the rhetoric of Moore and also of Ryan, who had reviewed Moore's book for the magazine. According to Farrell, "in modern Catholic argumentation against contraception I have seen no effective presentation of the argument from the intrinsic immorality of contraception"; he went on to say that it is "not sufficient to prove that contraception is against nature; that is almost self-evident. What we must show now is why this violation of nature is such a grave offense, a mortal sin."[31] Farrell was zeroing in on the very topic Ryan and Cooper had confronted back in 1928 in their *Ecclesiastical Review* articles but, unlike them, claimed he could prove contraception was a mortal sin.[32] With *Commonweal* concentrating on science-centered arti-

28. Advertisement in *Commonweal* 14 (September 23, 1931): iv.

29. "Memorandum" to Fr. Burke (June 8, 1931), in NCWC Papers, box 85, folder "Social Action Family Life Bureau 1930–1944," ACUA.

30. Walter Farrell, "Dwindling Populations," letter to the editor, *Commonweal* 14 (November 18, 1931): 72–73.

31. Farrell, "Dwindling Populations," 72–73. Farrell went on to provide a small lesson in neoscholastic philosophy, arguing both that every act against nature is a mortal sin and that contraception is intrinsically wrong because it violates the "primary" ends of humans from all possible angles. He evinced surprise at Ryan's failure to criticize Moore's book on that basis.

32. These 1928 pieces were discussed in chapter 4.

cles about contraception, some of its readers who focused on neo-scholasticism wrote to say that the magazine was not presenting an internally consistent Catholic viewpoint.

Catholic physician James J. Walsh, who himself wrote articles for *Commonweal*, penned a letter to the editor referring to the recently published antibirth control pamphlet of a New York Catholic doctor, Edward C. Podvin. Walsh gloried not only in the fact that many physicians personally opposed birth control but also in the fact that Podvin's claims revealed that "the most important medical organizations throughout the country not only do not approve but take up a definitely negative position on the subject."[33] But then Walsh went on to appeal to the expert authority of a known eugenicist who happened to oppose birth control: "Thoughtful physicians take the position described by Professor Paul Popenoe who stigmatizes birth control as 'pseudobiological' and declares that the propaganda for birth control 'has in fact become a quasi-religious cult.'"[34] Walsh closed by rousingly endorsing the following statement by Popenoe: "Like other new cults, [the birth control movement] is marked by zeal, fanaticism, intolerance and enjoyment of mild martyrdom."[35]

Meanwhile, as liberal Catholic figures lauded scientific authorities, several scientist-authored articles on supporting contraception appeared in *The Nation* after *CC* employed religious language. A number of these articles, especially those found in the January 1932 special issue dedicated to birth control, featured the increasingly prevalent position that scientists had the right to make theological claims in defense of their arguments.[36] According to physician

33. James J. Walsh, "The Birth Control Racket," letter to *Commonweal* 16 (July 27, 1932): 331.

34. Walsh, "Birth Control Racket," 331. For years, Popenoe was one of the most active and ardent members of the American Eugenics Association. He also became a close friend and correspondent of John Montgomery Cooper.

35. Walsh, "Birth Control Racket," 331. The irony, of course, was that the same, and more, had surely been said of the very eugenics movement from whose perspective Popenoe spoke these words and of which he was a longtime leader.

36. See Lake, "Spiritual Aspect of Birth Control," 110; and Pusey, "Birth Control and Sex Morality," 112. As an expert on sex, the physician should be heeded: "The physician ... of all men is constantly forced to a realization that sex is the dominant subtle influence in life." (Pusey, 111).

George Lake, scientists' assertions about contraception had to tran-
scend "hygienic, economic, and social aspects" so that they could
demonstrate "the great spiritual values which undoubtedly inhere
in it [birth control]."[37] Only scientists had the ability to glimpse this
new religious vision. Lake then offered a theological-psychiatric
argument for facilitating the next "step in [humanity's] spiritual
evolution," eliminating womankind's remaining boundary, which
prevented her from standing next to her husband "as the other half
of his soul."[38]

Arguing in favor of scientists' power to pronounce on such
spiritual and moral matters, Lake claimed that birth control was,
in fact, "entirely outside [the] field" of religious thinkers and "dogmatic theology" because, "like all other matters with which human
beings are concerned, it is neither right nor wrong in itself, those
qualities depending solely upon how it is used and by whom."[39]
Scientists, he averred would also be the ones to discover the new
values around which individual behaviors and broad social policies
could be molded. In this way, the scientists would be the ones to
foster what he called humanity's "spiritual evolution."[40]

The theme of science-minded reformers triggering humanity's
ability to control, and thus direct, nature and society dominated
the subsequent articles in *The Nation's* special birth control issue.
But religious arguments abounded here as well. Tying together
both themes, the pieces were reminiscent of the religiously tinged
pro-eugenics language in the 1920s. Henry Pratt Fairchild's article
"Birth Control and Social Engineering" offered a quasi-utopian vision of humanity that took for granted an ascending social development that would result in mastery over the "iron law" of nature,
a law that would otherwise deal brutally, in neo-Malthusian fash-

37. Lake, "Spiritual Aspect of Birth Control," 110.
38. Lake, "Spiritual Aspect of Birth Control," 111. By this "boundary," he meant involuntary motherhood. Lake's argument here seems an amalgam of theological monism and
scientific positivism.
39. Lake, "Spiritual Aspect of Birth Control," 110. The reader is left to puzzle over Lake's sud-
den characterization of birth control as "neither right nor wrong in itself" in light of his previous
and successive comments asserting the "great spiritual values" which "undoubtedly inhere in" it.
40. Lake, "Spiritual Aspect of Birth Control," 111.

ion, with overpopulation. Fairchild's use of imagery portrayed the birth control debate as a divide between reason and unreason; between rational, scientifically derived spirituality and an older-style, irrational religion; between light and darkness; and between suffering and social perfection.[41]

The focus on Catholicism as the prime opponent of enlightenment on the subject of birth control cut across most of the pieces in *The Nation*'s series.[42] The first paragraph of *The Nation* article by John Dewey invoked the bogeys of both Copernicus and Galileo to claim that dogma-centered religion had been, and was once again, the chief obstacle to scientific enlightenment: "The opposition to the birth-control movement is not a unique or isolated fact. It is an expression of an ever-recurring struggle between darkness and knowledge."[43] For Dewey, the key was society's ability to *control* that brought about advance: "New knowledge always means the possibility of new control.... The conflict between ignorance and knowledge becomes one between chance and control."[44] This quest for control, in Dewey's discourse, clearly tied birth control to eugenic goals: "I can think of no change which would be more beneficial than one which would make us prize quality more and quantity less."[45] On the topic of eugenic birth control, a final piece in *The Nation*'s series by Margaret Sanger tied together the major themes found in the journal's other articles.

41. Henry Pratt Fairchild, "Birth Control and Social Engineering," *The Nation* 134 (January 27, 1932): 106. Birth control, according to Fairchild, was a "modern," "socially conscious," "deliberate," "farseeing," "broad," "intelligent," "scientific," and "self directed" means to "eugenic" "social engineering" and to the "control" necessary to ensure the "revision [of society] upward" (106).

42. In another article appearing in the same issue, Robert Allen did not hesitate to aver that a female Catholic politician (Mary Norton) who had opposed the federal government's use of power to loosen access to contraceptive information was herself but a product of slimy and corrupt Catholic machine politics, a "henchman," in Allen's phrasing. Catholics were the ever-present "bitter and vociferous" rabble, evincing "bellicose hostility," who turned every attempt to demonstrate the social excellence of birth control into irrational "emotional melee." Robert S. Allen, "Congress and Birth Control," *The Nation* 134 [January 27, 1932]: 104–5.

43. John Dewey, "Education and Birth Control," *The Nation* 134 (January 27, 1932): 112.

44. Dewey, "Education and Birth Control," 112.

45. Dewey, "Education and Birth Control," 112. On the same page, Dewey added, "There is always wholesome sanitation where this is free circulation of intelligence."

Margaret Sanger and the Pope

Sanger expressed pleasure that *Casti Connubii* had de facto admitted what she had said all along—that a lot of Catholics used birth control. But she was by no means pleased with the encyclical on the whole, employing her trenchant wit in her piece in the *Birth Control Review*: "Evidently the Pope believes in birth control, although he countenances only one method, namely, continence."[46] Sanger, too, wrote in religious language, claiming that God must be in favor of the birth control movement, especially because of its eugenic blessings: "Assuming that God does want an increasing number of worshipers of the Catholic faith, does he also want an increasing number of feeble-minded, insane, criminal, and diseased worshipers? That is unavoidable if the Pope is obeyed because ... he forbids every single method of birth control except continence, a method which the feeble-minded, insane, and criminal will not use."[47] She also appealed to Dean Inge, the iconoclastic pro-eugenics Anglican modernist of St. Paul's Cathedral in London, to echo a point made by the aforementioned physicians in *The Nation*: the alternative to controlling conception is abortion.[48] Abortion, she pointed out, was a disgrace, but it would be the unintended consequence of following the Catholic position, as would be the neglect of "race improvement."[49]

Continuing with the religious themes and authorities appealed to in her argumentation, Sanger challenged the encyclical's interpretation of the oft-discussed thirty-eighth chapter of Genesis on the story of Onan.[50] She continued by contrasting the pope's view of the role properly given the individual—one of obeying the au-

---

46. Margaret Sanger, "Comments on the Pope's Encyclical," *Birth Control Review* 15 (February 1931): 40. Sanger wrote a year later in *The Nation* to emphasize that numerous Catholics were evidently ignoring the pope: "One-third of the women who come to the Birth Control Clinical Research Bureau are Catholics." Sanger, "Pope's Position on Birth Control," 102.

47. Sanger, "Pope's Position on Birth Control," 102.

48. Sanger, "Pope's Position on Birth Control," 103.

49. Sanger, "Pope's Position on Birth Control," 102.

50. Sanger, "Pope's Position on Birth Control," 103.

thoritative teaching of the Catholic magisterium—with the words
of Jesus himself from the Gospels. Her rhetorical effect was augmented by quoting from *CC* and then writing, "That is what the
Pope says. Now let us see what Jesus says."[51] Sanger invoked the
gospels of Matthew and Mark to reject what she characterized as
the papal view of God's will regarding procreation. She even went
so far as to ask, "Did [Jesus] ever say anything about the limit of
offspring? Did He ever say anything that by any twist of argument
can be interpreted to mean that He disapproved of contraception?
If He did, why does not the Pope cite chapter and verse?"[52]

Finally, Sanger invoked an argument fraught with irony, one
that would soon be employed by the very Catholics with whom
she disputed while our cadre within the latter continued to eschew
Biblical or theological language in courting the legitimacy that
science could ostensibly bestow on their cause. In her words: "In
many cases, according to medical science, continence in marriage
is positively harmful to health if practiced for any length of time. It
can bring on serious nervous derangement."[53]

Progressive Catholics' appeals to science in birth control discourse substantially increased when, in October 1932, a supposedly
scientific, rational method of birth regulation was disseminated in
a book published by a devout Catholic, a book that received imme-
diate popular attention and even acclaim. In that book, a twenty-
nine-year-old Catholic physician named Leo Latz described a
method recently articulated by the Dutch Catholic Jan Smulders,
a method that would purportedly enable couples to know when
their intercourse might lead to pregnancy and, crucially, when it
definitely would not. The measurement relied on the work of two
research physicians charting the hitherto inscrutable processes
of the female menstrual cycle. Both Catholic scientists, Smulders
and Latz, contended that the resulting method of controlling con-

51. Sanger, "Pope's Position on Birth Control," 103.
52. Sanger, "Pope's Position on Birth Control," 103.
53. Sanger, "Pope's Position on Birth Control," 103.

ception fit the stringent natural law criteria for marital sexuality established by *CC*. To some publicly influential Catholics, including Ryan, Cooper, and O'Brien, it appeared to be a literal godsend, and they treated it as such. These first impressions would later be second-guessed by third parties, but by then, the heavens had opened and the storm had arrived.

The Rhythm of Birth Control

Termed the scientific method of birth regulation, the system colloquially known as *the rhythm method* arrived on American shores from Austria and Japan just as the Great Depression was setting in. Based on a new scientific measurement of fertility and sterility periods in ovulation cycles, this calculated means of avoiding pregnancy contradicted an older approach rooted in the erroneous base of Frederick Hollick's and Felix Pouchet's *safe period*.[54]

American Catholic intellectuals began publicly extolling the new scientific approach to birth regulation by 1933. They were inspired by two books that explained and enthusiastically endorsed the method; both books were authored by American Catholic physicians and, crucially, were published with the explicit approval of key Catholic bishops in 1932 and 1933. The first of the two popular birth control books was Chicago physician-professor Leo Latz's *The Rhythm of Sterility and Fertility in Women* (1932). The other was *The Sterile Period in Family Life* (1933), coauthored by Fr. Valere Coucke and Pennsylvania physician James A. Walsh, the latter a neoscholastic enthusiast.[55] Both books received the official seal of

54. Reed, *From Private Vice to Public Virtue*, 12–13. Unsurprisingly, the pursuit of a scientific map for the ovulation process occurred within the same matrix of research and reform as the method of birth control dependent upon it. See Viterbo, "Promise of Rhythm," 294–95.

55. Leo Latz, *The Rhythm of Sterility and Fertility in Women: A Discussion of the Physiological, Practical, and Ethical Aspects of the Discoveries of Drs. K. Ogino (Japan) and H. Knaus (Austria) Regarding the Periods When Conception Is Impossible and When Possible* (Chicago: Latz Foundation, 1932); Valere J. Coucke and James J. Walsh, *The Sterile Period in Family Life* (New York: Joseph F. Wagner, 1933). Latz learned about the method when he was in Cologne, Germany, having heard a presentation on it at the Cologne Medical Society (Viterbo, "Promise of Rhythm," 252).

approbation of the dioceses in which they were published—Latz's by Chicago's Cardinal Joseph Mundelein and the Coucke-Walsh book from Cardinal Patrick Hayes of New York, well-known in the fight against artificial contraception.[56] Latz, whose book was first, received the most attention of the authors, particularly after he published his broader professional appeal in the *Journal of the American Medical Association* in 1935.[57]

These volumes explained mutually reinforcing conclusions, independently arrived at by Hermann Knaus of Austria and Kyusaku Ogino of Japan, on the natural workings of the ovulatory cycle in menstruating human females.[58] By mapping out what was itself a natural process, the Catholic presenters of this theory argued, one was not interfering with the system of reproduction implanted in creation, even if one used the knowledge to decide when to have sex without the possibility of conceiving a baby.

Some Catholics who endorsed the method insisted on calling it birth *regulation* as though that would differentiate it from supposedly illicit birth *control*. However, whatever philosophical distinction was intended did not inhere in the public discourse. Not just physicians and politicians but even a number of Catholics themselves referred to it as birth control. Others, critiquing Catholics, simply called it contraception. [59]

56. Technically, both books shared their lineage in the work of Dutch Catholic physician Jan M. Smulders, whose book popularizing the sterile period had appeared earlier in 1932 in Germany. See J. N. Smulders, *Periodische Enthaltung in der Ehe Methode: Ogino Knaus* (Regensburg: Manz, 1932). Knaus's own book had been given the seal of approval by one of Europe's most venerable Catholic dioceses: Regensburg.

57. Leo J. Latz and E. Reiner, "Natural Conception Control," *Journal of the American Medical Association* 105 (October 1935): 1241–76.

58. Although there was a one-day difference in their original estimates, Ogino and Knaus independently concluded that ovulation occurred between twelve and sixteen days prior to the next menstrual period. Allowing for the shelf life of sperm and ova, women with a perfectly "regular" cycle—said to be every twenty-nine days—had to abstain from intercourse for eight days while using the rhythm method. As both authors noted, most women do not have perfectly regular cycles. Women with irregular menstrual cycles would have to be abstinent for twelve days per month (Tentler, *Catholics and Contraception*, 105).

59. See, for example, the Catholic author Frank A. Smothers's article "New Light on Birth Control," *Commonweal* 17 (March 8, 1933): 511–13; Anthony M. Turano, "Contraception by Rhythm," *American Mercury* 35 (June 1935): 164–68.

For average lay Catholics who supported these books, the rhythm method was nothing other than new fruit stemming from the tree of God-given human intellect and its profound ability to investigate and understand the workings of nature. However, the method's advocacy predicated a novel position among Catholics: that it is both moral and scientifically valid to purposely exclude any possibility of procreation from the act of intercourse in non-exceptional circumstances.[60]

What is more, our liberal-progressive Catholics who endorsed the rhythm method in the public sphere did so almost exclusively on the basis of inductive evidence wedded to arguments for the social and economic good, rather than on overtly religious or deductive philosophical grounds. Because rhythm's efficacy could be—and, indeed, was—challenged by some scientists, many people began to wonder what exactly was distinctive and superior about this supposed-Catholic birth control over other methods of contraception. With respect to articulation of Catholic moral theology, increasing scientism in human origins discourse and in the sexual considerations of millions of people, these developments equaled something like shots heard round the world. By World War II, the question of birth control would not mainly be framed by religion, ethics, or debates about obscenity, even with respect to many Catholics' own discourse. It would often boil down to competing appeals to the available science most akin to own's own preferences.[61]

Practically speaking, by the early 1930s Latz had already set out to advise women how to use the rhythm method in his own medical practice, even before Ogino's and Knaus's books appeared in the United States in English translation. All the while, when featured in the popular press through the 1930s, Latz was characterized with

60. A pamphlet advertising a cardboard wheel device used to calculate the rhythms of ovulation and sterility found in John Ryan's papers declares that the device "Assumes Perfect Birth Control" (1937). Ryan Papers, box 17, folder 17, ACUA.

61. Interestingly, this was much the vision and goal articulated above in early 1932 by Henry Pratt Fairchild and physician George Lake in *The Nation*. Viterbo argues that by 1937, Leo Latz had advised more than 25,000 women, most by mail and at no charge ("Promise of Rhythm," 253n381).

epithets such as "deeply religious Catholic."[62] Latz himself made no bones about his own ardor for the Catholic faith.[63] Maxine Davis, who described Latz's deep zeal for Catholicism in 1938, contended that his missionary zealotry was equally strong for the rhythm method, saying "he teaches it with the ardor of an apostle." Indeed, just one year earlier, Latz referred to the rhythm method in an article he published in the *Illinois Medical Journal* as the "Knaus-Ogino biological law."[64]

The liberal *Commonweal* first endorsed the Latz-articulated rhythm method in the spring of 1933 in an article written by Frank Smothers. The article, entitled "New Light on Birth Control," basically summarized and elaborated on Latz's book. Smothers claimed this "natural" birth regulation "would go far toward effecting a solution to one of the most vexing moral problems now confronting the Catholic Church," that is, "if [it proves to be] as reliable as its more enthusiastic proponents believe it to be."[65] Although Smothers contended that he would also discuss the "moral considerations" of Latz's book, his article dealt mostly with Latz and Smulders's scientific contentions about the formula and their experiences applying it, including, in Smulders's case, his own personal use with his wife.[66]

Smothers added his own social scientific and demographic arguments that highlighted the need for some sort of birth control in the United States given soaring unemployment levels. He added medical arguments about the potential dangers of continence within marriage from the perspective of the day's psychological theo-

62. See, for example, Maxine Davis, "The Rhythm," *Pictorial Review* 39 (May 1938): 18.
63. See Tentler, *Catholics and Contraception*, 115.
64. Latz quoted in Viterbo, "Promise of Rhythm," 253.
65. Smothers, "New Light on Birth Control," 511.
66. Physician Halliday Sutherland (cited in chapter 5) and his contentions in this vein were also presented in support of the rhythm method: "Without suggesting that continence is impossible, or in itself harmful, I do suggest that prolonged continence in marriage may have a profound psychological effect" (Smothers, "New Light on Birth Control," 513). As stated above, the subsequent demographic argument was strangely similar to the one birth control activists had used against pre-rhythm-era Catholics who had called for continence as the only method of avoiding procreation (Smothers, "New Light on Birth Control," 513).

ries, some of the same theories that birth control advocates had themselves used throughout the 1920s to discredit moral and religious opposition to their cause.[67] Smothers added that Catholics around the country showed great enthusiasm for the method, in some cases even making it a community-wide cause: "In one parish ... it has been made a special work of Catholic Action to disseminate knowledge concerning the theory's practical application."[68]

Smothers followed this by contending that the authority of scientific and psychological pronouncements about the broader human need for sex should supersede the natural law argument's implication that one should have sex only when one was prepared to accept the possibility of creating a child. He also turned to physician Latz's theological argument that the Catholic contention about continence as the highest form of birth avoidance, or "the more perfect way," was itself impracticable and out of tune with the nature of matrimony itself.[69] Smothers added Latz's appeal to contemporary Catholic philosophers and moral theologians for his view of marriage and the rhythm method. Among them were the German philosopher Dietrich von Hildebrand and Arthur Preuss, editor of the standard-bearer textbook on moral theology at the time.[70] Smothers essentially asserted that the Catholic Church itself saw birth regulation as advisable, adding that marital continence was inadvisable on the basis of social scientific and other modern experimental and theoretical data.

67. Smothers, "New Light on Birth Control," 513.

68. Smothers, "New Light on Birth Control," 512. Latz helped alleviate women's reluctance by eventually exchanging data and questionnaires through the mail so that they could receive advice without the need for regular office visits after the physical examination and other tests were taken in person (Viterbo, "Promise of Rhythm," 253–54). This would seemingly have violated the prohibition under the Comstock Law of 1873 on circulating birth control information in the mails.

69. Smothers, "New Light on Birth Control," 512–13.

70. Smothers, "New Light on Birth Control," 513. Latz's theologizing ultimately got him into trouble with the more conservative elements within his church. On the initiative of a Jesuit irritated over Latz's widespread enthusiasm over the rhythm method, Latz was dismissed from his faculty position at Loyola University of Chicago's medical school in 1934 (Tentler, *Catholics and Contraception*, 115). He nevertheless maintained his enthusiasm both for Catholicism and for the rhythm method afterward.

Commonweal's Readers Discern a Game Afoot

A letter published in *Commonweal* in April 1933 featured reader Ernest Dimnet, a French Catholic priest and intellectual who had written the book *The Art of Thinking* (1928), previously reviewed in *Commonweal*. Dimnet pointed out in his letter the dramatic reorientation, even U-turn, that Smothers's article represented in public Catholic rhetoric that had hitherto appeared—even in that liberal forum. Dimnet stated "with astonishment" that Smothers's piece did not merely rephrase previous *Commonweal* articles on birth control but instead made quite a new argument. He noted "the contrast ... I have no doubt non-Catholic periodicals will notice—between Mr. Smothers's article and those on the same subject previously published ... where the stress was on the immorality and dangers of contraception," whereas in Smothers's article, it "is on the advisability and practical inevitability of contraception."[71]

Dimnet contended that Smothers's use of the phrase *birth regulation* failed in its intent to distinguish rhythm-based avoidance of pregnancy from all other kinds of birth control: "For the deliberate and scientific avoidance of contraception in marital relations may be called by any Latin or Greek name, but to people unused to theological subtleties, it will appear as mere contraception."[72] While Dimnet said he, too, approved of the rhythm method, he warned that readers might be scared off by what he said appeared as such a final "vindication of contraception." Perhaps, Dimnet suggested, "a plea [for consideration of it] would be more appropriate" at the present state of the discussion. He added, "Unquestionably the tone of the formerly abused resolution of the Anglican bishops on the same subject [the 1930 Lambeth Conference statement] was more productive of the right atmosphere than this," what he termed a "triumphant demonstration." He concluded by

71. Ernest Dimnet, "New Light on Birth Control," letter to the editor, *Commonweal* 18 (April 12, 1933): 663.
72. Dimnet, "New Light," 663.

saying the article implied to readers that contraception is both inevitable and necessary.[73] Another reader, Leo Sweeney, inspired by the progressive liberals' rhythm advocacy, wrote to *Commonweal* quoting from a John O'Brien article in *Homiletic and Pastoral Review* in order to argue in favor of an even more open position toward birth control.[74]

Within the next month and a half, a prominent advertisement for Latz's book appeared in *Commonweal*.[75] Boasting that eleven-thousand copies had been sold in six months, the advertisement featured various endorsements. Among them were the *Michigan Catholic* and *Catholic Daily Tribune* newspapers, the former having called it "'a remarkable book ... on rational birth control'" and the latter "a golden book for married people."[76]

Confusion had set in among both Catholics and non-Catholics over whether Latz's book advocated a position distinct in any important way from advocacies of different methods of birth control. Some Catholics tried to deny that such a question even needed to be asked. Editor Arthur Preuss of the Catholic *Fortnightly Review* magazine clearly disagreed with Dimnet's impression of Latz's and Smothers's arguments: "We do not know of a more potent antidote to the contraception heresy so widespread today than ... what Dr. Latz rightly calls 'the only rational method of birth control.'"[77] Whether Preuss was thinking wishfully or trying to divert attention from the cracks people were beginning to perceive in Catholics' discursive edifice, Dimnet's perceptions would turn out to be more than prescient.

73. Dimnet, "New Light," 663. *Commonweal* published a few other letters to the editor in subsequent issues, both pro and con, in response to Smothers's piece and Dimnet's critique. Dimnet himself wrote one of those letters for good measure to show that he was no stuffy conservative taking shots at the rhythm method (another letter writer had accused him of being opposed to rhythm. Dimnet, letter to the editor, *Commonweal* 19 (June 9, 1933): 162.

74. Leo Sweeney, letter to the editor, *Commonweal* 19 (May 26, 1933): 104.

75. "*The Rhythm of Sterility and Fertility in Women*" [advertisement], *Commonweal* 19 (April 26, 1933): 724.

76. "*Rhythm of Sterility and Fertility*" [advertisement], 724. The ad promised a "16 page descriptive circular sent free upon request" (724).

77. Preuss quoted in "*Rhythm of Sterility and Fertility*" [advertisement], 724.

The Reversals of 1933 and 1934

In the summer of 1933, John Ryan's Catholic University mentor and colleague William Kerby, editor of the *Ecclesiastical Review* since late 1927, asked Ryan to write an article about the rhythm method from a Catholic moral theology perspective. The resulting piece appeared as "The Moral Aspects of Periodical Continence."[78] In it, Ryan seemed to seriously compromise his own position as given in the very same magazine in 1928, which was discussed above. The new article was a watershed, but not in a way Ryan intended. It would eventually become a widely cited source by those who wished to demonstrate that Catholics, and Ryan himself, had truly abandoned their previous reasoning on contraception.[79] Ryan's argument in this subsequent article appeared to offer mutually contradictory claims that resulted from trying to drive on both deductive and inductive rails at once.

Ryan began by summarizing the question and pointing out that all three of the books published in support of rhythm—by Smulders, Latz, and Coucke and Walsh—had been granted ecclesiastical approval by prestigious dioceses, creating "an overwhelming presumption that the corresponding doctrine is morally sound." He finished by concluding that the rhythm method was, in fact, per-

---

78. See John A. Ryan, "The Moral Aspects of Periodical Continence," *Ecclesiastical Review* 89 (July–December 1933): 28–39.

79. Ryan had already been criticized in the late 1920s and early 1930s for particular inconsistencies and reversals. For example, the *New Republic* published a piece on how Ryan's (and other Catholics') stances on Prohibition and contraception were contradictory with respect to the state's authority over the individual. Unsigned editorial in "Education Viewed by Its Victims," *New Republic* (May 29, 1929), 33. A 1931 *Commonweal* review of Ryan's own book *Questions of the Day* even points out the same inconsistency. John A. Lapp, "Doctrine for Today," review of *Questions of the Day*, by John Ryan, *Commonweal* 15 (December 23, 1931). Likewise, Ryan's about-face on sterilization—provisionally approving of it in the wake of *Buck v. Bell* and then reversing himself after *CC*—certainly drew attention. Ryan had to admit at a priestly conference in 1933 that his own published pamphlet from 1930 sanctioning eugenic sterilization by the state had to be corrected with an erratum insert "less than 6 months later," that is, after *CC* repudiated sterilization on the last day of December 1930. See "Baltimore and Washington Clerical Conferences Dec 11 and 13, 1933" (1933), in Ryan Papers, box 60, folder "Sterilization articles, NCWC press releases, 1934," ACUA.

fectly "licit" from the Catholic moral perspective.[80] The material in between constituted attempts to parry possible dissenting positions. Ryan's tone was one of almost triumphalist self-assurance predicated on his claim that the pope's *CC* encyclical itself was his basis for argument. He pointed especially to the encyclical's passage that purportedly permitted rhythm-based birth control. While Ryan admitted that the expression "circumstances of time" in *CC* could not have specifically referred to the Ogino-Knaus theory since it had not yet been announced when the encyclical was written, he nevertheless assured the reader that "[*CC*'s] language is sufficiently comprehensive to cover it, and to authorize the doctrine that intercourse may licitly be limited to that period."[81]

Ryan went on to quote the encyclical's specifically neoscholastic wording on the primary and secondary ends of marriage, the latter being "promotion of mutual love and the satisfaction of concupiscence," while at the same time eliding the fact that this was exactly the ordering his own 1928 article had devalued—and which the present one would irredeemably conflate. Regarding secondary goals of marriage, he continued to quote, "the parties are not in the least forbidden to pursue, always under the condition, however, that their action preserves its intrinsic nature and, therefore, also, its necessary relation to the primary end."[82]

Ryan highlighted this particular *CC* material for two specific reasons. First, he did so because, for him, the scientific surety of the sterile period, shown by Latz, was what made the method worthy of recommendation to Catholics in lieu of artificial contraception. While not all the Catholic scientists were in total agreement as to how absolute it was, Ryan asserted, "I am discussing the morality of periodic abstinence on the assumption that the sterile period is absolute."[83] The second reason Ryan highlighted these particular

80. Ryan, "Moral Aspects," 28–29.
81. Ryan, "Moral Aspects," 29.
82. Ryan, "Moral Aspects," 30.
83. Ryan, "Moral Aspects," 33. One might note that if the rhythm method really was exact in that way, the "primary" purpose of sex would be ruled out in each instance because the sex

lines from *CC* was that later in the article he elaborated on the "intrinsic" evil of artificial contraception, purporting to corroborate the neoscholastic papal argument, that is, Vermeersch's argument. But could Ryan have forgotten that he himself had argued in the very same magazine, five years earlier, that the intrinsic-ends argument for contraception was itself wrong when justified by the "perversion of faculty" claim?

Here, in 1933, he stated "the users of artificial preventives are guilty of perverting a human faculty, frustrating the normal effect of intercourse in the very act itself.... On the other hand, [those who use the rhythm method] exercise the sex faculty in the normal manner, so that conception could take place if an ovum were present."[84] He appended a secondary-effects argument to this statement, criticizing "some Catholics" who "cannot think of any act as evil unless it produces evil effects; that is, effects which involve some positive injury to human beings."[85] Yet, back in 1928, Ryan had overtly doubted precisely these arguments that he was now making, as discussed above. He had said, "While I have consistently accepted and defended this view [the intrinsic evil of perverting the sex faculty] myself, I have never found it entirely free from difficulty [from as far back as 1915]."[86] He now focused on the fact that it was the intent—that is, whether one was deliberately frustrating the natural end—and the evil consequences the action had on one's self that determined whether or not an action was morally blameworthy. In 1928 he had also demonstrated that the secondary-effects claim could appear very cloudy. In addition, the whole point of the rhythm method was to use empirical scientific techniques to frustrate the possibility of conception for both one's self and one's spouse.

---

would not "preserve ... its intrinsic nature and, therefore, also, its necessary relation to the primary end" as the neoscholastics would have it. In fact, in order for the rhythm method to be accepted as sufficiently scientific and precise, this primary end *had* to be short-circuited.

84. Ryan, "Moral Aspects," 31.
85. Ryan, "Moral Aspects," 31.
86. Ryan, "Immorality of Contraception," 408.

Since Ryan was writing his 1933 article for a Catholic publication, he spent some time operating within the neoscholastic framework yet, even there, reverted to the "ultimate effects" argument. In other words, the social science-based claims about harm to the economy, population, and psyche created by artificial contraception served as the backbone of his points there too.[87] And some of Ryan's vagaries and backtracking were either inscrutable or leaned toward the absurd. At one point, he argued that since the question of a population decline—especially of Catholics—had been proffered as an argument against the viability of the birth control regime, one could not entirely exclude its danger. But he then immediately proceeded to give elaborate demographic rationales as to why this was likely not a legitimate concern. He followed that by saying that if it came to light that Catholic couples were using the rhythm method to keep families too small, he might change his position yet again: "the fact that restriction of intercourse to the sterile period is not in itself wrong does not forthwith justify it for all couples at all times."[88] He offered imprecise criteria for knowing when this change might need to be made and for knowing who, among couples already using it, were doing so legitimately.

The rhythm method was moral, he said, when couples faced "grave inconveniences" in categories "falling under the heads of health, economic needs, or real and proximate temptation to the practice of contraception."[89] But his explanation of the latter temptation was nowhere to be found. And how gravely "inconvenient" should the economic need be before one was clear of the danger of sinning by using rhythm? Ryan confused the case further when he added this disclaimer: "To be sure, they will not always be guilty of even venial sin when they enter upon this way [(rhythm), on] account of slight inconveniences, but they will have deliberately chosen to live on a lower moral level."[90] How a couple was to know

87. Ryan, "Moral Aspects," 32–33.
88. Ryan, "Moral Aspects," 35.
89. Ryan, "Moral Aspects," 36.
90. Ryan, "Moral Aspects," 36.

when they had reached any of these states was left unsaid. When Ryan discussed how soon a priest-confessor should recommend rhythm to confessees, there was similar vagueness: "prudence" was advised in explaining the exact procedures, but, in general, rhythm should be suggested even more than the 1880 Roman Penitentiary decision had decreed legitimate.[91]

In the end, Ryan's 1933 article only widened the fissure spreading through Catholic rhetoric on contraception, which he had helped open five years earlier. Not only had he contradicted himself, but by doing so he had effectively invalidated anything substantive left in his argument except for social and biological science. It was on these last remaining grounds that he and his colleagues would have to stand. An irony in all this was that in order for the scientific part of Ryan's argument to be sound—and the rhythm method to be valid—the neoscholastic position articulated by *CC* had to be ignored or even defeated. Yet if his scientific claim was unsound, that was to render it open to the very attacks it would soon face as simply an inferior form of birth control. He had tried to have it both ways but ended up having it neither way. As the 1930s wore on, the rhythm method's scientific effectiveness would be increasingly targeted by his opponents advocating artificial contraception. As if Ryan had not made the fissure in Catholic birth control discourse sufficiently glaring, O'Brien soon came along and turned it into an unbridgeable chasm.

John A. O'Brien and "A Way Out"[92]

After reading O'Brien's 1934 pamphlet *Lawful Birth Control*, and its expanded version *Natural Birth Control* (1938)—the distinction being the latter's inclusion of a detailed appendix showing exactly how to employ the rhythm method—one realizes that a comment

91. Ryan, "Moral Aspects," 37.
92. John A. O'Brien, *Lawful Birth Control*, 25. See also O'Brien, *Natural Birth Control*. The latter book taught the rhythm method using specific gynecological terms.

John Montgomery Cooper had made about Leo Latz's book *The Rhythm of Sterility and Fertility in Women* applied even more so to O'Brien's works: "I think he makes an excellent case for the birth controllers without intending to do so."[93] O'Brien's putatively scientific yet hyperbolic presentation was even more triumphalist than it had been in his earlier book on evolution. One understands why Sanger complained that it could be legally sent through the mails while information on other types of contraception could not. Even the books' titles reinforced contraception advocates' contention that the Catholics had reversed themselves and now openly taught that birth control was acceptable.

O'Brien's argument was predicated to an overwhelming extent on social and biological science with a few added contentions based on natural law. As seen below, it actually duplicated many of the claims birth control advocates had put forward over the years to support artificial contraception. Yet O'Brien employed these same arguments to plead for what he said was an entirely unique and natural yet scientifically perfect form of birth prevention.

O'Brien's birth control volumes amounted to something more than just two extra publications added to the pile already present in America around that time that explained the "OK" birth control method, as the rhythm method was then termed. Rather, O'Brien's publications were meant, as he put it, to "proclaim from the housetops the findings of medical science."[94] Indeed, O'Brien went far in attesting to the absolute scientific infallibility of Ogino's and Knaus's measurements of the female sterile period. Statements such as the following filled the book: "Great numbers of the outstanding leaders in gynecology have declared [Ogino's and Knaus's results] to be not a theory but a biological law, thoroughly tested and verified."[95] And he went beyond that, lauding the method as

93. Cooper to Edgar Schmiedeler, quoted in Tentler, *Catholics and Contraception*, 113.
94. O'Brien, *Lawful Birth Control*, 71; O'Brien, *Natural Birth Control*, 71.
95. O'Brien, *Natural Birth Control*, 147. O'Brien acknowledged that while he was "not a medical scientist," in preparing his book he had the assistance of the Belgian physician Raoul De Guchteneere; of Harry Schmitz, professor of gynecology at Loyola of Chicago medical

vastly more healthful and effective than almost any other form of contraception. Because of all its benefits, he intended it for "every fair-minded citizen, regardless of religious faith."[96]

Early on, O'Brien took care to assert that enthusiasm for the method existed within the Catholic Church, especially among priests.[97] This was done no doubt to assuage potential suspicions among Catholic readers that it was all too good to be true. He claimed to have been inspired to write *Lawful Birth Control* by the "joyous refrain which [sprang] spontaneously from the hearts of all upon learning how modern science confirm[ed] the Church's teaching and show[ed] the way out of the [economic] difficulty."[98] These plaudits ostensibly arose after people had read his earlier article lauding the rhythm theory in the popular devotional newspaper *Our Sunday Visitor*. O'Brien claimed to have received "an avalanche of letters from every state of the Union, averaging hundreds a day," as a result of the earlier article.[99]

O'Brien's progressive-liberal diocesan hierarch, Bishop John Francis Noll of Fort Wayne, Indiana, had not only given his official "ecclesiastical approbation" to publish the original pamphlet but also penned an introduction to the first edition, which said: "I believe this book by Father O'Brien is the best ever written on the subject of Birth Control."[100] O'Brien hoped his material would be sent in the mail to any who asked for it "on its errand of light and help ... acclaimed alike by science and by religion, [and promoting] the ideal of rational fecundity."[101]

---

school; and of the Austrian researcher Herman Knaus (O'Brien, *Lawful Birth Control*, i; O'Brien, *Natural Birth Control*, 146).

96. O'Brien, *Natural Birth Control*, 20–21; O'Brien, *Lawful Birth Control*, frontispiece.

97. See, for example, O'Brien's citation of the *Clergy Review* (London) from May 1933 (O'Brien, *Natural Birth Control*, 44). Raoul De Guchteneere was said to have written positive articles on the method in *Homiletic Monthly* (*Lawful Birth Control*, xvii–xix, 18, 41–42).

98. O'Brien, *Lawful Birth Control*, 28.

99. O'Brien, *Lawful Birth Control*, 28.

100. Noll quoted in O'Brien, *Lawful Birth Control*, xv. Noll later refused to officially endorse the 1938 expanded volume. Its Newman publisher still listed that second volume as printed with ecclesiastical approbation.

101. O'Brien, *Lawful Birth Control*, 148.

O'Brien framed the discovery of the safe period as God working through modern science as revealed in nature, and at a providential time, too, when help was urgently needed to ease the sufferings caused by the Great Depression. O'Brien claimed to echo the Jesuit Fr. Joseph Reiner, SJ, in this position.[102] The Jesuit order in the United States had been divided in its view of rhythm in the interwar era.[103] Interestingly, *America* magazine's somewhat conservative science editor, Fr. Joseph LeBuffe had actually just written to his fellow Jesuit, Reiner, in March of 1934 to complain of damage O'Brien was doing to Catholicism's positions through his birth control rhetoric. LeBuffe especially rued the extent to which contraception advocates were co-opting O'Brien's writings on rhythm to support their own cause.[104]

O'Brien went further than other American Catholics in claiming for science the role of actually opening up new religious experience. He argued, "the laws of nature [are] a reflection of the mind of the divine Legislator," and, therefore, understanding and using them to one's own advantage actually opened up opportunities to cooperate more freely with the Creator than had ever been possible before modern science. Because parents would know when they could expect to conceive a child (as well as when they could expect not to conceive), they could, in his words, "deliberately accept" or else decline the chance to "cooperate" with God "in His work of Creation" rather than relying on "blind chance."[105] In O'Brien's schema, modern inductive science appeared as the catalyst for greater religious advancement of individuals than was possible without such science. His claim covered both the technique of rhythm and the broader goal of controlling exactly when one would have children. The sense that modern science permitted

102. O'Brien, *Lawful Birth Control*, 44.

103. *America* magazine, for example, strongly criticized Latz, and the rhythm method in general, throughout the 1930s. For the internal workings behind this stance, see Gerald Garvey to LeBuffe (March 27, 1933), *America* Magazine Archive, box 1, folder 23, GURBSC.

104. See three letters exchanged between LeBuffe and Reiner on O'Brien from March 1934, in *America* Magazine Archive, box 3, folder 23, GURBSC.

105. O'Brien, *Lawful Birth Control*, 60, 73; O'Brien, *Natural Birth Control*, 73.

new and more intimate connections with God had been a characteristic claim of theological "modernists"—both within Catholicism and elsewhere—since the later nineteenth century. It was a point also found in O'Brien's book on evolution.[106]

To further persuade his readers that both he and his church had always been prime celebrators of science, O'Brien went on: "In her vast temple of truth every new secret teased from any of the varied segments of nature finds a prompt and hearty welcome. For the Church knows that every newly discovered truth ... will give additional reinforcements to [her known truths]."[107] O'Brien's rhetoric thereby made use of a motif widely used in eighteenth- and nineteenth-century rhetoric: the twin books written by God—the Bible and the book of nature—were coterminous parts of divine revelation.

O'Brien attempted to parry the complaint that books and pamphlets sent out by Catholics on technical aspects of natural birth control took contraception out of the hands of medical experts and put it in the hands of anyone, even young people. A number of these complaints came from Catholics. *Commonweal* had already printed an article in the summer of 1932 featuring a female Catholic civic leader arguing against loosening the restrictions on sending contraception information through the mail by saying, "the dissemination of birth control information ... is to let loose a flood of temptation upon a younger generation." She cited statistics "backed by the Birth Control League itself [that] show ... contraceptive articles sold in this country annually amount to one hundred million.... That the youth of the nation is being perverted in large and steadily increasing numbers is certain."[108]

O'Brien, reversing cause and effect, quoted from a 1934 AMA report on a survey taken in Florida two years earlier showing that

106. On this particular aspect of modernism, see Christopher Kauffman, *Tradition and Transformation*, 160–61.

107. O'Brien, *Lawful Birth Control*, 73; O'Brien, *Natural Birth Control*, 73–74.

108. Quoted in Michael Williams, "The Birth Control Racket," *Commonweal* 16 (June 8, 1932): 142.

contraceptives were already widely obtainable, sold "in 376 places besides drug stores, including gas stations[,] garages, restaurants, soda fountains, barber shops, pool rooms, restaurants, cigar stands, newsstands, shoe shining parlors, and grocery stores."[109]

In another tactic duplicating contraceptive advocates' arguments, O'Brien did not hesitate to invoke the implicitly abhorrent alternative to natural birth control—abortion—to defend advertising the rhythm method. Sanger, in particular, was always careful to dismiss abortion as a disgrace, but one that people would likely resort to if society ignored her recommendations. It was novel to have a Catholic use the same warning to sell readers on the necessity of a particular kind of birth control. Aside from immorality, O'Brien testified that abortion was tied to "a high maternal death rate," since women turned to it after having put their misguided trust in other contraceptive techniques that were both immoral *and* less effective than rhythm.[110]

Several of the book's later chapters consisted of antiphonal litanies of allegations and promises about what could happen if rhythm were not used or if other contraceptive measures were instead employed. O'Brien presented a series of quotes from contemporary experts—including some in physiology, psychiatry, psychology, and various social sciences—to support his claims about the ineffectiveness and recklessness of other methods of contraception. He did so with notable directness.

For example, O'Brien combined physiological and psychological advocacies and warnings to assert not only that women's genitalia benefited from the intake of spermatic fluid delivered during male orgasm but also that "fruitless stimulation of the genital organs leads to more or less serious chronic pelvis disorders [*sic*] and very frequently to sterility."[111] To this end, he also cited "the dis-

109. O'Brien, *Lawful Birth Control*, xxi; O'Brien, *Natural Birth Control*, 21–22.

110. O'Brien, *Lawful Birth Control*, 48–49.

111. Here O'Brien relied on the opening address of Dr. Hugo Sellheim to the 1929 Congress of German Gynecologists (O'Brien, *Lawful Birth Control*, 81–82; O'Brien, *Natural Birth Control*, 81–82).

tinguished scientist" Dr. H. L. Long, saying "the semen is the most powerful stimulant to all female sex organs and to the whole body of the woman. The organs themselves will absorb quantities of semen and it is most healthful and beneficial," and those women who have the sense to seek out these fluids "improve in physical well being after they are married by availing themselves of this healthful organismal nourishment."[112]

It is difficult to imagine O'Brien fearing this rhetoric too subtle; nevertheless, he followed it up with a stark quote from an address delivered in 1929 at the French Congress of Gynecologists: "It is perfectly well-known and universally admitted that the female organism absorbs spermatic products introduced during the sexual act and that these products act on woman in a manner favorable to her development."[113] Conversely, development-stunting disorders resulting from mechanical contraception included afflictions like "inflammations in the womb" that "nearly all scientific publications dealing with the subject" indicated could "lead to cancer."[114]

The development that semen putatively conferred on women manifested itself not just in the biophysical sense. O'Brien argued that substantive psychological and psychiatric warnings should certainly dissuade women from avoiding semen: "lack [of absorbed semen] leads to both physical and psychic disorders."[115] O'Brien called upon H. L. Long again to reinforce this view of ejaculation as the best psychological balm conceivable for the anxious woman: "There are multitudes of nervous women, hysterical even, who are restored to health through the stimulative effects of satisfactory coitus and the absorption of semen."[116] For further support on the psychological front, he appealed to British physician Robert Armstrong-Jones, "a recognized authority on neural diseases" who,

---

112. O'Brien, *Lawful Birth Control*, 87; O'Brien, *Natural Birth Control*, 87.

113. O'Brien, *Lawful Birth Control*, 87; O'Brien, *Natural Birth Control*, 87.

114. O'Brien, *Lawful Birth Control*, 82–83. In *Natural Birth Control*, the phrase "inflammation of the neck of the womb" was used (O'Brien, 82–83).

115. O'Brien, *Lawful Birth Control*, 82–83; O'Brien, *Natural Birth Control*, 87.

116. O'Brien, *Lawful Birth Control*, 80; O'Brien, *Natural Birth Control*, 88.

according to O'Brien, put matters very succinctly in an address to other physicians: "Birth control often leads to lunacy in women."[117] So, too, could excessive abstinence, a scientific discovery that must have troubled Catholics who had argued in previous years for positive value in such abstinence. One wonders, too, what these scientific revelations were to have meant for the many nuns cloistered in convents and thus deprived of healthful spermatic benefits.

Much of O'Brien's case on birth regulation amounted to redigested and re-presented arguments based in science and expertise that contraceptive advocates had themselves offered since the 1920s after Sanger and the birth control lobby chose to switch to a scientific defense of contraception. It also featured some of the contraception arguments' eugenic inflections when O'Brien warned of limits to the church's pro-marriage and pro-procreation stances: "She discourages those who are seriously tainted in body or mind from marrying. This is especially true when there is likelihood of transmitting such a taint to offspring."[118]

The early portions of O'Brien's books addressing natural law were in certain respects more legalistic from the Catholic perspective than even the neoscholastic argumentation he himself so derided. They were also manifestly dubious and incomplete even to the nonexpert in neoscholasticism, as though he inserted them without much thought and only to satisfy internal critics. They comprised, in effect, inductive (or hypothetico-deductive) arguments dressed up in ill-fitting classical deductive garb. O'Brien ultimately concluded that while not ideal, it was even permissible for a Catholic married couple to produce no offspring at all, provided

117. O'Brien, *Lawful Birth Control*, 84; O'Brien, *Natural Birth Control*, 84. Armstrong-Jones cited his own experience in medical practice with this warning: "If you are to have birth control on a large scale, you will have to add to your lunatic asylums for women" (O'Brien, *Lawful Birth Control*, 84; O'Brien, *Natural Birth Control*, 84). See also O'Brien's Freudian critique of women practicing artificial contraception (*Lawful Birth Control*, 85, 87; *Natural Birth Control*, 85–86). Freud's influence, of course, was not insignificant in these decades with his emphasis on the overriding power of the sex impulse and, concomitantly, the near powerlessness of the will to control it in any manner that was healthy.

118. O'Brien, *Natural Birth Control*, 63–64.

that "the propagation of the race is not being endangered."[119] It is
no wonder that by the 1940s, even Fr. Daniel Lord, SJ, an American Jesuit who had believed in the rhythm method, penned a story
where the Catholic priest-protagonist complained of his encounters with parishioners about children and birth prevention: "I'm
getting awfully sick of telling people just how far they can go without actually going to hell."[120]

Fallout: Birth Control Activists and Catholic Rhythm Enthusiasts through the Rest of the 1930s

It is not overly surprising that contraception advocates ran with
O'Brien, Ryan, and Cooper's progressive argumentation that supported the rhythm method and critiqued neo-Thomism not long
after such works were published. The first thing such opponents
did was attack the seeming paradox of Catholics' opposition to
some forms of birth control and defense of others. The ardent neoscholastic Catholics claimed that such critiques were the result of
non-Catholics' ignorance of the intricacies of natural law; after all,
the rhythm method was different because it was *natural*. But as we
have seen even in the famous example of Ryan himself, the impression of existing contradiction and confusion among Catholicism's
brightest intellectual lights was not wholly false.[121] Non-Catholics'
attacks drove home the idea that such Catholics were simply using
science to argue in favor of the rational effectiveness of the rhythm
method, with a token nod to natural law thrown in to mislead.

More conservative Catholics, too, were not hesitant to point
out instances where their more liberal brethren had opened themselves up to such criticism or found their science-centered argu-

---

119. O'Brien, *Lawful Birth Control*, 61.
120. Quoted in Tentler, *Catholics and Contraception*, 112.
121. It certainly did not help that some of them cautiously criticized rhythm in one setting
and heartily defended it in another. Viterbo noted that Ryan praised rhythm when writing as
an individual thinker but took a cautious approach when speaking as NCWC Social Action
Director. See Viterbo, "Promise of Rhythm," 289.

ments co-opted by the very people those liberals ostensibly opposed. Father Wilfred Parsons of *America* magazine wrote in 1934
to the same Fr. Joseph Reiner whom O'Brien had himself enlisted
in his cause, complaining that at a recent birth control conference
the president of the organization "read a passage which apparently
gave all the reasons for birth control; she then stopped and said that
[it] was written by the Catholic priest John O'Brien, and was tak-
en from the *Sunday Visitor*."[122] As averred above, *America* printed
harsh criticisms of the rhythm method early in 1933, but the more
progressive Catholics who defended it got the lion's share of publicity partly thanks to the pro-birth control lobby's co-opting.[123]

Pro-contraception thinkers also asked why, if Catholic arguments for rhythm were predicated on science, those Catholics
would champion a birth control method of dubious scientific effectiveness that was also difficult to employ from a practical perspective. Why not, instead, endorse the more scientifically and
practically reasonable versions they themselves advocated? The
uncomfortable predicament for such Catholics was that this critique often seemed valid. A singular set of scientific arguments had
essentially replaced theological argument as the basis for prominent progressive Catholics' public birth control discourse. The
tactic favored by mainline birth control proponents was simply
to criticize rhythm from the scientific point of view since Catholics who most advocated the rhythm method acceded to staking
their claims on the science.[124] The year following publication of
Coucke and Walsh's *The Sterile Period*, eugenicist Guy Irving Burch
penned an article in the *New Republic* attacking the rhythm meth-

122. Wilfred Parsons to Reiner (March 20, 1934), in *America* Magazine Archive, box 3
folder 23, GURBSC.
123. For Parsons's own published attack on rhythm, see Wilfred Parsons, "Is This 'Catholic' Birth Control?," *America* 48 (February 25, 1933): 496.
124. For example, O'Brien's frontispiece to *Natural Birth Control* opened with the quotation "Not one failure in 30,000 Cases," adding "In the April issue, 1938, of *Surgery, Gynecology,
and Obstetrics*, Dr. A. G. Miller, Director of the Miller Clinic" of Indiana said that when the
Ogino-Knaus law was "correctly applied," "not one failure in 30,000 cases" was documented
in the previous three years (O'Brien, *Natural Birth Control*, frontispiece).

od mostly on scientific grounds, arguing that "this confidence in the rhythm theory is not shared by the medical profession generally, [or] by specialists who have treated thousands of women in birth control clinics."[125] But Burch also attacked the philosophical and ethical positions typically employed by Catholic defenders of rhythm, contending that Catholics irrationally posited the moral superiority of one form of birth control over another. In his words, "The point appears to be a fine one indeed; the rhythm method ... 'avoids' conception, while contraception 'prevents' conception. The one may be as deliberate as the other, sexual intercourse indulged in, and the motives may be the same." Yet, he went on, "one is considered by the Catholic clergy to be a 'mortal sin' ... while the other is considered to be a holy and legitimate means of Catholic birth control. One method employs the use of mathematics and a calendar and the other employs the use of physics and chemistry."[126]

Logically, Burch appeared to be right. If the rhythm method was as effective as the Catholics maintained, was it not equally likely to prevent conception as a contraceptive device or chemical, which could also prove defective in a given instance? The practical problem for the progressive Catholics was that rhythm had to be simultaneously somewhat unreliable to sustain the moral argument yet also completely reliable to sustain the scientific argument. The rhythm method's opponents, on their part, mostly complained that the method was indeed ineffective.[127]

125. [Guy Irving Burch], "Catholics on Birth Control," *New Republic* 79 (September 5, 1934): 100. Burch made a nonspecific appeal to science and the "medical profession generally" but no indication of which authorities he meant, as though simply mentioning a greater scientific authority were enough to condemn the book as pseudoscience.

126. [Burch], "Catholics on Birth Control," 100.

127. Two studies appearing in the *American Journal of Sociology* in 1935 and 1936 suggested that American Catholic birth rates in various social classes were declining. Whether this meant American Catholics were resorting to mechanical contraception or employing rhythm effectively is debatable. See Stouffer, "Trends in Fertility"; Gilbert Kelly Robinson, "The Catholic Birth Rate: Further Facts and Implications," *American Journal of Sociology* 41 (May 1936): 757–66.

Sanger and Ryan in Congress

In the winter of 1933, Margaret Sanger wrote a letter to her friend and fellow contraception activist Juliet Barrett Rublee while reading Leo Latz's book *The Rhythm of Sterility and Fertility in Women.* In her letter, she said, "The Catholics have just issued a little book called "The Rythum" [sic]. Its [sic] annoying! at last they have come to say that marriage is not solely for the procreating of children! Nor is sex! I'm reading it carefully ... Really is significant."[128] After reading Latz, followed by Ryan's 1933 endorsement of rhythm, the disgusted Sanger was particularly determined to use the progressive Catholics' own arguments against them. She had handed off formal leadership of the American Birth Control League in 1929 to concentrate full time on political activism, for which she founded the National Committee for Federal Legislation for Birth Control.[129] In that latter capacity, she would have the opportunity to face Catholics several times in open debate over the next several years, most notably in five hearings Congress held between 1931 and 1934 on questions tied to contraception and obscenity. Sanger's reading of Latz occurred during the period of these hearings.

Sanger faced her nemesis, Ryan, in the halls of Congress several times during these hearings.[130] For his 1932 address to the Senate Subjudiciary Committee, Ryan appealed to the status of mainline professional expertise, referencing his own membership in the American Association of Social Workers and listing himself in his printed address as a "nationally known Economist and Sociologist."[131] He centered his presentation on deleterious social ends that would result from calls for open circulation of contraception

---

128. Sanger to Juliet Rublee (January 9, 1933), quoted in "She's Got Rhythm? A Safe Period for Sanger and the Church," *Newsletter* 31, Fall 2002, https://www.nyu.edu/projects/sanger/articles/shes_got_rhythm.php.

129. Tobin, *American Religious Debate*, 179–80.

130. On the hearings in this period, see Tobin, *American Religious Debate*, 199–205.

131. Ryan, "Economic and Social Objections to Birth Control: Statement by Dr. John A. Ryan, nationally known Economist and Sociologist, in opposition to s. 4432 before Senate Sub-Judiciary Committee" (May 19, 1932), in Ryan Papers, box 48, folder 12, ACUA.

materials. Among his contentions were that druggists would increase their habits of dispensing contraceptives without a physician's prescription; economic justice would be harmed by discrim-
inatory birth regulation that was itself called for by economic elites
who wanted to shirk their responsibility to the poor, surreptitiously
encouraging limitation of offspring rather than sharing their own
wealth; and contraception-centered decrease of offspring would
create a demographic disaster in America.[132] As to the basis of his
opposition to artificial contraception, Ryan did once mention the
phrase "intrinsically and everlastingly immoral" in the third paragraph, yet without context or any explication on what this specifically meant in connection to natural law.

In a much longer presentation in 1934 to a Judiciary Committee subcommittee dealing with further calls for repeal of Comstock
laws, Ryan said he would "submit to examination" the arguments
of the bill's proponents, which "relate exclusively to social issues
and social welfare."[133] However, possibly prompted by grumbling
already starting to make its way through the American Catholic
scene via Jesuits and others who complained that Catholic opposition to contraception was too often disconnected from moral theology, Ryan overtly mentioned the natural law position more fully
and with more clarity in his 1934 presentation as compared to his
1932 testimony. This time he even mentioned God and the Bible,
though the latter was seemingly triggered by his pro-contraception
opponents having done so first in their own commentary.[134] Nevertheless, as promised, he did spend the vast majority of his time
addressing social science arguments, even appealing to a University
of California eugenicist and the recent congressional testimony of
New York University eugenicist Henry Pratt Fairchild to point out

132. Ryan, "Economic and Social Objections to Birth Control."
133. Ryan, "Statement at the Hearing before the Subcommittee of the Judiciary Committee of the Senate" (March 20, 1934), 1, in Ryan Papers, box 48, folder 12, ACUA.
134. Ryan, "Statement," 2, 7. At one point, Ryan did manage to tie what looked like a
natural law argument to the practical views of Henry George's *Progress and Poverty*: "The law
of human progress, what is it but the moral law?" (Ryan, "Statement," 6).

Rhythm and Reverberation 269

dangers of future population stagnation as a result of contraception.[135] Ryan's science-centered approach was widely noted. Raymond Swing's critique of Ryan echoed others. Swing pointed out that Ryan focused almost wholly on demography and warnings about so-called race suicide in his public testimony on contraception and against repealing the Comstock laws.[136]

Concurrent with the congressional debates, a debate between Fr. Edward Roberts Moore and Guy Burch in the *Forum and Century* also focused on demography and social science to the exclusion of religion. Burch had the advantage of using Latz's and Coucke's books to redeploy against Moore. Claiming that the latter's "arguments are inconsistent with those of his church on the subject of birth control," Burch remarked:

It is surprising that a high official of the Roman Catholic Church should brand the advocates of the birth-control bill as "death" lobbyists when Catholic publishers are sending through the mails a method of birth control approved by the Roman Church to compete with contraception. *The Rhythm*, published with "ecclesiastical approbation," and *The Sterile Period in Family Life*, published with the Imprimatur of Patrick, Cardinal Hayes, explain in detail how a couple may participate in sexual union and avoid the conception of new life.[137]

As to Margaret Sanger's overall counterargument to Ryan in her testimony and writings, it boiled down to the following points, summarized on her behalf in the *New Republic*:

- Catholics were endorsing birth control and merely quibbling about methods;
- Even they realized it was a question to be resolved by rational science;

135. Ryan, "Statement," 4, 5.
136. See Raymond Gram Swing, "Birth Control and Obscenity," *The Nation* 140 (May 29, 1935): 621–22. NYU eugenicist Henry Pratt Fairchild also testified in these hearings. His arguments centered on the claim that Congress's wise 1924 Immigration Restriction Act would have to be supplemented with birth control if the country wanted to ensure that the "better elements" out-produced the putative racial riff-raff (Tobin, *American Religious Debate*, 200).
137. Guy Irving Burch, "A Eugenicist Replies," *Forum and Century* 92 (August 1934): 81; and Edward Roberts Moore, "The Death Lobby," *Forum and Century* 92 (1934): 78–80.

- Their science was inferior;
- They were hypocritical in telling other Catholics they could have sex without procreating since they were the biggest opponents of contraception and limiting family size;
- They could, and did, send their birth control information through the mail while Sanger and other contraception advocates could not; and
- This latter fact made Catholics not only hypocritical in arguing against the repeal of the Comstock laws but also socially irresponsible because their acts allowed birth control information to fall into the hands of laypeople instead of professional physicians.

In Sanger's own words: "Rhythm [was] loudly praised by Catholic prelates and press.... Most of us have long ago discarded the safe-period theory as a method available for general application. This book [*The Rhythm of Sterility and Fertility in Women*], however, was written by a physician and is published with 'Ecclesiastical Approbation,' which means it has the approval of the Roman Catholic Church." Sanger went on to argue that "On the general principles of limiting or controlling the size of the family—on the needs, rights and morality of the practice, we [the birth control movement and the Roman Catholic Church] seem to be in perfect agreement. *On methods we entirely disagree.*" The Catholics, she said, "advocate a safe period, the non-Catholic proponents desire to place all responsibility concerning methods in the hands of the medical profession."[138]

The scientized terms of the debate were set, and by that point there was little Catholics could do whether they hoped to reverse the tide or, alternately, embrace the tide and use science to win the debate using their preferred scientific method of birth regulation. Indeed, *The Nation*'s summary of Washington, D.C.'s American Conference on Birth Control and National Recovery in 1934

138. Margaret Sanger, "Catholics and Birth Control," *New Republic* 79 (June 13, 1934): 129.

showed both the medicine sessions and the round tables agreeing "that birth control is a medical problem which should be handled by physicians," while also ruling after the consideration of various methods that "the so-called safe-period method, permitted by the Catholic Church, ... [is] too uncertain for general use" and, therefore, "rejected."[139]

Despite the fact that Sanger could not persuade the U.S. Congress of her arguments in 1934, the tide of public opinion was turning, as was the tide of the discourse's ground rules to favor contraception as lying in the medical and economic spheres rather than in the realm of religious morality. In fact, Sanger repeatedly co-opted Catholic rhythm advocates' discourse to oppose conservative Catholic anti-contraception advocates. In the spring of 1934, Sanger wryly advised the latter to read Catholic-authored pro-rhythm books since in them "every argument they have ever [rejected from contraception advocates] is ... [employed] on behalf of the safe-period method."[140]

By the middle of 1934, some highly placed American Catholics sensed that the situation was getting away from them such that efforts by Catholics enthusiastically supporting the rhythm method as an alternative to full-on contraception were backfiring. In a shift signaling that key bishops believed American Catholicism had backed itself into a corner, in December the NCWC sanctioned a move to implement an about-face and vastly tone down Catholics' publicly expressed enthusiasm for rhythm. As an extended consequence of this shift, Bishop John Noll even refused his imprimatur to the second edition of O'Brien's book appearing in 1938. But it was too late. O'Brien, Latz, and the other rhythm books had already entered, and affected, the public birth control debate; the co-opting of their language by birth control advocates could not be reversed, though such reversal would be attempted.[141]

139. Stella Hanau, "The Birth Control Conference," *The Nation* 138 (January 31, 1934): 130.
140. Sanger, "Catholics and Birth Control," 129.
141. For details on the internal Catholic attempts to reverse course, see Tentler, *Catholics and Contraception*, 113–22; and Viterbo, "Promise of Rhythm," 282.

In early 1935 *Commonweal* attempted to reorient the terms of the public debate between Catholics and others away from accusations of scientific blundering and back to the realm of morality and moral theology. The defensive tone of editor Michael Williams suggests that realistic Catholics acknowledged how secularized and even disorganized their own arguments had come to be viewed. Williams claimed there was "an error very prevalent at the moment [that Catholicism has abandoned its teaching on the main purpose of marriage]." However, "as has repeatedly been pointed out in the many recent discussions of this subject, ... the Catholic Church teaches, now as always, that the chief natural end of marriage is procreation, and its chief glory children."[142] Later that year, *Commonweal* published an article on Cardinal Hayes's recent address in St. Patrick's Cathedral that reveals rhetoric clearly intended to reassert the idea of a unique and united Catholic voice in opposition to birth controllers' advances. The sermon was itself particularly designed to counter the proclamation made by the American Birth Control League on December 2, which "endorsed unanimously by a rising vote of the 2,500 men and women ... 'that all agencies administering family relief inform mothers on relief where they may secure medical advice as to family limitation in accord with their religious convictions.'"[143] Catholics had lost the battle to defend even the notion that a connection between marital sexuality and procreation was a religious truism.

One final behind-the-scenes attempt to turn the Catholics' train around came the following spring. The apostolic delegate to the United States, Amleto Cicognani, titular archbishop of Laodicea, addressed Archbishop Michael Curley of Baltimore as dean of American episcopal sees in a confidential letter dated May 23, 1936, labeled "not to be published." The letter instructed, "Your Excellency will kindly see that no Catholic periodical or newspaper ...

142. [Michael Williams], "Week by Week," *Commonweal* 21 (January 18, 1935): 330.

143. [Michael Williams], "Cardinal Hayes Speaks Out," *Commonweal* 23 (December 30, 1935): 197.

advertises the theory [rhythm] in question, or discusses it" other than in a very narrow way delineated by Cicognani.[144] But key progressive Catholics continued to loyally embrace their form of birth control throughout the rest of the 1930s. Indeed, O'Brien's aforementioned glorification of the rhythm method appeared in 1938 in revised form containing detailed practical instructions on how to employ it. And according to a study from 1960, between 1932 and 1939, Latz's *The Rhythm of Sterility and Fertility in Women* sold over 200,000 copies, almost all in the United States.[145]

Contraception by Rhythm? Catholics Help Redefine Terminology in the Public Square

The terms *rhythm* and *birth control,* even *contraception,* had become interchangeable by the mid-1930s, a result institutional Catholicism had fought to prevent. Dorothy Dunbar Bromley titled her *Nation* article of September 1934 on rhythm, "Sanctified Birth Control."[146] Alice Hamilton of Harvard Medical School said in January 1935: "Even the Catholic Church has suddenly reversed her age-long position with a suddenness that is amazing.... Now [women] are forbidden to use only certain methods of contraception."[147] Anthony Turano's 1935 article on Catholics and the rhythm method from the *American Mercury* magazine was titled "Contraception By Rhythm." It opened with the sentence: "The ancient holy war of the Catholic Church against birth control clinics has finally simmered down to a caustic wrangle about the best methods to effect the stipulated result."[148]

144. Cicognani to Curley (May 23, 1936), in NCWC papers, box 85, folder "Social Action: Family Life Bureau," subfolder "Family Life Birth Control: 1930–1944," ACUA.

145. Flann Campbell, "Birth Control in the Christian Churches," *Population Studies* 14 (November 1960): 140.

146. Dorothy Dunbar Bromley, "Sanctified Birth Control," *The Nation* 139 (September 26, 1934): 346–48. Right in the second paragraph, she used both O'Brien's and Latz's arguments in her favor but qualified their enthusiasm for rhythm with accusations of the technique's ineffectiveness.

147. [Michael Williams], "Week by Week," *Commonweal* 21 (January 18, 1935): 330.

148. Turano, "Contraception by Rhythm," 164.

Efficiency-centered editor Bruce Bliven of the *New Republic* could plausibly imply by the summer of 1937 that the church's pro-rhythm voices were the true pulse of the Catholic Church and that the church had itself turned to science as the grounding for its declarations, yet, inexplicably, had chosen to rely on science of demonstrably substandard quality. As Bliven put it, "Some years ago, the [Catholic] Church in America abandoned its previous opposition to birth control." But, he added, "for reasons it has never answered to anyone's satisfaction but its own, [it] turned its back on all competent medical experience ... and went in for the so-called 'Rhythm.' The Church ... clings to this fallacious technique in the face of perfected, genuine, birth control methods now accepted by medicine."[149] Bliven went on to stingingly characterize the church's "disturbing" development of "Catholic Science, ... paralleling the 'Nazi science' at which the whole world has laughed. Science with an adjective before it is not science."[150]

Just the previous summer, *Commonweal*'s editors had employed an AMA committee's expert statement to show Catholicism using the best genuine science so as to retrench their own position amidst the increasing strains of the Depression: "We feel that an entirely false sense of values with respect to the important function of childbearing and parenthood has been created by ... lay organizations" that issued "propaganda" about birth control options. The AMA statement said, "No evidence was found which would indicate the wider dissemination of contraceptive information would tend to establish a better social and economic equilibrium in society." Echoing eugenic rhetoric, the statement went on, "At present, the part of our population with the best education and presumably the most competent socially and economically is not reproducing itself."[151] *Commonweal*'s emphasis was that there was

---

149. Bruce Bliven, "For Al Smith," *New Republic* 91 (June 23, 1937): 185.

150. Bliven, "For Al," 185. The implication does not seem to be that Catholics are akin to Nazis but rather that they are not objective.

151. "The Medical Association on Contraception," *Commonweal* 24 (July 3, 1936): 265.

no evidence to support the prevalent claim that disseminating information about contraception would improve the economic status of lower-income groups. *Commonweal* maintained that artificial contraception was not a solution.

American Catholicism's role in the discourse remained firmly tied to rhythm. Perhaps some Catholic circles determined that the best that could be hoped for was tolerance and pleas for people to credit Catholics with trying to do something constructive to contribute to America's demographic and economic crisis, even if one did not endorse Catholicism's moral code. As a possible example of the latter perspective, an article in *Pictorial Review* magazine replete with charts on how to use the rhythm method appeared in the summer of 1938. There was no mistaking in it the method's clear association with Catholicism. Its author, who focused on Leo Latz as a positive figure, announced at the start: "'The Rhythm' is a system of natural family limitation or birth control.... [It is] the only system or method known to us which does not conflict with any church or religious creed. As popularized by Dr. Leo J. Latz, a Catholic, it has ecclesiastical approval."[152]

By 1937, the AMA definitively reversed its own hesitancy from the year before and endorsed medically supervised contraception as an aspect of preventive medicine.[153] By then, a series of court decisions had effectively dismantled the Comstock laws while birth control conferences had become respected scientific gatherings. On the latter point, long-time birth control activist Hannah Stone penned a triumphant piece in *The Nation* early in 1937: "Birth Con-

152. Maxine Davis, "The Rhythm," 18.
153. See "Report of the Study Committee on Contraceptive Practices and Related Problems [1936]," 53–55, and "Report of [...] [1937]," 65–67, *Proceedings of the House of Delegates of the American Medical Association*," 87th (1936) and 88th (1937) Annual Session, ama.nmt-vault.com. Noteworthy in the 1937 report is the committee signature of Catholic physician John Rock, later famous for his role in helping develop the first contraceptive pill, *Enovid*, released in 1960. Comparing the 1936 AMA report with the same name to the 1937 report, one finds substantially different and even opposing approaches. The 1936 report contained a short section titled "Moral considerations" whereas the 1937 report jettisoned that category. For some backstory and context on the overall shift, see Peter C. Engelman, *A History of the Birth Control Movement in America* (Santa Barbara: Praeger, 2011), 167–70.

trol Wins."[154] She was referring to a goal for physicians that had effectively originated at the Conference on Contraceptive Research and Clinical Practice of December 29–30, 1926, whose organizer had been Sanger. Stone stated that experts in medicine and laboratory science had concluded that contraceptive advice was essential for good medical practice. Further, she said, the nature and atmosphere of the conference had proven that birth control had been "remov[ed] from the field of controversy to that of scientific consideration, from the platform and the pulpit to the laboratory and the clinic," a transformation this 1937 decree had cemented.[155] For the discursive shift from pulpit to laboratory, Stone could have partly thanked, in addition to Sanger, progressive and modernist Catholicism's most respected public intellectuals of the interwar era.

Sanger's own reaction, in an article titled "At Long Last," did just that. She characterized the AMA decision for birth control, "a medical and a technical problem," as a new door opened for "preventive medicine," with birth control now understood as "a necessary part of medical practice."[156] Sanger credited Robert Dickinson, "a fearless crusader" who "fought against the taboos and inhibitions which made the medical profession as a whole ignore the field of sex." And she made sure to credit, with irony, the Catholic Church's turn to endorsing the rhythm method for the broader change. Arguing Catholicism had been "forced to recognize the need for family limitation," she named Latz's book, and its publication "with ecclesiastical approbation," as a crucial part of the story. With a seeming mixture of bitterness and delight, she characterized what was a Catholic reversal as a case of "wriggl[ing] out of its absurd and inconsistent position by conceding the truth of the *principles* of birth control."[157]

154. Hannah M. Stone, "Birth Control Wins," *The Nation* 144 (January 16, 1937): 70–71.

155. Stone, "Birth Control Wins," 70.

156. Margaret Sanger, "At Long Last: A Veteran Crusader for Birth Control Reflects on the Campaign in Terms of the Medical Association's Action," *New Masses* 24 (July 6, 1937): 19–20, in "Published Writings and Speeches, 1911–1959," microfilm S71:948, Sanger Papers Project.

157. Sanger, "At Long Last," 19.

By the eve of the second World War, religious considerations were mentioned in mainline public discourse on marriage and birth control mostly in the service of pointing out that organized religion championed the positive good of artificial contraception, with one purely obscurantist exception. Certain Catholics had played an outsized role in the broader outcome of what had once been considered a battle over birth control. They had themselves forfeited the chance to legitimately claim that there was much of a battle raging at all.

In Sum

The more the liberal-progressive Catholic intellectuals tried to fit in with the shifting American culture of intellectual scientific rationalism, the more they unintentionally contributed to dissolving the very religious certainties they were trying to uphold in the realms of human origins and development. Slowly, yet inexorably, they had opened the slippery slopes they had once been sure were the sole purview of their intellectual opponents.

An author published in the mainline Protestant *Christian Century* put the matter this way: "On the one hand, there is the exploratory and the speculative. On the other hand, there is the practical function of science in handling and using the truth, which we call 'applied science.'"[158] Applied science became a synonym for technology. As such, the author went on, "A Scientist's first duty is to discover the facts. His second duty, as he sees it, is to *utilize* these facts for *reforming, reorganizing, and rebuilding human life*. Mere knowledge is not enough." In something of an ode to the rejuvenated progressive impulse to master the natural world, the author went on, "This knowledge must be made relevant to the needs of men. Pure science must become applied science. Mankind, in other words, must not only know, but use what it knows in order to

---

158. John Haynes Holmes, "Religion's New War with Science," *Christian Century* (October 27, 1937): 1322.

create."[159] Reinforcing that growing faith in science's fruits as tangible, he asked, "Who can doubt that this faith of modern science is a faith justified by works?"[160]

159. Holmes, "Religion's New War," 1323.
160. Holmes, "Religion's New War," 1323.

Conclusion

> Convincing evidence of these outstanding facts of early
> human history rests upon ... evidence clearly interpreted
> by conscientious observers, drawn [also] from the ranks
> of ... clergy, especially of the Catholic Church
>
> —Henry Fairfield Osborn (1926)

In January of 1936, Oscar Riddle of the Carnegie Institution and the
Station for Experimental Evolution in Cold Spring Harbor, New
York, delivered a paper as part of a zoology panel at the annual
December meeting of the AAAS. The talk, ostensibly lying in the
realm of professional scientific scholarship, included the following
ominous warning: "The present restrictive influence of organized
religion on the teaching of the best in biology is intolerable....
They now curb or tie the tongues of biologic truth." Young men
and women, he complained, "leave our schools without having opportunity to learn that worthy facts concerning man's origin and

Henry Fairfield Osborn, "Facts of the Evolutionists," *The Forum* 75 (June 1926): 842. The
article notes at the start that Osborn specifically wrote it in response to a challenge issued by
conservative Protestant minister John Roach Straton to the directors of the Natural History
Museum. Amid Osborn's discussion—which includes his contention about humanity's origin
in Central Asia and paleontological work performed there by Jesuit priest-paleontologist Fr.
Teilhard de Chardin and other priest-scientists—he also endorses the infamous Piltdown man
(later uncovered as a forgery). Near the end of the article is a drawing delineating Osborn's
habitual intertwining of evolution with a purported biological racial hierarchy, depicted there
as the "ascent of intelligence" over time. Osborn's "races of man" in the drawing feature a ver-
tical arrangement of animated skulls, with a "Caucasian" skull sitting on a top tree branch and
the next lower rung occupied by a "Chinese" skull, followed by lower ranked human groups'
skulls on branches beneath them.

destiny come not from religious traditions but from the biological investigations made within the time of men now living."[1]

News of this talk was subsequently published in the *Tabloid Scientist*, the newsletter of John Montgomery Cooper's CRTS initiative, created in 1928 by Cooper to fully incorporate science-minded Catholics into the professional scientific community in America.[2] According to the report, 175 members of Cooper's CRTS club sat in on that session. In fact, the panel's chair was one of these very Catholics: Fr. Alphonse Schwitalla, SJ, dean of St. Louis University's medical school.

Faced with Riddle's overt philosophizing, or perhaps stump speech oratory, Schwitalla managed but the feeblest of responses when it came his turn to reply—a response which silently passed over much of the geologist's basic premise about "organized religion" as a whole. "If it is true," said Schwitalla, "that organized religion is a restrictive influence on the teaching of the best in biology, the statement cannot be universally applicable to all schools conducted under religious auspices."[3] Schwitalla, a personal friend of Cooper, appears to have shared a similar mindset with Cooper on how to react: give way to the authority of professionalized science as the best way to gain a broad hearing of progressive Catholics' rhetoric.

The next time CRTS met, its members agreed to deal with Riddle's claim about organized religion retarding science by simply doing a better job of advertising that science produced by Catho-

1. See Oscar Riddle, "The Confusion of Tongues," *Science* 83 (January 24, 1936): 73. This was the second part of a speech printed in two installments in *Science*.

2. "St. Louis Meeting Report," *Tabloid Scientist* (December 20, 1936): 1, 3, in JMC Papers, box 23, folder "Catholic Scientific Research—The Tabloid Scientist," ACUA. The CRTS was a formal club created by Cooper as a means of encouraging Catholics to align themselves with both the professional apparatus and the naturalistic research philosophy of the broader scientific community. Cooper's vision had called for a loosely structured national organization whose members would gather annually for a short meeting at the AAAS December conference. In between the yearly national meetings, CRTS members met in local branch chapters. For Cooper's original outline of CRTS goals, see "Prospective Letter to Those Who Might Be Interested" (n.d.), in JMC Papers, box 23, folder "Catholic Scientific Research 1927–1933," ACUA.

3. "St. Louis Meeting," 1.

lics was indistinguishable from that produced by non-Catholics.[4] They said nothing about Riddle's own violation of the naturalistic strictures purportedly marking off a professional scientist's argumentation from that of generalization-prone amateurs. Yet Riddle's comments had come as part of a conference panel paper, a scientific forum implying at least a minimal form of the empiricism that could be hoped for (as with science textbooks and articles). A baseline of empirical objectivity was also expected from the public square's popular science produced by professional scientists. These expectations were regularly reinforced by professional scientific societies. The public was led to expect them at least since the 1870s when Edward Youmans of *Popular Science Monthly* promulgated the sense that genuine scientists operated "from truths first derived from facts and phenomena by the method of induction and then systematically verified from principles already established," principles based in eternal natural laws.[5] Indeed, the level of generalization in Riddle's talk differed little from the generalizations found in the most amateur of science writers.

Three years after the talk in question, *Tabloid Scientist*'s editor published an open letter to the CRTS from a Catholic who did not agree so readily with CRTS's tactics in the case of Riddle and other professionals in the sciences making similar kinds of nonscientific claims. Its writer lamented that in the intervening time since Riddle's offending address, other decrees overtly hostile to traditional religion, but which posed as scientific statements of fact, had been published repeatedly in the official AAAS magazines *Science* and *Scientific Monthly*. The same, said the writer, was true of material in popular science books: "On the whole," the writer of the letter

4. "St. Louis Meeting," 1, 3.
5. E. L. Youmans, "Herbert Spencer and the Doctrine of Evolution," *Popular Science Monthly* 6 (November 1874): 42–43. As William Leverette noted, Youmans's "optimistic scientism" granted "his philosophical hero, Herbert Spencer," the title of one who had shown "the uniformity of the law of evolution throughout nature," a law which could be seen in "life, mind, man, science, art, language, morality, society, government, and institutions." Leverette, "E. L. Youmans' Crusade," 13.

moaned, "they have gone unanswered, at least in a decisive way."[6]
Cooper, seemingly unshaken in his stance that avoiding any critique of mainline science would eventually win over both Catholics
and non-Catholics to his way of thinking, assured listeners in his
1938 speech honoring the tenth anniversary of CRTS, "the trouble
between Religion and Science is now happily past, it is now time to
emphasize normal cooperation between the two."[7]

Perhaps Cooper, Schwitalla, O'Brien, Ryan, and others who
kept to this path felt vindicated by the notice that liberal-minded
scientific Catholics received when a University of California zoologist delivering the 1939 presidential address of the AAAS's Western division set, alongside "many philosophers and liberal-minded
theologians," "the more enlightened leaders of Catholic thought
who accept the doctrine of evolution."[8] It was an address reprinted
in full in *Science* magazine. Then again, this tribute had come from
Samuel J. Holmes, president of the AES, amid a speech criticizing
traditional ethics and the religious institutions that promulgated
them in favor of a relativist ethics that Holmes claimed was a necessary scientific inference from universal evolutionary law. Holmes
singled out the institutional Roman Catholic Church as a chief of-
fender even as he argued that "ethics is still closely affiliated with
metaphysics and theology ... [but] Darwin's views on ethics are the
logical outgrowth of his theory of the causes of evolution."[9]

In another article appearing in *Science* that same year, Holmes
had complimented the engagement with eugenics by Catholic figures, a cadre that we know had included Cooper and Ryan. In an
article criticizing opposition to eugenics, especially opposition
"on religious grounds," Holmes noted that there were a number

6. "A Plea for Action," letter to Rev. Anselm Keefe, editor, *Tabloid Scientist* 5 (December 12, 1939): 2, in JMC Papers, box 23, folder "Catholic Roundtable of Science Correspondence," ACUA.

7. "Richmond Meeting Held," *Tabloid Scientist* 5 (December 12, 1939): 1.

8. Samuel J. Holmes, "Darwinian Ethics and Its Practical Applications," *Science* 90 (August 11, 1939): 118. Holmes's perception of liberal Catholics as a laudable minority within the
mostly lamentable Catholic Church is apparent (121, 122).

9. Holmes, "Darwinian Ethics," 118.

of the Catholic Church's "official representatives and adherents [who] have espoused the cause of eugenics reform."[10] Ryan, in his pamphlet *Human Sterilization*, published in 1927 while he was a member of the AES, had left open the legitimate possibility of state-mandated sterilization as "self-protection by the State."[11] He had argued in it that "the amount of social incompetence" resulting from "idiots, imbeciles, and feebleminded persons actually existing and imminent" is sufficient to demand systematic preventive action by public authority, although he strongly preferred "segregation during the procreative period," advocating for such in the pamphlet.[12] Notwithstanding the caveat, by 1939 Holmes's category would technically include Ryan as one of "the few voices among prominent Catholics which had been raised in defense of sterilization on eugenic grounds," voices which, Holmes implied, "have apparently now been silenced."[13] Ryan's later view rejecting sterilization was not the result of silencing, but it was triggered by *CC*.[14] Works like Ryan's pamphlet were open to co-opting when scientists like Holmes sought to establish a contrast between the institutional church and an ostensibly enlightened, science-minded minority operating within it. Indeed, Holmes specifically pointed to the effect of *CC* in muting sterilization advocacy.

10. Samuel L. Holmes, "The Opposition to Eugenics," *Science* 89 (April 21, 1939): 355.

11. John Ryan, *Human Sterilization* (Washington, D.C.: National Catholic Welfare Conference, 1927), 2.

12. Ryan, *Human Sterilization*, 2, 3. Ryan argued that, in practice, forced sterilization would often be imposed unnecessarily and using unscientific rationale, hence his preference for segregation (3). Yet forced segregation of those classified as mentally or physically incompetent was also a prong of the organized eugenics movement. It was a prong invigorated after the 1927 *Buck v. Bell* Supreme Court ruling validated state-sponsored intervention to prevent the reproduction of those whom experts deemed eugenically unfit. States that did not enact forced sterilization plans often enforced segregation by sex, especially for "girls and women of childbearing age," as a method of preventing reproduction. For an example of a segregation "colony" plan, where an expert commission was to determine who belonged in "a eugenically segregated institution," see Edward J. Larson, *Sex, Race, and Science: Eugenics in the Deep South* (Baltimore: Johns Hopkins University Press, 1995), 59, 67–68, 84.

13. Holmes, "Opposition to Eugenics," 355.

14. For an example of public coverage of Ryan's stance after he reversed his views on the possibility of state-mandated sterilization, see "Mgr. Ryan Assails Sterilization Aim," *New York Times*, February 19, 1934, 5.

Given the fact that during the interwar era, professional scientists—including Holmes, Riddle, and others—repeatedly intertwined evolution with the inevitability of both eugenics and contraception in professional and popular scientific discourse—one wonders whether these endorsements by such members of the American scientific intelligentsia were really much of a victory for American liberal Catholicism. Over the first few decades of the twentieth century, an enthusiasm for evolution and contraception came to symbolize one's broader zeal for advancing the social order through science while at the same time demonstrating a progressive and forward-thinking orientation. This happened even as those topics themselves were being transformed through a process of cultural alchemy into wholly scientific, rather than at least partially religious or moral, matters. In a number of ways, these reversals are emblematic of the irony pulsing through progressive Catholics' attempts to walk the thin line of a via media between Catholic subculture and American culture writ large.

John Montgomery Cooper, John A. O'Brien, John Ryan, and some other liberal Catholics in the interwar era adopted what one might call an anthropological take on scientific discourse, one that viewed science as a kind of language that should be learned—and used—by Catholics if they were to be heard in a larger national tribe's public square. Holding this view of scientific authority, they sought the broader tribe's trust as well as access to its cultural thought matrices for purposes of both outreach and communion. But these liberal Catholics, too, believed in much of the potential of that science. In their enthusiasm, however, the possibility of such scientific language being unable to translate what they thought distinctive about their message, or even the ramifications of their being framed as "going native" for scientism, seems not to have occurred to them much.

Liberal-progressive Catholics also urged their co-religionists to adhere to the dialects of empirical naturalism when crafting rhetoric aimed at broader American debates involving human origin and development, whether macrocosmic or microcosmic. Our swath of surveyed evidence suggests that a lot of the science-centered rhetoric that liberal Catholics directed at mainline consumption was subsequently colonized by scientistic interlocutors. Such interlocutors not infrequently exploited the Catholics' rhetoric along with their professional affiliations and memberships. Indeed, the Catholics' words were even employed to support worldviews antithetical to those of institutional Catholicism, thus weakening the cultural authority and influence of the institution whose interests they claimed to represent.

The liberal-progressive Catholics' role was not simply one of hesitant passivity in this cultural process. Their extensive efforts to participate in mainline public discourse led them to introduce ideas into that discourse that had been forged in their own bifurcated intellectual realm, ideas containing elements and residues of theological modernism and progressive quasi-positivism. Mixed into an autoclave, or perhaps melting pot, of public debate, the liberal-progressive Catholics' efforts helped transmogrify the legitimate terms of debate for evolution and birth control from discourses that had room for religious or ethical concern into discussions about technical issues subject to controlled planning. Thus redefined, evolution and birth control served as prongs in a larger social-scientific reform worldview where applied science could appear to be America's only legitimate and pancultural engine of biological and social progress.

The progressive Catholics' actions even unintentionally added ballast to scientifically legitimized notions of race hierarchy when they saw their words redeployed to defend constructions of evolution that bore the symbolic function of legitimizing applied racialist eugenics.[15] The mainline contraception movement's efforts to rationally separate sex from pregnancy—while in the process controlling which of the scientifically reified subgroups, including im-

15. For more on the functionalist construction of evolution as racialist and eugenic in that period, see Pavuk, "American Association for the Advancement of Science."

migrant Catholics, would be permitted to reproduce in the effort to guard social evolution—were also unintentionally strengthened by the kinds of arguments progressive Catholics offered in favor of the rhythm method. Such programs for reconstructing society on a putatively rational, scientific basis were the unintended beneficiaries of such Catholics' rhetoric.

Put differently, the construct of public scientific discourse did not work as much like a Rosetta stone for seamlessly translating liberal Catholics' intellectual contributions into the public sphere's post-Protestant normative vernacular as the Catholics had hoped. Rather, their contributions blended with and strengthened that vernacular and, thus, such vernacular's social, philosophical, and cosmological implications. When others, both Catholic and non-Catholic, puzzled over the seeming acquiescence to cultural scientism of figures such as Ryan, Cooper, and O'Brien, they responded in books and periodical articles expressing confidence that as long as Protestant intellectual hegemony was dissolving in American public life—and as long as scientific popularizers like Henry Fairfield Osborn no longer operated like nineteenth-century scientific materialists—all would turn out well in the end.

Did liberal Catholics make a Faustian bargain to achieve public influence or were they simply operating as their progressivism, Americanism, and quasi-modernism dictated? Both interpretations are plausible in their own ways. Traveling down these roads, Frs. Ryan, Cooper, and O'Brien unintentionally helped realize a vision made by Riddle at the AAAS: all would benefit, he believed, when traditional religion yielded to science the right to authoritatively ask, and answer, the question *what is life?*[16]

16. See Oscar Riddle, "The Confusion of Tongues," *Science* 83 (January 17, 1936): 41–45.

Postscript

> The physiology underlying the spontaneous "safe period"
> [of the rhythm method] is identical to that initiated by the
> steroid compounds.... Indeed, the use of the compounds for
> fertility control may be characterized as a "pill-established
> safe period" and would seem to carry the same moral
> implications.
>
> —John A. Rock, MD (1963)

When Margaret Sanger's associate Gregory Pincus suggested one day that Catholic physician John Rock ought to be made chief public advocate of the newly packaged contraceptive cause of the 1950s, she was at the same time appalled and intrigued.[1] Sanger, of course, was a longstanding and fervent anti-Catholic. However, Rock's past and present research activity—as well as his long clinical advocacy for birth control and women's health—indicated that he might be the perfect choice. Pincus was able to convince Sanger of the strategic wisdom of co-opting Rock's authority not only as a scientific researcher and physician (to convince secular

---

Epigraph is from John A. Rock, *The Time Has Come: A Catholic Doctor's Proposals to End the Battle over Birth Control* (New York: Alfred A. Knopf, 1963), 168.

1. See Marks, *Sexual Chemistry*, 93. Rock and Pincus had met during the 1930s and reconnected in 1952 after losing touch for a time (Marks, 93). As seen in this book, Sanger's birth control efforts had been intimately tied to the eugenics movement before World War II. However, the eugenics movement had been disgraced and driven underground after the war. Sanger partly divorced her rhetoric from eugenics (but not from the notion of social control). For information on how the Model Sterilization Law published by the United States Eugenics Record Office had been the guideline, albeit in less extreme form, for the German National Socialist Party's Eugenic Sterilization Law of 1933, see Marks, 19.

science-centered intellectuals and conservative physicians) but also as a practicing Catholic (to satisfy Catholic women and others who respected basic Judeo-Christian morality).[2]

Rock himself was primed to accept the offer; he had become America's foremost reproductive specialist by the 1950s. Also, although a practicing (liberal) Catholic, he had long been disgruntled with what he considered the American Catholic Church's heavy-handed dealings with Margaret Sanger.[3] More importantly, he saw the offer as a chance to put reproductive decisions in the hands of families, particularly women. Thus was born the great irony of a devout Catholic and a devout anti-Catholic tied together forever as postwar America's foremost advocates of *Planned Parenthood*. Rock soon initiated the scientific leap into the new age of human birth control. *Enovid*, the first pharmaceutical regulator of reproduction, was to become known simply as "the pill." It was the 1960s' tiny shot heard round the world, one that made possible the final detachment of sexual intercourse from reproduction that the institutional Catholic Church had been fighting against for a very long time.[4]

Harvard University, a major center of American Progressivism in the early twentieth century, was Rock's home for both undergraduate and medical school.[5] While he was in the latter, he

2. William Clifford Roberts, "'The Pill' and Its Four Major Developers," *Proceedings (Baylor University Medical Center)* 28 (July 2015): 426, https://www.ncbi.nlm.nih.gov/pmc/articles/PMC4462239/.

3. Rock, *The Time Has Come*, 89–90. Rock had been born to second-generation Irish Catholic immigrant parents in the Protestant-populated town of Marlborough, Massachusetts. According to one biographer, his parents took Catholicism seriously but were "remarkably permissive" and "not narrow." When growing up, Rock "steeped himself" in reading material offering Catholic viewpoints. Later, as an undergraduate, he revived the Catholic Newman student club at Harvard. Loretta McLaughlin, *The Pill, John Rock, and the Catholic Church: The Biography of a Revolution* (Boston: Little, Brown, and Co., 1982), 8.

4. Rock went on to become a birth control celebrity. Right before the debut of his 1963 book on the pill, he appeared in a round of very visible magazine articles and interviews advocating the pill's legitimacy both to Catholics—lay and clerical—and to others in America. Rock was featured on the cover of *Time*; in *Life*, *Reader's Digest*, and the *Saturday Evening Post*; on television; and in other public media at the time (McLaughlin, *The Pill, John Rock, and the Catholic Church*, 155).

5. Rock's undergraduate years were spent in Harvard's class of 1915.

expressed an interest in both gynecology and psychiatry. In fact, ever since he was an undergraduate, Rock had closely followed the ideas of Sigmund Freud and the Vienna school's thought about human sexuality; one can see its intellectual influence in his rhetoric about birth control.[6] Rock was also deeply affected by evolutionary thought in its various incarnations. In fact, his own views combined Freud's philosophy of sexuality with development by evolution. Rock attributed human love itself to evolution: "In the evolution of the hominid family from his ape-like progenitors ... there arose ... not only the powerful coital urge but also the utterly particular emotional quality of love."[7] In his subsequent calls for use of the pill, Rock's trust in these verities saw him urge readers to put their trust in new, enlightened definitions of sex as constructed by both biological and social sciences (including physiology, biology, anthropology, and psychology). He also counseled people to accept the wisdom of demographic and economic calls for worldwide birth regulation or else face planetary catastrophe.[8]

John Rock's most famous extended argument for the pill came in his book, *The Time Has Come: A Catholic Doctor's Proposals to End the Battle over Birth Control* (1963). Both internal discourse among various liberal Catholics and discourse directed outside Catholic circles affected Rock's thinking about birth control; this is discernible both in his book and in other earlier writings. Near the beginning of his career, Rock established his long-time connection

6. He came to speak of the sexual drive as an overpowering biological impulse (McLaughlin, *The Pill, John Rock, and the Catholic Church*, 12). Rock indicated as far back as 1923 that his conscience was not in line with what Catholic priests told him about human sexuality and that his practical experience and research led him further afield from those teachings. He later articulated his thoughts thus: "Decades of dealing with marital relations and of facilitating the creation and delivery of new life ... [produced] realistic thoughts on the nature of human sexuality.... These thoughts, compared with those of other natural and social scientists—biologists, anthropologists, sociologists, and others—contributed to my understanding of the sexual nature of man" (Rock, *The Time Has Come*, xiii).

7. Rock quoted in McLaughlin, *The Pill, John Rock, and the Catholic Church*, 33.

8. Rock, *The Time Has Come*, 3, 18, 25, 147. Christian Herter's foreword to the book characterized Rock as "see[ing] the population crisis as providing a categorical imperative for ending the religious and political battle over birth control." Christian Herter, *The Time Has Come*, vii.

with Leo Latz. This put him in the same Catholic discursive circles as the latter.[9] As Rock got more involved with birth control, such contacts increased and diversified. Rock was also significantly influenced by the progress-centered theological and scientific claims of Catholic modernist Teilhard de Chardin, among others. Rock viewed the Catholic Church's (specifically the Jesuit order's) rejection of Teilhard as a sign of backwardness, himself calling Teilhard "perhaps the greatest philosopher of our time, ... the Socrates, the Aquinas of our epoch, and, like them in their day, denied by blind men in high places."[10]

Rock's ultimate defenses of the pill were extensions of liberal Catholics' arguments favoring rhythm that first appeared in the interwar public square.[11] In fact, Rock often explained the pill as nothing other than a more accurate and reliable way of practicing the rhythm method. Both, he emphasized, were *natural* and both were moral. His version was just more predictable.[12] Rock's theologizing also resembled that of interwar liberal Catholics in that he reassigned humanity's presumed role in the divine plan for marriage the same way as Leo Latz and John O'Brien had. In other words, instead of opposing the ability of the human mind to separate intercourse from pregnancy, he celebrated it.[13] Like his

9. In fact, in *The Time Has Come*, Rock offered an almost identical tripartite theology of sex—stacked in opposition to the papal view—as the theology that Leo Latz had articulated back in the 1930s (67). See chapter six for my discussion of Latz.

10. Rock quoted in McLaughlin, *The Pill, John Rock, and the Catholic Church*, 125.

11. Rock directly cited the rhetoric of John O'Brien and Leo Latz on rhythm in *The Time Has Come* (39, 137, 157, 181).

12. The connections were also clear in Rock's book. At one point, he said, "My reasoning is based, in part, on the fact that the rhythm method, which is sanctioned by the church, depends precisely on the secretion of progesterone from the ovaries which these [drug] compounds merely duplicate." He went on, "The physiology underlying the spontaneous 'safe period' is identical to that initiated by the steroid compounds and is equally harmless to the individual" (*The Time Has Come*, 168–69).

13. As Rock put it, "It is difficult not to believe that God gave man his intellect to safeguard him whenever his inner biology is inadequate." Continuing in this apparently purposeful vein, he says, "One might even tend to think it immoral for husband and wife [with the pope's injunctions in mind] to reject their God-given intellect and trust only the automatic action of female sex glands ... to suppress the powerful love urge which their Creator fused with their sex instinct" (*The Time Has Come*, 169–70).

discursive progenitors, he sometimes appeared to argue in natural law categories but actually did so on the basis of inductive empiricism.[14]

Rock's book, it should be remembered, was garbed primarily for Catholics—laypeople and bishops—in an attempt to make a holistic case for the pill's legitimacy and desirability. But it was clearly directed at all Americans. His loose redeployment of natural law to serve his cause, his celebration of changing views of sexuality, and his defense of birth control's social and health benefits, would likely have made John O'Brien and John Cooper proud.

It took the papacy several years to officially weigh in on the pill, but American Catholics were in no mood to wait while it deliberated. They turned to it in droves: a study on the pill's usage made by Catholic priest-sociologist Andrew Greeley concluded that between 1960 and 1965, Catholics' use of birth control methods not overtly approved by their church had gone from 38 to 51 percent. It was, of course, not just Catholic women who were taking the pill, and thus came Rock's monumental influence on broader American society. Reports suggested that about six million American women were taking the birth control pill by 1965.[15] One Rock biographer contended: "the fact that he was a deeply religious man, a superbly informed Catholic, with his own reasoned opinion of the pill's moral righteousness, undoubtedly was a factor in its near universal acceptance by people of every faith the world over."[16] Given the secular nature of many subsequent assumptions about the pill, it is interesting to see the claim that some people turned to it because they trusted it was morally sound. Many others took it without any concern for who, if anyone, claimed it was moral or not. It was not a question of morality but of practicality. Such developments as the

14. Sometimes Rock just mixed them all together. At one point, he went so far as to quote a contemporary Catholic professor who argued it was actually man's "vocation" to "frustrate nature" (*The Time Has Come*, 59).

15. Andrew Greeley study cited in McLaughlin, *The Pill, John Rock, and the Catholic Church*, 177.

16. McLaughlin, *The Pill, John Rock, and the Catholic Church*, 38.

foregoing undoubtedly contributed to the increasingly normative cultural stance that reproduction and contraception were technical, scientific problems rather than moral ones.

Set up by a modernist view of Catholicism, Rock truly believed that the Catholic hierarchy would approve of his birth control pill, especially when he saw the massive changes the church had made during the Vatican II council of 1962 to 1965.[17] Therefore, both he and other liberal Catholics were shocked and disgusted when Pope Paul VI (r. 1963–78) finally issued an encyclical *Humanae Vitae* in 1968, condemning the pill with other forms of artificial contraception.[18] According to the encyclical, which was steeped in standard Catholic readings of natural law, the pill was not natural after all. Many Catholics believed they saw in the document an attempt to backtrack in the face of the much-discussed inconsistencies in Catholic birth control rhetoric over the decades. It is hard to argue with that assessment.[19]

17. The Vatican II Council's papal visionary, sponsor, and convoker in 1959 was Pope John XXIII (Angelo Giuseppe Roncalli, r. 1958–63). One anecdote about Pope John's mindset is telling, especially since Rock said he was influenced by the spirit of Vatican II to continue working for the pill's acceptance. The first day Roncalli sat down to his desk as the new pope John XXIII in 1958, an aide placed a folder on his desk. Its earliest contents dated back decades to the years shortly after his papal predecessor, Pius X, had condemned theological modernism. Over time, the bulk of the folder had increased substantially. The file itself came from a secret collection of such records kept by the Roman Holy Office to monitor the activities of those within the Catholic Church it had reason to believe harbored genuine modernist inclinations. On the front cover was a name: *Angelo Giuseppe Roncalli*. The pope lazily waved his hand over the letters and, picking up a thin pencil, he indicated that the file was to be immediately deleted. As he did so, he wrote on the folder with a wry smile, "Ah yes, but now we are infallible" (Appleby, *Church and Age Unite!*, 284n3).

18. The encyclical was issued on July 29, 1968.

19. It was also the case that the new discursive expectations about sexuality initiated for Catholics by our interwar cast of characters made it increasingly unlikely that many were going to listen to this papal decree. Set up by steadily scientized expectations for sexuality and for the church itself, many Catholics left the fold. Rock was deeply embittered by the decision. Amidst opposition from his church hierarchy, Rock turned, as had his hero Teilhard de Chardin years before, to public agreement with agnostic humanist Julian Huxley. In a speech given at Ohio University, Rock commented, "As Sir Julian Huxley has said, 'It has become wrong and indeed immoral to put obstacles in the way of bringing the rate of increase down, as Roman Catholics, puritans, fundamentalists, Marxists, and other frightened, dogmatic, or reactionary groups have been doing.'" Rock added the statement, "It hurts me to have to say that he is right. Let those in high ecclesiastical places face what is already a fact of life in many parts of the world" (Rock quoted in McLaughlin, *The Pill, John Rock, and the Catholic Church*, 178). Rock eventually left the church, his faith in tatters.

Bibliography

Primary Sources

Manuscript Sources

American Philosophical Society, Philadelphia
    American Eugenics Society Papers
    Eugenics Record Office Papers
    Papers Relating to Leon F. Whitney
American Catholic History Research Center and University Archives (ACUA),
    The Catholic University of America, Washington, D.C.
    John Augustine Ryan Papers
    John Montgomery Cooper Papers
    National Catholic Welfare Conference Papers (now in United States
        Conference of Catholic Bishops Papers)
Georgetown University Archives and Rare Book and Special Collections
    (GURBSC), Washington, D.C.
    America Magazine Archive
    Francis Talbot Papers
    John Wynne Papers
    Lucile Swan Papers
    Wilfred Parsons Papers
The Margaret Sanger Papers Project, http://sangerpapers.org/
    Published Writings and Speeches, 1911–1959
    Sophia Smith Collection

Published Sources

Agar, William M. "Religion and Science [I]." *Commonweal* 25 (1937): 568–71.
———. "Religion and Science [II]." *Commonweal* 25 (1937): 599–600.
———. "Religion and Science [III]." *Commonweal* 25 (1937): 662–64.
———. "Religion and Science [IV]." *Commonweal* 25 (1937): 689–92.
———. "Religion and Science Today [I]." *Commonweal* 27 (1938): 371–73.
———. "Religion and Science Today [II]." *Commonweal* 27 (1938): 399–401.
———. *Catholicism and the Progress of Science.* New York: MacMillan, 1940.
———. *The Dilemma of Science.* New York: Sheed and Ward, 1941.

Allen, Robert S. "Congress and Birth Control." *The Nation* 134 (January 27, 1932): 104–5.

Allen, Frederick Lewis. *Only Yesterday: An Informal History of the 1920s.* New York: Harper and Brothers, 1931.

"Anglicans Accept Evolution." *Literary Digest* 106 (September 6, 1930): 24.

Augustine. *De Genesi ad Litteram (On the Literal Meaning of Genesis).* Vol. 2. Translated by John Hammond Taylor. New York: Newman Press, 1982.

———. *On Genesis: Two Books against the Manichees and On the Literal Interpretation of Genesis: An Unfinished Book.* Translated by Ronald J. Teske. Washington, D.C.: The Catholic University of America Press, 1991.

Aquinas, Thomas. "Question 88: Venial and Mortal Sin." *Summa Theologiae* (2017). https://www.newadvent.org/summa/2088.htm.

Barrett, E. Boyd. "Psychologists' Colored Glasses [I]." *Commonweal* 2 (1925): 152–54.

———. "Psychologists' Colored Glasses [II]." *Commonweal* 2 (1925): 183–84.

———. "Catholic Loyalty: 'Rejoinder to J. J. Walsh.'" *The Forum* 82 (1929): 48–51.

———. "Will American Catholics Secede from Rome?" *The Forum* 82 (1929): 89–94.

———. "Roman Catholicism and Birth Control." *Birth Control Review* 14 (January 1930): 11–12.

———. "The Sociology of Nunneries." *American Mercury* 34 (1935): 175–83.

Baschab, Charles R. *A Manual of Neo-Scholastic Philosophy.* 3rd ed. St. Louis: B. Herder, 1929.

Basil. "The Hexameron." In *Basil: Letters and Select Works*, vol. 8 of *Nicene and Post-Nicene Fathers*, 2nd ser., edited by Philip Schaff and Henry Wace, 51–108. Peabody, Mass.: Hendrickson Publishers, 1994.

Bateson, William. "Evolutionary Faith and Modern Doubts." *Science* 55 (1922): 55–61.

Beatty, Willard W. "A Normal-School Course in Sociology Introductory to Work in the Social Studies." *American Journal of Sociology* 26 (1921): 573–80.

Berdyaev, N. A. "Neothomism." *Journal Put'* 1 (1925): 169–71.

Bliven, Bruce. "For Al Smith." *New Republic* 91 (June 23, 1937): 184–86.

Bode, Boyd H. "Justice Holmes on Natural Law and the Moral Ideal." *International Journal of Ethics* 29 (1919): 397–404.

"Books on Evolution." *Commonweal* 2 (1925): 484–85.

Bradford, Gamaliel. "Darwin the Destroyer." *Harper's Magazine* 153 (1926): 397–407.

Briggs, Charles A. "Modernism Mediating the Coming Catholicism." *North American Review* 187 (1908): 877–89.

Bromley, Dorothy Dunbar. "Sanctified Birth Control." *The Nation* 139 (September 26, 1934): 346–48.

Bryan, William Jennings. *In His Image.* New York: Fleming H. Revell, 1922.

Burch, Guy Irving. "Population: Public Health." *Eugenics* 3 (December 1930): 474.

———. "Larithmics." *Eugenics* 4 (January 1931): 35.

————. "A Eugenicist Replies." *Forum and Century* 92 (August 1934): 81–83.

[Burch, Guy Irving]. "Catholics on Birth Control." *New Republic* 79 (September 5, 1934): 98–100.

Campbell, Clarence G. "Presidential Address of the Eugenics Research Association: Human Evolution and Eugenics." *Eugenical News* 15 (1930): 89–97.

"Cardinal Hayes Pays Tribute to Science." *The Outlook* 141 (1925): 179–80.

Carroll, Paul L. "A Survey of Textbooks in College Biology." *Bulletin: National Catholic Education Association* 37 (1940): 221–58.

Carter, Elmer. "Eugenics for the Negro." *Birth Control Review* 16 (June 1932): 166–70.

A Catholic Priest. "The German Conspiracy in 1886." *The Independent* (1897). John Ireland Papers microfilm, roll 6. Originals in the Catholic Historical Society of St. Paul.

"The Catholic View of Evolution." *Literary Digest* 86 (July 4, 1925): 34.

Chesterton, G. K. "Religion and Sex." *Commonweal* 1 (November 12, 1924): 9–11.

————. "Religion and Education." *Commonweal* 2 (1925): 553–55.

————. *Eugenics and Other Evils.* In vol. 4 of *The Collected Works of G. K. Chesterton*, edited by George J. Marlin et al., 297–418. San Francisco: Ignatius Press, 1987.

"The Churches and Birth Control." *Federal Council Bulletin* 14 (April, 1931): 19–20, 25.

Codex Iuris Canonici. 1917. http://www.jgray.org/codes/cic17lat.html.

Committee on Special War Activities. *Civics Catechism on the Rights and Duties of American Citizens.* Reconstruction Pamphlets, no. 13. Washington, D.C.: National Catholic War Council, 1920.

"Concerning Evolution." *Commonweal* 2 (1925): 119–21.

Conklin, Edwin Grant. *Heredity and Environment in the Development of Man.* Rev. 2nd ed. Princeton: Princeton University Press, 1917.

————. *The Direction of Human Evolution.* New York: Charles Scribner's Sons, 1921.

Cooper, James F. "The Birth Rate of Genius: Does Contraception Curb It?" *Eugenics* 2 (May 1929): 19.

Cooper, John Montgomery. "Some Recent Trends in Social Hygiene." *Catholic Charities Review* 5 (January 1921): 3–5.

————. "Sex Teaching in the Home." *Catholic Charities Review* 5 (September 1921): 217–22.

————. "Sex Training in the Home." *Catholic Charities Review* 5 (December 1921): 321–26.

————. *Birth Control.* Washington, D.C.: National Catholic Welfare Conference, 1923.

————. "If Evolution Were a Fact?" *Catholic World* 121 (September 1925): 721–28.

————. "The Catholic Anthropological Conference." Washington, D.C.: The Catholic University of America, 1926. JMC Papers, ACUA.

———. "Social Hygiene and Religion." *Journal of Social Hygiene* 12 (1926): 1–13.

———. "Birth Control." Letter to the editor. *The Forum* 77 (January–June 1927): 150.

———. "Biological Evolution and the Catholic Social Ideal." Chapter prepared for unpublished volume. 1928. ACUA, Washington, D.C.

———. "Birth Control and the 'Perverted Faculty' Argument." *Ecclesiastical Review* 79 (November 1928): 527–33.

———. "Is Eugenics Racial Snobbery?" *Eugenics* 2 (February 1929): 20.

———. "The Birth Rate of Genius: Does Contraception Curb It?" *Eugenics* 2 (1929): 18.

———. *The Northern Algonquian Supreme Being*. Washington, D.C.: The Catholic University of America, 1934.

———. "The Scientific Evidence Bearing upon Human Evolution." *Primitive Man* 8 (January and April, 1935): 1–52.

———. "The Catholic High School and Scientific Research." In *Catholics and Scholarship: A Symposium on the Development of Scholars*, edited by John A. O'Brien, 168–77. Huntington, Ind.: Our Sunday Visitor Press [1939].

———. "Family Limitation and Human Welfare." *Salesianum* (n.d.): 22–26.

Coucke, Valere J., and James J. Walsh. *The Sterile Period in Family Life*. New York: Joseph F. Wagner, 1933.

"The Curse of Abortion." *Birth Control Review* 13 (November 1929): 307.

Darwin, Charles. *The Descent of Man and Selection in Relation to Sex*. London: J. Murray, 1871. Reprint, Princeton: Princeton University Press, 1981. Page references are to the 1981 version.

———. *The Origin of Species*. A Variorum text. Edited by Morse Peckham. Philadelphia: University of Pennsylvania Press, 1959.

Darwin, Leonard. "The Aims and Methods of Eugenical Societies." *Science* 54 (October 1921): 313–23.

———. "The Field of Eugenic Reform." *Scientific Monthly* 13 (November 1921): 385–98.

"Darwinian Theory Denied." *Scientific American* 111 (1914): 144.

"Darwin's Theory No Longer Accepted." *Scientific American* 111 (1914): 385.

Davis, Forrest. "Tennessee—State of Brave Men." *Commonweal* 2 (1925): 283–85.

Davis, Henry. *Eugenics: Aims and Methods*. London: Burns, Oates and Washbourne, 1930.

Davis, Maxine. "The Rhythm." *Pictorial Review* 39 (May 1938): 18–19, 84.

Davis, Watson. "Recent Scientific Progress: The Evolution Theory Entering a New Phase." *Current History* 27 (February 1928): 707–12.

"Dayton and Great Britain." *Commonweal* 2 (August 5, 1925): 301–3.

De Ford, Miriam. "The War Against Evolution." *The Nation* 120 (May 20, 1925): 565–66.

Desch, C. H. "Pure and Applied Science." *Science* 74 (1931): 495–502.

Dewey, John. "Education and Birth Control." *The Nation* 134 (January 27, 1932): 112.

————. *A Common Faith*. New Haven: Yale University Press, 1934.

Dickinson, Robert L. "Birth Regulation." *Eugenics* 2 (February 1929): 34–35.

Dillingham, [William], ed. *Reports of the Immigration Commission*, vol. 4. Washington, D.C.: Government Printing Office, 1911. Reprint, New York: Arno Press, 1970.

Dimnet, Ernest. "New Light on Birth Control." Letter to the editor. *Commonweal* 18 (April 12, 1933): 663.

————. Letter to the editor. *Commonweal* 19 (June 9, 1933): 162.

Draper, John William. *History of the Conflict between Religion and Science*. New York: D. Appleton and Co., 1874.

Dublin, Louis. "Birth Control: What It Is Doing to America's Population." *The Forum* 96 (November 1931): 270–75.

East, Edward Murray. *Mankind at the Crossroads*. New York: Charles Scribner's Sons, 1923.

————. "Heredity—The Master Riddle of Science." *Scribner's Magazine* 78 (July 1925): 1–7.

————. "Heredity and Sex." *Scribner's Magazine* 78 (August 1925): 144–51.

————. "Tabu—A Defense of Birth Control." *The Forum* 77 (May 1927): 669–77.

————. *Heredity and Human Affairs*. New York: Charles Scribner's Sons, 1927.

Elder, Benedict. "A Law That is Not a Law." *Commonweal* 2 (1925): 245–47.

Eliot, Charles. "The American Social Hygiene Association." *Journal of Social Hygiene* 1 (December 1914): 1–5.

Ellis, Havelock. *Little Essays of Love and Virtue*. London: A&C Black, 1922.

Eulau, Heinz. "Proselytizing in the Catholic Press." *Public Opinion Quarterly* 11 (Summer 1947): 189–97.

"Evolution a 'Powerful Aid to Religious Faith.'" *Literary Digest* 76 (1923): 33–34.

Fairchild, Henry Pratt. "Birth Control and Race Improvement." *Birth Control Review* 13 (December 12, 1929): 341–43.

————. "Birth Control and Social Engineering." *The Nation* 134 (January 27, 1932): 105–7.

————. "When the Population Levels Off." *Harper's* 176 (1938): 596–602.

[Farrand, Livingston]. "The Social Hygiene Movement." *American Journal of Public Health* 3 (1913): 1154–57.

Farrell, Walter. "Dwindling Populations." Letter to the editor. *Commonweal* 14 (November 18, 1931): 72–73.

Federal Council of the Churches of Christ in America. "Moral Aspects of Birth Control." New York: FCCC Committee on Marriage and the Home, 1938.

"Feminism and the 'New Woman.'" *Eugenics* 3 (1930): 302–4.

"Finding God Behind Evolution." *Literary Digest* 76 (1923): 35–36.

Fisher, D. W. "In Defense of Science." *Commonweal* 3 (January 20, 1926): 290–92.

Fitzsimons, Simon. "Wasmann and Evolution." Letter to the editor. *Commonweal* 2 (July 8, 1925): 228–29.

Flannery, Regina. "John Montgomery Cooper, 1881–1949." *American Anthropologist*, New Series 52 (January–March, 1950): 64–74.

Fosdick, Harry Emerson. "Religion and Birth Control." *Outlook and Independent* 8 (June 1929): 301, 314.

Fosdick, Harry Emerson, and Sherwood Eddy. *Science and Religion: Evolution and the Bible*. New York: George H. Doran, 1924.

Frederick, M. "Religion and Evolution Since 1859: Some Effects of Evolution on the Philosophy of Religion." PhD diss., University of Notre Dame, 1934.

"Fresh Evidence of Our Apish Ancestry." *Current Opinion* 77 (1924): 484–86.

Freud, Sigmund. *Modern Sexual Morality and Modern Nervousness*. New York: Eugenics Publishing, 1931.

Furfey, Paul Hanly. "John Montgomery Cooper, 1881–1949." *Primitive Man* 23 (July 1950): 49–65.

Garrett, G. R. "A Pope, a Comet, and Mr. Darrow." *Commonweal* 2 (June 24, 1925): 181–82.

"Genesis and Evolution." *Science* 67 (1928): 162–63.

Gosney, E. S., and Paul Popenoe. "Progress in the Study of Eugenic Sterilization in California." *Eugenical News* 13 (1928): 101.

Gower, Joseph F., and Richard M. Leliaert, eds. *The Brownson-Hecker Correspondence*. Notre Dame: University of Notre Dame Press, 1979.

Grant, Edwin E. "Scum from the Melting-Pot." *American Journal of Sociology* 30 (1925): 641–51.

Grant, Madison. "Further Notes on the Racial Elements in European History." *Eugenical News* 13 (1928): 118–20.

———. "What Readers Write." *Eugenics* 2 (1929): 36.

Gregory Nazianzus. "The Panegyric on St. Basil." In *Cyril of Jerusalem; Gregory Nazianzan*, vol. 7 of *Nicene and Post-Nicene Fathers*, 2nd ser., edited by Philip Schaff and Henry Wace, 395–422. Peabody, Mass.: Hendrickson Publishers, 2004.

Gregory of Nyssa. "On Virginity." In *Gregory of Nyssa: Dogmatic Treatises, Etc.*, vol. 5 of *Nicene and Post-Nicene Fathers*, 2nd ser., edited by Philip Schaff and Henry Wace, 343–71. Peabody, Mass.: Hendrickson Publishers, 2004.

Grover, Elbridge C. "The Status of Education as an Academic Subject in American Colleges." *Educational Research Bulletin* 7 (January 11, 1928): 12–15.

"Guesswork Legislation." *Commonweal* 2 (1925): 357–58.

Hall, G. Stanley. "Eugenics: Its Ideals and What It Is Going to Do." *Religious Education* 6 (1911): 152–59.

Hanau, Stella. "The Birth Control Conference." *The Nation* 138 (January 31, 1934): 129–30.

Hauber, Ulrich A. "In the Matter of Evolution." *Commonweal* 1 (1925): 163.

———. "Evolution and Catholic Thought." *Ecclesiastical Review* 106 (1942): 161–77.

Hecker, Isaac. "An Exposition of the Church in View of Recent Difficulties and

Controversies and the Present Needs of the Age." *Catholic World* 21 (1875): 117–38.

Herzfeld, Karl F. "Scientific Research and Religion." *Commonweal* 9 (March 20, 1929): 560–62.

———. "Science and Religion." *Commonweal* 17 (1933): 132–34.

———. "Filling the Gap in Science," in *Catholics and Scholarship: A Symposium on the Development of Scholars*, edited by John A. O'Brien, 86–96. Huntington, Ind.: Our Sunday Visitor Press, [1939].

Hibben, Paxton. *The Peerless Leader William Jennings Bryan*. New York: Farrar and Rinehart, 1929.

Himes, Norman E. "Eugenic Thought in the American Birth Control Movement 100 Years Ago." *Eugenics* 2 (May 1929): 3–8.

———. "Robert Dale Owen, The Pioneer of American Neo-Malthusianism." *American Journal of Sociology* 35 (January 1930): 529–47.

Hoehn, Matthew, ed. *Catholic Authors: Contemporary Biographical Sketches 1930–1947.* Newark, N.J.: St. Mary's Abbey, 1948.

Hollingsworth, Leta S. "For and Against Birth Control." Review of *The Pivot of Civilization*, by Margaret Sanger, and *Birth Control*, by Halliday Sutherland. *New Republic* 32 (1922): 178.

Holmes, John Haynes. "Religion's New War with Science." *Christian Century* (October 27, 1937): 1322–34.

Holmes, Oliver Wendell, Jr. "Natural Law." *Harvard Law Review* 32 (1918): 40–42.

Holmes, Samuel J. "Books and Bibliography: The Catholic View." Review of *Eugenics: Aims and Methods*, by H. Davis. *Eugenics* 3 (May 1930): 200.

———. "The Opposition to Eugenics." *Science* 89 (April 21, 1939): 351–57.

———. "Darwinian Ethics and its Practical Applications." *Science* 90 (August 11, 1939): 117–23.

Hopkins, Mary Alden. "The Catholic Church and Birth Control." *Harper's Weekly* 60 (June 26, 1915): 609–10.

Hornsby, William L. "Evolution: Is the Tide Turning?" *Commonweal* 2 (1925): 19–21.

Hunt, Harrison R. "Why Birth Control?" *Eugenics* 3 (1930): 128–29.

Hunter, George William. *A Civic Biology, Presented in Problems*. New York: American Book Co., 1914.

Huxley, Julian. "Vital Importance of Eugenics." *Harper's* 163 (1931): 324–31.

Inman, Mary Louise. "In What Field?" *Eugenics* 2 (October 1929): 37–38.

———. "The National Birth Control Conference, Reviewed." *Eugenics* 3 (January 1930): 12–17.

Ireland, John. *The Church and Modern Society: Lectures and Addresses*, vol. 1. St. Paul, Minn.: Pioneer Press, 1904.

Jennings, H. S. "Biographical Memoir of Raymond Pearl, 1879–1940." In *National Academy of Sciences Biographical Memoirs: Third Memoir*, vol. 22, 295–347.

Washington, D.C.: National Academy of Sciences, 1942. http://www.nasonline
.org/publications/biographical-memoirs/memoir-pdfs/pearl-raymond.pdf.

John Chrysostom. "Homilies on Genesis 1–17." Translated by Robert C. Hill. In *The Fathers of the Church, a New Translation,* edited by Thomas P. Halton. Washington, D.C.: The Catholic University of America Press, 1985.

Karrer, Enoch. "On Applied and Pure Science." *Science* 58 (1923): 19–23.

Katz, Esther, Peter C. Engelman, and Cathy Moran Hajo, eds. *Margaret Sanger, Vol IV: Round the World for Birth Control, 1920–1966.* Urbana: University of Illinois Press, 2016.

Keefe, Anselm M. "Fourth Round Table of Catholic Scientists Held in New Orleans." *Science* 75 (February 26, 1932): 245.

———. "Biology Texts Used in Catholic Colleges." *Bulletin: National Catholic Education Association* 37 (1940): 219–20.

Kennedy, G. A. Studdert. "Is Birth Control Right? A Debate." *The Forum* 78 (1927): 7–14.

Kerrish, William E. "Companionate Marriage." Letter to the editor. *Commonweal* 13 (February 13, 1931): 438.

Kerwin, Jerome. "Enhancing Catholic Prestige." In *Catholics and Scholarship: A Symposium on the Development of Scholars,* edited by John A. O'Brien, 154–64. Huntington, Ind.: Our Sunday Visitor Press, [1939].

Krutch, Joseph Wood. "Tennessee's Dilemma." *The Nation* 121 (July 22, 1925): 110.

Lake, George. "The Spiritual Aspect of Birth Control." *The Nation* 134 (January 27, 1932): 110–11.

Lapp, John A. "Doctrine for Today." Review of *Questions of the Day,* by John A. Ryan. *Commonweal* 15 (December 23, 1931).

Latz, Leo. *The Rhythm of Sterility and Fertility in Women: A Discussion of the Physiological, Practical, and Ethical Aspects of the Discoveries of Drs. K. Ogino (Japan) and H. Knaus (Austria) Regarding the Periods When Conception Is Impossible and When Possible.* Chicago: Latz Foundation, 1932.

Latz, Leo, and E. Reiner. "Natural Conception Control." *Journal of the American Medical Association* 105 (October 1935): 1241–76.

Laughlin, Harry. "Presidential Address of the American Eugenics Society: The Progress of American Eugenics." *Eugenical News* 13 (1928): 89–90.

———. "The Progress of American Eugenics." *Eugenics* 2 (February 1929): 3–16.

Lawrence, Jerome, and Robert E. Lee. *Inherit the Wind.* New York: Ballantine Books, 1955.

LeBuffe, Francis P. Letter to the editor. *Commonweal* 2 (June 17, 1925): 163.

Leo XIII. *Aeterni Patris.* Encyclical Letter. August 4, 1879. http://www.vatican.va/content/leo-xiii/en/encyclicals/documents/hf_l-xiii_enc_04081879_aeterni-patris.html.

———. *Arcanum Divinae Sapientiae.* Encyclical Letter. February 10, 1880. http://www.vatican.va/content/leo-xiii/en/encyclicals/documents/hf_l-xiii_enc_10021880_arcanum.html.

———. *Rerum Novarum.* Encyclical Letter. May 15, 1891. http://www.vatican.va/content/leo-xiii/en/encyclicals/documents/hf_l-xiii_enc_15051891_rerum-novarum.html.

———. *Testem Benevolentiae.* Apostolic Letter. January 22, 1899. https://www.papalencyclicals.net/leo13/l13teste.htm.

———. *The Leonine Encyclicals, 1878–1902.* McPherson, Kans.: Agnus Dei Publishing, 2014.

LeSueur, W. D. "A Defense of Modern Thought." *Popular Science Monthly* 24 (1883–84): 780–95.

MacArthur, Kenneth C. "Eugenics and the Church: Answering Questions." *Eugenics* 3 (December 1930): 469.

Mahoney, Thomas. "The 'Perverted Faculty' Argument against Birth Prevention." *Ecclesiastical Review* 74 (August 1928): 133–45.

"Major Leonard Darwin's Address before the Eugenics Education Society." *Popular Science* 85 (1914): 205–8.

Mathews, Shailer. "The Evolution of Religion." *American Journal of Theology* 15 (1911): 57–82.

———. *Contributions of Science to Religion.* New York: Appleton, 1927.

———. *Immortality and the Cosmic Process.* Cambridge, Mass.: Harvard University Press, 1933.

———. *The Faith of Modernism.* New York: MacMillan, 1924. Reprint, New York: AMS Press, 1969.

Mayer, Joseph. "Eugenics in Roman Catholic Literature." *Eugenics* 3 (February 1930): 43–51.

McCabe, David. "The Path to Eminence in Economics," In *Catholics and Scholarship: A Symposium on the Development of Scholars,* edited by John A. O'Brien, 146–52. Huntington, Ind.: Our Sunday Visitor Press [1939].

McCann, Alfred Watterson. *God or Gorilla.* New York: Devin-Adair, 1922.

McClellan, William H. "Genesis 2:7 and the Evolution of the Human Body." *Ecclesiastical Review* 72 (1924): 1–10.

"The Medical Association on Contraception." *Commonweal* 24 (July 3, 1936): 265.

Mencken, H. L. Letter to the editor. *Commonweal* 20 (November 2, 1934): 35.

Messenger, Ernest C. *Evolution and Theology: The Problem of Man's Origin.* New York: Macmillan, 1932.

———, ed. *Theology and Evolution.* London: Sands and Co., 1949.

Millikan, Robert A. "A Joint Statement upon the Relations of Science and Religion." *Science* 57 (June 1, 1923): 630–31.

———. "What I Believe." *The Forum* 82 (1929): 193–201.

———. "The Present Status of Theory and Experiment as to Atomic Disintegration and Atomic Synthesis." *Nature* 127 (January 31, 1931): 167–70.

Mivart, St. George Jackson. "Scripture and Roman Catholicism." *The Nineteenth Century* 47 (1900): 425–42.

Montague, Ashley. "The Genetical Theory of Race, and Anthropological Method." *American Anthropologist*, n.s. 44 (1942): 360–75.

———. *Man's Most Dangerous Myth: The Fallacy of Race*. New York: Columbia University Press, 1942.

Moore, Edward Roberts. "Doctors Differ on Birth Control." *Commonweal* 13 (1931): 713–16.

———. "The Contraception of Prosperity." *Commonweal* 13 (April 15, 1931): 654–56.

———. "The Malice of Contraception." *Commonweal* 14 (May 20, 1931): 68–71.

———. "The Death Lobby." *Forum and Century* 92 (1934): 78–80.

Muckermann, H. *Attitudes of Catholics Towards Darwinism and Evolution*. St. Louis: B. Herder, 1906.

Murray, Raymond W. *Man's Unknown Ancestors*. Milwaukee: Bruce Publishing, 1948.

"Not Science but Philosophy and Religion Failed the World." *Science* 37 (1940): 351.

O'Brien, John A. "Some Factors in the Development of Speed in Silent Reading." PhD diss., University of Illinois, 1920. Published: *Silent Reading: With Special Reference to Methods for Developing Speed*. New York: MacMillan, 1921.

———. "Catholic Leakage." *Commonweal* 15 (1932): 710–12.

———. *Evolution and Religion: A Study of the Bearing of Evolution upon the Philosophy of Religion*. New York: Century Co., 1932.

———. "The Origin of Man." Review of *Evolution and Theology: The Problem of Man's Origin*, by Ernest C. Messenger. *Commonweal* 9 (March 9, 1932): 536–27.

———. *Lawful Birth Control: According to Nature's Law, in Harmony with Catholic Morality*. Fort Wayne, Ind.: Courtney Co., 1934.

———. "Man in an Expanding Universe." *Commonweal* 20 (1934): 423–25.

———. *Natural Birth Control without Contraceptives, according to Nature's Law in Harmony with Catholic Morality*. Champaign, Ill.: Newman Co., 1938.

———. *Religion in a Changing World: Christianity and Modern Thought*. Huntington, Ind.: Our Sunday Visitor Press, 1938.

———. "Catholics and Cultural Leadership." In *Catholics and Scholarship: A Symposium on the Development of Scholars*, edited by John A. O'Brien, 27–37. Huntington, Ind.: Our Sunday Visitor Press, [1939].

———, ed. *Catholics and Scholarship: A Symposium on the Development of Scholars*. Huntington, Ind.: Our Sunday Visitor Press, [1939].

Osborn, Henry Fairfield. Preface to *The Passing of the Great Race: Or, The Racial Basis of European History*, 2nd ed., by Madison Grant, i–ix. New York: Charles Scribner's Sons, 1918.

———. "Orthogenesis as Observed from Palaeontological Evidence Beginning in the Year 1889." *American Naturalist* 56 (1922): 134–43.

———. "William Bateson on Darwin." *Science* 55 (1922): 194–97.

———. *The Earth Speaks to Bryan*. New York: Scribner's, 1925.

————. "Credo of a Naturalist." *The Forum* 73 (January 1925): 486–94.

————. "The Earth Speaks to Bryan." *The Forum* 73 (June 1925): 796–803.

————. "Evolution and Education in the Tennessee Trial." *Science* 62 (July 17, 1925): 43–45.

————. "Facts of the Evolutionists." *The Forum* 75 (June 1926): 842–51.

————. *Man Rises to Parnassus: Critical Epochs in the Prehistory of Man.* Princeton: Princeton University Press, 1927.

————. "Biographical Memoir of Edward Drinker Cope, 1840–1897." In *National Academy of Sciences Biographical Memoirs: Third Memoir*, vol. 13, 127–31. Washington, D.C.: National Academy of Sciences, 1929. http://www.nasonline.org/publications/biographical-memoirs/memoir-pdfs/cope-edward.pdf.

————. "Birth Selection versus Birth Control." *The Forum* 88 (1932): 79–83.

————. "Recent Revivals of Darwinism." *Science* 77 (1933): 199–202.

Osborn, Henry Fairfield, and Edwin Grant Conklin. "The Proposed Suppression of the Teaching of Evolution." *Science* 55 (March 1922): 264–66.

O'Toole, Barry. *The Case against Evolution.* New York: MacMillan, 1925.

"Paradox of Birth Control." *The Nation* 139 (1934): 33–34.

Parsons, Wilfred. "Is This 'Catholic' Birth Control?" *America* 48 (February 25, 1933): 496.

"The Philosophy of Evolution." *Eugenical News* 15 (1930): 165.

Paul VI. *Humanae Vitae.* Encyclical Letter. July 29, 1968.

Pius X. *Pascendi Dominici Gregis.* Encyclical Letter. September 8, 1907. http://www.vatican.va/content/pius-x/en/encyclicals/documents/hf_p-x_enc_19070908_pascendi-dominici-gregis.html.

Pius XI. *Casti Connubii.* Encyclical Letter. December 31, 1930. In *The Papal Encyclicals in Their Historical Context*, ed. Anne Fremantle. New York: G. P. Putnam and Sons, 1956.

————. *Quadragesimo Anno.* Encyclical Letter. May 15, 1931. In *Seven Great Encyclicals*, 125–168. New York: Paulist Press, 1963.

Polyzoides, Adamantios. "Personal Factors in Immigration." *Eugenics* 2 (July 1929): 18.

Popenoe, Paul. "Sterilization: Its Legality, Need." *Eugenics* 3 (1930): 180.

————. "Eugenics and Family Relations." *Eugenical News* 25 (1940): 70–74.

[Preuss, Arthur]. Review of "The 'Perverted Faculty' Argument against Birth Prevention," by Thomas Mahoney. *Fortnightly Review* (August 15, 1928): 320.

"Progress in Eugenical Research: Report to the Annual Meeting of the AES May 16, 1940 by Frederick Osborn." *Eugenical News* 25 (1940): 24.

"Psalm L." *Biblia Sacra Juxta Vulgata Clementinam.* Edited by Michaele Tvveedale. 2005. https://www.wilbourhall.org/pdfs/vulgate.pdf.

"Psalms, Chapter 50." *Codex Sinaiticus.* Accessed February 10, 21. http://www.codex-sinaiticus.net/en/manuscript.aspx?=SubmitQuery&book=26&chapter=5.

Pusey, William Allen. "Birth Control and Sex Morality." *The Nation* 134 (1932): 111–12.

Pyle, Leo, ed. *The Pill and Birth Regulation: The Catholic Debate, Including Statements, Articles and Letters from the Pope, Bishops, Priests and Married and Unmarried Laity.* Baltimore: Helicon Press, 1964.

Rahill, Frank. "National Origins in Pennsylvania." *Commonweal* 9 (1929): 253.

"Resolutions Adopted by the Council." *Science* 57 (1923): 103–4.

Review of *The Gist of Evolution*, by H. H. Newman. *Eugenical News* 11 (November 1926): 11.

Review of *The Medical, Social, Economic, Moral, and Religious Aspect of Birth Control*, by S. A. Knopf. *Eugenical News* 13 (1928): 46–47.

Review of *What Is Eugenics?*, by Leonard Darwin. *Eugenics* 3 (May, 1930): 240.

Reyniers, James. "Ways and Means of Developing Catholic Scientists." In *Catholics and Scholarship: A Symposium on the Development of Scholars*, edited by John A. O'Brien, 107–29. Huntington, Ind.: Our Sunday Visitor Press [1939].

Rice, Frederick W. "A Catholic Physician's Views on Family Limitation." *Ecclesiastical Review* 103 (1940): 60–67.

"Richmond Meeting Held." *Tabloid Scientist* 5 (December 12, 1939): 1.

Riddle, Oscar. "The Confusion of Tongues." *Science* 83 (January 17, 1936): 41–45.

———. "The Confusion of Tongues." *Science* 83 (January 24, 1936): 69–74.

Riley, William B. *Inspiration or Evolution?* Cleveland: Union Gospel Publishing, 1923.

Ritter, William. "Osborn Versus Bateson on Darwin." *Science* 55 (1922): 398–99.

"The Road to Rome—and Back: By One Who Has Traveled It." *Atlantic Monthly* 149 (April 1932): 407–8.

Robinson, Gilbert Kelly. "The Catholic Birth Rate: Further Facts and Implications." *American Journal of Sociology* 41 (May 1936): 757–66.

Robinson, James Harvey. "Is Darwinism Dead?" *Harper's Magazine* 145 (1922): 68–74.

Robinson, William Josephus. *Sexual Truths versus Sexual Lies, Misconceptions, and Exaggerations.* Hoboken, N.J.: Critic and Guide, 1919.

Rock, John. A. *The Time Has Come: A Catholic Doctor's Proposals to End the Battle over Birth Control.* New York: Alfred A. Knopf, 1963.

Romig, Walter, ed. *Book of Catholic Authors.* 2nd ser. Detroit: Walter Romig and Co., 1943.

Ross, J. Elliot. "The Embattled Theory." *Commonweal* 11 (1930): 302–5.

Russell, W. H. "John M. Cooper, Pioneer." *Catholic Educational Review* 47 (September 1949): 435–441.

Ryan, John A. "The Method of Teleology in Ethics." *New York Review* 2 (January–February 1907): 409–29.

———."Theories of Population." In *Catholic Encyclopedia.* New York: The Encyclopedia Press, 1913. http://en.wikisource.org/wiki/Catholic_Encyclopedia_(1913)/Theories_of_Population.

———. "The Catholic Church and Birth Control." Letter to the editor. *Harper's Weekly* 61 (August 7, 1915): 144–45.

———. "Social Questions: 'Arguments' for Birth Control." *Catholic Charities Review* 9 (May 1925): 175–78.

———. "The Sociological Aspect of Birth Control." *Trained Nurse and Hospital Review* (ca. 1925): 734–39.

———. *Human Sterilization*. Washington, D.C.: National Catholic Welfare Conference, 1927.

———. "Legislation and Liberty." *Commonweal* 6 (1927): 462–63.

———. "Is Birth Control Right?—A Debate II—The Wrong of It." *The Forum* 78 (July 1927): 15–19.

———. "The Immorality of Contraception." Letter to the editor. *Ecclesiastical Review* 74 (October 1928): 408–11.

———. "Overcharitable to the Unfit?" *Eugenics* 1 (December 1928): 21.

———. "The Evolution of an Anti." *Commonweal* 10 (1929): 211–13.

———. "Personal Factors in Immigration." *Eugenics* 2 (1929): 18.

———. "Catholicism and Liberalism." *The Nation* 131 (1930): 150–52.

———. "The Commoner." *Commonweal* 11 (1930): 302–5.

———. *Questions of the Day*. Boston: Stratford Co., 1931.

———. "The Moral Aspects of Periodical Continence." *Ecclesiastical Review* 89 (July–December 1933): 28–39.

———. *Social Doctrine in Action: A Personal History*. New York: Harper and Brothers, 1941.

Ryan, John A., et al. *Anti-Evolution Laws*. New York: American Civil Liberties Union, 1927.

Sands, William Franklin. "*Casti Connubii*." Letter to the editor. *Commonweal* 13 (February 18, 1931): 439.

Sanger, Margaret. "Birth Control and Racial Betterment." *Birth Control Review* 3 (February 1919): 11–12.

———. *Woman and the New Race*. New York: Brentano's Publishers, 1920. http://www.gutenberg.org/cache/epub/8660/pg8660-images.html.

———. "Comments on the Pope's Encyclical." *Birth Control Review* 15 (February 1931): 40–41.

———. "The Pope's Position on Birth Control." *Nation* 134 (January 27, 1932): 102–4.

———. "Catholics and Birth Control." *New Republic* 79 (June 13, 1934): 129.

———. "At Long Last: A Veteran Crusader for Birth Control Reflects on the Campaign in Terms of the Medical Association's Action." *New Masses* 24 (July 6, 1937): 19–20.

Schuster, George. "Have We Any Scholars?" *America* (1925): 418–19.

———. "Insulated Catholics." *Commonweal* 2 (1925): 337–38.

Shallow, Michael. *Lessons in Scholastic Philosophy*. Philadelphia: Peter Reilly Co., 1905.

Shaner, Ralph F. "Lamarck and the Evolution Theory." *Scientific Monthly* 24 (1927): 251–55.

"She's Got Rhythm? A Safe Period for Sanger and the Church." Newsletter 31 (Fall 2002). Margaret Sanger Papers Project. https://www.nyu.edu/projects/sanger/articles/shes_got_rhythm.php.

Shriver, Mark O. "Reading the Bible in Public School." *Commonweal* 11 (November 27, 1929): 108–9.

Sinclair, Upton. "Letter to Cardinal O'Connell; Catholic Attitude toward Prohibition and Birth Control." *New Republic* 61 (1930): 330–31.

Smothers, Frank A. "New Light on Birth Control." *Commonweal* 17 (March 8, 1933): 511–13.

Smulders, J. N. *Periodische Enthaltung in der Ehe Methode: Ogino Knaus.* Regensburg: Manz, 1932.

Spencer, Anna Garlin. "What Readers Write: Eugenics and Catholicism." *Eugenics* 3 (October 1930): 429.

Spengler, Joseph J. "The Decline in Birth-Rate of the Foreign Born." *Scientific Monthly* 32 (January 1931): 54–59.

Stone, Hannah M. "The Birth Control Clinic." *Eugenics* 2 (May 1929): 9–11.

———. "Birth Control Wins." *The Nation* 144 (January 16, 1937): 70–71.

Stouffer, Samuel A. "Trends in Fertility of Catholics and Non-Catholics." *American Journal of Sociology* 41 (September 1935): 143–66.

Stouffer, Samuel A., and Paul F. Lazarsfeld. *Research Memorandum on the Family in the Depression.* New York: Social Science Research Council, 1937.

Suter, Rufus. "Galileo and the Modern World." *Scientific Monthly* 51 (1940): 168–71.

Sutherland, Halliday. "The Fallacies of Birth Control." *The Forum* 77 (April 1927): 840–47.

Sweeney, Leo. Letter to the editor. *Commonweal* 19 (May 26, 1933): 104.

Swing, Raymond Gram. "Birth Control and Obscenity." *The Nation* 140 (May 29, 1935): 621–22.

Taylor, Monica. *Sir Bertram Windle: A Memoir.* New York: Longman's, Green and Co., 1932.

Teilhard de Chardin, Pierre. *Christianity and Evolution.* 1933. Lucile Swan Papers. GURBSC, Washington, D.C.

———. "Our Most Ape-Like Relative." *Natural History* 40 (1937): 514–17.

———. *Letters from a Traveller.* New York: Harper and Brothers, 1962.

"Too Many People?" *New Republic* 69 (December 1931): 84–85.

Turano, Anthony M. "Contraception by Rhythm." *American Mercury* 35 (June 1935): 164–68.

Vecchierello, Hubert. *Catholics and Evolution.* Paterson, N.J.: St. Anthony's Guild, 1933.

———. *Evolution, Fact or Fancy?* Paterson, N.J.: St. Anthony's Guild, 1934.

[Villard, Oswald.] "The Battle of Tennessee." *The Nation* 120 (May 27, 1925): 589–90.

———. "Tennessee vs. Truth." *The Nation* 121 (July 8, 1925): 58.

Walsh, James J. *The Popes and Science: A History of the Papal Relations to Science during the Middle Ages and down to Our Own Time.* New York: Fordham University Press, 1911.

———. "Forget the Pope? No! Reply to E. Boyd Barrett." *The Forum* 82 (1929): 173–76.

———. "The Birth Control Racket." Letter to *Commonweal* 16 (July 27, 1932): 331.

Ward, P. J. "The Catholics and Birth Control." *New Republic* 61 (1929): 35–38.

Wasmann, Erich. "Evolution." In *The Catholic Encyclopedia: An International Work of Reference on the Constitution, Doctrine, Discipline, and History of the Catholic Church,* edited by Charles Herbermann et al., 5:654–70. New York: Robert Appleton Co., 1909.

Wells, H. G., Julian Huxley, and G. P. Wells. *Evolution, Fact and Theory.* Garden City, N.Y.: Doubleday, Doran and Co., 1932.

Wenninger, Francis J. Review of *Darwinism and Catholic Thought,* by Canon Dorlodot, translated by Ernest Messenger. *American Midland Naturalist* 8 (March–May 1923): 211–14.

Weston, M. W. "Is the Soul a Myth?" *Commonweal* 8 (December 26, 1928): 230–33.

White, Andrew Dickson. *A History of the Warfare of Science with Theology in Christendom.* 2 vols. London: Macmillan and Co., 1896.

Wickham, Harvey. "A Century of Evolution." *Commonweal* 11 (1930): 553–55.

Wiggam, Albert Edward. "Eugenics and Evolution." *Eugenics* 2 (May 1929): 19.

Williams, Michael. *American Catholics in the War: National Catholic War Council, 1917–1921.* New York: Macmillan, 1921.

———. *The Book of the High Romance: A Spiritual Biography.* New York: Macmillan, 1924.

———. "At Dayton, Tennessee." *Commonweal* 2 (July 22, 1925): 262–65.

———. "Summing up At Dayton." *Commonweal* 2 (August 5, 1925): 304–5.

———. "Sunday at Dayton." *Commonweal* 2 (1925): 285–88.

———. "William Jennings Bryan." *Commonweal* 2 (1925): 303.

———. "The New Population." *Commonweal* 5 (1926): 113–14.

———. "Who Is an American?" *Commonweal* 4 (1926): 421–22.

———. "The Ex-Jesuit Enigma." *Commonweal* 7 (1927): 715–17.

———. *Catholicism and the Modern Mind.* New York: Dial Press, 1928.

———. "Recruiting the Layman." *Commonweal* 9 (1928): 118.

———. "The Birth Control Revolution." *Commonweal* 13 (1931): 589–91.

———. "The Religion of Death." *Commonweal* 14 (1931): 234–36.

———. "The Birth Control Racket." *Commonweal* 16 (June 8, 1932): 141–42.

———. "Week by Week." *Commonweal* 17 (March 1, 1933): 480.

———. "Ten Years of The Commonweal." *Commonweal* 21 (1934): 5–7.

[Williams, Michael]. "On Teaching Evolution." *Commonweal* 1 (April 22, 1925): 647–49.

————. "Concerning the Scopes Case." *Commonweal* 2 (June 3, 1925): 85–87.

————. "On the Freedom of the Teacher." *Commonweal* 2 (June 24, 1925): 169–70.

————. "The Scopes Dilemma." *Commonweal* 2 (July 15, 1925): 241–42.

————. "Week by Week." *Commonweal* 2 (September 9, 1925): 407–11.

————. "Our Second Year." *Commonweal* 3 (November 11, 1925): 1–2.

————. "Religion and Science." *Commonweal* 1 (1925): 445–46.

————. "What Birth Control Means." *Commonweal* 1 (1925): 618–19.

————. "Osborn on Religion." *Commonweal* 3 (February 2, 1926): 343.

————. "Sir Oliver and Evolution." *Commonweal* 3 (February 10, 1926): 370–71.

————. "Neanderthal Man." *Commonweal* 3 (1926): 259.

————. "Soundings in Mystery." *Commonweal* 7 (November 16, 1927): 379–80.

————. "Week by Week." *Commonweal* 7 (March 7, 1928): 1139.

————. "The Conquering Cockroach." *Commonweal* 10 (September 11, 1929): 459–60.

————. "The Case of Mrs. Dennett." *Commonweal* 10 (1929): 62.

————. "Sir Bertram Windle." *Commonweal* 9 (1929): 475.

————. "Rome Has Spoken." *Commonweal* 13 (January 21, 1931): 309–11.

————. "The Pope and Education." *Commonweal* 11 (1930): 353–55.

————. "Week by Week." *Commonweal* 21 (January 18, 1935): 330.

————. "Cardinal Hayes Speaks Out." *Commonweal* 23 (December 30, 1935): 197–98.

Windle, Bertram C. A. *What Is Life?: A Study of Vitalism and Neo-Vitalism.* London: Sands and Co., 1908.

————. *The Church and Science.* 3rd ed. London: Catholic Truth Society, 1917.

————. "Science Sees the Light." *Commonweal* 1 (November 12, 1924): 17–18.

————. "Huxley and the Catholic Church." *Commonweal* 2 (1925): 77–78.

————. Review of *Augustine and Evolution*, by Henry Woods. *Catholic World* (1925): 421–22.

————. Review of *The Case against Evolution*, by Barry O'Toole. *Commonweal* 2 (June 10, 1925): 124–26.

————. "The Roman Catholic View of Evolution." *Current History* 23 (December 1925): 335–39.

————. Review of *Ether and Reality*, by Sir Oliver Lodge. *Commonweal* 3 (February 17, 1926): 415–16.

————. Review of *Evolution and Creation*, by Sir Oliver Lodge. *Commonweal* 4 (September 29, 1926): 508–9.

————. *The Catholic Church and Its Reactions with Science.* New York: Macmillan, 1927.

————. "Emergent Evolution." *Commonweal* 5 (1927): 460–61.

————. Review of *Modern Scientific Ideas*, by Sir Oliver Lodge. *Commonweal* 6 (1927): 244–45.

————. "The Challenge to Materialism." Review of *The Metaphysical Foundations of Modern Physical Science*, by Edward Arthur Burtt. *Commonweal* 8 (1928): 1045.

———. "Evolution and Faith." Review of *Creation*, by E. T. Brewster. *Commonweal* 9 (1928): 133–34.

———. Review of *Man Rises to Parnassus*, by Henry Fairfield Osborn. *Commonweal* 8 (1928): 1241–42.

———. "A Scientific Herald of Revolt." *Commonweal* 9 (1928): 134–35.

The World's Most Famous Court Trial: State of Tennessee v. John Thomas Scopes: Complete Stenographic Report of the Court Test of the Tennessee Anti-Evolution Act at Dayton, July 10 to 21, 1925, Including Speeches and Arguments of Attorneys. 3rd ed. Cincinnati: National Book Co., 1925. Reprint, Civil Liberties in American History, edited by Leonard W. Levy. New York: De Capo Press: 1971.

Youmans, E. L. "Herbert Spencer and the Doctrine of Evolution." *Popular Science Monthly* 6 (November 1874): 20–48.

———. "Scientific Literature: Popular Books." *Appleton's Popular Science Monthly* 49 (July 1896): 414–15.

Zahm, John A. *Evolution and Dogma.* Chicago: D. H. McBride, 1896. Reprint, Hicksville, N.Y.: Regina Press, 1975.

Secondary Sources

Aczel, Amir D. *The Jesuit and the Skull.* New York: Riverhead Penguin Books, 2007.

Agassi, Joseph. *Science and Culture.* Boston Studies in the Philosophy of Science 231, edited by Robert S. Cohen et al. Dordrecht: Kluwer Academic Publishers, 2003.

Ahern, Patrick Henry. *The Catholic University of America, 1887–1896: The Rectorship of John J. Keane.* Washington, D.C.: The Catholic University of America Press, 1948.

Alexander, Denis R., and Ronald L. Numbers, eds. *Biology and Ideology from Descartes to Dawkins.* Chicago: University of Chicago Press, 2010.

Allen, Garland E. *Life Science in the Twentieth Century.* Cambridge History of Science, edited by George Basalla and William Cohen. Cambridge: Cambridge University Press, 1979.

———. "The Eugenics Record Office at Cold Spring Harbor, 1910–1940: An Essay in Institutional History." *Osiris* 2 (1986): 225–64.

Appleby, R. Scott. *Church and Age Unite!* Notre Dame: University of Notre Dame Press, 1992.

———. "Exposing Darwin's Hidden Agenda: Roman Catholic Responses to Evolution, 1875–1925." In *Disseminating Darwinism: The Role of Place, Race, Religion, and Gender,* edited by Ronald L. Numbers and John Stenhouse, 173–208. Cambridge: Cambridge University Press, 1999.

Artigas, Mariano, Thomas F. Glick, and Rafael A. Martínez. *Negotiating Darwin:*

The Vatican Confronts Evolution, 1877–1902. Baltimore: Johns Hopkins University Press, 2006.

Ashley, Benedict M. "The Loss of Theological Unity: Pluralism, Thomism, and Catholic Morality." In *Being Right: Conservative Catholics in America*, edited by Mary Jo Weaver and R. Scott Appleby, 63–87. Bloomington: Indiana University Press, 1995.

Atkinson, J. W. "E. G. Conklin on Evolution: The Popular Writings of an Embryologist." *Journal of the History of Biology* 18 (1985): 31–50.

Bailey, James R., and Wayne N. Eastman. "Positivism and the Promise of the Social Sciences." *Theory and Psychology* 4 (1994): 505–24.

Baker, Graham J. "Christianity and Eugenics: The Place of Religion in the British Eugenics Education Society and the American Eugenics Society, c. 1907–1940." *Social History of Medicine* 27 (2014): 281–302.

Bannister, Roger. *Science and Myth in Anglo-American Thought*. Philadelphia: Temple University Press, 1979.

Barbour, Ian. *Issues in Science and Religion*. Englewood Cliffs, N.J.: Prentice Hall, 1966.

Barkan, Elazar. *The Retreat of Scientific Racism: Changing Concepts of Race in Britain and the United States between the World Wars*. Cambridge: Cambridge University Press, 1992.

Barnes, Rosanna L. "Birth Control in Popular Twentieth-Century Periodicals." *Family Coordinator* 19 (April 1970): 159–64.

Barr, Steven M. *Modern Physics and Ancient Faith*. Notre Dame: University of Notre Dame Press, 2001.

———. "The Design of Evolution." *First Things* 156 (2005): 9–12.

Berger, Peter L. *The Sacred Canopy: Elements of a Sociological Theory of Religion*. Garden City, N.Y.: Doubleday, 1967.

"Bibliography of John Montgomery Cooper." *Primitive Man* 23 (July 3, 1950): 66–84.

Billington, Ray Allen. *The Protestant Crusade 1800–1860: A Study of the Origins of American Nativism*. New York: Rinehart, 1952.

Binzley, Ronald A. "American Catholicism's Albertus Magnus Guild, 1953–1969." *Isis* 98 (2007): 695–723.

Blancke, Stefaan. "Catholic Responses to Evolution, 1859–2009: Local Influences and Mid-Scale Patterns." *Journal of Religious History* 37 (2013): 353–68.

Bleckmann, Charles. "Evolution and Creationism in Science: 1880–2000." *BioScience* 56 (2006): 151–58.

Bodnar, John. *The Transplanted: A History of Immigrants in Urban America*. Bloomington: Indiana University Press, 1985.

Boggan, Ashley. "A God-Sent Movement: Methodism, Contraception, and the Protection of the Methodist Family, 1870–1968." *Methodist History* 53 (2015): 68–84.

Borell, Merriley. "Biologists and the Promotion of Birth Control Research, 1918–1938." *Journal of the History of Biology* 20 (1987): 51–87.

Bowler, Peter J. *The Eclipse of Darwinism: Anti-Darwinian Evolution Theories in the Decades around 1900*. Baltimore: Johns Hopkins University Press, 1983.

———. *Reconciling Science and Religion: The Debate in Early-Twentieth-Century Britain*. Chicago: University of Chicago Press, 2001.

———. "Revisiting the Eclipse of Darwinism." *Journal of the History of Biology* 38 (2005): 19–32.

———. *Monkey Trials and Gorilla Sermons: Evolution and Christianity from Darwinism to Intelligent Design*. Cambridge, Mass.: Harvard University Press, 2007.

———. *Evolution: The History of an Idea*. Berkeley: University of California Press, 2009.

———. *Science for All: The Popularization of Science in Early Twentieth-Century Britain*. Chicago: University of Chicago Press, 2009.

Brattain, Michelle. "Race, Racism, and Antiracism: UNESCO and the Politics of Presenting Science to the Postwar Public." *American Historical Review* 112 (2007): 1386–413.

Bredeck, Martin J. "The Role of the Catholic Layman in the Church and American Society as Seen in the Editorials of *Commonweal* Magazine." PhD diss., The Catholic University of America, 1977.

Broderick, Francis L. *Right Reverend New Dealer: John A. Ryan*. London: Macmillan, 1963.

Brooke, John Hedley. *Science and Religion: Some Historical Perspectives*. Cambridge: Cambridge University Press, 1991.

Brooke, John Hedley, and Geoffrey Cantor. *Reconstructing Nature: The Engagement of Science and Religion*. Oxford: Oxford University Press, 1998.

Brooke, John Hedley, and Ronald L. Numbers, eds. *Science and Religion around the World*. Oxford: Oxford University Press, 2011.

Brown, Dorothy M., and Elizabeth McKeown. *The Poor Belong to Us: Catholic Charities and American Welfare*. Cambridge, Mass.: Harvard University Press, 1997.

Bruce, Steve, ed. *Religion and Modernization: Sociologists and Historians Debate the Secularization Thesis*. Oxford: Oxford University Press, 1992.

Brundell, Barry. "Catholic Church Politics and Evolution Theory, 1894–1902." *British Journal for the History of Science* 34 (2001): 81–95.

Cadegan, Una M. *All Good Books are Catholic Books: Print Culture, Censorship, and Modernity in Twentieth-Century America*. Ithaca, N.Y.: Cornell University Press, 2013.

Campbell, Flann. "Birth Control in the Christian Churches." *Population Studies* 14 (November 1960): 131–47.

Carey, Patrick W., ed. *American Catholic Religious Thought: The Shaping of a Theological and Social Tradition*. Milwaukee: Marquette University Press, 2004.

Carlen, Claudia, ed. *Papal Pronouncements: A Guide*. 2 vols. Ann Arbor: Pierian Press, 1990.

Chaberek, Michael. *Catholicism and Evolution: From Darwin to Pope Francis*. Kettering, Ohio: Angelico Press, 2015.

Chinnici, Joseph. *Living Stones: The History and Structure of Catholic Spiritual Life in the United States*. New York: MacMillan, 1989.

Church, Robert L. "Educational Psychology and Social Reform in the Progressive Era." *History of Education Quarterly* 11 (Winter 1971): 390–405.

Clark, Constance Areson. "Evolution for John Doe: Pictures, the Public, and the Scopes Trial Debate." *Journal of American History* 88 (2001): 1275–1303.

———. *God or Gorilla? Images of Evolution in the Jazz Age*. Baltimore: Johns Hopkins University Press, 2008.

———. "Anthropology and Original Sin: Naturalizing Religion, Theorizing the Primitive." In *Science without God: Rethinking the History of Scientific Naturalism*, edited by Peter Harrison and Jon H. Roberts, 216–34. Oxford: Oxford University Press, 2019.

Clements, Robert B. "The Commonweal, 1924–1938: The Williams-Schuster Years." PhD diss., University of Notre Dame, 1972.

Cohen, Lizabeth. *Making a New Deal: Industrial Workers in Chicago, 1919–1939*. Cambridge: Cambridge University Press, 1990.

Conkin, Paul L. *When All the Gods Trembled: Darwinism, Scopes, and American Intellectuals*. Lanham, Md.: Rowman and Littlefield, 1998.

Connolly, Michael. "The 'Grave Emergency' of 1909: Modernism and the Paulist Fathers." *U. S. Catholic Historian* 20 (2002): 51–68.

Conser, Walter H. *God and the Natural World: Religion and Science in Antebellum America*. Columbia: University of South Carolina Press, 1993.

Cooke, K. J. "A Gospel of Social Evolution: Religion, Biology, and Education in the Thought of Edwin Grant Conklin." PhD diss., University of Chicago, 1994.

Coppa, Frank. *The Modern Papacy, Since 1789*. London: Longman, 1998.

Cross, Robert. *The Emergence of Liberal Catholicism in America*. Cambridge, Mass.: Harvard University Press, 1958.

Curran, Charles E. "Thomas Joseph Bouquillon: Americanist, Neo-Scholastic, or Manualist?" In *The Catholic Theological Society of America: Proceedings of the Fiftieth Annual Convention*, edited by Paul Crowley, 156–173. Santa Clara, Calif.: Santa Clara University, 1995.

Daly, Gabriel. *Transcendence and Immanence: A Study in Catholic Modernism and Integralism*. New York: Clarendon Press of Oxford University Press, 1980.

Daniels, George H. "The Process of Professionalization in American Science." In *Science in America since 1820*, edited by Nathan Reingold, 63–78. New York: Science History Publications, 1976.

Daum, Andreas. "Varieties of Popular Science and the Transformations of Public Knowledge: Some Historical Reflections." *Isis* (2009): 319–32.

Davis, Edward B. "Science and Religious Fundamentalism in the 1920s." *American Scientist* 93 (2005): 254–60.

———. "Arthur Holly Compton on Science, Freedom, Religion, and Morality." *Perspectives on Science and Christian Faith* 61 (2009), 73–83, 175–90, 240–53.

———. "Robert Millikan: Religion, Science, and Modernity." In *Eminent Lives in Twentieth Century Science and Religion*, 2nd rev. ed., edited by Nicholas A. Rupke, 253–74. Frankfurt am Main: Peter Lang, 2009.

———. "Altruism and the Administration of the Universe: Kirtley Fletcher Mather on Science and Values." *Zygon* 46 (September 2011): 517–35.

De Bont, Raf. "Rome and Theistic Evolutionism: The Hidden Strategies behind the 'Dorlodot Affair,' 1920–1926." *Annals of Science* 62 (2005): 457–78.

Depew, David. "Darwinism's Multiple Ontologies." In *Darwinism and Philosophy*, edited by Vittorio Hosle and Christian Illies, 92–116. Notre Dame: University of Notre Dame Press, 2005.

DeVito, Michael J. *The New York Review (1905–1908)*. New York: United States Catholic Historical Society, 1977.

Diner, Steven. *A Very Different Age: Americans in the Progressive Era*. New York: Hill and Wang, 1997.

Dixon, Thomas. *From Passions to Emotions: The Creation of a Secular Psychological Category*. Cambridge: Cambridge University Press, 2003.

———. "The Invention of Altruism: Auguste Comte's *Positive Polity* and Respectable Unbelief in Victorian Britain." In *Science and Belief: From Natural Philosophy to Natural Science*, edited by David M. Knight and Matthew D. Eddy, 195–211. Aldershot, UK: Ashgate, 2005.

———. *The Invention of Altruism: Making Moral Meanings in Victorian Britain*. Oxford: Oxford University Press for the British Academy, 2008.

Dixon, Thomas, Geoffrey Cantor, and Stephen Pumfrey, eds. *Science and Religion: New Historical Perspectives*. Cambridge: Cambridge University Press, 2010.

Dolan, Jay P. *The American Catholic Experience: A History from Colonial Times to the Present*. Notre Dame: University of Notre Dame Press, 1992.

Dorr, Gregory Michael. *Segregation's Science: Eugenics and Society in Virginia*. Charlottesville: University of Virginia Press, 2008.

Dowbiggin, Ian. " 'A Rational Coalition': Euthanasia, Eugenics, and Birth Control in America, 1940–1970." *The Journal of Policy History* 14 (July 2002): 223–259.

Ellis, John Tracy. *The Formative Years of the Catholic University of America*. Washington, D.C.: American Catholic Historical Association, 1946.

———. "American Catholics and the Intellectual Life." *Thought* 30 (1955).

Engelman, Peter C. *A History of the Birth Control Movement in America*. Santa Barbara: Praeger, 2011.

Fogarty, Gerald. *The Vatican and the Americanist Crisis: Denis J. O'Connell Amer-*

ican Agent in Rome, 1885–1903. Miscellanea Historiae Pontificiae 36. Rome: Gregorian University Press, 1974.

Franks, Angela. *Margaret Sanger's Eugenic Legacy: The Control of Female Fertility*. Jefferson, N.C.: McFarland, 2005.

Freeden, Michael. "Eugenics and Progressive Thought: A Study in Ideological Affinity." *Historical Journal* 22 (1979): 645–71.

———. "Eugenics and Ideology." *Historical Journal* 26 (1983): 959–62.

Garroutte, Eva Marie. "The Positivist Attack on Baconian Science and Religious Knowledge in the 1870s." In *The Secular Revolution: Power, Interests, and Conflict in the Secularization of American Public Life*, edited by Christian Smith, 187–215. Berkeley: University of California Press, 2003.

Garwood, Christine. *Flat Earth: The History of an Infamous Idea*. New York: Macmillan, 2008.

Gaukroger, Steven. *Civilization and the Culture of Science: Science and the Shaping of Modernity, 1795–1935*. Oxford: Oxford University Press, 2020.

Gayon, Jean. "From Mendel to Epigenetics: History of Genetics." *Comptes Rendus Biologies* 339 (2016): 225–30.

Gieryn, Thomas F. "Boundary-Work and the Demarcation of Science from Non-Science: Strains and Interests in Professional Ideologies of Scientists." *American Sociological Review* 48 (1983): 781–95.

———. *Cultural Boundaries of Science: Credibility on the Line*. Chicago: University of Chicago Press, 1999.

Gieryn, Thomas F., George Bevins, and Stephen C. Zehr. "Professionalization of American Scientists: Public Science in the Creation/Evolution Trials." *American Sociological Review* 50 (1985): 392–409.

Gilbert, James, *Redeeming Culture: American Religion in an Age of Science*. Chicago: University of Chicago Press, 1997.

Gleason, Philip. *Keeping the Faith: American Catholicism Past and Present*. Notre Dame: University of Notre Dame Press, 1987.

———. *Contending with Modernity: Catholic Higher Education in the Twentieth Century*. New York: Oxford University Press, 1995.

———. "Boundlessness, Consolidation, and Discontinuity between Generations: Catholic Seminary Studies in Antebellum America." *Church History* 73 (September 2004): 582–612.

Glick, Thomas, ed. *The Comparative Reception of Darwinism*. Austin: University of Texas Press, 1972.

Gordon, Linda. *Woman's Body, Woman's Right: A Social History of Birth Control in America*. New York: Grossman Publishers, 1976.

———. *The Moral Property of Women: A History of Birth Control Politics in America*. Champaign: University of Illinois Press, 2002.

Gould, Stephen Jay. *Ontogeny and Phylogeny*. Cambridge, Mass.: Belknap Press of Harvard University Press, 1977.

————. "The Piltdown Conspiracy." *Natural History* 89 (1980): 8–28.

————. *The Mismeasure of Man*. New York: W. W. Norton, 1981.

Graebner, Alan. "Birth Control and the Lutherans: The Missouri Synod as a Case Study." *Journal of Social History* 2 (1969): 303–32.

Gruber, Jacob W. *A Conscience in Conflict: The Life of St. George Jackson Mivart*. New York: Columbia University Press for Temple University, 1960.

Gundlach, Bradley J. *Process and Providence: The Evolution Question at Princeton, 1845–1929*. Grand Rapids, Mich.: Eerdmans, 2013.

Habermas, Jürgen. *The Structural Transformation of the Public Sphere*. Translated by Thomas Burger. Cambridge, Mass.: The MIT Press, 1998.

Haller, Michael. *Creative Tension: Essays on Science and Religion*. Philadelphia: Templeton Press, 2003.

Halsey, William M. *The Survival of American Innocence: Catholicism in an Era of Disillusionment, 1920–1940*. Notre Dame: University of Notre Dame Press, 1980.

Hardin, Jeff, Ronald L. Numbers, and Ronald A. Binzley, eds. *The Warfare Between Science and Religion: The Idea That Wouldn't Die*. Baltimore: Johns Hopkins University Press, 2018.

Harp, Gillis J. *Positivist Republic: Auguste Comte and the Reconstruction of American Liberalism, 1865–1920*. University Park: Pennsylvania State University Press, 1995.

Harrison, Peter. "Miracles, Early Modern Science, and Rational Religion." *Church History* 75 (2006): 493–510.

————. "'Science' and 'Religion': Constructing the Boundaries." *Journal of Religion* 86 (January 2006): 81–106.

————. *The Territories of Science and Religion*. Chicago: University of Chicago Press, 2015.

Harrison, Peter, and Jon H. Roberts, eds. *Science without God? Rethinking the History of Scientific Naturalism*. Oxford: Oxford University Press, 2019.

Haskell, Thomas L., ed. *The Authority of Experts: Studies in History and Theory*. Bloomington: Indiana University Press, 1984.

Hazen, Craig James. *The Village Enlightenment: Popular Religion and Science in the Nineteenth Century*. Urbana: University of Illinois Press, 2000.

Heitmann, John A. "Doing 'True Science': The Early History of the Institutum Divi Thomae, 1935–1951." *Catholic Historical Review* 88 (2002): 702–22.

Hennessey, James. "Leo XIII: Intellectualizing the Combat with Modernity." *U. S. Catholic Historian* 7 (1988): 393–400.

Higham, John. *Strangers in the Land: Patterns of American Nativism, 1865–1925*. New Brunswick: Rutgers University Press, 1955.

Hinze, Christine Finer. "John A. Ryan: Theological Ethics and Political Engagement." In *The Catholic Theological Society of America: Proceedings from the*

Fiftieth Annual Convention, edited by Paul Crowley, 174–91. Santa Clara, Calif.: Santa Clara University Press, 1995.

Hogan, John D. "G. Stanley Hall and The Journal of Genetic Psychology: A Note." *Journal of Genetic Psychology* 177 (2016): 191–94.

Hollinger, David. "What Is Darwinism? It Is Calvinism!" Review of *The Post-Darwinian Controversies,* by James R. Moore. *Reviews in American History* 8 (March 1980): 80–85.

———. "Historians and the Discourse of Intellectuals." In *Religion and Twentieth Century Intellectual Life,* edited by Michael J. Lacey, 116–35. Cambridge: Cambridge University Press, 1989.

———. *Science, Jews, and Secular Culture.* Princeton: Princeton University Press, 1996.

———. "The 'Secularization' Question and the United States in the Twentieth Century." *Church History* 70 (2001): 132–43.

———. "Justification by Verification: The Scientific Challenge to the Moral Authority of Christianity in Modern America." In *After Cloven Tongues of Fire: Protestant Liberalism in Modern American History,* edited by Hollinger, 82–102. Princeton: Princeton University Press, 2013.

Hurley, Mark. *Unholy Ghost: Anti-Catholicism in the American Experience.* Huntington, Ind.: Our Sunday Visitor Press, 1992.

Hutchison, William R. *The Modernist Impulse in American Protestantism.* Cambridge, Mass.: Harvard University Press, 1976.

Ignatiev, Noel. *How the Irish Became White.* New York: Routledge, 1995.

Jacobson, Matthew Frye. *Whiteness of a Different Color: European Immigrants and the Alchemy of Race.* Cambridge, Mass.: Harvard University Press, 1998.

Jeansonne, Glen. *A Time of Paradox: America Since 1890.* Lanham, Md.: Rowman and Littlefield, 2006.

Jones, Greta. *Social Darwinism and English Thought: The Interaction between Biological and Social Theory.* Atlantic Highlands, N.J.: Humanities Press, 1980.

———. "Eugenics and Social Policy Between the Wars." *Historical Journal* 25 (1982): 717–28.

Jordan, John. *Machine Age Ideology: Social Engineering and American Liberalism, 1911–1939.* Chapel Hill: University of North Carolina Press, 1994.

Kane, Paula M. *Separatism and Subculture: Boston Catholicism, 1900–1920.* Chapel Hill: University of North Carolina Press, 1994.

Kauffman, Christopher. *Tradition and Transformation in Catholic Culture: The Priests of Saint Sulpice in the United States from 1791 to the Present.* New York: Macmillan, 1988.

Kaye, Howard L. "The Myth of Social Darwinism." *Contemporary Sociology* 11 (1982): 274–300.

Kazin, Michael. *A Godly Hero: The Life of William Jennings Bryan.* New York: Alfred A. Knopf, 2006.

Kevles, Daniel J. *In the Name of Eugenics: Genetics and the Uses of Human Heredity.* Cambridge, Mass.: Harvard University Press, 1995.

King, Thomas M., and Mary Wood Gilbert, eds. *The Letters of Teilhard de Chardin and Lucile Swan.* Washington, D.C.: Georgetown University Press, 1993.

Kinzer, Donald. *The American Protective Association.* Seattle: University of Washington Press, 1964.

Kohler, Thomas C. "*Quadragesimo Anno.*" In *A Century of Catholic Social Thought,* edited by George Weigel and Robert Royal, 27–44. Washington, D.C.: Ethics and Public Policy Center, 1991.

Kraut, Alan M. *The Huddled Masses: The Immigrant in Urban Society, 1880–1920.* Wheeling, Ill.: Harlan-Davidson Press, 1982.

Kuhn, Thomas S. *The Structure of Scientific Revolutions.* 3rd ed. Chicago: University of Chicago Press, 1996.

Kuklick, Bruce. *Churchmen and Philosophers: From Jonathan Edwards to John Dewey.* New Haven: Yale University Press, 1985.

Kurtz, Lester. *The Politics of Heresy: The Modernist Crisis in Roman Catholicism.* Berkeley: University of California Press, 1988.

Kutschera, Ulrich, Georgy S. Levit, and Uwe Hossfeld. "Ernst Haeckel (1834–1919): The German Darwin and His Impact on Modern Biology." *Theory in Biosciences* 138 (2019): 1–7.

Lacey, Michael, ed. *Religion and Twentieth Century American Intellectual Life.* Cambridge: Cambridge University Press, 1989.

Lagemann, Ellen Condliffe. "Contested Terrain: A History of Education Research in the United States, 1890–1990." *Educational Researcher* 26 (1997): 5–17.

Lagerway, Mary D. "Nursing, Social Contexts, and Ideologies in the Early United States Birth Control Movement." *Nursing Inquiry* 6 (1999): 250–58.

Langford, Jerome J. *Galileo, Science and the Church.* Ann Arbor: University of Michigan Press, 1992.

Larson, Edward J. *Sex, Race, and Science: Eugenics in the Deep South.* Baltimore: Johns Hopkins University Press, 1995.

———. *Summer for the Gods: The Scopes Trial and America's Continuing Debate over Science and Religion.* New York: Basic Books, 1997.

———. *Evolution: The Remarkable History of a Scientific Theory.* New York: The Modern Library, 2004.

Lasch, Christopher. *The True and Only Heaven: Progress and Its Critics.* New York: W. W. Norton, 1991.

Lears, T. J. Jackson. *No Place of Grace: Antimodernism and the Transformation of American Culture, 1880–1920.* New York: Pantheon Books, 1981.

Leclercq, Jean. *The Love of Learning and the Desire for God: A Study of Monastic Culture.* New York: Longman, 1961.

Leon, Sharon. "'Hopelessly Entangled in Nordic Presuppositions': Catholic Participation in the American Eugenics Society in the 1920s." *Journal of the History of Medicine and Applied Sciences* 59 (2004): 3–49.

———. *An Image of God: The Catholic Struggle with Eugenics*. Chicago: University of Chicago Press, 2013.

Lescher, Bruce H. "William J. Kerby: A Lost Voice in American Catholic Spirituality." *Records of the American Catholic Historical Society of Philadelphia* 102 (1991): 1–16.

Leverette, William J. "E. L. Youmans' Crusade for Scientific Autonomy and Respectability." *American Quarterly* 17 (1965): 12–32.

Lightman, Bernard. "The Theology of Victorian Scientific Naturalists." In *Science without God? Rethinking the History of Scientific Naturalism*, edited by Peter Harrison and Jon H. Roberts, 235–53. Oxford: Oxford University Press, 2019.

Lindberg, David C., and Ronald L. Numbers, eds. *When Science and Christianity Meet*. Chicago: University of Chicago Press, 2003.

Livingstone, David N. *Dealing with Darwin: Place, Politics, and Rhetoric in Religious Engagements with Evolution*. Baltimore: Johns Hopkins University Press, 2014.

Lofton, Kathryn. "The Methodology of the Modernists: Process in American Protestantism." *Church History* 75 (June 2006): 374–402.

Lombardo, Paul A. "A Child's Right to Be Well Born: Venereal Disease and the Eugenic Marriage Laws, 1913–1935." *Perspectives in Biology and Medicine* 60 (2017): 211–32.

———. "The Power of Heredity and the Relevance of Eugenic History." *Genetics in Medicine* 20 (2018): 1305–11.

Longfield, Bradley J. *The Prebyterian Controversy: Fundamentalists, Modernists, and Moderates*. New York: Oxford University Press, 2001.

Ludmerer, Kenneth M. *Genetics and American Society: A Historical Appraisal*. Baltimore: Johns Hopkins University Press, 1972.

Luker, Kristin. "Sex, Social Hygiene, and the State: The Double-Edged Sword of Social Reform." *Theory and Society* 27 (1998): 601–34.

Lurie, Edward. "Louis Agassiz and the Races of Man." In *Science in America Since 1820*, edited by Nathan Reingold, 146–61. New York: Science History Publications, 1976.

Magat, Richard. "The Forgotten Roles of Two New York City Teachers in the Epic Scopes Trial." *Science and Society* 70 (2006): 541–49.

Marks, Lara V. *Sexual Chemistry: A History of the Contraceptive Pill*. New Haven: Yale University Press, 2001.

Marsden, George M. "Evangelicals and the Scientific Culture: An Overview." In *Religion and Twentieth Century American Intellectual Life*, edited by Michael J. Lacey, 23–48. Cambridge: Cambridge University Press, 1989.

Marsden, George M., and Bradley Longfield, eds. *The Secularization of the Academy*. New York: Oxford University Press, 1992.

Marty, Martin E. *Modern American Religion.* 3 vols. Chicago: University of Chicago Press, 1989–96.

Massa, Mark. "'Mediating Modernism': Charles Briggs, Catholic Modernism, and an Ecumenical 'Plot.'" *Harvard Theological Review* 81 (1988): 413–30.

———. *Charles Augustus Briggs and the Crisis of Historical Criticism.* Minneapolis: Fortress Press, 1990.

McAvoy, Thomas. *The Great Crisis in American Catholic History, 1895–1900.* Chicago: Henry Regnery, 1957.

McCarraher, Eugene. *Christian Critics: Religion and the Impasse in Modern American Social Thought.* Ithaca: Cornell University Press, 2000.

McCarthy, John F. "Two Views of Historical Criticism." *Living Tradition* 77/78 (1988). http://www.rtforum.org/lt/lt78.html.

McCarthy, Timothy. *The Catholic Tradition.* Chicago: Loyola University Press, 1994.

McCool, Gerald. *The Neo-Thomists.* Milwaukee: Marquette University Press, 1994.

McGrath, Alister E. *The Twilight of Atheism: The Rise and Fall of Disbelief in the Modern World.* New York: Doubleday, 2004.

McGreevy, John. *Catholicism and American Freedom: A History.* New York: W. W. Norton, 2004.

McKeown, Elizabeth. "From *Pascendi* to *Primitive Man*: The Apologetics and Anthropology of John Montgomery Cooper." *U. S. Catholic Historian* 13 (1995): 1–21.

McLaughlin, Loretta A. *The Pill, John Rock, and the Catholic Church: The Biography of a Revolution.* Boston: Little, Brown, and Co., 1982.

McLaughlin, Peter. "Materialism, Actualism, and Science: What's Modern about Modern Science?" In *Darwinism and Philosophy*, edited by Vittorio Hosle and Christian Illies, 15–29. Notre Dame: University of Notre Dame Press, 2005.

McShane, Joseph. *Sufficiently Radical: Catholicism, Progressivism and the Bishops' Program of 1919.* Washington, D.C.: The Catholic University of America Press, 1986.

Mehler, B. A. "A History of the American Eugenics Society, 1921–1940." PhD diss., University of Illinois, 1988.

Mitman, Gregg. "Evolution as Gospel: William Patten, the Language of Democracy, and the Great War." *Isis* 81 (1990): 446–63.

Moloney, Dierdre M. *American Catholic Lay Groups and Transatlantic Social Reform in the Progressive Era.* Chapel Hill: University of North Carolina Press, 2002.

Moore, R. Laurence. *Religious Outsiders and the Making of Americans.* New York: Oxford University Press, 1986.

Moran, Jeffrey P. *American Genesis: The Antievolution Controversies from Scopes to Creation Science.* New York: Oxford University Press, 2012.

Morehead, James. "The Erosion of Postmillennialism in American Religious Thought, 1865–1925." *Church History* 53 (1984): 61–77.

Morrison, John L. "A History of American Catholic Opinion on the Theory of Evolution, 1859–1950." PhD diss., University of Missouri, 1951.

———. "American Catholics and the Crusade Against Evolution." *Records of the American Catholic Historical Society of Philadelphia* 64 (1953): 59–71.

———. "William Seton—A Catholic Darwinist." *Review of Politics* 21 (1959): 566–84.

Moynihan, James H. *The Life of Archbishop John Ireland.* New York: Harper and Brothers, 1953.

Mulloy, Clement Anthony. "John A. Ryan and the Issue of Family Limitation." *Catholic Social Science Review* 18 (2013): 91–103.

Muncy, Robyn. *Creating A Female Dominion in American Reform: 1890–1935.* New York: Oxford University Press, 1991.

Neenan, Benedict. *Thomas Verner Moore: Psychiatrist, Educator and Monk.* New York: Paulist Press, 2000.

Neusse, C. Joseph. "The Introduction of the Social Sciences in the Catholic University of America 1895–1909." *Social Thought* 12 (Spring 1986): 30–41.

———. "Thomas Joseph Bouquillon (1840–1902), Moral Theologian and Precursor of the Social Sciences in the Catholic University of America." *Catholic Historical Review* 72 (1986): 601–69.

———. *The Catholic University of America: A Centennial History.* Washington, D.C.: The Catholic University of America Press, 1990.

———. "William Joseph Kerby (1870–1936): The Approach to His Field of the First American Catholic Sociologist." *American Catholic Studies* 111 (2000): 77–96.

Noonan, John T., Jr. *Contraception: A History of Its Treatment by the Catholic Theologians and Canonists.* Cambridge, Mass.: Harvard University Press, 1965.

Numbers, Ronald L. *Darwinism Comes to America.* Cambridge, Mass.: Harvard University Press, 1998.

———. "Creating Creationism: Meanings and Uses Since the Age of Agassiz." In *Evangelicals and Science in Historical Perspective*, edited by David Livingstone et al., 234–43. New York: Oxford University Press, 1999.

———. *The Creationists: From Scientific Creationism to Intelligent Design*, expanded edition. Cambridge, Mass.: Harvard University Press, 2006.

———, ed. *Galileo Goes to Jail and Other Myths about Science and Religion.* Cambridge, Mass.: Harvard University Press, 2009.

O'Brien, David J. *American Catholics and Social Reform: The New Deal Years.* New York: Oxford University Press, 1968.

———. *Public Catholicism.* New York: Macmillan Publishing, 1989.

———. *Isaac Hecker: An American Catholic.* Mahwah, N.J.: Paulist Press, 1992.

O'Connell, Marvin R. *John Ireland and the American Catholic Church.* St. Paul, Minn.: Historical Society Press, 1988.

Ohlers, R. Clinton. "The End of Miracles: Naturalism's Rise in American Science, 1830–1931." PhD diss., University of Pennsylvania, 2007.

O'Leary, Don. *Roman Catholicism and Modern Science: A History.* New York: Continuum, 2006.

O'Malley, John W. *Vatican I: The Council and the Making of the Ultramontane Church.* Cambridge, Mass.: Belknap Press of Harvard University Press, 2018.

Orsi, Robert A. *Thank You, St. Jude: Women's Devotion to the Patron Saint of Hopeless Causes.* New Haven: Yale University Press, 1996.

Paul, Diane B. "Eugenics and the Left." *Journal of the History of Ideas* 45 (1984): 567–90.

———. *Controlling Human Heredity: 1865 to the Present.* Highlands, N.J.: Humanities Press, 1995.

Pavuk, Alexander. "Evolution and Voices of Progressive Catholicism in the Age of the Scopes Trial." *Religion and American Culture* 26 (2016): 101–37.

———. "Biologist Edwin Grant Conklin and the Idea of the Religious Direction of Human Evolution in the 1920s." *Annals of Science* 74 (2017): 64–82.

———. "The American Association for the Advancement of Science Committee on Evolution and the Scopes Trial: Race, Eugenics, and Public Science in the U.S.A." *Historical Research* 91 (2018): 137–59.

Pells, Richard H. *Radical Visions and American Dreams: Culture and Social Thought in the Depression Years.* New York: Harper and Row, 1973.

Pernick, Martin S. *The Black Stork: Eugenics and the Death of 'Defective' Babies in American Medicine and Motion Pictures since 1915.* Oxford: Oxford University Press, 1996.

Pickens, Donald K. "The Sterilization Movement: The Search for Purity in Mind and State." *Phylon* 28 (1967): 78–94.

Plopper, E. T. "Protestants and the Acceptance of Contraception in Britain and the U.S.A." PhD diss., University of Notre Dame, 2015.

Portier, William L. *Divided Friends: Portraits of the Roman Catholic Modernist Crisis in the United States.* Washington, D.C.: The Catholic University of America Press, 2013.

Powell, Arthur G. "University Schools of Education in the Twentieth Century." *Peabody Journal of Education* 54 (October 1976): 3–20.

Preston, Robert M. "The Christian Moralist as Scientific Reformer: John A. Ryan's Early Years." *Records of the American Catholic Historical Society of Philadelphia* 81 (March 1970): 27–41.

Rademacher, Nicholas K. *Paul Hanly Furfey: Priest, Scientist, Social Reformer.* New York: Fordham University Press, 2017.

Ramsden, Edmund. "Social Demography and Eugenics in the Interwar United States." *Population and Development Review* 29 (December 2003): 547–93.

Reed, James. *From Private Vice to Public Virtue: The Birth Control Movement and American Society since 1830.* New York: Basic Books, 1978.

Regal, Brian. *Henry Fairfield Osborn: Race and the Search for the Origins of Man.* Aldershot, UK: Ashgate, 2002.

Rehrer, Margaret Mary. "Americanism and Modernism—Continuity or Discontinuity?" *U.S. Catholic Historian* 1 (Summer 1981): 87–103.
———. *Catholic Intellectual Life in America*. New York: Macmillan, 1989.
Reingold, Nathan. "History of Science Today, 1. Uniformity as Hidden Diversity:
History of Science in the United States, 1920–1940." *British Journal for the His-
tory of Science* 19 (1986): 243–62.
Richards, Robert J. "Darwin's Metaphysics of Mind." In *Darwinism and Philosophy*,
edited by Vittorio Hosle and Christian Illies, 166–80. Notre Dame: University
of Notre Dame Press, 2005.
———. *The Tragic Sense of Life: Ernst Haeckel and the Struggle over Evolutionary
Thought*. Chicago: University of Chicago Press, 2008.
Roberts, Jon H. *Darwinism and Divine in America: Protestant Intellectuals and
Organic Evolution, 1859–1900*. Madison: University of Wisconsin Press, 1988.
———. "Religion, Secularization, and Cultural Spaces in America." In *American
Catholic Traditions: Resources for Renewal*, edited by Sandra Yocum Mize and
William Portier, 185–205. Maryknoll, N.Y.: Orbis Books, 1997.
———. "Religious Reactions to Darwin." In *The Cambridge Companion to Science
and Religion*, edited by Peter Harrison, 80–102. Cambridge: Cambridge Uni-
versity Press, 2010.
———. "The Science of the Soul: Naturalizing the Mind in Great Britain and
North America." In *Science without God? Rethinking the History of Scientific
Naturalism*, edited by Peter Harrison and Jon H. Roberts, 162–81. Oxford:
Oxford University Press, 2019.
Roberts, Jon H, and James Turner. *The Sacred and Secular University*. Princeton:
Princeton University Press, 2000.
Roberts, William Clifford. "'The Pill' and Its Four Major Developers." *Proceedings
(Baylor University Medical Center)* 28 (July 2015): 421–32. https://www.ncbi
.nlm.nih.gov/pmc/articles/PMC4462239/.
Roediger, David. *The Wages of Whiteness: Race and the Making of the American
Working Class*. New York: Verso Press, 1999.
———. *Working toward Whiteness: How America's Immigrants Became White*.
New York: Basic Books, 2006.
Rosen, Christine. *Preaching Eugenics: Religious Leaders and the American Eugenics
Movement*. Oxford: Oxford University Press, 2004.
Ross, Dorothy. *The Origins of American Social Science*. Cambridge: Cambridge
University Press, 1991.
———, ed. *Modernist Impulses in the Human Sciences 1870–1930*. Baltimore and
London: Johns Hopkins University Press, 1994.
Ross, Sydney. "*Scientist*: The Story of a Word." *Annals of Science* 18 (1962): 65–85.
Ruse, Michael. *Mystery of Mysteries: Is Evolution a Social Construction?* Cambridge,
Mass.: Harvard University Press, 1999.
———. "Darwinism and Naturalism: Identical Twins or Just Good Friends?" In

Darwinism and Philosophy, edited by Vittorio Hosle and Christian Illies, 83–91. Notre Dame: University of Notre Dame Press, 2005.

———. *The Evolution-Creation Struggle*. Cambridge: Cambridge University Press, 2005.

———. "Evolution and the Idea of Social Progress." In *Biology and Ideology from Descartes to Dawkins*, edited by Denis R. Alexander and Ronald L. Numbers, 247–75. Chicago: University of Chicago Press, 2010.

Russell, Jeffrey Burton. *Inventing the Flat Earth: Columbus and Modern Historians*. New York: Praeger, 1997.

Safford, John Lugton. *Pragmatism and the Progressive Movement in the United States: The Origin of the New Social Sciences*. Lanham, Md.: University Press of America, 1987.

Sedgwick, Peter. "The Lambeth Conferences on Contraception, 1908–68." *Theology* 123 (2020): 95–103.

Serpente, Norberto. "More than a Mentor: Leonard Darwin's Contribution to the Assimilation of Mendelism into Eugenics and Darwinism." *Journal of the History of Biology* 49 (2016): 461–94.

Shanahan, Timothy. *The Evolution of Darwinism: Selection, Adaptation, and Progress in Evolutionary Biology*. Cambridge: Cambridge University Press, 2004.

Shapiro, Adam. "Civic Biology and the Origin of the School Antievolution Movement." *Journal of the History of Biology* 41 (2008): 409–33.

———. *Trying Biology: The Scopes Trial, Textbooks, and the Antievolution Movement in American Schools*. Chicago: University of Chicago Press, 2013.

Slattery, John P. *Faith and Science at Notre Dame: John Zahm, Evolution, and the Catholic Church*. Notre Dame, Ind.: University of Notre Dame Press, 2019.

Slawson, Douglas J. *The Foundation and First Decade of the National Catholic Welfare Council*. Washington, D.C.: The Catholic University of America Press, 1992.

Sloan, Phillip R. "'It Might Be Called Reverence.'" In *Darwinism and Philosophy*, edited by Vittorio Hosle and Christian Illies, 143–65. Notre Dame: University of Notre Dame Press, 2005.

Slominski, Kristi L. "Cardinal Gibbons as a Symbol for Early Sex Education." *U.S. Catholic Historian* 34 (2016): 1–25.

Smith, Christian, ed. *The Secular Revolution: Power, Interests, and Conflict in the Secularization of American Public Life*. Berkeley: University of California Press, 2003.

Smith, Timothy L. "Religion and Ethnicity in America." *American Historical Review* 83 (1978): 1155–85.

Solberg, Winton U. "The Catholic Presence at the University of Illinois." *Catholic Historical Review* 76 (October 1990): 765–812.

Soloway, Richard A. *Birth Control and the Population Question in England, 1877–1930*. Chapel Hill: University of North Carolina Press, 1982.

———. "The 'Perfect Contraceptive': Eugenics and Birth Control Research in Britain and America in the Interwar Years." *Journal of Contemporary History* 30 (October 1995): 637–64.

Sommerville, C. John. "Post-Secularism Marginalizes the University: A Rejoinder to Hollinger." *Church History* 71 (2002): 848–57.

Spalding, Thomas W. *The Premier See: A History of the Archdiocese of Baltimore, 1789–1989.* Baltimore: Johns Hopkins University Press, 1989.

———. "John Carroll." In *The Encyclopedia of American Catholic History,* edited by Thomas J. Shelley and Michael Glazer, 224–30. Collegeville, Minn.: Liturgical Press, 1997.

Sparr, Arnold. *To Promote, Defend, and Redeem: The Catholic Literary Revival and the Cultural Transformation of American Catholicism, 1920–1960.* New York: Greenwood Press, 1990.

Spiro, Jonathan Peter. *Defending the Master Race: Conservation, Eugenics, and the Legacy of Madison Grant.* Burlington, Vt.: University of Vermont Press, 2009.

Stanley, Matthew. "The Uniformity of Natural Laws in Victorian Britain: Naturalism, Theism, and Scientific Practice." *Zygon* 46 (2011): 536–60.

———. *Huxley's Church and Maxwell's Demon: From Theistic to Natural Science.* Chicago: University of Chicago Press, 2015.

Stenmark. Michael. *Scientism: Ethics, Science, and Religion.* Aldershot, UK: Ashgate, 2001.

Tebbel, John and Mary Ellen Walker-Zuckerman. *The Magazine in America, 1741–1991.* Oxford: Oxford University Press, 1991.

Tentler, Leslie Woodcock. *Catholics and Contraception: An American History.* Ithaca: Cornell University Press, 2004.

Thurs, Daniel Patrick. *Science Talk: Changing Notions of Science in American Culture.* New Brunswick: Rutgers University Press, 2008.

Tobey, Ronald C. *The American Ideology of National Science: 1919–1930.* Pittsburgh: University of Pittsburgh Press, 1971.

Tobin, Kathleen A. *The American Religious Debate over Birth Control, 1907–1937.* Jefferson, N.C.: McFarland, 2001.

Tobin-Schlesinger, Kathleen. "The Changing American City: Chicago Catholics as Outsiders in the Birth Control Movement, 1915–1935." *U.S. Catholic Historian* 15 (1997): 67–85.

Van Allen, Rodger. *The Commonweal and American Catholicism.* Philadelphia: Fortress Press, 1974.

———. "*Commonweal* and the Catholic Intellectual Life." *U.S. Catholic Historian* 14 (1994): 71–86.

Verhoeven, Timothy. "'Apostles of Continence': Doctors and the Doctrine of Sexual Necessity in Progressive-Era America." *Medical History* 61 (2017): 89–106.

Vidler, Alec R. *The Emergence of Liberal Catholicism in America.* Chicago: University of Chicago Press, 1958.

———. *A Variety of Catholic Modernists: The Sarum Lectures in the University of Oxford for the Year 1968-69.* Cambridge: Cambridge University Press, 1970.

Viterbo, Paula. "The Promise of Rhythm: The Determination of the Woman's Time of Ovulation and Its Social Impact in the United States, 1920-1940." PhD diss., SUNY Stony Brook, 2000.

Wangler, Thomas. "The Ecclesiology of Archbishop John Ireland: Its Nature, Development, and Influence." PhD diss., Marquette University, 1968.

Wilson, R. J., ed. *Darwinism and the American Intellectual: A Book of Readings.* Homewood, Ill.: Dorsey Press, 1967.

Witkowski, Jan A., and John R. Ingliss, eds. *Davenport's Dream: 21st Century Reflections on Heredity and Eugenics.* New York: Cold Spring Harbor Laboratory Press, 2008.

Woods, Thomas E., Jr. *The Church Confronts Modernity: Catholic Intellectuals and the Progressive Era.* New York: Columbia University Press, 2004.

Young, R. M. "Darwinism *Is* Social." In *The Darwinian Heritage,* edited by David Kohn, 609-38. Princeton: Princeton University Press, 1984.

Yudell, Michael. *Race Unmasked: Biology and Race in the 20th Century.* New York: Columbia University Press, 2014.

Zochert, Donald. "Science and the Common Man in Ante-Bellum America." In *Science in America since 1820,* edited by Nathan Reingold, 7-32. New York: Science History Publications, 1976.

Index

〜

Respectably Catholic and Scientific: Evolution and Birth Control between the World Wars was designed in Minion and composed by Kachergis Book Design of Pittsboro, North Carolina. It was printed on 55-pound Natural Offset and bound by Maple Press of York, Pennsylvania.